Capital Markets
and Development

Other Sequoia Seminar Publications
available from ICS Press

Policy Reform and Equity
Beyond the Informal Sector
Development With Trade
More Taxing Than Taxes?

CAPITAL MARKETS AND DEVELOPMENT

A Sequoia Seminar

Edited by
Steve H. Hanke and Alan A. Walters

ICS PRESS

Institute for Contemporary Studies
San Francisco, California

Capital Markets and Development
Copyright © 1991 by the Sequoia Institute

Printed in the United States of America. All rights reserved. No part of this book may be used or reproduced in any manner without written permission except in the case of brief quotations in critical articles and reviews.

Inquiries, book orders, and catalog requests should be addressed to ICS Press, 243 Kearny Street, San Francisco, California 94108. (415) 981-5353; Fax: (415) 986-4878; book orders within the contiguous United States: **(800) 326-0263**.

The cover was designed by Irene Imfeld.

The index was compiled by Shirley Kessel.

This book is derived from the proceedings of one of the seminars in a series conducted by the Sequoia Institute. Both the seminar series and this publication were funded by the United States Agency for International Development.

PDC-0092-A-00-6050-00

U.S.A.I.D.

Library of Congress Cataloging-in-Publication Data

Capital markets and development / edited by Steve
  H. Hanke and Alan A. Walters.
        p.   cm.—(A Sequoia seminar)
    Includes bibliographical references and index.
    ISBN 1-55815-073-0 : $29.95.—ISBN 1-55815-091-9 (pbk.) : $12.95
    1. Capital market. 2. Economic development. 3. Capital market—Developing countries.   I. Hanke, Steve H.   II. Walters, A. A.
(Alan Arthur), 1926–   .   III. Sequoia Institute.   IV. Series.
HG4523.C347   1991
338.9′009172′4—dc20   91-17097
                                                                   CIP

Contents

Preface xi
Robert B. Hawkins, Jr.

Foreword xv
Jerry Jenkins

1 **Capital Markets and Development: Essential and Irrelevant** 1
   Jerry Jenkins

2 **Financial and Capital Markets in Developing Countries** 25
   Steve H. Hanke and Alan A. Walters

3 **Keynes's Russian Currency Board** 43
   Steve H. Hanke and Kurt Schuler

   Appendix 59

4	**Money and Capital in Economic Development: A Retrospective Assessment** Lawrence H. White	65
	Comment Ronald I. McKinnon	101
	Discussion	113
	Response Lawrence H. White	131
5	**Latin American Contrast: Capital Markets and Development in Chile and Argentina** Rolf J. Lüders	135
	Comment Murray Sherwin	177
	Discussion	185
	Response Rolf J. Lüders	203
6	**Capital Market Liberalization: The New Zealand Experience** Murray Sherwin	209
	Appendix	235
7	**Policy and Institutional Considerations in Equity Market Development** Flora M. Painter and Robert J. Rourke	241
	Comment Terrence C. Reilly	289
	Discussion	297
8	**The Dhaka Stock Exchange: Expanding Equity in the Development of Bangladesh** Khurshid Alam	335
9	**Confidence and the Liberal Economic Imperative** Steve H. Hanke and Alan A. Walters	347

Notes and References	**355**
Contributors	**371**
Seminar Participants	**373**
Index	**375**

Preface

Developed capital markets allow people to do more with their savings than they otherwise could. They also provide financing that enables people to do more with their ideas and talents than otherwise would be possible. People's savings are allowed to be matched with the best ideas and talents in society by the daily activities of equities or debt intermediaries ranging from stockbrokers to bank loan officers, the professionals within developed capital markets.

Conversely, to the extent that capital markets are inadequate, underdeveloped, or simply absent, a society suffers: it is less likely to benefit from the best ideas and talents of its members; the earnings thereby lost also mean lost savings; and what savings there are will be less productively employed. Where the converse holds, the development of people and societies cannot be reasonably expected.

Capital markets were not always so critical to development. Through the nineteenth century, when the United States and other developed countries were getting that way, central banks were the exception and appreciating currencies were the rule. Today, central banks are the rule and appreciating currencies are nonexistent. Hence, capital market institutions and instruments that did not exist before the twentieth century are now required for development.

The history of capital markets, thoroughly described in *Capital Markets and Development,* allows the recognition that countries need not have the same institutions, be it the World Bank or any other and that governments need not march in lockstep to any single drummer. More than that, it compels one to consider that people living in highly dissimilar circumstances and countries may be best served by correspondingly diverse institutions. In exploring these issues, this volume is highly responsive to a fundamental fact of political life: whatever institutional and policy reforms occur will be those that government officials agree *can* occur. Because such agreement is itself highly variable throughout the world, any single "answer" for developing capital markets will fall mainly on deaf ears. By recognizing and encouraging a multiplicity of answers, the authors of this book provide one or more answers that will be "heard" by almost everyone, even those whose hearing diverges greatly from that of other listeners.

The practicality of a multiplicity of simultaneously evolving institutions and policies throughout the world—indeed, within countries as well—is an operating premise of the Center for Self-Governance launched by the Institute for Contemporary Studies in 1990. So this particular volume is "heard" here perhaps more clearly than it is by most listeners. And this book is likely to expand both the receptivity and size of the audience for two successor volumes in the Sequoia Seminar series: *African Finance: Research and Reform* and *If Texas Were Chile: Financial Risk and Regulation in Commodity-Exporting Economies*. The different possibilities, probabilities, and practices of capital market development that are considered by these two volumes are largely responsive to the differing circumstances of the countries they address. Thus the present book provides a platform from which two successful launches have already occurred.

Many more should follow. A world of simultaneous multiplicities warrants no less.

> Robert B. Hawkins, Jr.
> President and CEO
> Institute for Contemporary Studies

San Francisco, California
April 1991

Foreword

This is the fifth publication resulting from a continuing series of seminars introduced by the Sequoia Institute in 1987. Consistent with its theme—Including the Excluded: Extending the Benefits of Development—the series has two primary objectives:

(1) to shed new light on critical issues of third world development and its assistance

(2) to serve as a catalyst for a new generation of thinkers and ideas that will accelerate the inclusion of *all* people in the process of individual and social development

An operating assumption of the series is that hastening the inclusion of *all* individuals in the *process* of development is the surest route to accelerating the development of the societies they live in. Attempts to broaden the distribution of the products of development (at whatever stage) to the neglect of the processes (and human opportunities) that enable them appear to incur dire consequences, most evident today in the communist world and its remnants.

This book and two successors in the Sequoia Seminar series address capital markets and development. One of the successors (*If Texas were Chile*) attends to circumstances of financial calamity, and the other (*African Finance*) considers situations in which even more dire financial conditions afflict—indeed, disable—a country's formal economy. A virtue of each of the three volumes is that no one "answer" is advanced. Indeed, the very diversity of circumstances requires that more, rather than less, be provided. Beginning with this one, these volumes meet both that requirement and the expectations of the principal sponsor of this series, the Agency for International Development (A.I.D.).

The series is an outgrowth of the agency's policy endeavors during the past several years. Support for these seminars continues a commitment by the agency to encourage the reexamination of established precepts and practices in order to formulate more effective development policies. In accordance with this objective, the series strives to enlarge the supply of talent and ideas that are dedicated to development issues. One component of this effort, of course, is the publication and dissemination of each seminar's proceedings. Another is to bring together, within each of the seminars, several promising scholars who are relatively new to the international development field, by virtue of their youth or the concentration of their previous scholarship on other subject matter, to interact with established scholars and practitioners of development.

The support and cooperation of numerous A.I.D. officials has been instrumental to the success of the seminar series. Among these have been three administrators of the agency, M. Peter McPherson, Alan Woods, and Ronald Roskens; two assistant administrators for the Bureau for Program and Policy Coordination (the A.I.D. technical office most responsible for this endeavor), Richard E. Bissell and Reginald Brown; and four project officers within the bureau, Edwin L. Hullander, Warren Weinstein, Neal S. Zank, and Fred Kirschstein. Neal Zank warrants particular mention for his provision of valuable technical assistance to *Capital Markets and Development*. The authors represented in this book join me in expressing appreciation to Ysbrand van der Werf and Janet Mowery of ICS Press, Frances Bowles, and Roger Magyar, in particular, for their unstinting editorial efforts in bringing this manuscript to press. I also wish to acknowledge the continuing encouragement for the series that is provided by the president of ICS, Robert B. Hawkins, Jr.

Though none of the particular opinions found in the series volumes is necessarily shared by either the Agency for International Development or Sequoia Institute, their diversity is expected to include more people in the process of development than would otherwise occur.

Jerry Jenkins
Series Director/Editor

April 1991

Capital Markets
and Development

1
Jerry Jenkins

Capital Markets and Development: Essential and Irrelevant

When, as in the whole of this century, the real value or purchasing power of national currencies is declining, capital markets are essential to prevent the underutilization and waste of resources.[1] This volume shows how grotesque this waste can become and also explains how it is most costly to those who can least afford it.

More positively, this book presents recommendations ranging from actions directed at negating the devaluation of currencies to those that would lessen its invidious effects. More positively still, most of the recommended actions have been successfully implemented in many parts of the world at various points in history. Though economic theory removes any mystery that might attend the success of these cases, the reader with no background in economics is less apt to be mystified than to see such positive consequences as those of common sense. The challenge, then, is to account for the common nonsense of this planet's far more abundant failures.

The real value of the currencies of all countries has declined precipitously since 1900. The flip side of their deflated value is the escalation in prices of all those things that the currencies might purchase. As illustrated in Figure 1.1 by the example of the United States, nine dollars, today, are required to buy what one dollar would have purchased in 1941 and what fifty cents would have purchased in 1900. (The United States is considered a developed country in spite of this decline because few other countries have done much better.) Thus all individuals whose employment incomes do not increase at the rate of price inflation become worse off—*unless* they are able to offset that loss with interest or investment income. Because interest and investment income require capital markets, these markets and their instruments are deemed essential in order for most people to be better off tomorrow than they are today.

That capital markets might also be irrelevant to the material betterment of most people requires nothing but a reversion to currency appreciation (as existed in the United States and most of the Western world during the nineteenth century).[2] When the currency in which savings are held is rising in value, an individual is able to purchase more over time with that currency. In these circumstances, the individual who does not increase spending for consumption may increase the return to savings in two basic ways: by lending money to other individuals (including re-lenders), thereby earning additional (interest) income, and by investing in one's own business and/or that of others in exchange for a pro rata share of the enterprise's profits and capital gains or losses.

The first of these two basic ways of saving corresponds with the financial, and the second with the securities or equities components of capital markets. Banks are the most prominent example of the first, stock markets of the second. Just one hundred years ago, most stock markets in the world were in an embryonic state.[3] The turn of the century transition from currency appreciation to currency devaluation parallels, for most of today's capital market institutions and their financial and equity instruments, the passage from "irrelevant" to "essential."

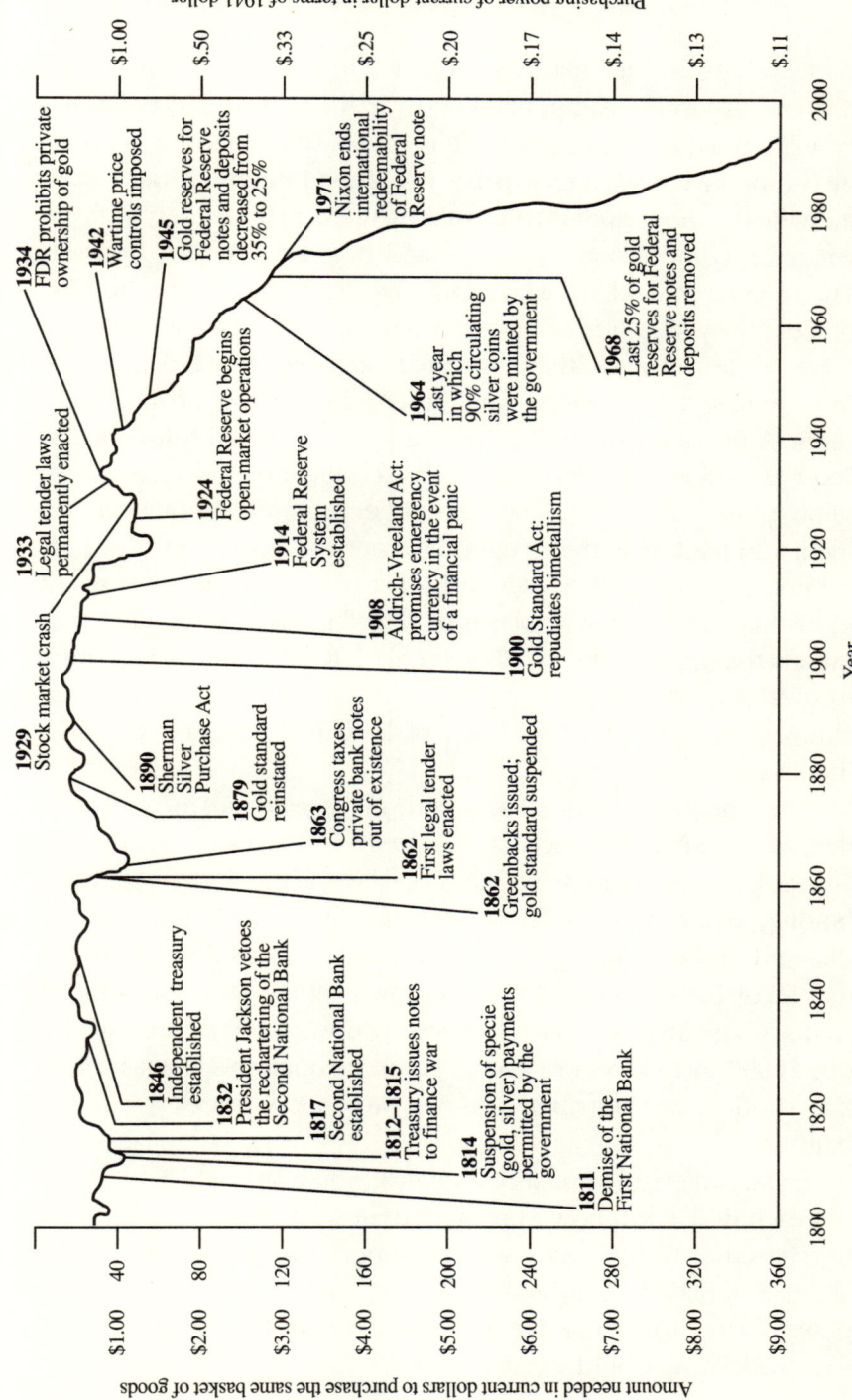

Figure 1.1. Declining Value of the Dollar (U.S. Price Index: 1800–1988; 1967 = 100) **Source**: The George Edward Durrell Foundation.

Developed capital markets, including most especially their equities and securities components, enable *all* individuals, no matter how limited their means, to share in the increased wealth provided by competitive private enterprise. Developed capital markets allow individuals who cannot own a given business in its entirety to invest whatever is individually possible and preferred *in* that business. They enable individuals who cannot by themselves *begin* the businesses they would like, to attract enough investment from others to make a start. Any of these investors can be wrong about their investments. The demand for (purchases of) the products and services provided by the business invested in may be less than is required to stay in business, in which case the investors lose. But the same individuals, even at the same time, may gain on other investments. Indeed, it is the maximization of the possibilities of both gaining and losing, simultaneously, that permits a guarantee to the individual saver-investor of something far more substantial than merely the opportunity to fail *or* succeed. By allowing an individual to diversify risk among many ventures, to offset losses and gains almost constantly, the likelihood of long-term, overall success is increased.

This phenomenon is subsequently elaborated, but for now, even the very possibility of success must be contrasted with what generally looks like a guarantee of failure, which is to say, the practice of holding savings in the form of government currency. Compare the illustration shown in Figure 1.1 with another (shown in Figure 1.2) that records the historical ups-and-downs of the Dow Jones Industrial Average and ask yourself where you would have preferred to put $1,000 in 1900 and to *keep* it (even through the Great Depression) until today? Distributed among two hundred stocks or in your mattress?

If you preferred the mattress deposit, you would still have $1,000, but each dollar will now purchase about what a nickel would have purchased in 1900; it will have all the purchasing power today that about $56 had then. In order to have the same real (purchasing power) value today that the $1,000 had when the mattress deposit was made, you would need $18,000.

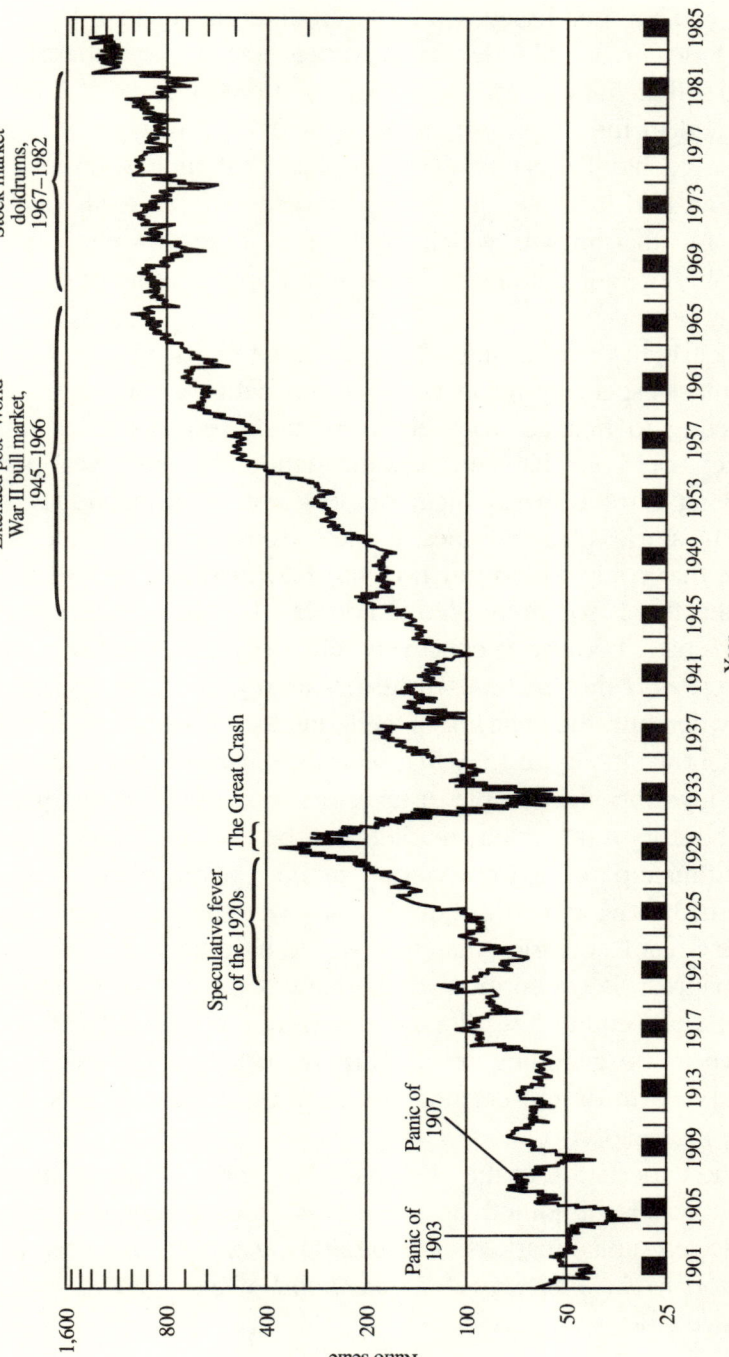

Figure 1.2. The Dow Jones Industrial Stock Average, 1900–1985 **Source**: Wonnacott and Wonnacott, 1986, 110.

If you had purchased two hundred different stocks listed in the Dow Jones Industrial Index (at an average cost of $5 per share),[4] you could sell them today for about $54,000 (a 1990 average of 2700, not included in the graph, was divided by a 1900 average of 50). Of course, each dollar is now worth 1/18 of its 1900 value, so instead of a fifty-four-fold increase, the original investment has really only tripled. But that growth, which does not include dividends, is considerably greater than even the currency appreciation of the nineteenth century.

Clearly, investors trying to make a living from playing the market, and most especially those who go into debt to purchase shares, expecting to finance that debt from their (equity) gains in the market, could only have survived throughout the ninety-year period by being extraordinarily lucky or prescient. Such individuals provide the stories of great riches, at one extreme, and of suicide, at the other, that comprise so much of the information about securities markets that is communicated to people. This focus on extremes is unfortunate, because it effectively tells people to see both equity markets *and* the infamous investors as representing exceptional risk, when only the behavior of the individuals qualifies as such. The story shown in Figure 1.2 is that securities markets are far kinder to saver-investors than to player-investors. Combine the two graphs, and the story is that equity markets may be essential to saving when the ultimate payoff is in monopoly money (government currency). Indeed, the savings of the equity investor were no worse at the depth of the Great Depression than they would have been if deposited in the mattress. Between the two alternatives, the holder of currency rather than equity has adopted the riskier position, but if he is known to be gambling on a sharp reversion to the nineteenth-century norm of appreciating currency, other descriptions would seem more appropriate.

The expectation of the obvious—that where failure is allowed, it will occur—is joined by the less obvious essential beauty of developed capital markets: *maximizing the opportunities for saver-investors to fail increases their likelihood of success*. This counterintuitive rule is attributable to

Capital Markets and Development

the desire of investors to apply insurance principles to investments. Many wanted to spread their risks by diversification, investing only a small fraction of their funds in any one enterprise or project. Marketable securities provided the means for doing so (Rosenberg and Birdzell 1986, 229).

Recognition of this benefit also indicates the weakness of an incipient market such as the Dhaka Stock Exchange (described in Chapter 8) relative to developed equities markets; *marketable* securities have been described as

> securities issued in sufficient quantity that there was regular trading in them, not securities that changed hands only once in a while. The advantage enjoyed by large issues was not merely an economy of scale in legal, accounting, and underwriting costs; the advantage was that a security issue which is large enough and widely enough held to generate frequent sales at an easily observable price is more valuable to investors than one which is not (Ibid., 255).

Without such quantity of regularly traded stocks, the insurance principle cannot be applied by investors in the securities market and the markets can grow little if at all. Absent the opportunity to diversify risk and thereby decrease the probable magnitude of either losses or gains, cows, jewelry, or other nonperishable assets will be preferred to either cash *or* shares.

Thus do the encouraging statistics provided by Khurshid Alam on the growth of the Dhaka Stock Exchange promise most saver-investors more for the future than can be delivered today. The market capitalization of the exchange, which is the sum of the market value (as determined by most recently traded price) of all exchange-listed stocks whose shares are issued and outstanding, is barely 1 percent of Bangladesh's gross national product (GNP). But, for the reasons quoted above, that measure of the contribution of equity financing to the total economic production of the country is less relevant to the individual investor-saver than are the volume and variety of securities traded. Though the individual elements of the Dhaka Stock Exchange have grown significantly, the value of shares traded as a *percentage* of market capitalization is extremely low. (The reader can make the calculation of 1 percent, at most, from the data provided in Chapter 8.) Comparable figures for the United Kingdom, Japan, and the United States range between 40 and 65 percent (the only exchanges having higher turnover rates than those are Taiwan, 532 percent; Korea, 101 percent; Thailand, 78 percent; and India (Bombay), 69 percent) (International Finance Corp. 1990, 16). High turnover (or the sum of the volume of shares traded multiplied by the value, that is, the most recent purchase price, of the respective shares in the market) is not sufficient to provide realization of the insurance principle by investors, but it is absolutely essential to that effect. Without it, for most people, equity finance cannot be a feasible (let alone superior) alternative to debt finance. In turn, the primacy of debt finance leaves most people maximally exposed to the vagaries of government currency, as they, and their bank deposits, were in most countries of the world (including the United States) during most of the 1970s.

The changing values of currency and equity in U.S. history depicted in Figures 1.1 and 1.2 mirror millions of choices and nonchoices made by individual Americans.[5] Unfortunately for most people on this planet, the graph shown in Figure 1.1 would be more negatively extreme than it is for the United States, and the graph shown in Figure 1.2 would not exist. The nonchoice in the latter fact is a function of the absence of an alternative rather than of individuals choosing not to choose. Furthermore, for most people the lack of choices is accentuated if the nominal rates of interest paid to savers on their deposits into banks and other financial institutions are less than the rate of inflation. Real rates of interest paid on deposits in the United States have been positive throughout most of the twentieth century, so in 1900 the saver-investor had a third alternative to either equity finance or mattress stuffing. An annually compounded interest rate of 3.27 percent on a deposit of $1,000 in 1900 could have been attained from then until today (U.S. Bureau of the Census 1960, 656) and would have yielded $18,100, at least keeping the individual saver approximately even with inflation. During the past ninety years U.S. government or municipal high-grade bonds have rarely exceeded the annual yields of common industrial stocks, and only once, during the Great Depression (a statistic that reinforces the point about risky investment behavior rather than the riskiness of the market) (ibid).

This assessment of self-finance without a capital market intermediary (the mattress), equity finance, and debt or deposit finance diminishes neither the importance of sound and stable currencies nor that of banks and the services they provide. Indeed, if currencies and bank finance do not meet some unspecified, minimal standards, the new "essentialness" of equities markets cannot be realized. In the vast panoply of extant capital market institutions, only banks arose before the nineteenth century and may be deemed essential to the economic development of the West. Our turn-of-the-century example shows that banks as they existed then have become either more irrelevant or more essential, depending on circumstances: *more irrelevant* in circumstances of depreciating currencies and appreciating equities, as in all developed countries, but *more essential—if* they are providing positive real interest rates on savings deposits—in most of the remaining countries wherein currencies conform to the twentieth-century norm but securities markets are nonexistent or embryonic. Equities markets and the securities traded therein are now essential in order for most individuals to be better off tomorrow than they are today unless their employment earnings increase at a rate greater than that of price inflation. This is true in the United States. What must it be like for most people in most countries of the world, where an option essential to many Americans is not an option at all?

Retarded Capital Markets and Choice Exclusion

Just as Chapters 7 and 8 might be ignored by many readers, most textbooks on economic development do not discuss equities markets. Indeed, it is often said, though rarely in print, that a stock market is irrelevant (or worse, an oxymoron) in poor countries. In a nineteenth-century world of appreciating currencies, this judgment would be reasonable, but *not* because a country is poor. In *that* world, Khurshid Alam would probably have no Dhaka Stock Exchange to write about, let alone one with increasing capitalization, trading volume, and consistent oversubscription of newly issued stocks. That Bangladesh, one of the poorest countries in the world, should be home to this phenomenon is testimony to the change in choice alternatives of individuals, which is correspondent with the transition from a world of currency appreciation to one of currency depreciation. The magnitude of this change in individual valuations of choice alternatives is inversely related to individual wealth. Without noncurrency resources, an individual on the brink of abject poverty literally faces starvation in consequence of currency deflation.

Thus it is that, in poor countries (particularly where deposit interest rates are exceeded by inflation rates), the poorest individuals wisely store their resources in cows, jewelry, or other tangibles that are less subject to taxation or depreciation by governments. It is a large, but not qualitatively different, step from cows and jewelry to issues of corporate stock. It is a far larger *and* qualitatively different step from any of those equity units, that *can* be worth more tomorrow than they are today, to currency that with certainty will be worth less. Making sense of a stock market in Bangladesh requires recognition of no more than the intelligent preference for cows over cash. And understanding why that preference is more intelligent than its opposite requires no more than our remembering the currency inversion that has occurred since the nineteenth century.

So it is that the contents of this book presume the predominance of neither uncommon nor nonsense. Instead, this volume, along with all others that address capital markets in contemporary circumstances, principally strives to ascertain the best of second-best solutions in a world of third-rate currencies.

In circumstances of currency depreciation (the twentieth-century norm), capital market development is essential in diminishing the waste of resources. Among the resources wasted and underutilized by retarded capital (and other) markets are individual human beings.[6] Because of this, actions that thwart the development of capital markets must be understood as discouraging the development of individuals and, therefore, societies. Unfortunately, the terms in which capital markets are typically addressed tend to obscure both their meaning and moment for any individual who is not a banker, a stockbroker, or rich. Those individuals already understand their interest in capital markets. Indeed, they already understand how they themselves can succeed in, or in spite of, the retardation of capital markets in their countries of residence.

Success *in* a retarded capital market requires either accident (good luck) or political advantage. Without either, individuals are not even assured of the minimal opportunity of being able to stay ahead of inflation by deposits in the market's financial institutions and instruments. In this circumstance it is highly dubious that those receiving loans from the institutions would be those whose investments would be most productive. Each part of this general failing exacerbates the other, further compounding the opportunity omissions by which most people are afflicted. People in general lose when those individuals who would most productively invest the proceeds of loans are unable to get them. Employment that would have been created is foregone, and that loss is compounded by the extent to which those receiving available loan funds apply them to less productive uses. Governmental rules that repress general financial opportunity can spawn particular benefits, at least in the short term, for both the government and the individuals who lobbied in favor of the rules.[7] The lucky are usually individuals whose circumstances are much the same as those who are lobbying government officials to obtain special benefits. Many, if not most, of these incidental beneficiaries would not accept their designation as "successes" because they either did or would oppose the special benefits.

Success *in spite of* a retarded capital market is very much a phenomenon of the late twentieth century; its exponential growth (and capital flight) is attributable mostly to the ongoing technological revolution. The corollary of this revolution is the exponential decline in the capacity of governments to confine the capital of their citizens within their respective sovereignties. An appreciation of this phenomenon appears to have been an integral component of the comprehensive financial reforms made in New Zealand during the 1980s, as detailed by Murray Sherwin in Chapter 6. It may also have influenced those of Chile; in Chapter 5, the recounting of those reforms by Rolf Lüders affords the reader parallel descriptions of the two most thoroughgoing financial liberalization endeavors of the past decade.

Because access to the new technology of this century (computers, modems, and so on) has been confined mainly to the relatively well-off in a country, capital flight and success are increasingly functions of wealth in all countries that have retarded capital markets. A corollary of this fact is that economic success among the poor in countries with retarded capital markets is most likely to be found in the informal markets of their underground economies.[8] The combination of these divergent exits from capital market repression has engendered an underground economy with external and domestic dimensions, the first principally of the rich, the second of the poor. Although the dimensions overlap to the extent that the poor are able to move themselves from one country to another, they are clearly distinguishable because most governments discourage poor immigrants but provide an open door to capital inflows. Nonetheless, their simultaneous occurrence means that extant measures of capital flight and underground economies systematically underestimate the magnitude of both, simply because a conceptualization of either phenomenon must include the other.

To the extent that potential emigrants' assessments of another country to which emigration is possible includes the benefits of an informal sector *within* the countries of current residence, human *and* capital emigration (flight) are underestimated. And, to the extent that modern technology eases the international movement of financial capital, individuals who would previously have moved themselves move their money instead. The most direct linkage of these two dimensions that I have seen or heard about is the characterization by Marcos Victorica (of the Institute of Contemporary Studies in Buenos Aires) of domestic informals as monetary emigrants:

> Informality is how people who don't want to leave the country emigrate. They don't emigrate physically, they just do it monetarily ... [and] capital flight is caused by the same factors as the informal economy. If the causes are the same, then the remedy is also the same. The problems of the foreign debt might be solved with the same kind of measures that would integrate the formal and informal economies (Sullivan 1987, 9).

This observation on informal economies is echoed by that of Cumby and Levich regarding capital flight:

> In the human capital literature, it was argued that, given the mobility of factors, human capital would migrate if it did not receive a competitive market wage. Now the analogy is that financial transactions and financial capital will migrate also if domestic depositors and investors are not offered financial services with competitive risks and returns. In this environment, capital flight ought to be viewed as a symptom of underlying economic problems, rather than as the source of the problem (1987, 50–51).

It is hoped that the reader will note that none of the preceding has required any reference to the formal taxation by governments that so inflames the emotions of taxpayers in developed countries. It is more accurate to consider these injuries of first world governments as no more than the insults that most other governments *add* to the taxlike effects (injuries) of their *non*tax policies. Thus does Richard Bird's book, *More Taxing Than Taxes?* (1991) pose more than a question. A profound irony is that the movement of both people and their money into external and domestic undergrounds deprives a formal government of much of what might have been its tax base.[9] The evidence strongly indicates that that base will diminish to nothing unless government officials recognize "cows or cash?" as an intelligent question when asked by those whose consent they desire, but whose answers they presume themselves able to provide. That presumption has been almost universally (in both time and space) misplaced. It is more worthwhile to look at the evidence.

Today, poorer citizens can reasonably expect their efforts and savings to result in substantial improvements of their life circumstances only if they are born in countries with well-developed capital markets or if they can emigrate.

Expanding Choice

It is apparent that the least wealthy among us would be most fully served by governments that ended their monopoly on the issuance of currency and the rules of entry, exit, and organization in banking. This judgment does not merely reflect a conventional antimonopoly position, for two reasons. First, the collapsing state monopolies of the communist world simply demonstrate that government cannot avoid the effects of private efforts to abrogate market forces.[10] Second, national money monopolies are not like other monopolies.

Capital in Currency. National money monopolies are the only ones that legally require the acceptance and use of their product. All governments have established their currencies as legal tender. This means that acceptance of government currency in discharge of debt is compelled by law and that private contracts specifying payment in anything other than government currency cannot be legally enforced. On the face of it, one might think that such a truly unique monopoly—one that legally requires consumption of its product—could not possibly fail. But this is only true if the magnitude of the product's irrelevance—and, conversely, the relevance of the "cows or cash" question—is not incorporated in the conception of failure.

To the extent and rate that a country's fiat money is becoming worthless, employees will prefer another medium of exchange in compensation for their work, and employers who want to retain them will provide it, even though (as debtors, in this instance) they are not legally required to do so. The employer (as creditor) will in turn seek payment for goods and services sold by the business in tangibles (or other currencies) that are most valued by the employees and other creditors of the business. All of these exchanges are, at the least, extra-legal and, depending on tax law on income and sales, may be illegal as well. Either way, the costs of transacting business and economic inefficiency are inversely related to the value of (demand for) government currency by its citizens. The exchanges contribute to the size of the country's informal or underground economy and reflect the extent to which the formal economy is irrelevant to its own citizens.

If escape from use of the currency by which the formal economy is monetized is not deemed a failure of the especially monopolistic institution of government money, it is doubtful that anyone would consider it a success. But apart from the scholarly literature on competitive currencies and free banking, a quotation such as the following is rare except when truly extraordinary circumstances are addressed.

> A market economy . . . is not established by a one-time reform. It requires a lasting commitment to limiting the role of the government in economic activity. The existence of a central bank provides a continuing incentive for politicians under pressure to confuse money creation with wealth creation. The resulting inflation then leads to myriad interventions in the economy in the form of wage, price, interest rate, exchange market, and capital controls. Eliminating the central bank is one way of committing to a limited role for the state (Hetzel 1990, 19).

An alternative, a currency board (advanced by Hanke and Walters 1990a, 1990b, and in the two chapters following this), is deemed a "close substitute for the proposal to eliminate the central bank," but concludes that the "disadvantage of a currency board is [that] there is no absolutely binding way to keep the government from forcing it to devalue for domestic political reasons" (Hetzel 1990, 19). The uncommon expression of common sense in both this article and the proposal by Steve H. Hanke and Alan A. Walters was a response to uncommon circumstances; indeed, the recommendations were directed to East European countries. Further accenting the uniqueness of the recommendation for eliminating the central bank is the publication in which it appeared, the *Economic Review* of one of the twelve regional Federal Reserve Banks of the United States. Its author disavows uniqueness, however: "A few years ago, this proposal would have seemed radical. Today, it is quite conventional. It simply telescopes the likely evolution of monetary arrangements in Eastern Europe into a one-time reform" (ibid.).

But if the proposal is no longer unique, its implementation, anywhere, will be. Almost any proposed change in almost any status quo engenders as many visions of increased costs as of increased benefits, and positive support by a country's citizens for putting capital back into currency (redeemability, at minimum, and appreciation, at maximum) requires a broader understanding than does perhaps any other policy recommendation. Should such a change in any national currency transpire, therefore, it might be most accurately attributed to the citizens' antipathy toward the status quo, an antipathy most probable during a country's financial and economic collapse—when the flow of citizens escaping from the national currency has become so rampant that government follows, limiting itself, or its paper authority, because its effective authority has already been eroded.

The possibility that many countries other than those of Eastern Europe have crossed this threshhold is reflected by one of two successor volumes in this series for which the present book provides a wide-ranging introduction, *African Finance: Research and Reform* (forthcoming, ICS Press), and by its editor, Lawrence H. White, who is one of the foremost authorities on the history (and possible futures) of free banking and competitive currencies.[11] More important, both this volume and White's introduce to thoughtful African citizens and political leaders a positive alternative to— indeed, an escape from what might otherwise be deemed inescapable—the perpetuation of government's currency monopoly.

The question of where the radical-cum-conventional reforms of free banking and competitive redeemable currencies will be implemented, however, is secondary to that of how.[12] Which of the alternative measures and sequences of their implementation will work better than the others remains to be discovered and may vary somewhat among countries. Nonetheless, the sequence of steps taken in establishing a new, competitively determined unit of account in many countries of Eastern Europe, Africa, and elsewhere should be far less disruptive to the ongoing exchanges of economic life than it would be in developed countries where, for better or worse, the unit of account is also the prevailing and presently preferred medium of exchange.

Somewhat ironically, the more time that elapses in the determination of how in various settings, the greater the likelihood that international government will preempt the possible evolution of competitive currencies,[13] thus replicating the exercises of national governments within countries that reached full steam in the early 1900s. This appears to be one response to the combination of deflated national currencies and the revolutionary changes in applied technologies since World War II that has impelled the creation of new financial market instruments for insuring that the savings of individuals will not be inflated away.

As the twenty-first century begins, the essential and the irrelevant may be expected to continue changing. For example, a company such as American Express (AMEX), operating worldwide and exchanging the currencies of all countries against one another, is but a step removed from the currency boards advocated in Chapter 2 by Steve Hanke and Alan Walters and further illustrated by the unique and virtually unknown case recounted by Hanke and Kurt Schuler in Chapter 3. If AMEX units were made redeemable in whatever commodity or commodities the company decides is most prudent (as were national and other currencies before this century), those units could become the currency against which national currencies are valued.[14] Banks, as we know them today, might survive only where AMEX is least accessible. Should this transpire, there would be entrants into the market to compete with AMEX. They would advertise and perhaps provide stronger backing for their currencies and deposits than AMEX could. Ironically, this state of affairs would be but an interrupted echo of what banks outside London were doing before the limitations imposed on them by the Bank Act of

1844,[15] and free banking (with neither an explicit nor an implicit lender of official last resort) might be reintroduced in today's developing countries as it existed during the development of others before the current century.

Indeed, in marked contrast with the historical correspondence between economic development and competition among note-issuing banks and their currencies, there is no evidence that central banks are or ever have been essential to any country's development. The evidence strongly indicates, instead, that the contributions of central banks to the process of economic development are, at best, irrelevant.[16] The almost universal ascendance of central banks can be most sensibly attributed, therefore, to factors that are themselves not essential to development. But the very fact of their universality also suggests that, should the future imagined by the foregoing actually transpire, there are likely to be calls for government (governments, in the future case) to intervene. If the situation does arise, only one thing is certain: The new order will be characterized (perhaps even believed) by many of its proponents as serving the public interest. AMEX may be among the proponents of the new order.[17]

In the midst of what may be an unending technological revolution, an imagined future escape from a world of deflating currencies is not farfetched. The effective authority of individuals having access to the technology is clearly being enhanced relative to the authority of any collectivity and its rules. These same reasons mitigate against a return in that future to today's circumstance. At the same time, all too frequently, in too many places, people are still adopting courses of action that simply defy so-called common sense. In 1920, for example, Argentina was on the brink of being one of the world's most developed countries. The actions of its governments since then have ensured that it did not succeed. In Chapter 5 in this volume, Rolf Lüders provides more than enough of the gruesome details of this case. Argentina constitutes but one of the more extreme instances of an all too general phenomenon that has been virtually impossible to ignore since the publication in 1973 of Ronald I.

McKinnon's book, *Money and Capital in Economic Development*. In the present volume, in Chapter 4, he provides the lead comment on a reconsideration of that classic by Lawrence H. White. White's scholarly specialization in free banking and competitive currencies provides not only a bridge between this book and one of its two successors, *African Finance*, but also a perspective for both distinguishing and interrelating the sound money considerations embodied in Chapters 2 and 3 and the remainder of this book.

Enabling Capital Creation with Currency. All of the contributors to this volume uphold the preeminent importance of sound currency. Indeed, all would view most of the remainder of the book as being irrelevant to the economic development of any country to the extent that the currency of residents' employment income is unreliable for purposes of economic transactions. If, for example, dollars are demanded by sellers in payment for the goods and services they provide, but employment earnings in the country are paid in zlotys, the discussions on the development of equities markets (Chapter 7, by Flora M. Painter and Robert J. Rourke, and Chapter 8, by Khurshid Alam) should be read last, if at all, by that country's residents. The first three chapters and Chapter 9, by Hanke and Walters, would be the four most relevant. Of these, the most appropriate might well be the third, a description of the North Russian currency board promoted by John Maynard Keynes during World War I.

Because the restoration of capital in currency (by institutional changes that enable its appreciation) cannot be reasonably expected except in the collapse of a country's economy, not just of its currency and formal (government-authorized) financial institutions, this book and especially its other successor volume, *If Texas Were Chile: Financial Risk and Regulation in Commodity-Exporting Economies* (forthcoming, ICS Press), edited (inspired and molded) by Philip L. Brock, attend almost exclusively to reforms that a far greater number of both citizen-consumers and governments will find to be readily responsive to the more immediate and tractable shortcomings of capital markets in all countries in the twentieth-century circumstance.

Indeed, *If Texas Were Chile* provides both implementation and operational guidance for governments of those countries, such as the United States, and states, such as Texas, in which the taxpayers are suffering from enormous losses because enormous losses are occurring within their extant financial markets. In Chapter 5 of this book, Rolf Lüders provides a valuable introduction to the policies adopted by Chile to reform its capital markets. *If Texas Were Chile* discusses the practical day-to-day implications and difficulties of implementing such reforms and includes the first English-language translation of Chile's new banking law (a law that this author would like to see imported into the United States) and an account, coauthored by the superintendent of the country's banking system, of the operation and effects of that law.

Circumstances clearly condition what is possible and probable with respect to the reform of either currencies or capital markets. Clearly, too, governments are essential to their occurrence. To ask whether government is the problem or the solution is somewhat misplaced; it is both. Whether government officials advance institutional and policy reforms because they feel they must or because they truly support them, it is they who will act because it is they who *must* act if reforms are to be implemented and not merely proposed.

These considerations accentuate the value of Terrence C. Reilly's comments (in Chapter 7) on the paper by Flora Painter and Robert Rourke, and on the kinds of reforms that are most likely to redress the inducements (implicit subsidies) to citizens to engage in debt finance rather than equity finance. As may be expected of one of the world's foremost practitioners of securities law, his recommendations are detailed, specific, practical, and immediately actionable. They launched a spirited discussion and highlight the classical liberal conundrum: If one is opposed to government interventions in economic markets, but government has already monopolized currency, should one be opposed in principle to government interventions that actively promote the development of equities markets (as illustrated by the discussion of the Korean case in those pages), or should one, being in favor of the desired effect of competitive market processes, support only those government interventions that negate or diminish the antimarket effects of other government interventions? If principle wins the day, would it matter if one *knew* that the new interventions increased the likelihood that other, more deleterious government interventions would subsequently be eliminated? In practice, no one can know one way or the other; thus much of the discussion found in this book reflects differing assessments of associated likelihoods.

Furthermore, as discussed earlier in this essay, to the extent that twentieth-century capital markets develop *in spite of* governments and their policies, choices available to the poor are likely to become even poorer. This dire possibility follows from the probability that the individuals who are succeeding best are those with the greatest capacity for influencing the reformation or transformation of those government institutions and policies in spite of which they are succeeding, and are, simultaneously, less likely to continue succeeding if they reallocate their time from what they are presently doing in order to influence government. The probability is compounded by the understandable reluctance of such people to call official attention to themselves and those activities that enable them to succeed in spite of government policies. One can hardly expect a person who is succeeding in spite of having but one foot to shoot the remaining foot.

Continuing currency devaluation in tandem with underdeveloped capital markets will minimize success and maximize failure for millions of people and, the poorer they are and the poorer their country of residence, the greater the likelihood of this result, and the greater the human loss. To the extent that foreign aid on this planet responds to the consequences of failure (as it does in the basic human needs approach) and neglects the institutional and policy elements that guarantee it, continuing basic human needs are guaranteed. It sounds ironic, but what people most need in order to escape from guaranteed failure is the guarantee of the *opportunity* to fail—and its converse, the *opportunity* to succeed—a basic human opportunities approach. Capital markets are integral to the approach because they enable the diversification of risk—insurance, not against any and all failures, but against the worst consequences *of* failing (including the perverse perpetuation of unrequited basic human needs).

So it is that the poor not only suffer most from continuing inflation and benefit least from the capital market instruments devised for escaping its consequences, but—unless governments change existing incentive structures—are also likely to have their suffering compounded in the future. So too, most people in countries with appreciating currencies and/or developed capital markets are far better off than are people in countries with neither. Because appreciating currencies and capital markets are essential to other competitive markets (with which they empirically covary), they even provide some fundamental guarantees: that what consumers want most will be provided and that what consumers want least will not be forced upon them. "Let the buyer beware" is reasonable advice to any consumer anywhere, but what developed capital markets guarantee is the even more appropriate maxim, "let the producer or seller beware."

At bottom, the alternative to the caveat, "let the buyer beware" and the development of capital markets is the question, "why should the buyer care?" Wherever producers and sellers are few, or even one and the same, so that consumer choice ranges from the narrow to the nonexistent, the answer must be that there is no reason for the buyer to care. Once this is understood, the more positive corollary of "let the buyer beware" can be recognized: that consumers have choices. The consequences of the absence of such choice is being dramatically revealed, at the outset of the 1990s, by the collapse of governments that established themselves as sole producer-sellers.

The root lesson is that, even as the individual consumer will always be well-advised to beware, consumers in general are king. In some places, even for extended periods of time (more than seventy years in the Soviet Union), this predominance may be belied—but it still remains.

Capital Markets and Development

A derivative set of lessons may emerge from the ongoing efforts to "marketize" or otherwise reform either socialism or previously communist countries. One of these lessons may be a greater appreciation of the inefficacy of dichotomizing citizen choice and consumer choice, as if the preferences and demands of individuals are not simultaneously those of both; as if an individual is not both citizen and consumer. From that, the disutilities of conceptually separating democracy and market, polity and economy can be appreciated. This is not to say that *no* separation is appropriate. Obviously, polity and economy comprise different instruments for responding to the preferences of individuals, and some combination of instruments may be essential to maximizing the breadth and depth of individual consent to the processes and consequences of either. But, clearly, the development of capital markets should not be expected in places where the potential choices of individual citizen-consumers are routinely arrogated by governments. Unfortunately, that usurpation is further routinized by the failure to develop capital markets in the twentieth-century circumstance of another—the continuing depreciation of currencies that individuals receive in reward for their efforts, and the corollary devaluation of any savings in those currencies. In this circumstance, especially—where capital is not restored to currencies—the development of capital markets is no more nor less than an exercise in restoring arrogated choice.

2   *Steve H. Hanke and Alan A. Walters*

Financial and Capital Markets in Developing Countries

The Liberal Economic Order

Before World War II, the liberal economic order was looked on favorably. It was generally agreed, for example, that economic progress could best be achieved by a minimalist state that secured private property rights, promoted financial stability, and allowed individuals to pursue their own affairs unmolested by government intervention.

Most developing countries were still colonies of the great powers of Europe. Not surprisingly, the colonies imported many metropolitan institutions and attitudes about the desirability of the liberal economic order. For example, the colonial monetary and financial systems were offshoots, indeed often quite sizable branches, of those of their metropolitan centers. In some cases, the colonies actually used the metropolitan currency; in many, perhaps most, the monetary link between the colonies and the metropolitan centers was through a currency board that exchanged domestic currency for the foreign reserve currency of the metropolitan center at a specified and fixed rate.[1] To perform this function, currency boards were required to hold realizable financial assets in the reserve currency. Amounts were at least equal to the value of the outstanding domestic currency. In consequence, there could be no fiduciary irresponsibility because at least 100 percent of the domestic currency was backed.

As colonies became independent states in the 1950s and 1960s, many institutions that were identified as colonial were maligned and condemned. In consequence—with notable exceptions, such as those of Singapore, Brunei, and Hong Kong—currency boards were discarded in favor of central banks. This change was rather unfortunate because the currency board system had a number of important advantages: exchange rates were fixed, colonial monetary policies were passive, and transactions on both current and capital accounts were relatively unimpeded. In consequence, colonies always enjoyed roughly the same relatively low rates of inflation as did the metropolitan centers to which they were linked. Because colonies with currency boards did not have central banks, they simply did not have the means to create money, manipulate exchange rates, and finance government deficits by borrowing from the central bank. By depoliticizing the monetary system and insulating the public purse from plundering politicians, the currency board system gave credibility to the fixed exchange rate. Citizens would willingly hold both currency and deposits, knowing that their value would be maintained.

The currency board system had another major virtue. It facilitated natural links between the colonies and metropolitan capital markets. Branch banks from the metropolitan centers were found in most colonies. With these banks and unimpeded capital flows, colonial residents had access to large pools of capital that were available on competitive terms. Hence, interest rates in the colonies were somewhere near those that prevailed in the metropolitan centers. The colonies also had easy access to metropolitan financial expertise and training. In consequence, markets and indigenous firms, often with correspondence arrangements in the home countries, developed to intermediate between local savers and investors.

These financial arrangements facilitated an extraordinary expansion of savings, investment, exports, and income in many countries in colonial Africa and Southeast Asia. For example, before 1885 there was not a single rubber tree in Malaya (now Malaysia) or a single cocoa tree in British West Africa. By the 1930s, rubber, cocoa, and other export crops were being produced on millions of acres, most of them owned and cultivated by non-Europeans. Such a transformation from subsistence to market agriculture required a massive capital investment. Although considerable capital flowed into these enterprises from abroad, much of it was generated by indigenous savings. This is clear evidence that freedom and financial stability—which accompanied the liberal economic order and specifically the currency board system—were crucial elements in stimulating sound investments in projects with very long maturities.[2]

The Interventionist Economic Order

The various vicissitudes of the financial regimes of the colonial powers, particularly during and after World War II, caused some difficulties, but, in general, inflation was modest, growth was satisfactory, and the satellite stability of the colonies continued until well after their independence. However, even though the liberal economic order had produced satisfactory if not spectacular results, an appeal to the interventionist economic order became a siren song to politicians in most newly independent nations. This appeal was underwritten by economic theorists who argued that the developing nations faced a "vicious circle of poverty." Although this argument takes many forms, the general line of reasoning is represented thus: incomes are low; hence, savings are low; hence, the capital accumulation that is necessary for economic progress is low; hence, developing nations are caught in a vicious circle of poverty (Myrdal 1957). To break this so-called vicious circle, the interventionist argued that, with the help of foreign aid, governments should employ intervention, regulations, income redistribution programs, and public works projects to create the conditions for economic growth and material progress.

Armed with a theoretical rationale for intervention, its popular appeal in the anticolonialist era, and the means to intervene, the politicians did not take long to transform most newly independent nations from liberal into interventionist economies. Even the rulers of countries that had achieved independence long before, such as those in Latin America, learned quickly how to control their economies in order to garner and deploy political power.

In the financial sector, central banks replaced currency boards, allowing governments to create money and finance their deficits by borrowing from the newly created central banks. Irresponsible fiscal policies, explosive monetary policies, and runaway inflation followed. If this were not enough, entry and operational restrictions were imposed on financial institutions, particularly those that were foreign-owned.

Intervention in financial and capital markets was designed so that governments could expropriate much of the seigniorage and control and direct the flow of credit for politically favored uses. For example, high reserve requirements were mandated and financial intermediaries were required to hold a certain portion of their assets in low-yielding government bonds. These mandates allowed governments to tap savings on a low or even no-cost basis. To reduce the ability of the private sector to compete for national savings, governments suppressed private bond and equity markets through taxes, duties, and overburdensome regulations. The private sector's ability to mobilize domestic resources was further limited by interest rate ceilings on deposits. Selective credit policies were also imposed to channel capital into investments that governments regarded as desirable. In practice, this resulted in the channeling of subsidized credit to political friends, rather than to sound projects.

Under the interventionist economic order, restrictions on the financial sector were designed to do two things: generate seigniorage for the government and allow politicians and/or civil servants to make credit allocation (investment) decisions. Judged on these criteria, the restrictions have been a success. However, there have been substantial costs associated with these policies. Restrictions on financial and capital markets have greatly reduced the material progress of the countries that have employed them (Scully 1988).

A Taxonomy of Selective Credit Policies

Although the details differ across countries, there are certain generic types of intervention in financial markets and they can be found in most developing countries. Selective credit policies represent one generic type, and interest rate ceilings on deposits are a form of selective credit. (For a complete review of selective credit policies, see Fry [1988].) Rate ceilings are an implicit tax on returns to savings. Indeed, when inflation rates are high and deposit rate ceilings are employed, real rates of return on savings are typically negative. Most developing nations also mandate that loan rates for priority sectors be set below market levels. To induce commercial banks to lend at these low rates, central banks rediscount priority loans on concessional terms. Hence, through the rediscount mechanism, central banks act as allocators of subsidized credit, and their assets represent a large share of the financial sector's total assets. In addition, by engaging in substantial rediscounting, central banks jeopardize their role as purveyors of monetary policy.

Central banks that engage in extensive rediscounting of priority paper usually use high required-reserve ratios. These requirements represent an implicit tax on savings. Moreover, they reduce the ability of commercial banks to engage in nonpriority lending and increase the collection of seigniorage. In some cases, the negative differentials between priority loan and deposit rates are financed by direct government subsidies. This form of selective credit policy is, of course, much more transparent than is the rediscounting mechanism, but the effects are largely the same.

Credit floors, whereby the monetary authorities simply set the minimum proportions of total credit or deposits that must be lent by private institutions to favored borrowers, are often used in conjunction with mandated, low-cost loans. This policy restricts the ability of private institutions to manage their portfolios in a manner that they consider most attractive.

With floors, most developing nations also have ceilings. A selective credit policy dictates either the maximum proportions of total credit or deposits that can be lent to nonpriority borrowers or the maximum aggregate volume of loans that can be made, thereby establishing credit ceilings. Aggregate ceilings are usually used in conjunction with exemptions for priority loans or credit floors for priority sectors.

Selective credit policies may also be implemented by specialized financial institutions established to cater to the needs of priority borrowers. Funds are often extracted from nonspecialized depository institutions through high reserve requirements. These funds are then channeled, through specialized financial institutions, to priority sectors on concessional terms. State-owned banks represent yet another means used to direct credit to priority sectors on concessional terms.

Israel's Mastery of Selective Credit Policies

Israel is but one example of a country that uses a wide range of selective credit policies. (For an analysis of selective credit policies in Israel, see Rabushka and Hanke [1988].) To illustrate how pervasive they can become, we present a brief review of Israel's policies. The basic legal instrument that allows the government to dominate the financial and capital markets is the Law for the Encouragement of Capital Investment. The law identifies two broad criteria that are used to determine "socially desirable" investments: the dispersal of population and the improvement of the balance of payments. If projects pass the eligibility tests that are based on these two criteria, they receive sizable subsidies in the form of direct government

Financial and Capital Markets in Developing Countries 31

grants and loans from the state-owned and/or private financial institutions at below-market rates. In consequence, between 50 and 80 percent of the total investment cost of eligible projects is financed by grants and subsidized credit. The scale of these benefits is truly staggering. For example, in the 1980s grants amounted to 4.3 percent of the gross national product (GNP), and the subsidies embodied in cheap credit averaged 5.2 percent of the GNP.

Because of the government's generous terms, applications for grants and cheap credit exceed the state's capacity to finance all of them. To pick the happy winners from the applicant pool, the government has established an Investment Center. Hence, it is the Investment Center's bureaucrats, not entrepreneurs operating in markets, who decide which projects will be carried out.

In order to obtain the means to finance socially desirable projects, the government nationalizes a large portion of Israel's savings by restricting investors' direct access to finance. For example, firms cannot issue stock or bonds without permission from the Overseer of the Capital Market and Insurance at the Ministry of Finance.

Faced with these restrictions, bond and equity markets are virtually squeezed out of existence, and investors must rely on credit from the government and/or financial intermediaries. However, financial intermediaries cannot use depositors' savings freely. For example, the government mandates that 75 to 85 percent of the intermediaries' portfolios be invested in nonnegotiable government bonds. The portfolios of commercial banks are further restricted by high reserve requirements. Bank deposits linked to foreign exchange are subject to a 100 percent reserve ratio and most other deposits require reserves of about 40 percent. Portfolio discretion is further limited because financial intermediaries are required, by means of credit floors and ceilings, to direct credit through seven separate funds, such as the Diamonds Fund, the Long-Term Export Fund, and the Aid to Industry Fund. Not surprisingly, these segmented funds are required to charge different, but below-market, interest rates.

Israel illustrates how selective credit policies can be employed to limit private bond and equity markets and channel private savings through financial intermediaries. By controlling intermediaries' use of these savings, the government directs virtually all private savings toward priority projects. In consequence, by 1983, Israel had effectively nationalized its citizens' savings without actually nationalizing the nation's financial institutions. In 1983, with the now-infamous Banking Shares Collapse, the nationalization of savings became overt because the government was "forced" to nationalize Israel's commercial banks.

The Ill Effects of Selective Credit Policies

Selective credit policies create substantial economic waste and retard economic progress. Returns on savings are reduced, and savers usually have little or no incentive to accumulate domestic financial instruments. Not surprisingly, a large share of domestic savings is either exported or accumulated through underground channels at relatively high resource costs. In consequence, total domestic resource mobilization is suppressed.

Selective credit policies also affect the allocation of the suppressed pool of domestic savings. Low-yielding investments displace high-yielding investments. Interventionists claim that this displacement does not generate economic waste because investments that are favored by selective credit policies generate social returns that are much higher than their private returns. However, evidence suggests that selective credit policies usually favor investments with relatively low social and private returns. Indeed, selective credit policies often promote investments that yield negative social and private returns. In consequence, these policies direct the suppressed pool of domestic savings to relatively inferior projects.

Selective credit policies also distort the term structure of loan rates. In free markets, with neutral inflation expectations, a rising loan-rate term structure (relatively high long-term rates) is generated because of time and liquidity preferences and risk aversion.

However, to encourage long-term investments, selective credit policies create a downward sloping term structure of loan rates (relatively low long-term rates). As a result, factor prices are artificially tilted in favor of capital-intensive, long-lived projects and against labor. This distortion adds to the waste.

Selective credit policies also destroy normal entrepreneurial activity and risk taking or drive them underground. The entrepreneurial-market process is replaced by a political-bureaucratic process in which investment decisions are made by politicians and bureaucrats rather than by private risk takers. Successful participants in economies that employ selective credit policies are not those who can innovate, assess risks, and make prudent investments; they are those who are well connected. They know their way around the political corridors and through the bureaucratic maze. The true entrepreneurial class is usually a small endangered species that operates underground.

Selective credit policies also lead to spectacular failures. Entrepreneurial-market processes typically generate many new, small enterprises. The market test is always sifting and sorting new enterprises to determine which ones will prosper and grow and which ones will fail. This sifting and sorting process is characterized by a relatively large number of small-scale failures.

In contrast, political-bureaucratic processes typically generate relatively few, large investments. Both the politicians and bureaucrats who make investment decisions desire visibility and lack the patience to create an economy bit by bit. Hence, there is a preference for large projects. Without a market test, the sifting and sorting function is left to politicians and bureaucrats. Not surprisingly, they tend to look the other way when large projects that they have financed go sour; politicians and bureaucrats suffer from a "not on my watch" syndrome. In consequence, although the political-bureaucratic process might not generate investment failures as frequently as does the entrepreneurial-market process, it generates failures on a much more colossal scale. Moreover, in contrast to markets, the political-bureaucratic process does not have the capacity to pick winners, and *everyone* has to pay for its failures. In the final analysis, selective credit policies suppress domestic savings, allocate credit to relatively inferior investments, and seriously slow economic growth.

Discriminatory Taxes on Financial Intermediation

Private financial intermediaries in developing countries face a wide variety of discriminatory explicit and implicit taxes in addition to the selective credit policies. These taxes reduce the flexibility of financial intermediaries because they reduce the funds available for discretionary lending and widen the spread between deposit and loan rates of interest. For example, in Israel, where taxes reach confiscatory levels, real spreads have exceeded 100 percent (in 1985). The wedge created by taxes reduces the real volume of savings that flow through financial intermediaries.

Explicit taxes include taxes on loan interest, withholding taxes on deposit interest, transaction taxes, stamp duties, value added taxes, and profits taxes. Implicit taxes are more subtle and perhaps more damaging. To finance what are often huge public deficits at low cost, many governments require private intermediaries to commit a large portion of their assets to the purchase of low-yielding, nonnegotiable government bonds. This is illustrated, in Israel, by the requirement that pension funds hold 75 percent and commercial banks hold 85 percent of their assets in nonnegotiable government bonds. This allows the government to finance its deficits and lay claim to a huge chunk of the nation's investable funds at below-market rates: a tax on savers. It also results in the displacement of relatively high-yielding private investment by relatively low-yielding public sector spending. If this were not enough, these investment requirements limit the ability of financial intermediaries to diversify their portfolios, which results in another implicit tax on the intermediaries and savers.

Because interest is usually not paid on bank reserves or excess reserves, reserve requirements represent another implicit tax on financial intermediaries and savers. If we ignore bank capital and excess reserves, banks' earning assets equal their deposit liabilities when there are no reserve requirements. As the required reserve ratio is increased, the volume of earning assets that can be sustained by the same deposit base is necessarily decreased. For example, a required reserve ratio of 50 percent reduces the volume of earning assets for each dollar of deposit base by 50 cents, thereby doubling the ratio of operating costs to earning assets. In consequence of this implicit tax wedge, the average interest rate paid to savers on their deposits can be no more than half the return that is generated on a bank's earnings assets. In addition, by reducing the ability of financial institutions to manage their portfolios, discriminatory taxes increase the costs of financial intermediation, driving a wedge between savers and investors and reducing the ability of intermediaries to mobilize domestic resources.

Uncompetitiveness and the Cost of Intermediation

Developing countries have received a considerable amount of criticism precisely because their financial systems tend to be uncompetitive. Uncompetitiveness increases intermediation costs and hinders the ability of intermediaries to mobilize domestic resources. Four measures of competitiveness confirm the general validity of this criticism. First, payments efficiency is typically low. This is evidenced by slow growth in demand deposit rates, low ratios of clearings to demand deposits, long time periods to cash checks and process accounts, and high costs of effecting payments. Second, the efficiency of resource mobilization (the ability to attract savings) is low. Third, the costs of intermediation are high. Last, the efficiency in allocating funds is low.

The uncompetitive nature of financial systems, in large part, is the result of government policies. Perhaps the most important determinant of competition in the banking systems of developing countries is the role that foreign banks are allowed to play. There is a strong positive correlation between the presence of foreign bank branches and competition. Given that many developing countries impose entry and operational restrictions on foreign banks, the dearth of competitive financial systems in these countries should not be too surprising.

Other government policies also act to reduce competition and increase intermediation costs: discriminatory taxes and reserve requirements, as previously discussed; selective credit policies that impose substantial administrative costs on financial intermediaries and thereby increase operating cost ratios; and interest rate ceilings. The latter induce financial intermediaries to engage in nonprice competition that further increases operating cost ratios. Government policies that stimulate inflation, when employed in combination with interest rate ceilings, reduce the real money demand. Hence, the real volume of resources available to the banking system is reduced, and operating cost ratios rise. Inflation-induced increases in operating cost ratios also occur because the average maturity on deposits is reduced as inflation rates rise. This requires more frequent deposit rollovers and higher operating cost ratios. Government policies toward labor unions can also greatly increase operating cost ratios for financial intermediaries. In many Latin American countries, for example, governments grant unions monopoly privileges. In consequence, labor contracts often contain work-rule clauses that raise operating costs. In some countries, nontermination clauses are included in union contracts. For example, all union employees of failed banks in Uruguay are guaranteed employment in other "healthy" banks at the same pay scale, a provision that further increases operating cost ratios.

Arrears, delinquency, and default costs, which are symptomatic of repressed, uncompetitive financial markets, also increase the cost of financial intermediation, thereby reducing the net returns to savers while raising the gross costs to borrowers. Of course, selective credit policies are among the major contributors to the huge volume of nonperforming loans in developing countries, because below-market loan rates (often negative in real terms) give borrowers a strong incentive to postpone repayment.

Excessive arrears and default rates, which are all too common in developing nations, indicate inefficiency of one sort or another. The causes are typically interventionist government policies and the lack of proper bank regulation and supervision. If this were not enough, the legal systems within which financial intermediaries operate are totally inadequate. Banks typically have great difficulties in securing loans and obtaining legal redress in the event of nonpayment. Inadequate bankruptcy laws contribute to the explosion in nonperforming assets because many creditors cannot use bankruptcy proceedings and have no legal recourse when state-owned enterprises fail to service their loans. All of these dire results reflect poorly defined property rights, slow court procedures, incompetent court officials, political influence in the legal process, and corruption. In consequence, banks and other financial intermediaries attempt to avoid legal recourse because the legal systems are most unsupportive.

Specialized Credit Institutions and State-Owned Banks

To correct for so-called market failures and assist in channeling credit to "socially worthwhile" projects, specialized credit institutions and nationalized financial institutions are often employed by interventionists in developing nations. With an unintended irony, these institutions are often called Development Finance Corporations (DFCs) or Institutions (DFIs). Specialized institutions are often designed to handle sector-specific credit "needs." These needs usually arise because traditional banks have avoided making loans, particularly long-term loans, to high-risk, marginal sectors. The specialized institutions are therefore established to lend to high-risk, marginal borrowers but are usually not allowed to charge loan rates commensurate with high-risk, marginal loans. In consequence, the specialized institutions simply segment credit markets, increase the costs of financial intermediation (through financial layering), promote uneconomic projects, and either go bankrupt or receive large operating subsidies from governments.

State-owned financial institutions are also used to achieve the interventionists' goals. These financial institutions typically perform, as do other state-owned enterprises, in an inferior manner. For example, when compared to similarly situated private banks, nationalized banks have higher operating costs to assets, to deposits, and to capital. Inferior performance results because property rights arrangements are not neutral. The incentives created by private property rights—through the link between the consequences of the use of private assets and their owner's wealth—have profound consequences. Private owners face significant incentives that make it desirable to monitor the behavior of enterprise managers and employees. Consequently, private managers and employees find it relatively difficult to engage in wasteful shirking behavior or behavior that is inconsistent with the enhancement of the present value of the enterprise (owners' wealth).

The market for shares acts as a court of last resort to reinforce these monitoring incentives. The expected effects of current actions are capitalized into the present value of shares. If the actions of incumbent managements are inappropriate, share prices will fall, and the returns from the purchase of shares for the purpose of a corporate takeover, which is designed to replace current management, will increase. In consequence, the threat of corporate takeovers is a disciplinary force on incumbent managements. Residual claimants (owners) monitoring managers and the market for corporate control—both of which are absent in state-owned enterprises—act to generate superior performances by private enterprises vis-à-vis public enterprises. This performance gap is largest when output, input, and capital markets are competitive.

Underdeveloped Bond and Equity Markets

The uncompetitive, costly nature of financial intermediation in developing countries should give rise to formal markets for bonds and equities to permit direct access to capital. However, bond and equity markets play a minor role, at best, in domestic resource mobilization. This is largely the result of government policies. For example, through inflation, discriminatory taxes, and regulations, Israel has discouraged the development of equity and private sector bond markets because the government does not want its monopsony over that nation's private savings to be challenged.

In the final analysis, once a government decides to control credit policies and financial intermediation, it cannot allow private bond and equity markets to develop. After all, if they did, enterprises would have direct access to the nation's pool of savings, and the government would lose a source of seigniorage and its control over the allocation of savings.

The Bitter Fruits of Interventionism

One of the most serious consequences of interventionism has been the *shrinkage of the financial sector*. When subject to effective expropriation through low deposit interest rates, people naturally seek a proper reward elsewhere—either through capital flight, so popular in Latin America, through a retreat to the underground or informal economy, or through the hoarding of goods that will depreciate less than a bank deposit does. People keep their savings out of the financial markets, and large firms find ways of shifting finance without entering the expensive portals of the banks. In the nine most indebted countries, we find that only some 20 to 25 percent of savings are injected into financial markets. This compares with about 85 to 90 percent in industrialized western countries. (For illustration of various measures of the extent to which savings are channeled through formal financial systems, see the World Bank [1989].)

The informal or underground sector is of immense importance in marshalling savings and allocating capital. By its nature we know little about it, but some of the inefficiencies are manifest. For example, when a man accumulates capital to build a house, he does so by gradually acquiring bricks and timber, rather than by depositing cash in the bank. The large commodity stocks and the many unfinished buildings and assets that we see in developing countries are testimony to the inefficiency caused, inter alia, by the restriction on overt financial and capital markets.

The informal sector has developed its own structure of exchange and markets. Because informal markets are usually quite illegal and, in many countries, severe penalties are imposed for transgressing the credit and currency laws, they tend to be limited and capricious and often require a wide arrangement of bribes and kickbacks to keep the authorities at bay. Nevertheless, these markets do contribute enormously to development and they do so relatively efficiently. For example, the informal sector responds to customers' financing needs rapidly, its transaction costs (operating and default costs) are lower than those of traditional financial intermediaries, and it enhances domestic resource mobilization (Holst 1985).

One of the most efficient ways for governments to contribute to the creation of wealth is for them to cease suppressing or attempting to suppress the myriad financial transactions in the informal sector. The economic climate would then be propitious for the development of indigenous financial and capital market institutions, such as the borrowing companies of Malaysia, the credit clubs in the *favelas* of Rio de Janeiro, the rotating savings and credit associations of Africa, and the curb markets of South Korea and other Asian countries.

A second major consequence of dirigiste policies has been the *insulation of developing countries from world capital and credit markets*. It has shielded domestic markets from competition. Visitors who view these protected domestic financial institutions are always appalled at the waste, inefficiency, and often bribery involved. In many countries, protected domestic banks become little more than extensions of government bureaucracies. This insulation has also cut developing countries off from the normal interchange of banking transactions, capital market instruments, and foreign expertise. The numerous instruments available to the international investor, such as currency swaps, interest rate swaps, commercial paper, liability management, and so on are all restricted or nonexistent. Also absent is bank management expertise. Not only is there a severe shortage of personnel to carry on normal banking functions, such as project appraisal, portfolio management, foreign exchange management, auditing, and so forth, but also there is virtually nobody with the training and experience to deal with the sophisticated financial transactions that have become prominent during the financial revolution of the 1980s.

Developing nations' main link to outside financial centers is through ubiquitous government agencies, a link that should be privatized. Perhaps the fastest way to gain financial expertise, increase available sources of capital, and improve domestic financial market competitiveness and efficiency would be to eliminate the restrictions on the entry of foreign banks and security dealers into domestic markets. By lifting these entry restrictions, developing nations would become privately linked to competitive international capital markets. This linkage would be greatly enhanced if developing countries also abolished their central banks and replaced them with currency boards. The currency board system would generate the monetary stability required to attract more foreign expertise and capital.

A third main effect of interventionism is that the *financial sector inhibits, instead of promotes, efficient change in industry and commerce*. Rigidity of the financial system begets rigidity in the economy that it services and is particularly important in the wake of financial distress. The system of regulated interest rates and credit rationing reduces the volume of credit and channels most of it to politically preferred firms that tend to be large employers of labor and are sheltered from the winds of change by trade restrictions and sometimes by outright subsidies. Typical examples include iron and steel companies, automobile assembly plants, textile firms, and petrochemical plants. As relative prices on world markets change, the cost of maintaining such inefficient industries becomes very high. Indeed, most of the enterprises in these favored sectors should go into receivership. But the banks that have channeled so much money into these firms have a great incentive to keep on lending the lion's share of the diminished total quantity of credit to these enterprises. Keeping them liquid avoids the costs of bankruptcy and makes it more likely that the government can be pressured into bailing out both the protected firms and their supporting banks. The most important element in this sorry story, however, is the fact that new firms in efficient lines of production cannot get their hands on credit because it is virtually all being used to prop up old moribund firms. This suggests how important it is for governments and their agencies to enforce bankruptcy and to prevent the Rube Goldberg behavior of banks and development finance institutions.

Finally, we should mention that, although there is considerable agreement about the necessary elements of reform, the sequencing of the reforms leaves much room for dissension. Everyone would agree that the reform of government finance (the reduction of deficits and control of monetary emissions) is crucial. But should it precede, follow, or accompany the deregulation of domestic labor and goods markets? Perhaps even more important are issues that surround the debates about the liberalization of capital markets. Just when should these markets be opened up? Many argue, for example, that the premature opening of capital markets will result in massive capital movements that will inhibit further reforms. No doubt many of these issues cannot be resolved without discussing particular countries and institutional systems. These items remain on the agenda.

Stable financial systems and free and open capital markets have played a major role in the development of many advanced or rapidly developing countries. Free capital markets do not guarantee rapid development; other ingredients are needed. Nevertheless, an ossified financial system will inhibit or even stop development. Therein lies the hope for reform.

3   *Steve H. Hanke and Kurt Schuler*

Keynes's Russian Currency Board

For an economy to function well, it needs a currency that people can use to purchase a wide variety of goods and services, that is readily convertible into foreign exchange, and that is a reliable store of value. The currencies of most less-developed countries, as well as those of the Soviet Union and the newly democratizing nations of Eastern Europe, do not possess these qualities. Unless successful currency reforms can be implemented, these nations will not be able to sustain economic progress.

A promising currency reform would require that the central banks in these countries be replaced by currency boards (Hanke and Walters, 1990a). The principal attributes of currency boards are: (1) the issuance of domestic currency that is readily convertible into a foreign-reserve currency at a specified and fixed rate; (2) a domestic currency backed by liquid reserves held by a board and denominated in a foreign-reserve currency; and (3) reserves equal to or greater than the value of the domestic currency issued. With the discipline of convertibility at a fixed rate and reserve-currency backing, reliability and confidence in the domestic currency would be established, and the domestic currency would acquire the properties that are necessary for a well-functioning economy.

As evidence that these results would be obtained, we need only look at the record of currency boards. Boards were ubiquitous in the British colonial regimes of Africa, Asia, and the Caribbean. Indeed, they are still employed in Singapore and Hong Kong. In addition, there were several outside of British colonies, including one in Russia. We will discuss that board in detail below. In all cases, the boards successfully issued domestic currencies that were as good as the reserve currencies that supported them. Moreover, the boards captured noninflationary seigniorage from their domestic note issues because they held a portion of their reserves in high-grade, interest-bearing bonds.

An Introductory Note

A jumble of currency reforms has been proposed recently for the Soviet Union and newly democratized nations in Eastern Europe as well as for other less-developed countries. We examine an instance of a successful currency reform that occurred in Russia itself. Although this reform is virtually unknown today, it provides us with concrete evidence to support recent "sound-money" proposals (Hanke and Walters 1990b and 1990c; Hetzel 1990).

What makes this Russian currency reform even more noteworthy is the fact that it was the idea of none other than John Maynard Keynes. Surprisingly, there are no references to Keynes's scheme in the standard biographies about him or in his *Collected Writings*. The only published discussion of Keynes's North Russian currency reform of 1918 is an article by Dominick Spring-Rice that appeared in the *Economic Journal* of September 1919. Spring-Rice was an official sent by the British War Office to advise the Allied forces on financial matters. His grasp of currency matters was solid, and he wrote from first-hand knowledge of most of the events he discussed. Although his article is quite useful, it represents a progress report rather than an analysis of a completed episode. Later the Bolsheviks overran North Russia and the North Russian currency went out of circulation.

From the perspective of over seventy years later, the North Russian currency has fresh importance. We shall supplement Spring-Rice's description and partial account with information from British Foreign Office archives. Moreover, we analyze the North Russian currency in light of current events taking place in the Soviet Union and Eastern Europe.

The Allied Invasion of North Russia

The Bolshevik party opposed Russia's involvement in World War I. Within days after it seized power in the revolution of November 1917 (according to the New Style calendar), it began peace talks with the German government. While the talks dragged on, the fighting continued. The main supply route for goods from the other Allied nations to support Russia's war effort was the sea route to the northern ports of Archangel and Murmansk. Archangel, the larger and more established city, was connected by railroad to Moscow. Murmansk did not become an important port until the war. It had the advantage over Archangel of usually being ice-free all winter. Murmansk was connected by railroad to Petrograd.

The Bolsheviks upset the Allies by seizing some of the Allied military goods stored in Archangel during the winter of 1917–1918. The Allies could do nothing to stop the Bolsheviks, though, because the port was icebound. The Bolsheviks signed the Brest-Litovsk peace treaty with Germany on March 3, 1918. On March 6, the British quietly landed a party of fewer than two hundred marines at Murmansk. The Murmansk soviet had been quarreling with the central government over the Allied presence in the North. The Murmansk soviet favored that presence because the Allies supplied the North with badly needed food. The central government distrusted the Allies. Matters came to a head on June 30, when the Murmansk soviet broke with the central government. A large British force landed in Murmansk on July 26 and proceeded toward Archangel. While the British were overpowering an island fortress guarding Archangel, White Guard forces in the town staged a coup against the Bolsheviks on the night of August 1. The Allies found a local government well disposed toward them when they entered the city (Kennan 1967). White forces across the North joined together to form a provisional government for the region, with headquarters in Archangel. It was headed by N. V. Chaikovski. In consequence of a series of accidents and blunders, the Allies became entangled in the Russian civil war, supporting the Northern provisional government.

French, American, Italian, and Canadian troops soon joined the original British force in North Russia, making a force of about ten thousand troops. One of the force's pressing needs was a way to pay for the local services it needed. To promote good will, the Allies decided not to seize goods or to force laborers to work for free, as the Germans were doing. Currency in the North was quite heterogeneous: czarist, Kerensky, Bolshevik, and local White government notes all circulated (Foreign Office 1918, 3295: 102). The Russian state bank branch at Archangel declared itself independent of the Petrograd head office after the White coup and issued its own notes as the State Bank of Northern Russia. Even though none of the currencies had a reliable value—they were inflated or often forged—the Allies, lacking adequate supplies of notes to pay dock and railway workers, were sometimes forced to acquire notes by selling imported goods locally. Indeed, on occasion, the Allies were so desperate for notes that they dumped goods on the market for less than they had paid.

The Emission Caisse

Spring-Rice began thinking immediately of how to improve the Allies' financial situation. In a memorandum written on July 3, 1918, at Murmansk, he suggested that "the task of providing currency for local needs should, if possible, fall on the local authority," perhaps in combination with a loan to the provisional government in British pounds (Foreign Office 1918, 3344: 249–50). On July 9, the British general at Murmansk asked the British government to print notes for British military use at Murmansk (Spring-Rice 1919, 282).

The precise form that the note issue would take was to be decided later. Spring-Rice, in a memorandum written on July 28, proposed five possible ways of ensuring an adequate supply of currency. Two involved British-issued or British-backed currency. Spring-Rice favored "a special issue of currency created by the Murmansk authorities," to be called the Murmansk ruble, in terms of which the Allies would agree to sell, at fixed prices to the local populace, food and other goods they imported (Foreign Office 1918, 3344: 256–60). War Office officials in London went to work in July to arrange a British printer for Murmansk ruble notes.

John Maynard Keynes, who at the time was a high British Treasury official responsible for war finance, became involved in establishing a North Russian currency in August. Both Spring-Rice (1919, 284) and Foreign Office records (1919, 3970: 22) credit Keynes with thinking up the details of the currency issue scheme. Indeed, Keynes wrote two notes on the subject, which we discovered in the Foreign Office archives (1918, 3295: 52, 62–64) and have reproduced in the Appendix to this chapter. On September 11, the British commissioner in Archangel received a telegram outlining Keynes's scheme (Spring-Rice 1919, 284).

The American and French governments were at first hostile to the scheme. They feared that it would become a tool of British economic dominance in North Russia. At the same time as the North Russian intervention was occurring, all three governments and Japan were jockeying for influence in Siberia. Their cooperation was strained because each suspected the others of wanting to establish spheres of influence as they had already done in China. The British government argued that the situation in North Russia urgently demanded action, which it was best poised to take. By mid-October, the American and French governments agreed to the scheme (U.S. Department of State 1932, 3: 66–87; Carley 1988, 130).

The essential elements of the note issue scheme were outlined in a resolution of the Northern provisional government's Financial and Economic Council on October 9. The following points were officially published on November 11 (Spring-Rice 1919, 286):

The provisional government established an agency called the National Emission Caisse (North Russia). (*Emission caisse* is French for "note issue office.") The Caisse was to be an organ of any successor government to the Northern provisional government. The president of the Caisse for the first six months was to be a British banker, Ernest M. Harvey.

The Caisse was to issue notes in denominations of one up to five hundred rubles and small-change coins or notes. It was to exchange its rubles for British pounds at a fixed rate of 40 rubles per pound sterling by issuing checks on banks abroad (mainly in London). The Caisse was also to accept U.S. dollars and French francs at their rates of exchange against the then-floating British pound. Anyone wishing to buy the Caisse's notes had to do so with foreign currency. The provisional government guaranteed the notes with its whole property. But, more important, the Caisse's note issue was backed with a pound sterling reserve equal to at least 75 percent of the issue. This reserve was on deposit in British pounds with the Bank of England. The Bank of England deposit was the Caisse's inviolable property and could not become a Bolshevik possession should the provisional government fall. The Caisse was also allowed to buy the provisional government's bonds up to 25 percent of its note issue.

The Caisse was expected to make profits from its deposit at the Bank of England and its holdings of provisional government bonds, because both paid interest whereas the notes it issued did not. The Caisse and the government were to share profits equally until the Caisse accumulated a further reserve of 10 percent of its note issue. Any profits beyond that were to go entirely to the government (Foreign Office 1918, 3295: 343–47, 529–31).

The Caisse worked like the West African Currency Board, which had been established for Britain's colonies in that region in 1912 and became the model for many similar boards in other British colonies in the first half of this century (see Keynes 1913a for his assessment of the West African Currency Board). The Caisse was also somewhat similar to the Indian monetary system, with which Keynes was very familiar: He had served on a British government commission of inquiry into that system and had published his first book (*Indian Currency and Finance* on that subject in 1913). The idea behind currency boards was to enable local governments to capture the seigniorage from note issue that would have accrued to the Bank of England had its notes been used instead.

It was typical of currency boards to issue only notes and coins. They usually did not conduct deposit business. British currency boards maintained a fixed exchange rate between local currency and the British pound. Orthodox currency board practice called for keeping reserves of between 100 and 110 percent in British pounds sterling in London (Walters 1988). Reserves above 100 percent would provide a cushion should the bonds or other sterling assets suddenly fall in value. Some later currency boards operated with reserves of less than 100 percent, as the North Russian Caisse did.

The Emission Caisse in Operation

The British government bought 100 million rubles of notes from the Emission Caisse to provide for the Caisse's reserve. The notes entered circulation at Archangel (where the Caisse had its headquarters) and at Murmansk by British military payments to the local populace. The first shipment of notes arrived in Archangel on about November 3, 1918. Because the printers had made the notes as quickly as possible, they had used plates of czarist notes for the basic design. In their haste, the printers had not noticed that the notes still bore czarist insignia. To circulate the notes as they were would have upset antimonarchists and would have been an enormous propaganda blunder. Several days were lost while the Caisse's staff blotted out the imperial insignia by hand on each note (Foreign Office 1918, 3295: 273, 276; Ironside 1953, 81). The Caisse's board of directors met for the first time on November 27, and the official gazette announced the Caisse's opening for business the next day (Foreign Office 1918, 3295: 527).

The British commissioner in Archangel estimated that, as of mid-October 1918, about 600 million rubles of all types were in circulation in North Russia (Foreign Office 1918, 3295: 89), which had a population of about 600,000. When the new Emission Caisse rubles were introduced, British military authorities, who still needed old rubles for some purposes, fixed the exchange rate at 48 old rubles for 40 new rubles as the Caisse directors and British government officials had proposed. (The prewar rate had been 9.57 rubles per British pound.) Curiously, the Northern provisional government and the State Bank of Northern Russia tried to prop up the exchange rate at 45 to 40, perhaps because they had issued some of the old ruble notes in circulation. They were waging a losing battle, however, because the supply of old rubles was growing rapidly as the Bolsheviks and White governments elsewhere inflated the currency rapidly to finance their civil war expenditures. At this time, there were more than 2000 separate issuers of fiat rubles, and all the old rubles issued by them exchanged at the same rate. The rate that the British military offered for 40 new rubles stayed at 48 old rubles until April 1919, when it fell to 56. By the beginning of May it was 64, by mid-May, 72, and by the second half of June, 80 (Foreign Office 1919, 3969: 455; 3970: 48, 80, 149). The depreciation of old rubles overcame the initial reluctance of many people to use the unfamiliar new ruble, which was maintaining its purchasing power (Foreign Office 1919, 3970: 23).

After the Caisse opened, the Northern provisional government was not inflating its currency as were other Russian governments at the time. It financed its deficits by selling bonds to the public and to the Caisse and, most important, by receiving an Allied subsidy. Before the civil war, the government in Petrograd had subsidized public works and food in North Russia. The North's only significant export was timber. When the war came, the North found itself cut off from its normal sources of food supply. Moreover, it was saddled with the expenses of government on an imperial scale (Foreign Office 1919, 3970: 291). In April 1919, the provisional government estimated that its revenue for the year would be 200 million rubles, and its expenses, 400 million rubles (probably an underestimate) (Foreign Ofice 1919, 3970: 158). The British government lent the provisional government £334,821—almost 13.4 million rubles— little or none of which the provisional government ever repaid (Foreign Office 1919, 3970: 575). The Allies' outright subsidy was about 120 million rubles in 1918. According to the Emission Caisse's president, the subsidy would have been about the same in 1919 had they kept troops in the region for the whole year (Foreign Office 1919, 3970: 391).

The Caisse, had it had a longer life, could have contributed approximately 5 million rubles a year to government revenue in profits. During the Caisse's first year, however, its president projected that it would lose about 2.6 million rubles because the rush job to print the first notes had been very expensive, costing 7.2 million rubles. Administrative expenses were a moderate 400,000 rubles (Foreign Office 1919, 3970: 135). The British government agreed to lend the Caisse money to make up the first-year deficit, and the Caisse promised to repay the loan out of future profits, which, as it happened, never materialized. The British government later bargained with the note printers and the printing bill was reduced by about one-third.

Although the Caisse did not exist long enough to turn over any profits to the provisional government, it did help the government by lending money. By law, the Caisse was allowed to purchase government debt up to 25 percent of its note circulation. This was for all practical purposes an indirect British loan to the provisional government. The Caisse lent the government 2 million rubles on December 16, 1918 (U.S. Department of State 1932, 3: 95) and 27 million rubles later. In consequence, the total amount of loans was slightly in excess of the legal ceiling (Foreign Office 1919, 3970: 591). The loan was for five years and it carried an annual interest rate of 5 percent. The government was to pay interest semiannually in Caisse notes or in British pounds.

The Caisse reported its financial condition monthly in the Northern provisional government's official gazette. Unfortunately, we were unable to find copies. The following short series of statistics on the Caisse's note circulation is from dispatches by the British commissioner in Archangel: May 31, 1919: 37,762,385 rubles; June 30, 1919: 39,657,235 rubles; July 31, 1919: 52,734,935 rubles; and August 31, 1919: 48,715,000 rubles (Foreign Office 1919, 3970: 152, 318, 429, 433). The rest of the 100 million rubles that the British government bought were unspent notes still in its hands. The British commissioner in Archangel estimated total nominal circulation of old rubles to be about 300 million as of mid-April 1919 (Foreign Office 1919, 3969: 478), down from 600 million six months earlier, before the Caisse began operation. The old rubles had fallen in purchasing power, so in inflation-adjusted terms their circulation was down even further. The new rubles were making progress in driving the old rubles out of use.

By a decree published on April 14, 1919, the Northern provisional government called in all old rubles in the region to be registered and stamped. The official reason for the decree was "to prevent the flooding of the Northern Region with currency printed by the Bolsheviks, and in order to ascertain the amount of currency there is in the Region." All old rubles not stamped by local banks by May 15 (June 1, for remote parts of the region) would not be accepted by the State Bank of Northern Russia, nor would any private person be required to accept them as legal tender in payment (Foreign Office 1919, 3970: 61). The provisional government intended the stamping of old notes to be a first step toward removing them from circulation and replacing them with new rubles. It is not clear how the provisional government expected such a currency unification scheme to work. The British Treasury correctly observed that there was no similarity other than the name between the old rubles, which were not backed by anything, and the new rubles, which were backed by reserves in the Bank of England (Foreign Office 1919, 3970: 22). At any rate, the change in military situation in the next few months made the question insignificant.

Some additional details of the Caisse's operation deserve mention. Notes could be redeemed either in Archangel or London.

In London, Barclays Bank acted as the Caisse's agent for exchanging notes that soldiers returning from Archangel had carried with them. In Russia, Archangel seems to have been the only place where redemptions were made; the Caisse had no branch offices in Murmansk or elsewhere. The purpose of having so few redemption points was to be sure that German agents would have little chance of redeeming ruble notes for British pounds, which were a more acceptable currency in trade with neutral countries than was the German mark. Redemptions before the Caisse decamped to London seem to have been small: a report made on August 12, 1919, estimated that redemptions to the end of the month would be 120,000 rubles. There is some mention of the Caisse obtaining revenue from a 1 percent tax, but we were unable to determine the tax base (Foreign Office 1919, 3970: 355). It was probably an exchange commission for writing checks payable in London.

The End of the Emission Caisse

The Allied intervention in North Russia became increasingly unpopular in the Allied countries after World War I ended in November 1918. The intervention no longer served any purpose related to war against Germany and it was entangling the Allies in a bloody civil war. The British government decided in March to withdraw its troops from North Russia. The other Allies took similar action. There were also troubles at the front. By the spring of 1919, morale was very low. Even though Allied troops, in their confrontations with the Red Army, seem to have inflicted high losses while suffering few themselves, they were tired of fighting. In July, British, French, and American units mutinied and refused to go to the front. (A similar mutiny had taken place among White Guard troops on April 23.) The mutinies hastened the Allies' determination to withdraw. By September 27, the last Allied troops left North Russia (Rhodes 1988, 121).

Despite its legal status as an organ of the Northern provisional government, the Emission Caisse was in reality a British financial scheme, as shown by the fact that its president at the time, G. R.

Young, was a former official at the British embassy in Archangel. Young proposed to the British commissioner in Archangel that the Caisse buy some of the British government's "all-Russia" ruble notes (issued by the White government in Omsk) for those noteholders who did not wish checks for British pounds on London banks. The British Foreign Office agreed because the commissioner had an excess of all-Russia notes that the British would have little occasion to use once they withdrew their troops (Foreign Office 1919, 3970: 381–82).

The Caisse announced that it would close in Archangel and redeem all the notes presented to it. The British military command still held about 55 million rubles in unused notes. To prevent them from falling into Bolshevik hands, the War Office instructed the British military commander to burn them. Because the notes were wrapped in bundles and had become damp, they would not burn. They were dumped at sea (Ironside 1953, 81), and the British government received a book-entry credit for them.

The Caisse officially closed to the public in Archangel on October 4, 1919, despite the provisional government's protest. It continued to redeem notes collected by the provisional government and the State Bank of Northern Russia until October 15 (Foreign Office 1919, 3970: 492, 498). The Caisse moved to London. Its main business there was redeeming the 55 million rubles that the British government held. About 13.5 million rubles remained in circulation. British troops returning from northern Russia held small amounts of rubles, but most other rubles in circulation were still in Russia. The Caisse's president suggested that the North Russian provisional government and a bank that was serving as the Caisse's agent in Norway be allowed to redeem notes as long as Archangel did not fall to the Bolsheviks. He proposed accordingly that the British government refrain from redeeming all the rubles it held. Such action would have provided a sufficient reserve for the rubles still in circulation. He argued that "the assertion of our financial integrity is well worth £300,000. The Northern Rouble is known throughout North Russia and Scandinavia as the English Rouble. . . . It is the only good money seen in Russia since the Bolshevik revolution" (Foreign Office 1919, 3970: 507–21).

Without Allied troops, the existence of the North Russian provisional government was precarious. It held on for several months because the Bolsheviks were concentrating their forces elsewhere. When the Red Army mounted a campaign in North Russia early in 1920, the provisional government's army disintegrated. The government fled on a ship to England on February 19, and two days later the Bolsheviks entered Archangel. The Emission Caisse remained open in London until April 30, 1920 (Foreign Office 1919, 3970: 597). After that date, note redemption ceased. There seem to be no records in Foreign Office archives of the Caisse's final disposition, but judging from correspondence from the last few months of its existence, most of the 13.5 million rubles in the hands of the public never were redeemed, inflicting a loss on their holders. The British government, therefore, ended up losing about 15.5 million rubles (£378,500), the difference between the now worthless North Russian government bonds the Caisse held and the notes that were never redeemed.

The Relevance of the Emission Caisse Today

The North Russian currency issue scheme was on the whole quite successful. The currency never deviated from its fixed exchange rate with the British pound. In contrast to currencies being issued by other Russian governments at the time, the Northern currency was a reliable store of value. In consequence of the Caisse, the Allied army was able to buy and sell goods almost as easily as if it had been at home on maneuvers. Moreover, the difficulties that plagued the Allies in having enough currency on hand to pay railroad and dock workers disappeared after the new currency came into circulation.

As well as being useful to the Allies, the Caisse could have earned profits for the North Russian government had both institutions continued to exist. During its first and only year, the Caisse suffered a loss because of the high cost of printing notes quickly and because its North Russian government bonds became worthless. It would probably have shown a profit from its second year forward. The cost of printing the first batch of notes was an atypical expense. Later issues could have been printed less quickly at lower cost. Furthermore, many of the notes would have stayed in circulation for years before wearing out and needing to be replaced. The North Russian government bonds that the Caisse purchased at the start of its operations would have been redeemed had the Whites triumphed over the Bolsheviks. The North Russian government would no doubt have redeemed the bonds, if only to avoid arousing British ire. As matters turned out, the bond sales became a sort of gift from the British government, which bought a supply of the Caisse's notes to use in paying for Allied military activity.

The currency scheme suffered from two problems. The first was that for many months, the provisional government and the State Bank of Northern Russia did not throw their full support behind the new currency. British officials in Archangel were quite irritated at the State Bank's behavior, but their dispatches do not make clear why it acted so. The most plausible explanation is that the North Russian government and the State Bank itself had issued some of the old, rapidly depreciating currency and that they both wanted to leave the way open for further issues should the government have been unable to finance its deficits any other way. The scheme's second problem or defect was the purchase of North Russian government bonds as collateral for 25 percent of the note issue. Orthodox finance required a 100 percent reserve in foreign exchange only. British colonial currency boards, which resembled the Emission Caisse in other respects, generally kept a reserve of between 100 and 110 percent. When the time came to liquidate the Caisse, the worthlessness of the North Russian bonds left it bankrupt. Fortunately for the British government, the major holder of Caisse notes, some notes were in circulation too far away to make redemption in London feasible before the Caisse closed. That reduced the British losses.

When we consider how difficult the circumstances that faced the Caisse were, its problems seem minor. The scheme worked as well as anyone could reasonably expect. The Caisse's performance deserves a close look today. Indeed, this currency board episode suggests a way that the Soviet Union, as well as the newly democratized nations in Eastern Europe and other less-developed countries, could establish convertible hard currencies.

A currency board could work as follows. The Soviet government, for example, would set aside foreign exchange assets in hard currencies sufficient for a reserve of between 100 and 110 percent against its ruble note issue. How much foreign exchange the currency board would need would depend on the exchange rate between the ruble and hard reserve currencies. This rate would best be determined by allowing the ruble to float against hard currencies. After a prudent period of observing floating exchange rates, the currency board could fix a "proper" rate for the ruble vis-à-vis its reserve currency (or currencies). If the Soviet government did not have enough foreign exchange, it could borrow from Western governments and/or multinational organizations, pledging to repay from the interest from the currency board's holdings of foreign exchange assets. Recall that a board's gross profits would arise from the difference between interest on its investments and its note issue, which would pay no interest to noteholders. As long as the interest rates on a board's investments exceeded its borrowing rates, it could probably raise a considerable amount of foreign exchange for backing of note issues.

A fixed exchange rate with a reserve currency is also vital. All successful currency boards have had a fixed exchange rate. The fixed rate enforces a discipline that presumably would not be so strong under purely discretionary monetary policy. Indeed, one potential weakness of *government* currency boards is that there is no absolutely binding way to keep the government from forcing the board to devalue for domestic political reasons (Hetzel 1990).

Perhaps one way to insulate currency boards from the possibility of political meddling with the exchange rates would be to franchise *private* currency boards. The franchises would be awarded on the basis of competitive bidding (Demsetz 1968). Franchises would entitle the franchisees to issue private domestic notes based on specific terms contained in the franchise agreements. Such private boards would probably also operate more efficiently and evoke more public confidence than would public boards.

Currency boards have worked well in the past in many countries, mostly British colonies or former colonies, but also in a handful of other quite diverse countries. They were replaced by central banks mainly for *political* reasons, not economic ones. Hong Kong and Singapore, which have had the world's most rapid economic growth since World War II, have currency boards today. The experience of the Emission Caisse of Northern Russia provides a particularly interesting model for those countries that are attempting to liberalize their economies and establish sound, convertible domestic currencies.

Appendix

Both Spring-Rice (1919, 284) and Foreign Office records (1919, 3970: 22) credit John Maynard Keynes with thinking up the details of the currency issue scheme described in this chapter. Two notes that Keynes wrote on the subject are reproduced in this Appendix. They could not be reproduced in their original form because of their poor condition in the Foreign Office archives (1918, 3295: 52, 62–64).

Sydney Peel was a war finance adviser to the British Foreign Office, Baron Robert Chalmers was joint permanent secretary of the British Treasury. Rufus Daniel Isaacs, Earl of Reading, was Lord Chief Justice of England as well as High Commissioner and special ambassador to the United States.

The telegram to which the following note is attached is printed in U.S. Department of State (1923:75–76), with minor changes. It addresses American concerns about the North Russian currency scheme.

14.10.18

Dear Peel,

I enclose two copies of a telegram to Washington (speak kindly) about Russian currency. Will you tell Lord Robert that this telegram has been seen and approved by Lord Reading.

Yours,
JM Keynes

I have seen Lord R.C. and he approves the telegram.

S.P. 14/10/18

Aimé-Joseph de Fleuriau was a counselor in France's London embassy with responsibility for financial affairs. Josef Avenol was French delegate to the inter-allied financial commission in London. Charles Sergent was under-secretary of state in the French Ministry of Finance. Major General Frederick Poole was commander of the British forces in North Russia.

15 October, 1918.

Dear Peel,

I suggest that the note to De Fleuriau might be on the following lines.

"Some weeks ago Monsieur De Fleuriau and Monsieur Avenol were informed of certain proposals of His Majesty's Government for dealing with the immediate necessities of the currency situation in Northern Russia. The representatives of the French Government at Archangel have also been kept continuously informed of the developments in that centre.

Reproduced with the permission of Her Majesty's Stationery Office (HMSO).

Appendix

The French Government for their part have furnished His Majesty's Government with a memorandum making proposals of a somewhat different kind on the lines of the establishment of an Inter-Allied bank for Russia. It was accordingly suggested that with a view to ensuring a common policy between the two Governments Monsieur Sergent should be invited to come to London at once with a view to a conference on these questions. Owing to Monsieur Sergent's unfortunate accident it has not been possible for this visit to take place and in the meantime the pressure of events in Northern Russia is making it necessary for immediate steps to be taken for the provision of currency there. H.M. High Commissioner at Archangel Lindley has telegraphed that it is essential for the new currency to be put into operation at a very early date. General Poole agrees and considers that the result of any further delay in putting the scheme into force would be "disastrous". He telegraphed further on October 11th that he anticipated that in the absence of a supply of currency there would shortly be local outbreaks due to the inability of the Government to find cash for the wages of essential services such as the railways, the port, and the Fire Brigade. The French and United States Ambassadors in Archangel are well acquainted of the urgency of the situation and have doubtless kept their Governments informed.

In view of the above His Majesty's Government trusts that the French Government will not object to their proceeding with their currency scheme without prejudice, however, to later developments or to such subsequent proposals for permanent arrangements as the Allies may eventually agree upon. The military necessities of the situation and the absence of any alternative proposal which can be put into force at an early date render this course unavoidable. His Majesty's Government regret that pressure of events makes it impossible to evolve a complete and final Inter-Allied scheme at the present moment. When such a scheme has been completed it could of course absorb the scheme of limited application and experimental character which the position requires as an immediate military necessity.

His Majesty's Government anticipate that it may be necessary to make some announcement about the new currency arrangements in Archangel not later than October 19th. If therefore the French Government wish to make any further communication on the question, His Majesty's Government beg that they will do so at a very early date.

In the above connection I desire to emphasize that the proposed Office of Conversion is to be under Russian auspices, that the new notes will carry no British guarantee and that the special connection of Great Britain with the scheme will be limited to the appointment of a British financial advisor to the Russian Office of Note Issue. I would also point out that there will be no connection between the operations of the Office of Conversion and such Allied control as it may be necessary or advisable to exercise over the expenditure of the Government of Northern Russia, even though this expenditure may be met by means of the new note issue. His Majesty's Government propose to invite the French Government to participate with them in any such control. They would welcome any further suggestion from the French Government emphasizing the purely Russian complexion of the new Office of Conversion and its entire dissociation from the political situation or from the relations, political or financial, between the Allied Governments, and the authorities of Northern

Russia. The scheme is strictly limited to what it purports to be, namely an arrangement for overcoming the immediate difficulties of the situation arising out of the absence of suitable currency, under auspices which are as purely Russian as is possible in present circumstances, and on experimental lines which will not prejudice the absorption of the present note issue into such larger scheme as may be eventually developed for Russia as a whole."

Yours sincerely,
JM Keynes

4
Lawrence H. White

Money and Capital in Economic Development: A Retrospective Assessment

One way of approaching the assignment reflected in the title of this chapter—to provide a retrospective assessment of Ronald I. McKinnon's book, *Money and Capital in Economic Development* (1973)—would be to focus on the impact the book has had on the thinking of economists and policymakers in the field of development finance, on the formation of actual policy, and ultimately on the performance of developing economies. Such a review of the fortunes of the book's ideas in the real world would be of considerable interest, for the book has clearly had a tremendous impact on both thought and practice of monetary and financial systems in less-developed countries (LDCs). It has cemented as an undisputed cornerstone of modern development economics the proposition that the money, banking, and finance sector is crucial in the development process. It has raised at least to predominant acceptance the proposition that the financial sector better promotes development when liberalized, that is, freed from regulations that repress intermediation through formal financial institutions.

References to the book's impact often pair it with a contemporaneous and like-minded book written by Edward S. Shaw (1973). The joint influence of the two books on economic thought is evident in a comprehensive text on development finance by Maxwell J. Fry (1988, xv), which begins by citing "the path-breaking work of Ronald McKinnon and Edward Shaw in 1973." Fry refers repeatedly to the work of the "McKinnon-Shaw school" (of which he confesses to being a member) and devotes the first three chapters of his book to "McKinnon-Shaw models." The current edition of the leading collection of readings in development economics (Meier 1984) includes an excerpt from a piece by McKinnon (1980) that, in effect, summarizes the message of his book.

Evidence that McKinnon's book has influenced policies and events in the world of development financial systems is not difficult to find. Reviewers of the Chilean experience with financial liberalization often prominently link McKinnon's ideas with the reforms adopted there (Diaz-Alejandro 1985, 1; Edwards 1985, 250).

The retrospective assessment provided here is nonetheless primarily internal, offering a detailed critical assessment of the text from the perspective of today. This approach reflects the present assessor's comparative advantage (or disadvantage) as an academic monetary economist only recently attracted to modern development issues. What we have here, then, amounts to an unusually long and unusually delayed book review. The external impact of the book is traced only as far as the boundaries of the economics profession, and even there only in a few instances.

Fry's review (1988) of the development finance literature fortunately makes it unnecessary to attempt a systematic survey of that literature here. To others closer to the action is left the task of tracing the influence of McKinnon's thought on policymaking in such places as the International Monetary Fund (IMF). (Two suggestions can be made, however, to those who would undertake that task. The first is that, in the case of the IMF, McKinnon's ideas have undoubtedly been transmitted in part by his student and collaborator, Donald J. Mathieson, who in 1975 became an officer in the Financial Studies Division of the IMF's Research Department. The second is that the interests of the IMF and others in adopting the ideas of liberalization need to be explored. Is it possible that we have here a counterexample to George Stigler's (1982) stricture that the economist acting as preacher is wasting his time? The job of reviewing the experience of LDCs with McKinnon-esque policies is left to Rolf Lüders (1991). It has also been undertaken by McKinnon himself (1986).

The retrospective herein proceeds as follows. The following section briefly reviews previous contributions to the literature of financial liberalization in order to provide a background for an appreciation of McKinnon's contribution. Shaw's book, for the same reason, is compared and contrasted with McKinnon's. Then *Money and Capital in Economic Development* is critically reviewed, chapter by chapter. Finally, the message of the book is summarized through a recapitulation of its reception by reviewers.

The Earlier Literature of Financial Liberalization

The idea that a liberal policy toward banking, interest, and finance is favorable to economic growth and development is as old as classical liberalism itself. Among the earliest expressions of liberalism were defenses of usury by such seventeenth-century writers as Hugo Grotius (see Böhm-Bawerk 1959, 1:23). The argument for financial liberalization is clearly articulated in the work of Adam Smith. His statements are worth quoting as examples of the venerable wisdom that has led Douglas Rimmer (1973, 59–60) to remark: "The [development] policies defensible by economic canons have an old-fashioned look. . . . They invoke Adam Smith rather than Dr. Raoul Prebisch or Professor Jan Tinbergen."

In his *Lectures on Jurisprudence*, Smith (1978, 505–6) argues: "it is manifest that banks are beneficial to the commerce of a country, and that it is a bad polic[y] to restrain them." In the *Wealth of Nations* ([1776] 1976, 297), he testifies that its free banking industry had "contributed a good deal" to the "very considerabl[e]" growth of his native Scotland. The contribution Smith emphasizes is the formation of productive capital allowed by the banks' replacing metallic money with banknotes, that is, outside money with inside money: "It is . . . by rendering a greater part of [the nation's] capital active and productive than would otherwise be so, that the most judicious operations of banking can increase the industry of the country" (1976, 320).

In an oft-quoted passage, Smith conveys the vital message that the wealth of nations is better served by the decentralized and self-interested strivings of private investors than by central government direction:

> What is the species of domestic industry which his capital can employ, and of which the produce is likely to be of the greatest value, every individual, it is evident, can, in his local situation, judge much better than any statesman or lawgiver can do for him. The statesman, who should attempt to direct private people in what manner they ought to employ their capitals, would not only load himself with a most unnecessary attention, but assume an authority which could safely be trusted, not only to no single person, but to no council or senate whatever, and which would no-where be so dangerous as in the hands of a man who had folly and presumption enough to fancy himself fit to exercise it. (1976, 456)

Below we will quote a like-minded statement by McKinnon.

A second landmark of classical liberalism relevant to our theme is Jeremy Bentham's *Defence of Usury* published in 1787 and reprinted in Stark (1952). In criticizing Smith's suggestions ([1776] 1976, 357) for fixing a legal maximum rate of interest, Bentham emphasizes the growth-promoting function of market-determined high interest rates. The very title of his open letter to Smith invokes the "discouragements opposed . . . to the progress of inventive industry" by restraints on interest rates. Shaw (1973, 157) cites Bentham's tract.

In the twentieth century the importance of banking and finance in economic development has been stressed by Joseph A. Schumpeter in his classic book, *The Theory of Economic Development* ([1934] 1974), and by Raymond W. Goldsmith's book *Financial*

Structure and Development (1969). In neither book is liberalization stressed.

The dual message—the joint importance of finance to development and of liberalization to finance—is significantly advanced in two collaborative volumes put together by Rondo Cameron to provide a survey of the historical role of banking in the early growth of the industrialized nations, *Banking in the Early Stages of Industrialization* (1967) and *Banking and Economic Development: Some Lessons of History* (1972). These volumes offer a historical focus rather than the theoretical thrust of McKinnon and Shaw and emphasize past rather than current development. Nonetheless the essays of Cameron (and to a lesser extent those of his collaborators) anticipate McKinnon's dual message in many specific points.

There is clear common ground between Cameron and McKinnon-Shaw regarding the relationship of finance to the development process. Cameron (1967, 1) notes that development goes hand in hand with "a proliferation of the number and variety of financial institutions," as Shaw emphasizes, and with "a substantial rise in the ratio of money and other financial assets relative to total output and tangible wealth," as McKinnon emphasizes. He recognizes that "obstacles to financial innovation, whether legal, social, or other, may hinder the growth of financial institutions and thus retard the progress of industrialization" (p. 8). As McKinnon later does, he points out that "improvement of financial markets should... produce a narrowing of the dispersion of interest rates among different types of users, among geographical regions, and over periods of seasonal fluctuation" (p. 9). Cameron notes (p. 10) that credit-rationing criteria are particularly important in the allocation of funds in economies where markets are less perfect. A greater availability of funds would allow entrepreneurs to assume more debt and to make larger investments. Monetization of the subsistence sector is important in encouraging production for market, specialization, greater effort, focus on higher yield products, greater responsiveness to relative prices, and increased output.

The merits of liberal financial policy are clearly emphasized in

Cameron's concluding remark that "insofar as the criterion for judging bank performance is the contribution of banks to growth, the best results have been achieved when competition was freest and most unfettered" (p. 313). The same theme permeates his discussion of the free banking system of Scotland in the eighteenth and early nineteenth centuries. Cameron traces "the superiority of the Scottish system" to the "freedom and competition" (p. 97) that allowed the banks to innovate and to develop naturally. In particular, the freedom of note issue "facilitated the establishment of new banks, increased competition, and immediately provided the banks with the means to engage in productive credit creation." Together with freedom in the establishment of branch banking, it produced "the resulting popularization of the banking habit, which led to the early development and widespread use of bank deposits as both outlets for saving and means of payment."

Cameron's program for liberalization goes beyond McKinnon's in a provocative way: He thinks freedom of private note issue a reform worth considering in LDCs today. His survey of the historical experiences of various countries indicates that (p. 295), in a country with an underdeveloped banking system, the right of note issue is an effective means of eliciting growth in the number of banks and in the public banking habit. Hence it promotes saving and economic growth. He concedes (p. 319) that central bank note monopolies may be here to stay (a "not necessarily felicitous conclusion"), but persuasively maintains that there is still much to be said for the "local banks of issue" that have historically played the role of "habituating the populace to the use of financial instruments and institutions." Cameron makes the interesting proposal that experiments along these lines today, which would be "highly instructive," may yet be possible in LDCs where traditions of regional autonomy remain. The present author has elsewhere (White 1987) made a similar proposal for allowing private note issue in LDCs.

Cameron summarizes the "lessons" of his second volume in an unmistakably liberal way. The case studies in the volume reinforce the view that where banking was left most free to develop in response to the demand for its services, it produced the best results. Restrictions on freedom of entry almost always reduce the quantity and quality of financial services available to the economy, and thus hinder or distort economic growth. Competition in banking, on the other hand, acts as a spur to the mobilization of idle financial resources and to their efficient utilization in commerce and industry. (1972, 25)

This summary of Cameron's work is intended to show that the link between financial liberalization and development had been made by economic historians. Their work certainly did not anticipate McKinnon and Shaw in every important respect. To cite again the most obvious dissimilarities, Cameron's volumes neither study modern-day LDCs nor offer an explicit reformulation of monetary theory. Nor do they have anything to say about the impact of interest rate restrictions, the keystone of the "financial repression" studied by McKinnon and Shaw. Evidently interest restrictions were nowhere, in the cases studied, deemed to have been binding enough to have had a significant distortive effect.

McKinnon's Book and Shaw's

A final preliminary necessary to set the stage for McKinnon's book is a brief discussion of its relationship to the already mentioned book by Edward Shaw, *Financial Deepening in Economic Development*, that appeared in the same year, 1973. Many commentators have noticed the similar themes (and even similar titles) of the two books, and the books have been reviewed jointly. McKinnon (1973, 2) credits Shaw with convincing him of the importance of financial processes in economic development. He notes that Shaw was an adviser on the Korean reforms of 1965–1966, the effectiveness of which stimulated McKinnon's further research.

Shaw (1973, viii) in turn thanks McKinnon for his "collaboration in antecedents" of his volume. The two Stanford economists were at one time working jointly on a book about monetary and financial policies in economic development. An extant, jointly written typescript from about 1968, "Policies in Restraint of Development" (n.d.), offers insight into their common ground and will no doubt be useful to future historians of economic thought. The typescript is seventy-five pages in length. The co-authors split, so the Stanford oral tradition has it, over the relative importance to be attached to outside money balances (McKinnon) versus a wider range of financial instruments (Shaw) as vehicles for saving and capital accumulation. Maxwell J. Fry explores this difference (1978) and renders an empirical judgment on which view is more applicable to the semi-industrial Asian LDCs. (It is Shaw's.)

A detailed account of the similar and dissimilar points of the two books is beyond the scope of the present discussion. But it is worth making the general observation that one finds a more nearly laissez-faire outlook in Shaw's book. Shaw (1973, 80, 87) is far more apt to formulate his policy advice as a case for "free-market rates of interest" and for "financial authority in lagging economies . . . to let deposit and loan rates alone, for the market to determine." He proclaims openly that his work "implies a bias toward decentralization of economic choice" (p. vii), a bias that is not quite as obvious in McKinnon's writing. In a *festschrift* for Shaw, edited by McKinnon (1976, 280), Donald J. Mathieson remarks that "in Shaw's optimal system, there would be free banking with no required reserve ratios." Shaw indeed describes such a system (1973, 129–30) though his belief in its supremacy over alternative systems is left implicit. There is no evidence of a similar view on McKinnon's part.

As far as such a thing can be measured by citation counts, McKinnon's has been the more influential of the two books. Articles citing *Money and Capital*, as recorded in the *Social Science Citation Index*, number 28 for the period 1971–1975 (17 these book reviews), 65 for 1976–1980, 102 for 1981–1985, and 44 for 1986–1987. The corresponding numbers for *Financial Deepening* are 18 (12 reviews), 44, 56, and 25. The respective totals are 239 and 143. Both are healthy sets of numbers. It is probably invidious to seek an explanation for greater recognition of McKinnon's book, other than to hypothesize superior pricing and distribution by its publisher, the

Brookings Institution. One reviewer (Price 1974, 189), however, has praised its superior readability, organization, and succinctness.

A Critical Review of the Text: Chapter 1

Main themes are briefly stated in the first chapter. McKinnon (1973, 3) makes it clear at the outset that the lion's share of blame for poor growth in LDCs, contrary to the prevailing ideology of the 1960s, is not to be laid at the door of the wealthier economies. As long as other nations do not raise tariff barriers, "successful development rests mainly on policy choices made by national authorities in the developing countries. Correspondingly the inadequate economic performance of many LDCs is attributed to repressive, though understandable, policies that they themselves have pursued." In this respect McKinnon's message is complementary to that of P. T. Bauer, who in the book *Dissent on Development* (1971) had raised a lonely voice in favor of liberal policies.

The central policy choice to McKinnon is whether authorities "decide to nourish and expand the 'real' stock of money . . . or allow it to remain shrunken and heavily taxed (p. 3)." Evidence shows that growth in real M2 coincides with greater saving and income and with greater efficiency of investment. Existing theory, with its assumption that real money balances and physical capital are substitutes, could not explain why. McKinnon will set out a theory in which they are instead complements.

Fragmentation and Intervention: Chapters 2 and 3

In Chapters 2 ("Capital in a Fragmented Economy") and 3 ("The Intervention Syndrome"), the patient's ills are diagnosed.

Chapter 2. McKinnon is quite critical, in Chapter 2, of the consequences of the interventionist policies practiced by LDC governments, taking as the first question to be answered, "Why is public intervention so pervasive and generally so unsuccessful?" In the retrospective light of the last fifteen years of public choice economics, he is surprisingly charitable—even naive—about the motives behind the policies:

> Intervention is usually prompted by the perception—sometimes correct—that a particular market is functioning badly, so that authorities feel pressed to "do something." An infant textile firm is helped by a tariff; or the price of an agricultural product may be raised to permit farmers to use a new fertilizer-intensive technology; or a tax exemption may be granted to a foreign firm for automobile assembly. This pressure for public intervention is the result of severe fragmentation in the underdeveloped economy (1973, 5).

No mention is made here of the possibility that intervention is instead usually prompted by the desire to augment the revenue or power of government, to create artificial rents, or to redistribute wealth for the sake of favored beneficiary groups. Such activity is generically known in the public choice literature as "rent-seeking." Stanislav Andreski in *Parasitism and Subversion* (1966, 77), an important sociological analysis of Latin America, speaks of it as the "parasitic involution of capitalism," which he defines as "the tendency to seek profits and to alter market conditions by political means in the widest sense of the word." Andreski cites as an important aspect of such acquisitive interventionism in Latin America "the stranglehold which cliques of big capitalists have on credit facilities" (p. 84).

As Douglas Rimmer (1973, 54) has written, we need to "consider the hypothesis that the primary purpose of so-called 'developmental activities' and 'growth policies' is to control the distribution of the national income, not to raise it."

Though the beneficiaries of the rents created by a policy may attempt to justify it by complaining about the inadequacy of the domestic capital market, such complaints may be no more than camouflage. After all, very similar rent-seeking goes on in nations with highly developed capital markets, though apparently to a lesser degree. McKinnon's examples are all perfectly explicable under the rent-seeking hypothesis. Particular markets are "functioning badly" according to firms who find their profits squeezed. The "infant" textile firm pleading for a protective tariff is a prime example. The price of an agricultural product may be raised simply in order to make its producers wealthier. Talk about the supposed benefits of using a high-cost, fertilizer-intensive technology is beside the point, because an increase in the selling price of a product by itself does nothing to change the least-cost input combination. The prevalence of an argument for a policy actually designed to promote the use of high-cost fertilizer should lead one to suspect that the producers of fertilizer have been spreading it. In none of these cases does the pressure for public intervention stem from the severe fragmentation of the underdeveloped economy.

As McKinnon elsewhere recognizes (1973, 7), modern fragmentation is the result of intervention. It is not clear why he chooses to regard it also as an initial cause (p. 8). It is unlikely that McKinnon's reluctance to emphasize the rent-seeking origins of repressive LDC policies could have originated in the belief that nothing was to be gained by appearing to impugn a particular government's motives, for such a point can be made quite generally. Something is surely to be gained by frank appraisal of the problem.

In a similarly charitable vein we have McKinnon's statement that LDC governments have chosen to offset the legacy of colonialism "by interfering directly to help some individuals or sectors of the economy at the expense of others" (p. 6). What McKinnon regards simply as the unfortunately chosen means—helping a few at the expense of the majority—may instead have been the deliberate goal of these policies. It would be more than a bit ironic for such favoritism to masquerade as the inverse of colonialism. McKinnon later recognizes this point when he characterizes as "neocolonial" LDC banking systems in which "favored private and official borrowers still absorb the limited finance available at low real rates of interest" (p. 70). If favoritism is the very point of official policy, advice for improving the operation of factor markets will not be sufficient "to persuade authorities to cease intervening in commodity markets" as McKinnon hopes (p. 8).

With regard to the *consequences* of interventionist financial policies, McKinnon's analysis is cogent and compelling. A government that fragments the capital market "causes the misuse of labor and land, suppresses entrepreneurial development, and condemns important sectors of the economy to inferior technologies" (p. 8). Thus capital market liberalization is the key to a general improvement in economic performance.

The internal dynamic to interventionism, as Shaw (1973, 12–13) and Basil Moore (1975, 124) emphasize, can lead a government that begins with capital market interference to impose successively more general fetters on economic activity. Controls on loan interest rates and foreign-exchange rates create excess demands for loanable funds and foreign-currency funds. These shortages call forth discretionary official rationing of funds. The allocation of the underpriced funds creates a new round of distortions. Typically the favored recipients of funds are firms that propose long-term and heavy investments in plant and capital equipment, investments that look profitable only because of the artificially low interest and exchange rates. These overly capital-intensive firms, mimicking the production techniques of more developed countries, employ a small proportion of the labor force at relatively high wages. The unduly capital-poor remainder of the economy can provide only low-wage jobs. A dual labor market results. The industrial labor force may gain union monopoly power and a minimum wage law. Rural laborers are drawn into the pool of the numerous urban unemployed until the probability of landing a high-wage job becomes low enough to discourage further migration, a situation analyzed by the well-known model of Harris and Todaro (1970).

McKinnon (1973, 31–32) adds to this explanation for the coexistence of overly capital-intensive and unduly capital-poor production techniques. Ceilings on *deposit* interest rates deter the owner of a profitable enterprise from placing his "surplus" funds with intermediaries. Because the high marginal returns to capital funds elsewhere in the economy are not conveyed to him by intermediaries as a relevant opportunity cost, he will reinvest his funds internally until the marginal rate of return is driven quite low. Thus the lack of outlets for savings leads to excess use of capital equipment in some enterprises while others suffer from inadequate capital.

McKinnon's analysis of the market for capital is built on the fairly solid microeconomic foundation provided by Irving Fisher (1930). In accordance with Fisher's focus on the preferences and opportunities facing individual savers and would-be investors, McKinnon (1973, 11) rightly emphasizes the dispersion of knowledge among numerous entrepreneurs concerning the economy's best investment opportunities. Though McKinnon attributes it to the dispersion of technical expertise and factors of production, an important source of the dispersion of relevant knowledge is simply the specialized familiarity with local and immediate circumstances (the land, labor, machines, and other resources available, and the production techniques to which their particular capabilities are suited) held by the individual on the spot. Hayek made this point vigorously in his classic critique of the view that general equilibrium theory provides a useful blueprint for central planning: "We need decentralization because only thus can we insure that the knowledge of the particular circumstances of time and place will be promptly used" (1948, 84).

An undistorted market system is indispensable for allowing the economy to take full advantage of the specialized knowledge of entrepreneurs on the spot. It communicates to them through prices the accurate information about relative scarcities and demands they need to dovetail their individual investment plans with the plans of other actors in the economy. As McKinnon puts it, echoing Adam Smith in spirit, "there is no single authority or narrow class of individuals who can extract saving and allocate investment according to a neoclassical menu of best-practice production techniques" (1973, 11). In this respect, LDC economies are no different from developed economies. Where LDC governments have attempted to steer investments, particularly into modern plant and equipment, the results (p. 14) have been "highly perverse" from the point of view of improving rates of return. Andreas Fuglesang (1984) has provided complementary examples from agriculture in Africa, where the overriding of local farmers' knowledge by outside technicians' plans has resulted in disastrously poor yields.

What is different about less-developed economies is the greater dispersion in realized rates of return to investment. For McKinnon (1973, 9), this is a matter of definition (he unconventionally defines "economic development" as the reduction of dispersion in rates of return), but it is true even when "less-developed" means "poor" or "backward." The persistence of low-payoff uses of capital while high-payoff uses go wanting is indeed a major cause of poverty. To quote Andreski (1966, 119): "Although in a country like Paraguay or Bolivia there is very little wealth available for anything, in the richer countries of Latin America the unproductive use of existing funds constitutes as important an obstacle to economic progress as the paucity of wealth." McKinnon (1973, 15) justifiably insists that "the release of resources from inferior uses in the underdeveloped environment is as important as new net saving per se." Certainly it is a less costly source of increases in output.

Wasteful uses of capital persist in LDCs because governments encourage them. The encouragement comes through ceilings on loan interest rates, the rationing of artificially low-priced loans, and direct credit subsidies. Small-scale entrepreneurs with potential high-mean-payoff projects cannot outbid the well-connected sponsors of established low-payoff projects for the scarce funds available through the organized banking system. These entrepreneurs lack the wherewithal for self-finance. Pockets of profitability go unexploited. McKinnon tells this story persuasively, and wisely relegates technical diagrams to an appendix.

Chapter 3. McKinnon analyzes, in Chapter 3, seven categories of government policies commonly found in LDCs. Again he charitably considers them all to be "policies for circumventing the [inadequate] domestic capital market," and thus justifiable at least in principle under the theory of the second best.

McKinnon is certainly not blind to the monopoly rents that the policies create, but insists that an LDC government's "favoritism toward an 'in' group of entrepreneurs cannot be explained away as pure corruption. . . . In an appropriately liberalized economy, one would expect it to be no more common than elsewhere" (p. 25). This suggests that McKinnon does not wish to attribute *all* rent-seeking, but only the *extra* rent-seeking apparent in developing countries, to attempts to circumvent inadequate capital markets. There is an alternative hypothesis to be considered. In accordance with the framework proposed by Douglass C. North (1979), one could attribute the extra "favoritism" or wealth-transfer activity to lesser constraints against exploitation by the national government. The relevant constraints are informed and ideological public opinion, effective democratic or constitutional processes, and the mobility of the citizenry. An empirical test of the competing hypotheses would be of great interest.

The chapter includes a list of common interventionist policies: (1) tariffs for "infant industries," (2) import licenses, (3) other monopoly privileges, (4) artificial cheapening of capital goods, (5) manipulation of agriculture's terms of trade, (6) land redistribution, and (7) restrictions and concessions toward foreign direct investment. The common element of capital-market circumvention that McKinnon (p. 30) finds in these policies is that they "relieve the constraint on external finance by enriching the holder of a production opportunity, or by making that opportunity appear to be more profitable so that the immediate cash flow from it increases." In other words, they create flows of artificial profits or rents. The capitalized value of the flows constitutes wealth for the beneficiary. Certainly the flows can be used as evidence of creditworthiness to enable the beneficiary to borrow more readily in the present, or can be used for self-finance as they accrue. Nonetheless one suspects that the enrichment of the beneficiary and not the circumvention of constraints on external finance per se is typically the real reason for which the policies are enacted.

McKinnon quite forcefully criticizes these policies for creating expensive and corrupt bureaucracies, for creating monopoly power, for distorting the allocative function of spot prices, and for tilting the aggregate distribution of income toward the relatively rich. Most emphatically, he insists that they provide an inefficient reward structure for encouraging saving and truly productive investment.

Only one reservation needs to be expressed concerning his argument, namely, that his strictures against foreign direct investment seem to extend unjustifiably even to unsubsidized cases. The statements that "direct investment may be expensive" because of the greater risk perceptions of foreigners and that "relying on direct investment from abroad may break the external financial constraint at the cost of relinquishing investment opportunities to foreigners at bargain-basement prices" (p. 29) are difficult to accept as reasons to block domestic residents from selling labor services and land to, or buying products from, foreign capitalists. No matter how high a risk premium is required by foreigners, it is difficult to see how their supplying of capital can make a capital-poor economy worse off. So long as foreigners lack the local entrepreneurs' knowledge of time and place, they will be unable to take up all the investment opportunities available. So long as foreign capitalists are not prevented from competing with one another, they will be unable to take up many opportunities "at bargain-basement prices." In any event, it is better for the domestic resource owners, labor suppliers, and consumers that a foreign investor fill an opportunity to buy domestic inputs at "bargain-basement" prices, in order to transform them into more highly valued outputs, than that no investor does. It is the mission of profit-seeking entrepreneurs everywhere to find inputs that are underpriced relative to the outputs they can produce (Kirzner 1973).

Against the view that fiscal devices (taxes and subsidies) may be useful to remedy factor price distortions caused by financial repression, McKinnon (1973, 34) cogently argues that useful subsidies would have to be "tailored to a degree of fineness beyond the knowledge and administrative capacity of the government," given the fragmentation of markets in developing countries. He instead indicates that fiscal policies should be confined to the tasks of

Money and Capital in Economic Development

stabilizing the macroeconomy, providing public goods, redistributing income, and "mobilizing an economic surplus of revenues over current expenditure for capital formation" in both the public and private sectors (p. 36).

It is clear from the extensiveness of this list of tasks that McKinnon is not wedded to a laissez-faire ideal. Leaving disagreements over the first three tasks aside, we find that the last fits particularly ill with what one would have supposed is the point of a program of financial liberalization. Surely the point is to allow resources to be allocated by markets so as to reflect the genuine preferences, particularly time-preferences (Irving Fisher's "impatience"), of the economy's participants. (McKinnon indicates that he accepts a time-preference theory of the equilibrium rate of interest.) There is no warrant for a policy of forced savings through taxation. Even if nondistortive taxes were available, there is no case for forcing members of the public to sacrifice more current consumption than they are voluntarily willing to sacrifice at the trade-off rate against future consumption represented by an undistorted interest rate.

Money, Banking, and Financial Repression: Chapters 4 through 9

Chapters 4 through 9 highlight the role of commercial banking as the most important component of the financial system in a developing economy. Because there is little financing of enterprise through bonds and equities, intermediation through banks provides the predominant means of finance. The public holds a large share of its claims on intermediaries (two-thirds is the figure McKinnon cites) as claims on the banking system (central bank included). The importance of commercial banking means that, to "nurture" capital markets, a government must stop discouraging the holding of bank deposits.

McKinnon chooses to call all deposits of the banking system "money." So long as this remains merely a matter of terminology, there is no reason to object to it on any grounds other than its awkwardness. But it is important not to lose sight of two potentially important distinctions that this terminology blurs. The first is the distinction between basic money (full-bodied commodity money or fiat money, which is no one's redeemable liability) and secondary money (bank liabilities redeemable for primary money).[1] The holding of basic money can be a vehicle of saving but, unlike the holding of secondary money, it does not provide the banking system with funds for intermediation. Secondary money can be either deposits or banknotes. During the nineteenth century, the holding of banknotes constituted a major source of bank funding. The second important distinction is between checkable (M1) and noncheckable (M2) bank deposits. The advantages of holding a means of payment are crucial to explaining the holding of currency and checkable deposits, but are not relevant to the holding of noncheckable deposits.

Chapter 4. McKinnon's approach to inflation, the price level, and money demand and supply, embodies the standard principles of monetary theory. The equilibrium price level, P, is determined by the ratio of the central-bank-determined nominal stock of money, M, to the public's real money balances demanded, $(M/P)^d$, thus equating the actual real stock of money, M/P, with the public's real money balances demanded. He emphasizes the importance of the real return to holding money, its nominal interest yield (zero in the case of currency and some demand deposits) minus the expected rate of inflation, in determining the real money balances demanded. In a liberalized financial system we are accustomed to thinking that inflation appreciably affects only currency's real yield, with the nominal yields on deposits adjusting like all other competitive interest rates to changes in expected inflation; in an economy where the authorities impose binding nominal deposit ceilings (or require heavy holdings of non-interest-bearing reserves against deposits), we find that inflation directly penalizes the holding of deposits as well. The authorities determine the real returns on currency and deposits by their choices of inflation rate and deposit interest rates. Thus the demand for real money balances is particularly at the mercy of government policy.

The point to which McKinnon brings novel emphasis is this: As goes the quantity of real money balances, so go the quantities of real saving, intermediation, and capital formation in the less-developed economy. One measure of the accomplishment of the book is that today such a conclusion makes obvious sense. In 1973 the economics profession was under the sway of neoclassical money growth models from which the opposite conclusion emerges. In those models, real money balances and physical capital are treated as alternative forms of wealth for households. A lower real return to holding money, as created by inflation, is thereby found to encourage capital accumulation. Inflation promotes real growth. This notorious result is known as the Tobin effect in recognition of work by James Tobin (1965).

Chapter 5. Because the Tobin effect and the models generating it have been widely accepted in the economics profession as valid, McKinnon quite justifiably devotes Chapter 5 of his book to "a critique of prevailing monetary theory." He exposits an archetypal neoclassical money growth model and quite appropriately notes that it harbors a bias toward inflation. His initial indictment that "the neoclassical model does not transfer well to poor, fragmented economies" (1973, 50), is from today's perspective rather mild. It suggests, perhaps unintentionally, that the model provides adequate guidance in analyzing and making policy for developed economies. McKinnon later (pp. 52–53) notes its real shortcoming: the model fails to incorporate the transactions purpose for holding money. Once this purpose is given its place, real money balances become complementary to the accumulation of physical capital.

This insight is somewhat obscured by McKinnon's choosing to associate the transactions-facilitating function of money with "imperfections in capital markets," on the grounds that in a perfectly frictionless economy, everyone could arrange his payments without anyone having to hold any special moneylike instruments that yield less than the rate of return to capital. Given this association, there is more than meets the eye in his pointing out (p. 52) that the "imperfections in capital markets" that undermine the applicability of the model to less-developed economies "also exist in advanced countries, albeit in less extreme forms." In fact, the key condition—the transactions purpose for holding money—that McKinnon identifies for less-developed countries is every bit as applicable to advanced economies: "Cash balances are needed to intermediate between income and expenditures" (p. 53).

The current state of professional debate on the Tobin effect directly reflects McKinnon's insight. Alan Stockman (1981), twice citing McKinnon's argument (1973), has presented an influential model in which a "cash-in-advance" constraint is used to capture the idea that cash balances already acquired are needed in order to make expenditures on consumption and capital goods. Inflation then reduces the net return from accumulating capital by making more costly the temporary holdings of money needed to buy capital goods and to trade the income from capital for consumption goods. The result is that capital accumulation is discouraged by higher inflation, contrary to the Tobin effect. Empirical work by other authors, using data from developing countries, has generally found neither a Tobin effect nor its inverse (see Danthine, Donaldson, and Smith 1987, 476).

Chapter 6. McKinnon presents, in Chapter 6, an alternative model of the relationship of money to growth. The central result of this model is the complementarity between money and physical capital. A straightforward way to establish such a result would be to note that most of the measured money stock consists of bank liabilities, matched on the banks' balance sheets by investment loans. As George A. Selgin (1987, 441) has argued, an increase in the public's willingness to hold bank money at a given price level "is tantamount to an outward shift in the supply schedule of loanable funds to be intermediated by the banking system." In the literature, this line of thought is known as the debt-intermediation view and is associated with Edward S. Shaw (1973). McKinnon, however, takes a more roundabout route.

In McKinnon's model, the stock of money is assumed to consist entirely of basic fiat money. Commercial bank liabilities are excluded from consideration. The government's proceeds from creating fiat money are assumed not to be used for capital formation, so that neither does the central bank act as an intermediary. These assumptions are meant to duplicate the usual money-supply assumptions of the neoclassical money growth model. The contrast in results between the two models must then arise elsewhere, namely from differing assumptions concerning money demand. In McKinnon's model, "all economic units are confined to self-finance" (1973, 56), so that the temporary accumulation of money balances is the only vehicle for financing discrete (or "lumpy") investments in physical capital. It follows from these assumptions that desired real money balances will vary directly with desired investment activity. More to the point, desired investment activity will vary directly with the desirability of holding money. The reasoning foreshadows that later embodied in Stockman's model: A higher real return to holding money, say due to a lower rate of inflation, reduces the cost of saving up for the purchase of capital goods. McKinnon calls this the "conduit effect" of money. It produces the reverse of the Tobin effect. Inflation discourages real growth.

For the sake of completeness one should, as McKinnon does, note that, even in his model, the Tobin effect (which he calls the "competing-asset effect") can potentially return to dominate the conduit effect. If the real return to holding money rises high enough, money holding becomes an attractive alternative to holding physical capital as a means of accumulating wealth. This is likely to occur only when the rate of inflation becomes significantly negative.

The enduring value in McKinnon's money demand model lies in the backing it gives to his surely warranted conclusions that "inflation is a poor way to deal with the scarcity of real capital," and that "monetary mismanagement resulting in high inflation may be much more damaging than prevailing theory would suggest" (p. 67). Economists who take the neoclassical model of inflation seriously have had a notoriously difficult time understanding why inflation should be considered any more burdensome than a minor excise tax on currency holding. Axel Leijonhufvud (1981, ch. 9, 10) has offered an extensive critique of this misconception that in some respects overlaps with McKinnon's.

McKinnon ventures onto less secure ground when he deploys his model as a guide to "optimization" by monetary authorities. In this exercise we find the real return on money that maximizes the rate of self-financed investment. No reason is given for supposing that government ought to impose such a goal on society. The exercise suggests—perhaps unintentionally—that the authorities should not allow the real rate of return on money to rise "too high," a suggestion that one would certainly not want to see carried over to an economy with bank-issued money or employed as a rationale for government monopoly over money. Here the intuition of Cameron is persuasive: "the theoretically optimal growth path of the ratio of bank assets to national income is also the 'natural' growth path that would result from free competition" (1967, 313).

Chapter 7. The analysis of "financial repression" for which *Money and Capital in Economic Development* is best known appears in Chapter 7. The "formal" banking and financial sector is repressed primarily by interest rate ceilings (on both sides of the balance sheet) that are particularly binding when inflation is high. Artificially low (sometimes even negative) real returns discourage the holding of bank liabilities, holding down intermediation through the banks and saving in total. Artificially low loan rates create an excess demand for loanable funds that is rationed through favoritism to licensed importers, large-scale exporters, protected manufacturers, and (naturally) government agencies and the national treasury. Unfavored enterprises are excluded from the long-term finance of the formal banks and left to borrow at much higher rates from the "informal" financial sector or "curb market" of local moneylenders, shopkeepers, pawnbrokers, and cooperatives.

Far from making cheaper loans available to the small borrower, then, interest-rate ceilings have the opposite effect. Loans are more expensive to all but the favored few. McKinnon makes this point vividly by citing a truly alarming difference between official and unofficial lending rates in Ethiopia: 6 to 9 percent versus 100 to 200 percent. He then considers government attempts to patch over the problem by further interventions. Extending the usury ceiling to the informal sector does not remedy the problem, but worsens it by making credit still less available. Relieving farmers of the need to finance inventories by having government buy and store farm produce does nothing to relieve the shortage of capital (government borrowing is now larger) and shifts the pricing of produce into the political realm. This in turn leads to the central planning of agriculture.

The route to economic sanity is clear: Eliminate financial repression so that bank-intermediated funding becomes available to entrepreneurs throughout the economy. The expansion of bank lending to small-scale, rural, and other formerly excluded enterprises can make use of the specialized knowledge about potential borrowers held by the informal lenders who had been serving them. As McKinnon (1973, 78) suggests, banks can lend funds to the moneylenders for relending or can hire them as loan officers. Alternatively, with free entry into banking, the moneylenders can transform their own operations into formal or quasi-formal banks.

The importance of private ownership and free entry for competitive and efficient results in banking is unfortunately neglected by McKinnon and, in one uneasy passage, seems even to be denied. He proposes (pp. 78–79) that "banks can be organized . . . to simulate competitive lending and deposit practices, even if the banking structure remains highly concentrated." Instructions for the simulation of competitive practices are then given, presumably for the benefit of monopolistic government-run or government-fostered banks. Profit-motivated private banks, constrained by genuine competition, would find such instructions unnecessary or irrelevant.

The fact of the matter is that competitive results cannot be attained by asking state-owned or state-sheltered banks to "simulate competitive practices." This is so for two reasons—lack of knowledge and lack of incentive—that should be familiar to students of the classic debate over the feasibility of "market socialism" (see Lavoie 1985 for a secondary account).

Though one can specify roughly the directions in which practices in a particular noncompetitive system would have to move to be more like those observed in competitive systems in similar developmental settings—and such a rough specification is all that McKinnon's instructions provide—the pattern of activities that competition would produce in a given time and place cannot be known in any detail without letting actual competition operate. We simply do not know, but must rely on the competitive selection process to show us, which activities and practices will allow banks to survive and prosper in a particular economy. Competition is not just a means for enforcing static cost-minimization in a world of given products, known production techniques, and given input prices. It is also an essential means for uncovering previously unknown higher-valued products and lower-cost production methods appropriate for a specific setting (see Hayek 1978). McKinnon's instruction to price loans to reflect "the general scarcity [cost] of capital and the peculiar administrative costs of serving each class of borrower" (p. 79) would be operational only if those costs were somehow already known.

No method analogous to profit competition has yet been devised for compelling a public agency or sheltered private monopoly to act as if it were *trying its best* to produce competitivelike results. An institution created by politics faces political incentives that pull it in quite another direction.

For these reasons a case can be made for the privatization of state-owned financial institutions and for free entry into financial markets that applies with special relevance to developing countries (White 1987). McKinnon may well accept this case. He may intend his instructions merely as second-best policy advice for a government that refuses to privatize and open up its economy's financial sector. Or he may not. His position is not clear. Discussion concerning the rules of the game necessary for "first-best" banking—private ownership and free entry in particular—is conspicuously absent from

McKinnon's book. Its absence is highlighted by the emphasis on the importance of genuinely competitive conditions in the more recent literature. Fry rightly insists that where government-owned or -controlled banks misallocate resources and operate wastefully, "financial liberalization cannot by itself rectify the problem" (1988, 299; see generally 261–322).

The lack of clarity about the ideal continues when McKinnon (1973, 79) speaks of relieving financial repression through a "preferred strategy of high real rates of interest—where real finance is plentiful at those rates." This suggests that the real interest rate and the real quantity of loanable funds can appropriately be regarded as policy instruments rather than as a price and quantity whose correct determination must be left to competitive markets. The following paragraph likewise considers the adjustment of nominal interest rates to variation in the inflation rate as a strategic problem for "the banking authority" rather than as a market outcome in a regime of competing financial firms. In neither paragraph is a second-best apology offered.

The final section of Chapter 7 introduces McKinnon's novel prescription for relatively painless disinflation (which he persistently calls "deflation") in financially repressed economies. The orthodox method of disinflation is to slow the growth of the nominal money stock, thereby in quantity-theoretic fashion lowering the equilibrium growth rate of the price level. This approach is typically painful, in monetarist analysis (Darby 1976, for example), because the momentum of the price level keeps it rising at the old rate for a time even while the rate of money growth is being reduced. During this period, the prices of goods in general are too high given the slowed growth of money balances: there is not enough money in circulation to support such high prices. An excess supply of goods (corresponding to an excess demand for money) develops at the existing price level and is reflected in unsold inventories. This leads to cutbacks in production, layoffs, and all the other features of recession, until the price level decelerates to its newly warranted path.

McKinnon's diagnosis is different from, though not inconsistent with, the foregoing. In his account (1973, 87) a reduction in nominal money growth, given the momentum of the price level, means a fall in the quantity of *real* money balances and thereby (given that most of M2 consists of bank liabilities matched on the balance sheets by loans to business) a reduction in the real supply of bank credit to manufacturers. (Here McKinnon implicitly drops his own self-finance model in favor of something akin to Shaw's debt-intermediation view of money.) Firms dependent on bank credit must contract operations for lack of working capital to finance their inventories and wage bills. Unemployment and recession ensue. In this account, the excess demand for money constrains firms through its effect on the banking system's real balance sheet rather than through its effect on final sales.

The key to avoiding recession when disinflating, in the orthodox monetarist view, is to make the lower growth path of the money stock credible in advance. Then price-setters will moderate their periodic price adjustments so as to avoid setting prices too high. In the limit, the price level will shift immediately onto its new equilibrium path, unsold inventories will not accumulate, and recession will be avoided. The major problem is how to make an announcement of lower money growth credible. One method often discussed in developed countries is to bind the government's hands through some constitutional constraint so that it can no longer expand the stock of base money at its discretion. That method may be presently impracticable in a developing country that lacks effective constitutional mechanisms for binding government in any respect. There may simply be no method for the monetary authority of such a country to make a credible precommitment.

McKinnon does not explicitly consider the question of whether a disinflation can be made credible in advance, but implicitly answers in the negative with his quite general assertion that "orthodox direct restraints on the *supply* of money and credit are indeed likely to bring misery and hardship in their wake" (p. 88). As the use of italics in that statement suggests, he goes on to recommend that disinflation be driven by way of the alternative route: by increasing the real *demand* to hold money. Increasing the public's real money balances demand, as seen in the simple price-level analytics of Chapter 4, brings down the price level so as to equate actual with demanded real balances. People trying to acquire greater real balances will be more eager to sell and less eager to buy commodities, thus bidding down their prices.

The authorities of a financially repressed economy have a ready means at hand for increasing the real demand to hold money balances: they can raise the real return to holding money (broadly defined) by raising their ceiling on deposit interest rates. In accord with McKinnon's diagnosis of recession, this route avoids the shrinkage in the real stock of money and accompanying credit contraction that make an orthodox disinflation so painful. In fact the real stock of money can rise at the outset of the disinflation. In the orthodox disinflation, the real stock of money shrinks at first and only much later (as lower inflationary expectations become established, raising the expected real return to holding money balances) does it rise.

What McKinnon's advice offers here is not a "price stabilization without tears" (p. 88), as he puts it, so much as a price stabilization in which a spoonful of sugar helps to mask the bitterness of the medicine. The sugar is of course the removal of financial repression: lifting interest rate ceilings allows real intermediation to increase as the market for loanable funds clears at the greater quantity supplied. The medicine is the establishment of a lower growth rate for the nominal money stock. Its bitterness, due to the creation of an excess demand for money during the transition to a lower path of prices, is unavoidable in the absence of credibility for the announced disinflationary path for money. McKinnon's demand-led disinflation does not avoid creating an excess demand for money as part of the process of bringing down the path of prices. Correspondingly an excess supply of commodities and, presumably, some layoffs and idling of capital cannot be avoided. The only way to avoid the tears associated with disinflation is to avoid inflating in the first place.

Rather, the boost to the real economy from the removal of financial repression helps to offset the monetary shock. So too would other policies to promote the aggregate supply of real income. One suspects that McKinnon would be at most ambivalent about being associated with supply-side economics, but there is some similarity in their respective prescriptions for disinflation. There is also, we will see below, similarity in their support for a value-added tax.

Chapter 8. McKinnon provides, in Chapter 8, several case studies of LDCs that, in the years before 1973, had successfully liberalized their financial sectors. The important empirical issues to be resolved are whether the quantity of real money balances in fact exhibits complementarity with investment and growth, and how sensitive private saving is to the rise in real interest rates produced by liberalization. Germany and Japan in the postwar era are studied as examples of sustained growth in both real output and in real money balances per unit of real output. Argentina, Brazil, and Chile in the same period show similar joint movement, only in reverse. The financial reform of South Korea in the 1960s provides a fairly persuasive picture of "financial reform without tears."

The Korean reform abruptly reduced inflation (measured by the wholesale price index) from between 20 and 35 percent in 1963–1964 to between 6 and 10 percent between 1965 and 1970, without creating a recession in the growth of the Korean economy. From the perspective of the present, it is interesting to contrast McKinnon's view of how this was possible with the current wisdom on ending inflations, as represented by the rational-expectations view of Thomas J. Sargent (1986). Sargent emphasizes the credibility issue: Inflation can be stopped quickly and without tears *if* inflation-rate expectations can be reduced. With expectations being formed rationally, lower inflation-rate expectations can only be created by the announcement of *credible* change in the path of money growth. The chief condition for credibility, in Sargent's view, is a simultaneous change in fiscal policy such that less revenue from money creation is needed.

Money and Capital in Economic Development 93

From McKinnon's account we do find the fiscal-reform condition fulfilled in the Korean case. Indeed he cites it, much as Sargent would, as an important factor lending credibility to the government's control over nominal money growth, and thereby dampening inflation-rate expectations. In McKinnon's account, however, the dampening of inflation-rate expectations acts indirectly rather than directly to mitigate any painfulness of disinflation. Lowered expectations of inflation increase the expected real yield from bank liabilities, thereby increasing real deposit holding and correspondingly real intermediation, and thereby boosting aggregate supply. A more detailed historical investigation would be necessary to disentangle the direct and indirect contributions of the lowering of inflation-rate expectations to the painlessness of the disinflation.

Chapter 9. A theoretical digression on the topic of "optimum" monetary policy, that is, policy that allows for the maximization of the benefits of money holding net of cost, is provided in Chapter 9. In general, optimum money holding occurs where the marginal opportunity cost of holding money (the difference between the real rates of return to money and to capital) equals the marginal benefit of holding real money balances rather than physical capital (the implicit payment-service or "convenience" yield of money), which in turn equals the marginal cost of producing real balances. In the standard neoclassical model, real balances consist entirely of fiat money, on which a real yield equal to the rate of return on physical capital can be provided without cost by perfectly anticipated deflation and whose payment services are available at zero cost. The point of optimum money holding is thus obtained where the marginal payment-service benefit of holding real balances goes to zero, and where the rate of return on money equals that on physical capital.

McKinnon presents a geometric model that modifies the assumption of zero-cost money in a straightforward and sensible way. In his model, real money balances are provided at a positive marginal cost by a banking system. Optimum money holding therefore occurs where the marginal benefit of holding money equals the positive cost of providing the services of a bank account and where the real return on money is lower than the return on physical capital by that same cost.

Implicitly, McKinnon's approach assumes that the cost of providing the payment services of a bank account is identical to the cost of intermediation (which transforms claims to the returns on physical capital into bank accounts). In principle these two costs are distinct. The first can be covered by explicit transactions fees (per-check and per-account charges). In that case the spread between the rates of return on bank assets (reflecting the returns on investments in physical capital) and on bank liabilities reflects only the cost of intermediation.

For monetary policy purposes, the addition of banking costs to the model seems to make no difference. Both McKinnon's model and the neoclassical model conclude that the optimal rate of seigniorage extraction by government is zero. The process of extracting seigniorage by issuing new fiat money imposes a distortive tax on holders of existing money, because new issues dilute the purchasing power of existing money. Positive rates of seigniorage drive a wedge between the economically necessary and the actually perceived costs of money holding, inefficiently depriving the public of potential benefits.

McKinnon (1973, 123) correctly emphasizes that seigniorage collection is typically the prime motivation behind high rates of monetary expansion in LDCs. He then proposes that "the temptation to divert seigniorage to the public exchequer" depends on the capacity of the government to raise revenue by other methods of taxation being "unduly limited." This proposal is easier to accept once we remove the modifier "unduly." Given the natural temptation of government to consume and disburse revenue, seigniorage is a tempting revenue source so long as the capacity to raise revenue through other taxes is limited, period. Which is to say: Seigniorage is always tempting. It is more tempting when revenue is wanted more urgently, which is why high rates of monetary expansion so regularly accompany warfare, particularly because the quickest way to raise so much revenue is by printing money. To limit a government's appetite for seigniorage, it is necessary either to persuade it that it should reduce its spending or that its attempt to raise revenue through seigniorage has entered the region of negative returns.[2]

To government, seigniorage is an attractive way to raise revenue at all times because the public is not prepared to resist or evade it. Its incidence is hidden. Its collection, unlike overt taxation, requires little apparatus for coercion. The only coercion involved is that supporting the domestic government's exclusive monopoly on the issue of basic money. It is not always appreciated (and McKinnon does not mention) that such measures extend to devices that reduce the availability of legal substitutes. By reducing the elasticity of the real demand for government-issued money to changes in the inflation rate, such devices enhance seignorage revenue. Foreign exchange controls and other policies to prevent the "dollarization" of the economy can be understood in this way. Interest-rate ceilings on bank deposits serve the same purpose (Nichols 1974). Much of the apparatus of financial repression then, to return to an earlier theme of this paper, serves the revenue interests of government.

The remainder of the chapter emphasizes that the complementarity earlier noted between money and physical capital runs both ways: not only does increased saving in the form of money holding (as promoted by financial liberalization) feed capital formation, but also growth in capital and wealth stimulates the acquisition of additional money balances. The "portfolio effect" of growth on saving thus completes a "virtuous circle." Liberalization boosts saving and hence growth, which *itself* promotes additional saving and hence more growth. This helps to explain (1973, 129) "why a discrete improvement in monetary policy can have such a sharp impact on observed growth and saving rates," and why the impact can persist over time.

Foreign Trade, Currency, and Capital: Chapters 10 through 12

Chapter 10. The case for the liberalization of foreign trade and its implications for the fiscal policy of a government that relies heavily (as LDC governments do) on tariffs for revenue is discussed in Chapter 10. Setting forth a now widely accepted case against import-substitution policies, McKinnon sagely argues not for new policies in the direction of export-encouragement, but simply for an end to trade-distorting policies. The dismantling of protective tariffs and quotas on imports will alone do enough to encourage exports through the two-sidedness of international trade.

The remainder of the chapter frets over the failure of indirect taxes (sales taxes, customs duties, excise taxes) to raise proportionately more revenue as gross national product (GNP) grows. It is taken for granted that government should grow at least in proportion to GNP. A value-added tax (VAT) is recommended as a remedy. In common with supply-side economists, McKinnon likes the fact that the VAT excludes saving from the tax base, increasing the incentive for saving over consumption. Unlike supply-siders, McKinnon complains that the VAT is "not a suitable vehicle for effecting significant income redistribution from the rich to the poor" (p. 147). The ethical merits or demerits of such a wealth transfer receive no discussion. More surprisingly, no mention is made of the possibility that expropriation from the rich, or at least from those who acquire their riches through honest enterprise and accumulation, may discourage saving and growth.

Chapter 11. Through a parable of the alpha economy and the beta economy, McKinnon argues, in Chapter 11, for liberalization without reliance on inflows of foreign capital.

Chapter 12. He reinforces the argument, in Chapter 12, with anecdotal evidence. Taken as a case against international agencies providing subsidized rates or credit guarantees on loans to LDC borrowers as an inducement for liberalization, or LDC governments themselves providing firms with artificial incentives to use foreign financing, the argument is compelling. Taken as a case for erecting artificial barriers against capital flows, even temporarily, it is not. Used to support interest-rate and exchange-rate manipulations, capital controls, and discrimination against foreign direct investment in the name of "balanced indigenous development," the argument is ironic if not perverse. Here McKinnon seems to forget the principle expressed in Chapter 10, that past distortions do not justify future distortions in the opposite direction. He also seems to contradict the principle announced in Chapter 1: "Complete rather than partial liberalization is more likely to be ultimately successful" (p. 4).

One sees here the first steps being taken into that tangled thicket that is known as the "order of liberalization" literature. The essential point to be made in rejoinder to McKinnon's case for transitional capital controls has been made by Alan Stockman in a comment on an article by McKinnon (1982, 190):

> The issue is whether capital flows facilitate mutually beneficial exchange and help promote economic growth. McKinnon's argument for controls rests on the assumption that the "authorities" (the government) can make better decisions about foreign investment issues than the investors who are risking their own money.

One only need add, in light of the bailouts that seem to have compromised the Chilean liberalization, that it is vitally necessary for both foreign investors and domestic banks to believe that they really are risking their own money.

The Policy Message Conveyed

The reception accorded to *Money and Capital in Economic Development* by economists reviewing the book was overwhelmingly positive (see Lüders 1974, Waters 1974, Grubel 1974, Price 1974, Caves 1974) with only an occasional dissent (Reubens 1974) from the old guard. One senses in reading their reviews that the old paradigm in development theory was ripe for replacement. We can glean an answer from these reviews to the question: What was considered novel in McKinnon's message? The reviewers in 1974 stressed the following points.

(1) Development begins at home. The policy choices made by the LDC governments themselves are responsible for their various

growth performances in the postwar era. McKinnon himself calls his approach "heavily 'bootstrap' in emphasis" (1973, 2). Successful development can therefore proceed without reliance on foreign aid or foreign capital.

Regardless of the policy route to be recommended to LDC governments, the message that praise or blame belonged with them, not with the already developed nations, was in 1973 an unusual point of departure.

(2) Well-functioning domestic financial and monetary sectors are crucial to economic development. Grubel (1974, 333) comments that development theory had previously focused almost entirely on the "real" sector, a "gap in the literature" that McKinnon helps to fill.

(3) Monetary and financial regulatory policies that stifle domestic intermediation, creating "financial repression," are primarily responsible for poorly functioning domestic monetary systems and capital markets, and thus for poor growth. Interest rate ceilings on deposits and loans, combined with inflationary rates of monetary expansion, are the most important policies creating "financial repression."

The combination of point 3 with point 1 means an emphasis not on the overall scarcity of capital in the LDC (difficult to remedy except by massive capital transfers from abroad), but on its misallocation as a result of policy-induced distortions (possible to remedy simply by eliminating the bad policies).

The contrast of these three points to the intellectual status quo then prevailing is obvious.

> For a quarter of a century the dominant prescription in much of the literature of economic development for poor countries has been to seek foreign capital through grants and loans, through so-called planning to control investment and all markets including the capital market, and to follow a protectionist policy with respect to foreign trade. . . . In most poor countries in the fifties and sixties little or no attention was given to development of domestic capital markets that would provide necessary incentives for saving and provide an

efficient means for allocating financial resources among investment opportunities (Price 1974, 188).

(4) Liberalization reduces the painfulness of stabilization, because inflation can then be brought down by an increase in demand for money (as interest rates on deposits are allowed to rise and as increased intermediation augments the volume of real income) rather than by a reduction in its supply.

(5) The liberalization of domestic financial markets is the key to growth. This conclusion follows from the first three points. As Reubens puts it, the book offers "a bootstrap approach to economic development, using monetary straps" (1974, 500). Grubel distills from it the message that "the road to economic development is paved with competitive financial intermediaries operating in free markets and under price stability" (1974, 333).

Whatever dissents have been registered above with respect to the details of McKinnon's argument, the essential message reflected in these five points is surely correct and vital. The vitality of his thesis as an intellectual achievement is evidenced by its continued citation in the literature and by the very assignment of this retrospective. Its vitality as a policy manifesto is evidenced by the extent of liberalization thus far achieved and by the extent remaining to be achieved. For the citizens of the third world, on whom the crushing weight of poverty is increased by financial repression, the essential message of Ronald McKinnon's modern classic is especially vital.

Ronald I. McKinnon

Comment

It is indeed a pleasure for me to comment on Lawrence White's paper because it has been a long time since the previous review of *Money and Capital in Economic Development* (McKinnon 1973) was published. Eighteen years later, this may be the best of all, certainly in terms of depth of insight. Since I am in an odd position, being a lead commentator on a review of my own book, let me provide some perspective on how the book came to be written. Consider the mindset of people back in the 1960s on the role of finance in economic development and then consider the way in which our thoughts have changed subsequently.

I was trained as a mathematical economist at the University of Minnesota in the late 1950s and early 1960s. At that time, one of the key ideas in the development area, sort of a shortcut to rapid development, was the large-scale planning model. For example, you would build a large planning model for India, with a big input-output structure including maybe twenty or thirty industries, and people would then estimate in some detail the values of pertinent variables. The World Bank would project one for Turkey, one for

Korea, and so on. Each country would get its own large-scale planning model.

Because the planners did not know much about resource allocation within the economy and about what individual entrepreneurs were doing, they projected in the model a course of development based on import substitution. Customs statistics were available, so they could look at the pattern of imports coming into the economy. Implementation of the model would be directed by the government, presumably on the basis of fiscal processes—taxes and subsidies—and by official directives.

This was the formal aspect of the import substitution approach to economic development led by Hollis Chenery at the World Bank and also people such as Alan Manne. At the same time, there was the Ranis-Fei model of labor market distortions. The main message of this model was that labor was somehow too highly priced in the industrial sector. There was a labor market distortion. They believed that future development success required industrialization, so they felt that the government had to take action to somehow grab resources from the rest of the economy and pour it into the industrial sector. Then it could use the large-scale planning model as a method of guiding that resource transfer.

I am caricaturing things a little bit. You will have to excuse me. However, the financial process and how it could help to produce the saving surplus needed for industrial development just lay in the background. Nobody talked about capital markets in less-developed countries. People thought of the monetary system more in a Keynesian sense: It was something to be mined by the government for fiscal purposes.

You could tax it with inflation if necessary, but keep interest rates as low as possible, because real money balances were thought to be a substitute for real capital accumulation. Directed credits were the order of the day. Government mandated where credits should go according to the plan. All of this was to be supported by foreign aid. External capital was thought to be very important in the development process.

If you went further, one could think of other ways of raising the surplus necessary for development. Protectionism in foreign trade would turn the terms of trade against farmers and essentially extract the surplus forcibly for the benefit of the industrial sector. The whole idea of having a voluntary financial system, where people actually parted with their saving on a quid pro quo basis at an equilibrium real rate of interest, was neglected as a mechanism for future development.

The words "financial repression" had not been used in the economics I learned as a graduate student. We were beginning to learn about the repression in foreign trade through tariffs and quotas and the damage that protectionism did to the export capability of the economy. Because of obvious resource misallocation, by the end of the 1960s people became concerned that there might be something wrong with import substitution as a development strategy.

But the equally important repression of the domestic financial system was not obvious to people at the time. So, the purpose of my book was to draw attention to the fact that there was internal repression of capital markets that paralleled the repression of foreign trade.

This concern was prompted by a visit to Korea in 1966. As some of you may remember, from 1954 to 1964 the Korean economy languished. After the Korean War there was virtually no growth on a per capita basis. There was high and variable inflation, and there were commentators, such as Joan Robinson of Cambridge University, who used to make speeches comparing the economic development of North Korea very favorably to what was going on in the South. I remember her coming to Stanford and giving the speech to a delighted group of students.

Then, fortunately, in the mid-1960s there was a series of reforms in finance and foreign trade. Moving away from a multiple exchange rate mechanism that had greatly overvalued the Korean currency, the government unified exchange rates in 1964. There was big fiscal reform; suddenly the ability of the government to collect tax revenue doubled as a share of GNP. There was a military government and they had just put a new general in charge of inland revenue.

In 1965, my colleagues, Edward Shaw and John Gurley, and Hugh

Patrick, of Yale University, wrote a report suggesting how the financial system could be liberalized. Fiscal reform made possible this liberalization because the government no longer had to tap the financial system, principally the banks, as a source of finance. So, it became possible to reduce the official reserve requirements imposed on the Korean banks and to raise rates of interest on deposits to positive and quite high levels in real terms. Previously, Koreans had been acquiring virtually no new net financial assets as a share of GNP. Suddenly, bank deposits looked really attractive to the average Korean household, rural or urban.

There was a great flow of savings into the financial system out of inflation hedges or out of low-productivity investments within households. Along with the foreign trade reform that was making the economy externally competitive, this internal financial reform was the beginning of the great growth spurt in South Korea. Entrepreneurs could now bid for the capital they needed to finance profitable domestic and export activities.

I was there as a tariff adviser in the mid-1960s. It was clear to me that the academic case for free trade was well established in principle, provided that the financial system was stable. If high rates of inflation and great changes in real exchange rates and real interest rates could be avoided, the analytical basis for free trade would be well established—even though, politically, free trade was often difficult to implement.

On the financial side, however, it was quite clear that there were the technical problems of preventing inflation or deflation that people had not solved, even with the best intentions and no political restraints. You had to decide how fast the money supply should grow, what should be prudential regulations for the banks, what interest rate policies should be established, and what kinds of financial intermediaries should work best in different circumstances. These are open technical issues on which reasonable people can disagree. That set the course for my future research in trying to understand these issues.

Optimal financial policy seemed to be a more interesting technical problem to address than tariffs or quotas on foreign commerce, which were equally important as a policy issue but were more or less resolved conceptually in favor of free trade. My moving away from an emphasis on foreign trade to an attempt to understand domestic finance is what motivated me to write the book.

In analyzing *Money and Capital in Economic Development*, Lawrence White mentioned some errors of omission and a few of commission in what is generally a very nice review. The omission he correctly points to is my lack of historical perspective. Coming from a fairly technical background as a young man, I had insufficient perspective on the importance of financial processes in nineteenth-century Europe and North America when I wrote the book. It is just as lucky. I would have been inhibited if I had known that people had written similar things earlier.

White points out a tradition among economic historians of analyzing financial processes going back through Rondo Cameron, Raymond Goldsmith (whom I was somewhat familiar with), Joseph Schumpeter, and Adam Smith. However, I came to the importance of finance as a revelation out of my own Korean experience and not by reading economic history proper. The key role of financial institutions in the late nineteenth century for European and American development was neglected in the postwar literature emphasizing economic theory. The importance of finance in mainline macroeconomics, for example, was (and is) suppressed. So my neglect of economic history was a good criticism for White to bring out.

Now, I have a couple of other points to which Lawrence referred. In most less-developed countries, there are incredibly detailed state interventions in most spheres of economic activity: credit allocations and interest ceilings in the finance area, and quotas, tariffs, special licenses, and so on in foreign trade. In Chapter 3 of my book, I considered the motivation of the state for intervening to be fairly benign. If, for any reason, the domestic capital market is malfunctioning, it appears to everybody that resources are not being allocated correctly. Thus tremendous pressure is placed on government to get in there and replace the moribund capital market with some other incentives.

For example, the infant industry argument for protection is

based largely on capital market failure. The infant industry argument suggests that a new firm making a new product may incur losses for a while. Because learning-by-doing takes time, several years may elapse before the firm moves down its learning curve and becomes efficient. But, during the period when it is making losses, it will not be able to survive and therefore will need at least temporary tariff protection.

But this argument implies that the domestic capital market is not working, that the entrepreneur cannot borrow over the long term to cover his losses in the present against the time in the future when the firm will be profitable. As a second-best response, the government may feel impelled to jump in there with a tariff to protect the nascent entrepreneur.

Apart from carefully planned infant industry protection, however, there may be second-best arguments for protection in foreign trade in any less-developed economy that is in financial chaos. In Brazil, for example, the rate of inflation can be anywhere between 50 and 300 percent per year, and changes in the nominal exchange rate do not necessarily match the rate of inflation. Therefore, the real exchange rate is all over the place. Sometimes the cruzeiro is highly overvalued. Sometimes it is highly undervalued. Rates of interest can be anything. The long-term capital market may cease to exist, and short-term rates vary all over the map. In any sector of the economy, new entrepreneurs face tremendous uncertainty from real exchange risk and real interest fluctuations. If they do not get protection, they will not invest in promising new technologies.

Consider the Brazilian computer industry. The American government has been complaining bitterly about the lack of access for American firms and the fact that the market is sealed off for Brazilians. With the real exchange rate variance that Brazilian entrepreneurs face, I can see a second-best argument for trying to protect the nascent computer industry. Otherwise, it could not survive, even though in a stable financial world it would be viable. Thus having the financial system under control, stabilizing the price level, and getting the capital market working right are very much necessary for eliminating protection in foreign trade.

Lawrence White suggests that governments intervene for a lot of other reasons beyond just trying to correct for the moribund capital market. There is patronage, rent-seeking, and just outright corruption in trying to siphon off resources to political clients. I do not deny that these other motivations can be also very important. But, if we can figure out a way to stabilize the financial system, then it is much easier to expose these other interventions for what they really are.

The problem of optimal bank regulation is a very subtle matter. As those of you who have read Rolf Lüders's paper [Chapter 5 in this volume.—Editor] already know, we have all been chastened by the fact that the apparent success of the Chilean liberalizations of the late 1970s was followed by the financial collapse of 1981–1982, which really set back the whole development program. Although they have now partially recovered, the Chileans did not have their financial regulations right in the initial liberalization phase. This bears on a point that Lawrence White made in his criticism, that is, that I was too cautious regarding free banking.

In my book, I mentioned that interest rates on deposits should be set at fairly high levels in real terms, but that note issues would remain the province of the central bank. In contrast, White would allow free entry into banking and allow banks to issue their own private bank notes. He criticized me for being too restrictive on what banks could do. But, in fact, there is tremendous moral hazard in the banking sector. Unlike nonmonetary financial intermediaries, banks, either implicitly or explicitly, are insured by their governments because of the central importance of the money mechanism. The Chileans did not have explicit deposit insurance. Nevertheless, everyone believed that the government would come to the rescue of the banks if a crash occurred—and the government did come to the rescue when the crash occurred.

Because it sets up terrific moral hazards with which we are now familiar, you cannot have uninhibited free banking. In 1973, I was not familiar with the Stiglitz-Weiss model of credit rationing. It is in Adam Smith, which again reflects my absence of historical perspective. It is now quite well known that interest rates break down as a rationing mechanism if you have a period of very high real rates of interest in the capital market. The quality of credit will deteriorate substantially because of adverse risk selection. The only people willing to borrow at those very high real rates of interest are those who think there is only a small probability that they are likely to repay.

In the Stiglitz-Weiss model of credit rationing, the financial intermediary sets an interest rate below the market clearing level, thus rationing credit, to prevent this adverse risk selection from being so severe. If, however, you are dealing with a monetary financial intermediary, then there is moral hazard in the bank itself, which is not in the Stiglitz-Weiss model. So, instead of behaving in a prudent and conservative way by keeping interest rates lower than the market clearing level and rationing credit to limit adverse risk selection, the insured banks may instead raise real rates of interest and embark on extremely risky lending.

Then, banks will not be a restraining or prudent force on the natural adverse risk selection associated with a high real interest rate environment. This is one thing I did not realize when I wrote the book in 1973. I could not have predicted what happened in Chile in the late 1970s when real interest rates rose so high and there was a lot of very bad lending. But it is clear that as far as the monetary system is concerned, we need very careful prudential regulation of what institutions we have. We do not necessarily want free entry for monetary intermediaries.

The American savings and loan (S&L) system today is a shambles because of free entry combined with deposit insurance by the state. It is very easy to get S&L charters. In the state of California, every year a hundred new S&Ls come into existence. After getting the deposit insurance privilege from Uncle Sam, each of these fledgling entrepreneurs can raise capital at the government's expense, even though they could never raise it on their own. The quality of the individual in the S&L business has changed completely because of deposit insurance—many are now high rollers, or scoundrels, or both.

It is clear in this circumstance that insurance creates a distortion, so that you should not have free entry. You must have very strict prudential controls. You can have free entry, but the results are terrible. In the early stages of development, the monetary system is everything to the capital market: about 90 percent of all borrowing and lending. But, as development proceeds, you want the regulated monetary system (subject to moral hazard) to diminish in size and the unregulated nonmonetary financial intermediaries, primary securities markets and so on, eventually to supplant the monetary system as the main financial artery.

It is very hard to justify the case that Lawrence makes for free banking. He referred to Scotland, one generation away my home and native land, and the Scottish clearing banks that issued their own bank notes without restraint. But this was under very favorable circumstances in which they had fixed exchange rates with England so that the price level in Scotland was pegged and the monetary control was quite good. The Scots are naturally quite prudent anyway.

[Laughter]

I will make one more point. What I liked most about Lawrence's review was his analysis of the problem of disinflation. We all know we have this incredibly high inflation in Latin America. Government imposes the inflation tax because it cannot collect ordinary taxes. But that inflation tax is extremely debilitating to the financial process.

In my book, I emphasized the importance of a major fiscal reform, as the Chileans succeeded in doing in the 1970s, so you can collect regular taxes and balance the government's budget. Then, there remains the problem of phasing inflation out of the system. If price inflation is several hundred percent per year, how can you disinflate efficiently without some major calamity occurring? Lawrence White mentions the standard argument, now associated with Tom Sargent, that to get inflation under control you must slow down the rate of increase in the money supply after you have the fiscal wherewithal to do it.

Credibility is everything. The people must have confidence in the government if this slowdown in money growth is to be successful. But there is a dilemma. Once the government embarks on a program of slowing money growth, people see that there is some chance that it will be successful in stabilizing the price level. Then there is a big surge in the demand for money. If the government does not satisfy that surge, there may be a precipitate deflation. This is an acute policy dilemma. To establish credibility, you want to slow money growth but, once you successfully do that, there is a big surge in the demand for money. It is very difficult to accommodate that surge in demand and retain your credibility as a government if you emphasize controlling the rate of increase in the money supply.

In Chapters 7 and 8 of my book, I approach the problem of disinflation somewhat differently. Start with the typical repressed financial system, where deposit rates of interest are too low and real cash balance holdings are also low. Then, after your fiscal reform, raise deposit rates of interest and make money much more attractive from the demand side.

You can deflate the price level either by raising the demand for money or by slowing growth of the money supply. But if you operate on the demand side, then financial repression is released at the time the reform occurs. People may remain very suspicious of the government's efforts to carry through the price stabilization. Still the very high interest rates on cash balances will make money much more attractive than holding rice in your backyard or holding excess inventories if you are a businessman.

So there will be a big flow of funds into the banking system. That itself will tend to deflate commodity markets and, at the same time, could channel real credit flows to productive activities in order to release the supply constraints in the economy. By operating on the demand for money and releasing financial repression, it is possible to disinflate without any turndown in real output and without requiring the full credibility of the government. Everyone need not have full confidence that the government is actually going to pull it off. People just operating in their own self-interest will build up their cash balances if you give them a higher rate of interest. This happened in Korea in 1965 and resulted in a big surge of funds into the banking system. Price inflation, which had been 30 or 35 percent, fell to nothing in 1965, but real output expanded enormously as a result of the financial stabilization.

Lawrence has very nicely brought out the parallels between this approach, which is demand-oriented, and the dilemmas associated with the traditional approach, which operates on the supply of money.

By operating from the demand side, one can avoid using growth in the supply of nominal money as the indicator governing inflation expectations. As long as people see higher real deposit rates, we get a favorable disinflationary effect *even if credibility in the overall success of the program is lacking*. Thanks to Lawrence White's analysis, I now see that the strength of my approach is that it depends much less on people having confidence that the government will stick to its reforms. Indeed, Koreans didn't have much confidence in their government at the time the 1964–1965 reform actually succeeded. This success followed on the heels of a botched monetary reform in 1961—when the government introduced a new money to replace an old one without successfully curbing its fiscal deficit or its rate of price inflation.

I think that the analysis encouraged by Lawrence's retrospective look at my work has implications for the new "heterodox" approach to price stabilization in LDCs. In the heterodox approach, people try to play on expectations too much by introducing price and wage controls as well as new currencies—as with the failed austral and cruzado plans in Argentina and Brazil. Instead, the dominant consideration should be to get the fiscal fundamentals right—and then work on improving the financial efficiency of the economy with only minimal "expectational" interventions to set forward wages and exchange rates. Certainly, general price controls can be ruled out (as being very damaging and difficult to get rid of) if one concentrates on increasing the demand for money rather than on limiting its supply.

Discussion

MR. WALTERS: With much of what Ron McKinnon said I agree. But I am afraid we are in danger of unwarranted or even exaggerated claims for financial sector reforms.

Japan, in the 1960s, is one of the countries that developed rapidly in the absence of a competitive capital market. It did not have one then, nor does it today. In France, another country that developed very rapidly in the 1960s and 1970s, credit markets were certainly not free.

Japan has done some things that certainly increase the degree of financial intermediation. For instance, even on its post office accounts it pays a reasonable rate of interest not far below market rates. But credit was allocated in Japan for quite a long time.

The example of Korea that Ronald McKinnon talked about did have these various reforms in the capital markets. But be careful. The Korean capital markets have highly directed credit arrangements and still ration credit.

The same thing is true of Taiwan, another wonder economy.

Four years ago, you could not get a hold of a new Taiwan dollar. The system is very restricted in many ways.

These countries—Japan, Korea, Taiwan—operated their controls rather sensibly. This does not mean that I believe that capital markets should be controlled or regulated. On the contrary, I believe there is very strong evidence—Hong Kong and Singapore come to mind here—that free capital markets can be very important elements in development.

Restricted capital markets, the highly regulated ones such as you see in India, in many parts of Africa, and in the highly repressed markets in Latin America, have undoubtedly retarded in a very considerable way the development of those economies. But I think that it is very important not to have exaggerated claims about what development can be induced solely by free, competitive capital markets. In my view, a competitive financial system is normally an important ingredient for growth. And it should be viewed as an important ingredient—not absolutely necessary, but a very important ingredient, for enabling the adoption of policies, more generally, that give rise to prosperity rather than immiseration.

Mr. Pastore: I liked the historical introduction in Larry White's paper. In reference to it, I noticed that you mentioned both Smith and Bentham. In particular, you included Bentham's criticisms of Smith's suggestion that a legal maximum rate of interest ought to be fixed even though he did very strongly favor financial liberalization. Could you elaborate a bit on that particular point?

Mr. White: It is a very surprising passage in Adam Smith, and Professor McKinnon mentioned it because it does conjure up the Stiglitz-Weiss idea to a modern reader.

Smith says—to put it in more explicit and more modern terms—that the market rate of interest on loans naturally reflects the rate of return on capital and serves the important role of matching the supply and demand for loanable funds. He argues against a legal interest rate ceiling of zero and against a ceiling that would exclude all but the lowest-risk borrowers from the legal market.

But, he says there ought to be a legal maximum rate of interest somewhat above the lowest market rate, in order to keep unworthy borrowers out of the market. People who want to borrow at a rate much above the lowest market rate can only be very risky borrowers who will likely waste the money on very speculative projects that are better avoided. "Prodigals and projectors," Smith called them.

Bentham criticized that argument on the grounds you would expect: there is no reason to want to discriminate against potentially high-payoff projects in cases where both the borrower and the lender have their eyes open and are willing to take those risks. Lenders have every incentive to evaluate the risks and returns of borrowers' projects soberly and not to lend their own money where the risk-adjusted returns are low or negative. To suppress risky loans would be to suppress the entrepreneurship that produces economic progress.

MR. PASTORE: But I wonder if he had more in mind than just that, because when we read Smith we find a number of references to things that we now think are maybe mistakes or statements that he should not have made, and this seems to be one of them. I wonder if you regard it as an off-the-cuff comment, or if you see more implications in it.

MR. WHITE: Smith's argument was not made casually. As did Bentham, I find it very difficult to integrate with the rest of Smith's ideas. There is some evidence suggesting that Bentham's critique changed Smith's mind on the question.

MR. LÜDERS: I think the remark on Smith's ideas about the interest rate is very interesting, based on the Latin American experience. I would like to relate it to one of Alan Walters's comments.

In Latin America, and I presume elsewhere too, if real interest rates are at low or negative levels that induce capital flight to other countries, this has a cost for the development of the capital market as well as for savings and investment processes and, therefore, for the economic development process. But if interest rates are too high, let's say 15 or 20 percent, the stability of the financial system might be significantly affected. And, therefore, this idea of Adam Smith of having positive, but not excessively high, interest rates, makes some sense to me.

A different question is the method used to control the interest rates; you could fix maximum rates directly or you could manage the economy otherwise, to avoid excessively high market interest rates.

In any event, from the point of view of the Latin American experience, this idea of having prudently high positive real interest rates makes sense.

Mr. Walters: I think your argument has a fallacy in the sense that I do not believe the issue is the real interest rate's being positive. For instance, in the 1970s, real interest rates around the Western world were substantially negative. So, what you mean is, it should not be too different from the market rate adjusted for risk.

Mr. Lüders: Exactly. This is correct if we think in terms of the international market rate.

Mr. McKinnon: I would like to follow up on Rolf Lüders's comments about setting the interest rate to limit risk. When we talk about the real interest rate, we mean the nominal interest rate deflated by some anticipated rate of inflation in the economy.

My own experience in looking at different economies is that, if you are going to limit risk, it is much easier to do it in the context of a stable price level, where there is zero price inflation. Then you can have very substantial nominal rates of interest, as Taiwan has managed in the last thirty years, and the risk to the financial system and to the borrowers is minimal in that circumstance, because they can predict what the future real rate is going to be, roughly.

But, if you are in a world of turmoil where you cannot predict the rate of inflation, but you must contract at some nominal interest rate, then the risk is inevitably much greater. You may have to regulate the banks to a lower real rate of interest in those circumstances. Even if you have a rate of inflation of 200 percent a year, having interest rates rise to 220 percent might be too risky.

Nobody quite knows what the real rate is going to be. Unfortunately, you might have to be more repressive, in the sense of keeping nominal interest rates somewhat lower, than if you had a successful program of absolutely stabilizing the price level.

Alan Walters mentioned the great success of the Japanese economy despite the fact that there seemed to be quite a lot of intervention in the credit markets. One thing they did manage, measured in terms of the wholesale price index, is that they stabilized their price levels completely in the 1950s and 1960s. Then they had nominal rates of interest that were a point or two above American interest rates, if you can believe it given the current circumstance. If American interest rates were 4 or 5 percent, typically, Japanese interest rates in this period would be 7 or 8 percent, reflecting the underdeveloped state of the Japanese economy.

It is true that these were controlled rates. Nevertheless, there was a very robust flow of finance through this very stable system, and real rates of interest were substantially positive in that system.

MR. WHITE: There is one point, I think, that needs to be made here. It is clearly true that, in some sense, extremely high interest rates are a bad thing. There is no disagreement about that. But it would be unwarranted to jump to the conclusion that, therefore, we need to manage interest rates to prevent them from becoming too high.

High interest rates are a price. They are a reflection of what is going on in the economy. They are a symptom of the scarcity of capital or they are a symptom of a monetary policy whose conduct is temporarily changing interest rates.

The way to avoid interest rates that are too high is to avoid the policies that make them too high. It is not effective to impose low interest rates because you think low interest rates would be better. Low interest rates would be better if they were the equilibrium market outcome, if they were sustainable. But simply to impose low interest rates, when conditions call for high rates to clear the market, is not going to improve things.

MS. FERNANDEZ: There seems to be a divergence among those economists who see growth as a strategic issue and those who see growth as arising naturally from competitive forces. Professor McKinnon and Professor White seem to be on somewhat opposite sides, although I think Professor McKinnon is close to Professor White in many of the issues.

Some people can point to Japan as a vision of an economy in

which people decided which industries were to be targeted. For example, loans were given to the auto industry in both good times and bad times, and a purely competitive banking industry might not have done so. Other economists might point to Hong Kong or to other favorite examples of economies that managed to grow through purely competitive mechanisms. There seem to be a lot of examples on both sides.

I wonder if perhaps the question could be tackled more directly by saying that there might be moments when intervention in credit markets might be called for. You brought up the example of Brazil and the computer industry. You said a tariff might be a good idea when we have highly frustrating real interest rates. From theory of the first-best approach, maybe intervening in Brazil's credit markets and guaranteeing loans to the computer industry in bad times is better than using tariffs.

Mr. McKinnon: You are right. Not only is there a tremendous real interest rate risk in Brazil, there is a terrific real exchange rate risk, which can easily wipe out the computer industry at the next roll of the die. So, government is incited to provide guaranteed credits at some ridiculous real, though high nominal, rate of interest, or to seal off the domestic industry with protection.

And protection is not by tariffs in this case. Because if you just have a tariff and the real exchange rate is going up and down, you will still get the same variance in the domestic price over the tariff. You need an absolute quota to shield the domestic industry against that real exchange rate risk. And that is terrible from the point of view of resource allocation. It is the second- or third-best approach. By far the best system is to stabilize the price level and regularize the business of borrowing and lending at positive and predictable real rates of interest, and stabilize the exchange rate.

But let me come back to something you said: Hong Kong grew fast without controls, Japan grew fast with controls, so what is going on here? Both of them were financially stable, for a start. They were not in financial chaos. The price level was quite predictable in each case. Hong Kong went through a nasty bit in the early 1980s when

Discussion

they mistakenly devalued. There was doubt as to the future of the colony and a big outflow of capital. But, other than during that very short period, they were both stable financially. However, the Japanese case was somewhat more managed.

There is now a revisionist view of Japanese financial history of the 1950s and 1960s. A man at the University of Tokyo by the name of Horiuchi has gone back and looked at the degree of intervention of the Japanese government in the flow of finance in that period. He calculates that real rates of interest were positive and substantial and that the price level in tradable goods was stable. He concludes that there was much less official intervention than we casually think. The main areas of intervention were in failing industries to ease them out of their misery. But internationally competitive industries, by and large, did what they wanted and competed for loanable funds at something like a market rate of interest.

Ms. FERNANDEZ: Is that true for the auto industry?

MR. McKINNON: I cannot say exactly for the automobile industry, but the Japanese government never thought that the automobile industry would be internationally competitive in the form that it now is. They actually wanted the various firms to combine into much larger entities, a plan that the firms ignored. Each had its own access to finance, and you have this structure now of seven or eight very internationally competitive automobile firms. But that is not what the Ministry of International Trade and Industry (MITI) envisaged for the automobile industry.

MR. BROCK: I would like to make a few comments on the topic of rent-seeking as an explanation for financial controls in developing countries. Professor White suggests in his paper that Professor McKinnon was too charitable in his analysis of the causes of government intervention in financial markets. Professor McKinnon argues that governments initially intervene in financial markets in response to market failures, but then let regulation get out of control. Professor White is much more inclined to explain all intervention as the result of rent-seeking behavior. Although the concept of rent-seeking behavior is a powerful one when applied to many interventions in market economies, it is worth reconsidering Professor McKinnon's idea of market failure as the primary initial reason for government intervention in financial markets of developing countries.

Many developing countries are the size of one of the states in the United States. For example, Chile with 12 million people and 290,000 square miles is approximately the same size as Texas with 16 million people and 260,000 square miles. Chile (or any other typical developing country) is as subject to severe shocks as is the Texas economy, but Chile must rely on its own government to deal with the financial consequences of shocks. If Chile were part of the United States, the Federal Deposit Insurance Corporation (FDIC) would bail out failed Chilean banks. Better still, if there were large global banks with branches in all countries, the banks would absorb those losses.

It is widely agreed among economists that interstate banking in the United States is desirable for reasons of economies of scale and the diversification of risk. In fact, had the United States allowed interstate banking before the 1980s, banks in Texas would have been branches of larger U.S. banks at the start of the 1980s. With interstate banking, the current financial traumas of Texas banks would have been handled by the marketplace (via the effect on the market value of large, diversified U.S. banks) rather than by government bailouts as they are at present. In developing countries, the absence of international deposit insurance means that global banks with country branches are probably the only satisfactory way to ensure financial stability.

In the absence of such global banks, a government faces the task of regulating or not regulating a domestic banking system that must cope with large, undiversifiable (to one country) shocks. Failure to regulate brings with it the possibility of bank runs and additional instability. The act of regulating creates problems of moral hazard that encourage excessive risk taking by banks because bank deposits are backed by the government. To cope with the moral hazard problem, financial regulators are forced to regulate the asset composition of banks to keep them from taking undue risks. Reserve requirements, portfolio guidelines, and interest rate controls can all theoretically be justified by the need to prevent excessive risk taking by banks when the government insures bank deposits.

Intervention in credit markets occurs because the possibility of bank runs represents a pecuniary externality caused by the absence of sufficient markets for bearing risk [see Loong and Zeckhauser 1982, for a general discussion of this problem]. One of the great economists of the 1930s, Henry Simons, of the University of Chicago, considered this pecuniary externality and the accompanying government intervention a threat to free societies. Simons argued (1936) that financial systems must be set up with rules so that the arbitrary authority of government regulators would not undermine the functioning of financial markets.

Simons believed that banks must somehow be converted into mutual funds so that the value of bank deposits does not have to be guaranteed by a government in order to prevent bank runs. In practice, however, there are many reasons that bank deposits cannot generally be converted into shares of a mutual fund. The most important of these is the inability of depositors to monitor a bank's operations, because information connected with long-term bank lending is private. These information problems are resolved by a banking structure that contains a large component of noncontingent debt (bank deposits) and a smaller buffer of bank equity.

In the absence of worldwide deposit banking in global banks, and in the presence of information requirements for investment projects that prevent the conversion of bank deposits into mutual funds shares, the pecuniary externality related to bank runs and the resulting government intervention will remain a primary cause of restrictions placed on banks in developing countries (as well as in the United States). It is almost surely the case, as Professor McKinnon argues, that regulation of financial markets takes on a life of its own in developing countries. Much of this added life is undoubtedly driven by rent-seeking behavior. But I think it would be a mistake to suggest, as does Professor White, that all or even the most important part of government intervention in credit markets in developing countries is unrelated to market failure, especially market failure associated with markets for risk.

MR. WHITE: If you would like me to respond to that, I think it is important to avoid genuine externalities or spillover effects. And certainly it can be a problem in financial systems if there are spillover effects from one financial failure to another.

The important point here, though, is that government policies can have perverse consequences, unforeseen at the time they are instituted. For example, some regulatory policies can, in fact, increase financial fragility, even as they attempt to reduce it.

The problem I have in mind is exemplified by the early nineteenth-century American regulations placed on the portfolios that banks could hold. The avowed objective was to have them hold only safe assets. But the unintentional result was that all the banks held the same assets, so that, if you saw one bank fail, you knew your own bank was about to fail, and bank runs could spread. The regulations actually made the system less stable.

MS. SAGARI: Along the lines of Phil's comments and apart from the issue of scale economies, I am worried about information asymmetry that is particularly relevant in the case of financial markets, a problem we come across every day in our work. It is very clear that there are at least three instances where information asymmetry has a tremendous impact.

One is the matter of long-term financing and how information asymmetries can explain the lack of long-term financing among other sources in the banking system.

Another is the funding of new ventures and how information asymmetries have an impact on everything that is new because there is a lack of background information on new people with new ideas. This is very important in cases of trial evaluation where we want to change the types of things that the industrial sector is producing.

Third is the support of small- and medium-sized enterprises.

We come across these issues in Latin America, in Africa, in Asia, and I would be very interested in listening to what practical suggestions the authors here have to give us concerning the matter of deposit insurance. What I have seen across the world is that avoiding implicit insurance in the case of large financial intermediaries appears almost impossible.

MR. MCKINNON: One of the first victims of high and variable inflation is long-term finance. It is just not possible to organize a long-term capital market and many other longer-term contractual arrangements with inflation rampant. That is why the whole issue of price stabilization is more important to development than it might first seem.

Let me say a good word for the nineteenth-century system based on an international gold standard. There were some periods of deflation and others of very mild inflation, but these movements were small in light of modern experience. There was a common monetary standard in which people worldwide had confidence over a long period of time.

Thus, to build railways, ports, and so forth, countries all over the world—such as Canada, Argentina, Uruguay, Chile, and Brazil—could borrow at long term by issuing thirty-year bonds in the London capital market because there was a common monetary standard that was known to be stable.

We had that briefly in the 1960s when the world dollar standard was stable, but then the system collapsed into inflation and great fluctuations in exchange rates and interest rates. World finance reverted to a short-term mode, except for official agencies.

We had a tremendous flow of short-term bank finance into the third world in the 1970s at artificially low real rates of interest. The use of short-term funds for financing what is essentially long-term infrastructure turned out to be disastrous. And some of the borrowing was just for consumption.

To restore their access to long-term foreign finance, developing countries should be more like Taiwan with a stable internal price level. However, there is also a degree of chaos in the international economy right now that makes it very difficult to restore those institutions that worked quite well in the late nineteenth century. Stable exchange rates among the major industrial countries would be a precondition for giving developing countries good access to long-term finance in the world capital market.

MR. WHITE: With regard to information asymmetries, I am not quite sure what you mean by that phrase. It covers a wide array of phenomena. One example that is relevant to our discussion is that of a situation in which loan officers from large formal banks in the urban centers go out into the countryside and try to evaluate investment projects without having a clue as to what they are looking at because there is an information asymmetry. That is, the would-be borrowers know a lot more than the loan officers do.

The way to remedy that situation and to make finance possible is to use people on the spot who have relevant information about local borrowers. I think that through liberalization, local money lenders or local financiers, whose information is not so asymmetrical with that of the borrowers, will be able to mobilize resources and be in a position to fund those projects about which the loan officers sent out from the city have no clue.

MR. SPOSATO: Professor McKinnon, I am very interested in knowing more about the motivations of the Korean banks in increasing their deposits and loan portfolios after the liberalization. Also, what types of loans did they go into in the first stage of their development?

The reason I ask this is that we have seen that, after banking liberalizations in other countries, banks remain very conservative in terms of making short-term commercial loans and remain very reluctant to expand their portfolios and deposits into what they consider much more risky areas. I wonder how this situation was addressed in Korea and how it might be addressed elsewhere.

MR. MCKINNON: I mentioned this very successful reform in the mid-1960s. There was an initial spurt of growth in which the lending was for what you might call light-industry projects. At first the export products were wood veneers, for example, plywood paneling from logs imported from the Philippines processed into wood veneers for dashboards in automobiles and that kind of thing. That was one of their first big exports. Textiles were also important because long-term finance was not terribly necessary for this kind of industry.

Then unfortunately, in the early 1970s, the Korean government lost control over the price level again. I gave you the favorable story for the mid-1960s. But the Koreans left a major gap in their regulatory framework. Any exporter who wanted credit for any reason could get it from the banking system. He could go to a commercial bank and get a loan at a low—less than the going—rate of interest. The commercial bank could automatically rediscount it with the central bank and that was the principal method of export subsidy.

In the mid-1960s, these credit subsidies did not much hamper the central bank as long as Korean exports were very small. For the overall macroeconomic stability of the Korean banking system, they could be tolerated. But, as Korean exports grew so dramatically and this built-in subsidy forced the central bank to lend to the commercial banks, the authorities lost control over the monetary base and the price level.

The Koreans went through a period of variable inflation in the 1970s with a return to financial repression to some extent. The government began to intervene very strongly to direct the flow of credit. They tried to build up heavy industries by directing the banks to lend long-term at low rates of interest to petrochemicals, to shipbuilding, and to construction companies. Many of these loans turned out to be quite bad and they are still carried on the banks' portfolios as nonperforming loans.

Yields to depositors fell, along with growth in bank deposits. During this period of slow growth in domestic finance, Korea had to rely on foreign borrowing and incurred its very large external debt. Taiwan, in contrast, maintained a liberalized financial system throughout the 1970s and it is now a big international creditor. But Korea went through this bad period where they repressed domestic finance.

Fortunately, in the early 1980s, the Koreans again had a big stabilization. Their price level is now more stable than the American one and their domestic financial system is again robust. They have now reached the point where they are actually developing nonmonetary intermediaries. Stock and bond markets are providing sources of long-term finance within the economy in a proper way that had not existed earlier.

MR. SHERWIN: I am fortunate enough to represent Korea on the board of the World Bank, so I have had a little exposure to them over the last year or two, and I have been intrigued by the various references to the Korean experience. Obviously, one admires enormously the phenomenal growth rates that they have managed to achieve over the last few years. But, when one starts talking about issues of capital market liberalization, I do not think you look to Korea for examples. In fact, I would say that at this point, the financial markets represent probably the biggest challenge that Korea faces.

You have already mentioned, Mr. McKinnon, the issue of poor assets in the banking system, which is a real problem. The more fundamental problem is that, having come this far in their development process with what is a quite tightly directed financial system, at least it has been in various respects, they now face this rather daunting Pandora's box. To continue their growth, they are going to be forced into some sort of financial liberalization in much the same way the Japanese and one or two others have been pushed a little down that track.

To give you an example, Korea is an exporting nation. They export a lot of heavy industrial products, ships, and increasingly other heavy industrial items. In the framework that they have right now, it is almost impossible to get reasonable forward cover for exchange risks. When you are signing a contract for a supertanker and the delivery is coming a few years down the track and you cannot find a market to protect your risks in any way, you have a pretty substantial dent in your overall competitiveness and capacity to manage risks.

You cannot get forward cover while you have exchange controls because exchange controls and effectively operating forward exchange mechanisms are simply incompatible. You take off exchange controls and you have got all sorts of problems with the exchange rate. How do you manage that? That leads into a whole range of other issues on monetary control techniques.

Right now, the government and the central bank are busy firing out "monetary stabilization bonds" to try to soak up the consequences of the current-account surpluses. These things have to go somewhere and in an environment of controlled interest rates, it is difficult to sell increasing volumes of government debt on a voluntary basis. This is the enormous Pandora's box that I think the Koreans are having to deal with and are finding it rather difficult.

The implications of not just how to approach the problem in the financial sector but also the linkages from that back through the real economy are really quite profound. In fact, the lessons in Korea are about what is still to come, rather than what has occurred.

MR. WALTERS: I entirely agree with Murray Sherwin, but I think that we ought to look at the problem more generally. Ronald McKinnon and Lawrence White have taken us around the garden, and we tend to be sniffing the individual flowers, rather than looking at the landscape and seeing what sort of garden we should be tilling.

I would like to distill some of the things that have been said and identify what the real issues are. As I understand it, this is the nature of the problem: In the developing countries, contrary to what the development economists said and still do say, savings are fairly high. In fact, the average savings rate for Latin American countries is between 20 and 25 percent. Their savings are almost at Japanese levels.

In the United States, the savings rate is much lower, about 10 percent. Europe is quite low. Germany is about 12 percent; Britain, 10 percent; France, 10 percent. Then you say, what happens to those savings of developing countries? Well, on the average, only 25 percent of the savings in the developing countries goes into the financial system. In the case of the United States, it is 85 percent. That is a critical statistic. Roughly 25 percent of this large number goes into the intermediation process in developing countries, whereas 85 percent or so is intermediated in Western countries.

This is the statistic that illustrates many of the problems to which

Ronald McKinnon referred. Suppose 20 percent of the GNP of developing countries is saved. If only 25 percent of that goes into intermediation—that is, put in deposits or financial instruments or something like that—then that is only 5 percent of GNP that enters the financial system. Whereas in the United States, 8.5 percent of GNP finds its way into intermediation.

What happens to all those other savings that do not find their way into intermediation? If you walk around the villages of developing countries, you will see a man saving to buy a house. He does not put his money in the bank, however; he buys bricks and stores them and bags of cement. Why does he avoid putting his money in the bank? Because his savings will be expropriated by regulated low interest rates combined with high inflation. Not only do they not earn a positive real rate of interest, but also they are expropriated by a negative real rate of interest regulated by the authorities. That is the supply side problem of the intermediation system.

I think the McKinnon and White story here is entirely correct. They identify the major problem as inducing more intermediation of savings—getting people to put their money into banks and financial intermediaries, rather than to store it, most wastefully, in bricks.

A rather dramatic contraction of the financial sector has occurred in Latin America, particularly in Mexico and Argentina. It is a major problem but it is overcome to some extent in Korea, Japan, and Taiwan. It has not been overcome in other countries, even Brazil, for instance, where they guarantee a real rate of return of 5.16 percent. Nobody believes that 5.16 percent, because the government has played around with the indexing rules and it may do that again. That creates the fear that they will expropriate the savings.

The informal sector is by far the biggest capital market in all LDCs, accounting for between 15 and 20 percent of GNP. Undoubtedly, there are some investments that the curb market or the informal market finances with enormous rates of return. Others, such as the bricks or the cement or all of the other forms of storing, such as in gold bangles and other precious metals of one sort or another, are basically unproductive.

This is, in my view, a very serious indictment of the system. I think the idea that the developing world is short of capital is nonsense. There is, however, a shortage of other things: trust, intermediation, stable prices, stable administrative systems, law and order, and other conditions that we take so much for granted in at least parts of the West.

The opposite side of the coin is the allocation of credit. What is being said is that it is generally a very good idea to have competitive allocation. But at times a controlled allocating system may be superior. I think it is true that most allocated credit systems are inefficient and politicize and inhibit growth; the exception is possibly Korea, but I share Sherwin's view there.

What happens is that credit is allocated to those who have political pull. It is a gift at very low, even negative, interest rates, and those who have political pull collect. The classic cases of this are in Latin America and also in India. You see this being perpetuated in Latin America, in Argentina, and so on, where credit is allocated at negative interest rates.

Let me give you an example. Inflation in Mexico when I was there in 1985 was running at about 40 or 50 percent. Interest rates on housing loans were 15 percent. It does not take much arithmetic to see that, if you get an allocated credit, it is really a gift. The only people who got those loans were those who had political pull.

I do not think you can avoid facing the issue that the effect of credit controls does depend very much upon the political economy. I think we need to look at that very carefully.

Mr. Callison: I want to make a comment with respect to the last comment, which bears, I think, on the enormous complexity of this subject that we are considering. What struck me is the implication that the accumulation and storage of construction materials might be a bad use of one's savings.

If you assume that financial intermediaries are operating in a competitive environment and that they are allocating credit along efficient lines to stimulate sustained economic development, then I think your statement is true. If the financial system, and the exchange rate, and the rate of inflation, and all these other things are promoting investment from financial intermediaries into capital-intensive industries that are import-dependent and are otherwise economically white elephants, then I would much prefer to see the poor families store up house construction materials. It is a labor-intensive investment that will apply labor that will otherwise be unutilized. To me that is one of the best forms of investment in a poorer country because it stimulates the domestic economy with all sorts of multiplier effects.

MR. WALTERS: I quite agree. My argument was premised on having the right signals. If you have the wrong signals, then organizing efficiently the distribution of resources into the areas where they are least efficient is not effective. In other words, it is useless having an efficient financial system to allocate resources, if all your signals are pointing exactly in the wrong direction.

Lawrence H. White

Response

I did my best to try to keep the idea of private currency out of my review of Professor McKinnon's book. I did not entirely succeed, as his remarks indicate. It somehow weaseled its way in there. But perhaps it is a good thing that it did, because it gives us something to disagree about.

McKinnon and I are in the difficult position of agreeing on an awful lot. We seem to agree about the basics of monetary theory and interest theory: that inflation is a monetary phenomenon and that the interest rate is a price that rations resources between present and future uses. Most fundamentally, we are in agreement on the importance of liberalization for improving resource allocation through the financial system.

My discussion, after acknowledging these agreements, gets down to disagreements at a somewhat secondary level. Two of the disagreements that have been mentioned already are, first, that I would place more emphasis on rent-seeking as a explanation for the policies adopted to repress financial markets; and second, that I would consider the greater degree to which the financial system, particularly the banking system, can be opened to entry and to private note issue. In addition, I take a somewhat less gradualist approach than Professor McKinnon. Jerry Jenkins, of Sequoia Institute, in organizing this seminar may have thought it would be refreshing for Professor McKinnon to be criticized from that perspective, rather than from the more common perspective that accuses him of going too far.

Let me say just a few words about his reservations regarding uninhibited free banking, as he called it. I did not talk about the Stiglitz-Weiss analysis in my paper because it is not a part of his book, although I recognize that in more recent papers he has written about it.

To regard what banks do as credit rationing has always struck me as a curious idea. The contention is that if banks do not take all borrowers who want to borrow at the interest rate they post, then they are engaged in credit rationing. Well, movie studios are engaged in movie star rationing in the same way. They pay $2 million a picture, but they do not take all comers who want to work at that price. You can regard that as rationing, I suppose. What is really happening, of course, is selection according to the perceived star quality of those who audition for roles. Likewise a bank selects among loan applications according to the perceived risk quality of the would-be borrowers.

Adverse risk selection of the Stiglitz-Weiss sort would pose a problem if banks were unable to judge the risk quality of loan applicants with sufficient accuracy. It is precisely the job of loan officers, however, to make accurate judgments of the riskiness of would-be borrowers.

The importance of moral hazard as a danger in banking is something I certainly do not disagree with Professor McKinnon about. That is, under conditions of implicit or explicit bailout and insurance guarantees, it is certainly true that the banking system will make loans that it otherwise would not make. Each bank will take on riskier gambles because its potential losses are limited.

This prospect does not lead me to conclude that we therefore need prudential regulation and need to block entry. We do not have to take it for granted that bailouts and deposit insurance are here to stay. Instead, what seems prudent to me is to eliminate the subsidization of risk taking implicit in underpriced deposit insurance. Each bank should be made to face fully the risks of loss that are carried by the loans it makes.

The moderate way to do that is to price deposit insurance so that it reflects those risks, rather than doing what the Federal Deposit Insurance Corporation (FDIC) and the Federal Savings and Loan Insurance Corporation (FSLIC) do in the United States, which is to charge a flat premium regardless of what kind of loans a bank or S&L makes.

A more radical way to do it is simply to eliminate the government-provided deposit insurance and bailout guarantees, and let the financial system operate on a privately insured or caveat emptor basis. Once you take the underpriced government insurance guarantees for granted, you are led to want to limit entry, and then to appoint a regulator who will decide which banks get to come in and which do not. Going down that path gets you into the same sort of planning problems that are involved in trying to allocate credit generally.

In his book, Professor McKinnon is quite cogent in arguing the impossibility of having government efficiently allocate credit. Government officials simply do not know enough to pick the winners and losers among projects. I think that for the same reason, the government does not know enough to pick which banks ought to be allowed to enter and which banks should not be allowed to enter. Our goal ought to be to make it possible for free entry to operate, that is, for the market to decide which banks are pursuing the right policies and which are not. That means something like a caveat emptor policy or at least allowing a system in which it is possible for banks to fail. Such a policy seems to me to be the only way to avoid the sort of miasma of second-best and third-best regulations piling upon regulations.

I do not know what else to add, except to reiterate that I am very much in agreement with the fundamental points in Professor McKinnon's book. It is a policy message that has made a splash but has yet to be fully implemented or attempted in enough countries.

5

Rolf J. Lüders

Latin American Contrast: Capital Markets and Development in Chile and Argentina

This chapter provides an analytic and comparative history of financial developments in Argentina and Chile during the years 1970–1987. Until the mid-1970s, the role of government in each had become highly expansive, protecting and intervening in their respective economies in accordance with their very similar import substitution strategies. In consequence, their economic development problems largely mirrored each other's. Then both countries experienced military takeovers. Several changes effected by the new governments continued the close parallel between the two countries, including their respective efforts to move toward relatively free market economies.

In 1981, however, the economic policies of the two countries began to diverge sharply, Argentina reverting back to pre-1976 economic policies in the wake of a financial crisis, while Chile sustained its so-called social market economy in spite of a financial crisis that was even more severe than was Argentina's.

Thus do Argentina and Chile present a combination of long-standing correspondence and (since 1981) vivid contrast that provides a unique opportunity to draw some lessons on financial development from the experience of two middle-income countries of similar cultural and historic background.[1]

As in most developing countries, capital markets, in the sense of purchases and sales of stocks, bonds, and other instruments for providing enterprises with long-term finance, are underdeveloped in Chile and (especially) Argentina. The financial and investment activities of their economies are dominated by depository institutions (commercial banks and finance companies) comprising "financial markets" that are clearly distinguished, in developed economies, from "capital markets." In contrast, the capital market in most developing countries *is* the financial market. Accordingly, the two terms are used interchangeably throughout this chapter, except in its concluding pages. There, the more circumscribed (and demanding) meaning of "capital markets" is employed in addressing the substantial developments in the market for shares and other variable return investment papers in Chile.

The two sizable sections of the chapter following this introduction are each divided into two parts, one referring to Argentina and the other to Chile. The first of these sections summarizes the main overall economic development features of the two countries during the period of study. The second section relates financial developments to those features. Throughout the chapter, comparisons between the experiences of the two countries are highlighted.

Some striking lessons, consistent with established theory, but also suggesting new approaches to capital market development, emerge from the study and are summarized in the remainder of this introduction.

During most of the period addressed by this chapter, Argentina had a severely repressed financial system, while Chile liberalized its internal financial market early during its overall liberalization experience. As a result, and as expected, financial deepening, as measured by official indexes (money to gross domestic product [GDP] ratios) almost tripled in Chile, while declining (except for a brief liberalization period) by about 30 percent in Argentina.

During the first phase (1974–1982) of the Chilean financial liberalization, interest rates rose to extraordinary levels, contributing decisively to the severity of the 1982–1983 financial crisis. These high rates appear to be a consequence of macroeconomic conditions and management that are unrelated to the liberalization. The Chilean experience clearly indicates that interest rate levels should become a primary policy concern of any government engaging in financial liberalization.

The study also suggests the difficulty, perhaps impossibility, of sustaining a financial liberalization in tandem with a large government deficit (as in Argentina). In contrast, the Chilean case indicates that fiscal discipline decreases the likelihood of government's crowding out the private sector in order to finance a fiscal deficit; accomplishing this, it is also apparent that undue problems of business insolvency, balance of payments, and inflation can be simultaneously avoided without the necessity of intervening directly in the financial markets.

The Chilean experience also strongly suggests that privatization that incorporates the objective of spreading share ownership can become a very powerful instrument for capital market development in countries where state-owned enterprises (SOEs) constitute a large portion of the business enterprise sector. Furthermore, countries with sizable foreign indebtedness can generate, through debt-to-equity conversions, a capital market development process while facilitating privatization and reducing the burden of their debt.

Finally, the chapter discusses some findings about the relationship between the particular financial policies followed in Argentina and Chile and their observed rates of growth. The increase in the

Chilean financial savings rate is impressive; the development of the formal financial market and the existence of a positive interest rate have almost certainly contributed to this. However, the behavior of the remaining macroeconomic variables (terms of trade, changes in permanent income expectations, the financial crisis, and so on) overshadowed these effects, and the resulting average savings and investments rates for the entire period of study are relatively low. The trend of these rates during 1979–1981 and 1985–1987 offer some encouragement. In contrast, savings and investment rates in Argentina have been declining since the mid-1970s, although during the 1976–1980 period of its brief financial liberalization, considerable financial deepening took place. More important, perhaps, since financial policies are (and were, in these two countries) an integral part of the overall economic development strategies, the resulting growth rates might help to answer the implicit question posed at the beginning of the paragraph. Over the whole 1970–1987 period, GDP grew by about 22.5 percent in Argentina and 50 percent in Chile. Moreover, in spite of its financial crisis during the period between 1980 and 1987, Chile's GDP still grew 10 percent while Argentina's dropped by 5 percent.

Development Policies, 1970–1987

Argentina's stop-and-go: a case of policy reversal. One hundred years ago Argentina was one of the ten richest countries in the world. Its per capita income reached 73 percent of that of the United States of America. Today it barely exceeds 35 percent of U.S. per capita income (De Long 1987, 18).

The import substitution policy of the 1940–1976 period. Argentina is a richly endowed country, and therefore most analysts attribute the relatively bad performance of its economy to the application of wrong economic policies. Since the 1940s and up to 1975, Argentina followed the so-called import substitution development strategy (Lüders 1976). This approach was adopted by most Latin American countries as a reaction to the catastrophic effects of the Great Depression of the 1930s. It sought to promote domestic industrialization by reducing imports. The policy package associated with this strategy began only with protective customs duties. The strategy's components and rationales included most (and usually all) of the following: the creation of state-owned enterprises (SOEs) to produce essential inputs for the industrialization process (steel, petroleum, electricity, and so on); public sector credits at subsidized rates to foster private sector investments in industry; commercial bank credit for industrialization; import taxation of luxury goods to save foreign exchange; foreign exchange controls; income redistribution measures, such as wage and price controls; and steeply progressive income taxation, starting at relatively low income levels.

Price distortions generated by the system were typically compounded by controls imposed to check the inflationary process ignited by associated public sector deficits. Thus did adherence to the strategy of import substitution invariably lead, over time, to expanded and increased interventions by governments in economies. Ironically, their interventions made import substitution more difficult by reducing domestic productivity and production. Short of rejecting the strategy itself, new interventions were the predictable response of governments attempting to "correct for" the negative consequences of other interventions.

In Argentina, the import substitution strategy was adopted during the mid-1940s by the authoritarian President Juan Domingo Perón. It was still in effect—in spite of a few, temporary efforts to modify it—during the early 1970s, when the aged Perón returned from exile. He was elected to return Argentina to a path of growth, price stability, and economic welfare. During his absence, the country had experienced relatively low average rates of economic growth, increasing and eventually very high rates of inflation, and growing balance of payments problems. Not rejecting the strategy, neither Perón nor his wife Isabel Martinez, who assumed the presidency after his death, were able to reverse these trends. Instead, conditions reached a crisis stage, and on March 24, 1976, a military takeover occurred.

The Economic Liberalization Experiment of 1976–1981. The new military government appointed José Martínez de Hoz as the new economic minister. He led a relatively brief period (1976–1981) of economic liberalization. A few years before, the economic team of General Augusto Pinochet had initiated, with more vigor, but for similar reasons, the same task in Chile. The Chilean liberalization policy has been maintained up to now, in spite of the negative impact of two deep "imported" recessions and some macroeconomic management errors. In contrast, the first downturn that Argentina's economy experienced during the liberalization effort of Martínez de Hoz resulted in its abandonment. Indeed, Argentina's economic policies reverted toward interventionist and protectionist development strategies. Therefore, the economic model that is operative in Argentina today is very different from that in Chile.

Beginning in 1976, Martínez de Hoz clearly aimed to transform the protectionist and interventionist economic development strategies of Argentina. He intended to limit government intervention in the economy to the "proper functions" of the state, which he understood to be the provision of guidelines to the private sector, by means of monetary, fiscal, exchange rate, and commercial policies. He also intended to correct the price distortions attributable to customs duties. Finally, the government tried to reduce drastically the rate of inflation, without affecting the rate of unemployment. The first two objectives reflected the government's intention to liberalize the economy, the third pointed toward fiscal discipline.

During the four years of the liberalization experiment, substantial progress was achieved in some aspects. The exchange rate was unified early in the period, and foreign capital movements were freed. Taxes on exports were eliminated, and domestic taxes were reimbursed to exporters. Price controls were eliminated early, and wage and interest-rate controls were subsequently lifted. The exchange rate was fixed, up to 1978, as a crawling peg on the basis of past price movements, and then, as an active-crawl-reduction scheme based on the preannouncement of future rates of depreciation (known as the *tablita*). The last *tablita*, announced in late 1980 and to be in effect during several months of 1981, had a low implicit inflation rate. However, progress was slow, or nil, in some other respects.

After some "water" was eliminated from the tariff scheme during 1976, a tariff reduction program was announced in 1978, to come into effect over a five-year period starting in 1979. But by 1980, the average tariff on manufactured products still exceeded 50 percent, although some progress was made in removing import quotas, prohibitions, and licenses for tariffs. In spite of a significant increase in tax revenues, and a temporary reduction in the public sector deficit from 14.1 percent of GNP during 1975 to 9.0 percent during 1979, the deficit increased again to 16.4 percent during 1981 (Cavallo and Peña 1983). The inflationary pressures of these deficits were temporarily reduced, initially through internal indebtedness, and during 1980–1981 through foreign indebtedness.

By 1980 Martínez de Hoz had achieved a relatively free financial system, free international capital movements, and, by a labor law reform in 1976, a more freely working labor market. However, because the protectionist trade policies of the past changed only modestly, the order in which the liberalizations were implemented seems to have been exactly the opposite from that considered desirable by most experts (see, among others, Edwards 1985; Edwards and Wijnbergen 1983; Khan and Zahler 1985; McKinnon 1982; Mussa 1983). Moreover, the size of the public sector had rapidly grown, few and relatively minor privatizations had taken place, and the high public sector deficit remained unchanged. Led by the public sector, total expenditures in the country had grown, while the inflation rate had been reduced slightly below the three-digit level, and unemployment had reached record lows. But these achievements were obtained at the expense of a somewhat reduced investment rate and a very significant foreign indebtedness.

The economic and financial crisis of 1981–1982. The foreign debt of Argentina increased during the Martínez de Hoz period to about U.S. $36.6 billion, from U.S. $8.2 billion in 1976. This phenomenal increase parallels that of most other Latin American countries, including Chile, suggesting its relationship to a supply-of-foreign-funds shock having its origin in the recycling of petrodollars. Nevertheless, there also had to be willing takers of those funds to explain the levels of indebtedness that were reached; the nature of these takers as well as the reason for their willingness varied from country to country and even within countries. In Argentina, two phases can be distinguished. During the first stage, up to 1979, the government financed a significant part of its deficit by increasing its internal indebtedness. This resulted in crowding out the private sector, which, in turn, took advantage of the freeing of the international capital movements to finance part of its own expenditures through foreign indebtedness. After 1979, the government financed its deficit mainly by increasing the debt of public sector firms (SOEs) directly abroad. The private sector, betting that the growth of the public sector deficit would result in the government's abandoning the *tablita* and perhaps even confiscating local deposits of foreign currency, withdrew its foreign funds (which had to be monetized to pay for the government expenses in pesos) and sent them abroad in a record capital flight of about U.S. $7 billion (most of it in early 1981).[2] During the latter part of the fixed exchange rate period, interest rates in Argentina rose significantly, reflecting devaluation anticipations.

In early 1981, economic uncertainty was compounded by political events, because a change of government was about to take place. The rise in the interest rates, and the dramatic change in relative prices between tradable and nontradable goods brought about by the massive inflow of foreign resources (and their effect on the real exchange rate), had started a financial crisis. Many businesses were no longer in a position to service their debt because of the interest rate level. Also significant numbers of these firms were facing operational losses. Some of the largest financial institutions in the country were unable to finance their losses because of nonperforming assets. Because the central bank was guaranteeing deposits, pressures on the foreign exchange market increased even more. The country was losing its foreign exchange reserves very rapidly, in spite of the also rapidly rising (and already very high) real interest rate. Because the incoming government, also military, did not declare its support for the existing *tablita,* pressures on the foreign exchange market became unbearable, and the peso was devalued. The liberalization experiment—never completed, unaccompanied by the necessary fiscal discipline, and perhaps involuntarily tied in the minds of the population to a certain (mistaken) exchange rate and macroeconomic policy—had in fact ended. The country was submerged in a deep economic and financial crisis, reflected, among other things, in GDP declines of 7.1 and 3.8 percent during 1981 and 1982 respectively.[3]

Recovery from the economic crisis, 1982–1988. After the devaluation of 1981, Argentina returned gradually to the economic system that prevailed before the liberalization episode. After the devaluation, the desire to sterilize the monetary base expansion associated with the fiscal deficits and the commercial bank rescue operations induced the central bank to raise reserve requirements of the banking system to their pre-1976 level of 100 percent during the second half of 1982. Although later reduced, they have averaged close to 75 percent since then. In addition, interest rates on most banking operations were again fixed by the authorities, and the government intervened heavily in the allocation of credit.

In spite of the partial sterilization effected by the new reserve requirements, inflation rates rose rapidly and selective price fixing was again introduced. Wage levels were regulated by the authorities. Voluntary foreign capital movements became unthinkable after the international debt crisis broke out during 1982. In short, the country returned to a relatively closed economy, with heavy (and discriminatory) government intervention in the financial sector and in the determination of basic prices (interest rate, wage rate, foreign exchange rate). The public sector continued to play an important role in the management of the large existing SOEs (Artana and Szewack 1988).

Within this economic framework, and faced with rapidly declining terms of trade, governments of Argentina tried to solve the problems generated by the economic crisis (solvency of the banking system, overindebtedness of the private sector, and the level of the country's foreign debt), as well as to satisfy in the relatively short run the main economic demands of the citizen (full employment, significant real wage increases, and price stability). These latter demands, in all likelihood, weigh more heavily in the Argentine economic policymaking process than they do in the Chilean. In Argentina, the government had changed to civilian hands during 1983, possibly as one consequence of the War of the Malvinas (Falklands). The Chilean government, strongly in power, was in a position to take a longer view on such demands and, in part perhaps because of it, to satisfy them better and sooner.

It is well known that internal adjustment to strong adverse foreign shocks (terms of trade, international capital movements) is no easy task. Argentina, faced with political restrictions, found that more often than not, because the basic disequilibria had not been eliminated, an acceptable solution to any one of the problems inherited from the crisis generated another problem. For example, the solution to the internal indebtedness problem was obtained by fixing the interest rate, both on deposits and credits, while the rate of inflation was allowed to rapidly rise. The resulting income transfer from depositors to creditors reduced, as expected, the debt-to-equity ratio of the business enterprise sector, but at the cost of a big inflationary push and a rapid reduction in the financial deepening levels (Baliño 1988).

Another example is afforded by policies that are intended to manage aggregate demand with a consistently low unemployment rate (a first priority in Argentina) and high wages. Given the severe foreign resource restriction, these policies contributed decisively to the rapidly increasing inflation rate during 1984–1985 and to the declining savings-investment rate during the whole 1982–1988 period. Finally, the different policies implemented in attempting to reduce the foreign indebtedness level (which have included a debt service suspension and the temporary decision not to negotiate with the International Monetary Fund [IMF]) actually may have worsened the yearly foreign exchange restrictions. Chile adopted the opposite stance and has been far more successful in its efforts. Very little progress was made on this front. As a matter of fact, the effect of uncertainty generated by such negotiations on foreign trade and direct investment operations in all likelihood reduced the availability of such resources and may have reduced income growth rates. To compensate, Argentina had to keep the real exchange rate at higher levels than would otherwise have been likely, and this produced additional short-run pressures on the rapidly increasing price level. (Reflecting these differences, between September 1986 and May 1988, the price of Argentine foreign debt instruments declined from 64 to 28, while those of Chile moved from 67 to 60.)

The Austral Plan. In 1985 inflation in Argentina eventually reached almost 700 percent per year. Late that year, the government of Raúl Alfonsín tried an unorthodox anti-inflationary program (the Austral Plan) aimed at practically stopping the inflation from one month to the next. To this end, prices were frozen, a monetary reform was implemented, after a readjustment in real terms (virtually foreshadowing the plan's failure) wages were fixed to eliminate undue cost pressures, nominal interest rates were adjusted, and some measures were announced to reduce the public sector deficit and increase the money supply. The fiscal measures taken were modest in order to make them politically acceptable and turned out to be insufficient to control the budget deficit to the extent required by the price freeze. In addition, some features of the plan were attracting foreign resources and thereby producing an unexpected increase in the supply of money (Lanús de la Serna 1987). As a result, after a sharp reduction in the rate of inflation to about 90 percent during 1986, it accelerated again, reaching annual levels, during early 1988, that even exceeded those of 1976 and 1985.

The record of the Austral Plan was one of failure: unemployment, still relatively low, was rising; wages, temporarily higher, fell to their 1980 levels during 1987; the economic growth rate, although still positive, was low and declining; savings and investment levels were at an all-time low; and only one problem of those generated by the crisis, the high level of internal indebtedness, had probably been solved. (Baliño [1988] estimated that during the period from mid-1982 to the end of 1983 borrowers benefited from the interest-fixing scheme at the rate of 10.8 to 13.4 percent of GDP, while holders of deposits lost the equivalent.)

Chile's sustained liberalization: a market economy for a developing country. Chile's economic development record over the long run is only slightly better than that of Argentina. Its per capita income was 50 percent of that of the United States in 1870. In 1979 it reached about 29 percent of U.S. per capita income. However, after the financial crisis of the early 1980s Chile has recovered significantly faster than have Argentina and most other Latin American countries. The relatively slow long-run average rate of growth in Chile has been attributed in large part to the effects of the economic development strategy of import substitution applied during 1940–1973 (Ibañez and Lüders 1983). The fast recovery from the recent financial crisis is related to the fiscal discipline and the social market economy policies presently followed.

Economic policy under Allende. Chile adopted an import substitution strategy in the late 1930s, even before Argentina did. During the following decades, the degree of protectionism and government intervention in the economy increased faster and became deeper than in most other Latin American countries, although the process was not necessarily continuous. During the 1960s a land reform, eventually expropriating over 60 percent of the arable land, extended government intervention into the domain of property rights (the long-term bonds with which owners were paid had face values equal to the tax assessment value of their property, but were sold in the market at a very high discount). During the late 1960s, the unsatisfactory results of the import substitution strategy package led to the consideration and advocacy of alternative strategies for economic development. Such options were advanced by interests across the entire political spectrum, from right to left. Then, in 1970, the country elected Salvador Allende, a Marxist socialist to the presidency. Allende's economic team deepened significantly the protectionist and interventionist policies that had been followed, including the nationalization and/or management intervention of about 500 medium- and large-sized firms. This, together with the political consequences of his election, and disastrous macroeconomic management, generated a major sociopolitical and economic crisis: during 1973 GDP dropped by 5.6 percent, the fiscal deficit reached 25 percent of GNP, the annual rate of inflation increased to 353 percent (very high at the time, even by Latin American standards), foreign reserves had all but disappeared, and so on. Elected by little more than 30 percent of the popular vote, the regime saw its popular support dwindle. When Allende tried to impose measures that Congress and the Supreme Court deemed unconstitutional, these bodies in effect invited the military to intervene.

The social market economy. The military opted from the beginning for a market economy. To institutionalize what they termed a social market economy, they chose an economic team whose members changed from time to time, but whose leaders were known as the Chicago Boys because so many of them had been trained at the University of Chicago.

The economic team was led by Sergio de Castro. Initially, he operated behind the scenes but, between 1976 and 1982, as minister of finance, he concluded that the economic development strategy of import substitution had to be drastically changed. In particular, he concluded that the role of the state had to be reduced to the bare minimum and that the state should perform only those tasks necessary to achieve the common good that the private sector could not or would not perform. Private initiative, freedom of choice, and initially, increased investment financed with foreign resources, were to be the key elements of the new development strategy.

Between September 13, 1973, and the early 1980s, the protectionist and interventionist regime was dismantled and replaced by a relatively liberal economy. This move initially enjoyed considerable support because the experience under Allende had been so disastrous, and it was accepted after 1976–1977 by an even larger percentage of the population because the results of the system's application were, in general, very satisfactory. The economic team freed all prices of goods and services, unified the exchange rate, reduced customs duties to a uniform 10 percent, eliminated all quotas and other trade restrictions, freed interest rates and international capital movements (at the right time, that is, after trade and the internal financial system had been freed), eliminated all existing credit rationing devices and reduced required reserves of financial institutions to those normally existing in the developed countries, introduced free collective bargaining at the enterprise level (allowing strikes and lockouts), transformed the social security system to one of capitalization in which the employees can choose among several privately administrated funds, and so forth. At the same time, the government privatized all nationalized and intervened business enterprises, except those created or purchased by law (which, however, did include the major SOEs), and distributed for private ownership the land previously expropriated. Finally, it reduced fiscal expenses somewhat below the high levels of 1970 (mainly by requiring SOEs to be self-financing), and paid for those expenses through increased taxation, to the extent of generating a surplus. Even with its implementation of fiscal discipline and free markets, the government continued to control directly over 30 percent of GDP, the major industrial sectors through the SOEs (petroleum, steel, electricity, communications, airlines, railways, shipping, coal, nitrate, and so on), and a key price, the exchange rate. Moreover about 50 percent of the national budget was spent on social goods and services (education, health, housing) to try to give all citizens an equal opportunity to participate in the benefits of the system (Ibañez and Lüders 1983).

The unexpected crisis of 1982–1983. Between 1976 and 1981, the country experienced record economic growth rates while inflation rates were rapidly approaching modern lows. The expansion was being led by private sector expenditures for both consumption and investment. The boom could be felt almost everywhere. However, foreign capital inflows, attracted by very high real interest rates and the favorable business climate, and made possible by the petrodollar recycling and the opening of the Chilean capital account, were also reaching record levels. In the process, the production of tradable goods was facing difficulties. Though the real exchange rate and purchasing power of the Chilean peso were rapidly falling, and the government had fixed the nominal exchange rate (a *tablita* starting in 1978 and a fixed rate in mid-1979) and, according to the principles of the monetary approach to the balance of payments, was following a neutral monetary policy. It had confidence that the mechanism would produce an automatic adjustment in the expenditure levels, if external conditions required it. Up to early 1981, the system seemed to be working well. The increases in the money supply generated by the capital movements were fueling an impressive expenditure expansion and the desired reduction in the interest rate.

Then, during May 1981, a large conglomerate went broke. This changed the attitude of foreign bankers (who became less willing to lend to Chile) and that of the local business community, which suddenly realized that the flow of foreign funds could dry up. Some started to speculate about a likely devaluation, speculation that increased significantly when the recent deterioration in the country's terms of trade became evident. The internal interest rate shot up, and, soon after, a significant group of financial institutions became insolvent. In late 1981 the government intervened in the first group of financial institutions to fail and bailed out depositors and lenders. This increased the speculative dollar movement so much that President Pinochet, trying to stop the capital flight, personally declared twice that the government would not devalue. However, the high interest rate, the falling economic activity levels, the rising unemployment levels, the insolvency of business enterprises in the tradable sectors, the relatively slow reduction in the price and wage rate levels, and so on, eventually induced the president to accept the resignation of Sergio de Castro as finance minister, and, soon thereafter (May 1982) to devalue.

The "automatic macroeconomic adjustment" mechanism had

been abandoned. But, unlike the case of Argentina, the social market economy was going to be saved. This, in spite of the fact that during 1982 real GDP dropped by 14.1 percent, the unemployment rate increased from 9 to 20 percent (together with a significant increase in the official minimum employment program), and real wages started to fall.

Adjustment and growth. During the remainder of 1982 and the following years, the government centered its attention on foreign resource restriction and on engineering the recovery of a deeply hurt financial system. The private sector, through the free workings of markets for goods, labor, and credit, was to carry the main burden of the adjustment (profit rates fell dramatically during 1982–1984, and wages dropped steadily until 1987). Although tactical compromises were reached with some sectors (especially in foreign trade), the basic elements of the free market economy were not only retained but also reinforced (for example, the privatization process was significantly deepened *after* the crisis). Public sector expenses were also temporarily increased, especially for public works, housing, and social items, but during the last few years the public expenditure to GDP rate has again been steadily declining. Great care was taken to have the full-employment budget in balance, so much so that during 1988 a surplus was again likely, in spite of requirements imposed by changes in the social security system and the after-the-crisis transformation of the income tax into something like a progressive expenditure tax at the same rates. Both of these latter structural changes contributed, as expected, to increases in the traditionally low Chilean savings rate.

The effort to rehabilitate the financial system will be analyzed below. At this point it is sufficient to indicate that the rescue operations of most institutions, and the bailout of depositors (and foreign lenders), was related to the need to ease as much as possible the foreign exchange restriction. The strategy to achieve the latter included three key elements. First, as in Argentina, a low real exchange rate policy was adopted to expand exports as fast as possible. This policy required low customs duties that, though temporarily raised (reaching 35 percent during 1984) from their 10 percent level of 1982, have since been reduced to 15 percent. Further complementing this policy, a 10 percent drawback has been institutionalized on nontraditional exports. Second, renegotiations of the foreign debt with the international banking community took place. Conditions (spreads, new money, and so on) of these renegotiations were similar to those of the larger Latin American countries (with the exception of Mexico), even though Chile's debt as percentage of GNP was the highest.[4] Its negotiations with the IMF, unlike those of Argentina, were seen by Chile as an essential condition to achieving its objective of ameliorating the negative effects of its foreign exchange restriction. Thus fiscal and monetary discipline was accepted by the government as being valuable in and of itself, quite apart from any aid it might provide the negotiations. Finally, the country increased sharply its credit operations with the official Washington-based banks (World Bank Group, Inter-American Development Bank), with which operations had been almost suspended during the 1970s.

Since 1984, this three-pronged strategy has allowed a simultaneous expansion of imports and reduction, between 1986 and 1988, of its foreign indebtedness level as a percentage of GDP and exports. It not only stemmed the flight of capital from the country, but also resulted in new direct foreign investment in Chile. Debt-to-equity swaps were U.S. $303 million during 1986 and U.S. $674 million during 1987; other direct investments during the same years averaged U.S. $340 million.

The recovery has been successful on almost all accounts. The solvency of the Chilean financial system has been reestablished. Financial deepening reached record levels, and an interesting institutional capital market is emerging. As a result of adequate and timely private-sector adjustments conjoined with the success in dealing with the foreign resource restriction, GDP has grown around 5 percent per year since 1984. Fiscal discipline has allowed the inflation rate to remain at rather modest levels, if compared with Latin American standards, and its 1987 level of 21.5 percent was only slightly higher than the relevant international inflation for Chile. Starting in 1984, employment creation has been impressive, and the unemployment rate (still relatively high) is approaching pre-crisis levels. Of course, salary levels are lower (reflecting the adjustment to the deteriorated terms of trade and diminished foreign resource flows), but they are now expected to begin to increase, together with the already rising (but still low) net investment levels.

Financial Repression and Capital Flight in Argentina and the Contrast in Chile

Development of the financial system in Argentina and Chile, including the specific financial sector policies adopted in the two countries, was generally consistent with their respective overall economic development strategies.

In Argentina, except for the 1976–1981 liberalization period when financial markets were substantially deregulated, the formal financial system was heavily controlled by the government. Real interest rates in the banking sector were generally negative and below those to be obtained on foreign assets or in the informal local markets. The system was repressed, and informal financial operations (including capital flights) became at times very important. Argentine private holdings of financial assets (in the country and abroad) increased from about 36 percent of GDP in 1970, to a recent peak of 49.44 percent in 1982. During the same period, the monetary assets (the main component of the official financial market) to GDP ratio fell from about 23 percent to 13 percent (Arriazu 1988). Most of the difference in this ratio over time can be attributed to capital flight. According to one estimate, foreign currency holdings by Argentinians abroad are estimated to have increased from less than $1 billion in 1970 to over $17 billion during 1983 (ibid). Others estimate that today those holdings total approximately $30 billion, which would be well over 30 percent of GDP (Lanús de la Serna 1987).

In contrast, Chile's financial market was gradually freed after

September 1973, together with the other markets of the economy. Since late 1975 interest rates have been completely free, positive in real terms, and competitive with rates of return on foreign assets. Because the market remains regulated in some ways, described later, some informal activity continues to take place, but this is relatively insignificant in terms of the size of the formal market.

The different policies of the governments of the two countries have yielded no less divergent results. Financial deepening in Chile is now substantially greater than it is in Argentina, and the difference is growing, as revealed in Figure 5.1. The M2 numerator of Figure 5.1's M2/GDP index includes M1 (all money in circulation and demand deposits) plus other money holdings, such as time deposits, that cannot be converted to cash on demand. (Argentina's M2 does not include time deposits, so its nearest equivalent, M4, is relabled M2 in the chart for simplicity and meaningfulness.) Increasing values of M2/GDP often (perhaps usually) reflect financial deepening. Exceptions exist to the extent that monetary assets broadly defined (M2) are accounted for by their more narrowly defined M1 component. In those instances, liquidity appears to be a higher priority for individuals than are savings and investment and can become quite extreme—as it did during the 1971–1973 Allende period, when M1 accounted for almost all M2, as evidenced by comparing Figure 5.2 with Figure 5.1.

In order to place the pairs of M1/GDP and M2/GDP percentages (in 1987, 6 and 15 percent for Argentina; 6 and 30 percent for Chile) in a more inclusive context, consider the corresponding percentages for Colombia (12 and 18 percent), Korea and Brazil (both about 12 and 40 percent), and Germany and the United States (both about 16.5 and 70 percent). This additional information may assist the reader in understanding that, although the evidence of either figure viewed separately might be taken as indicative of financial deepening, that possibility can be contradicted if both are viewed together. The sharp increase in monetization in Chile during 1971–1973 reflects not an increase in the demand for money, but a money supply shock in a completely closed economy in which the government allocated

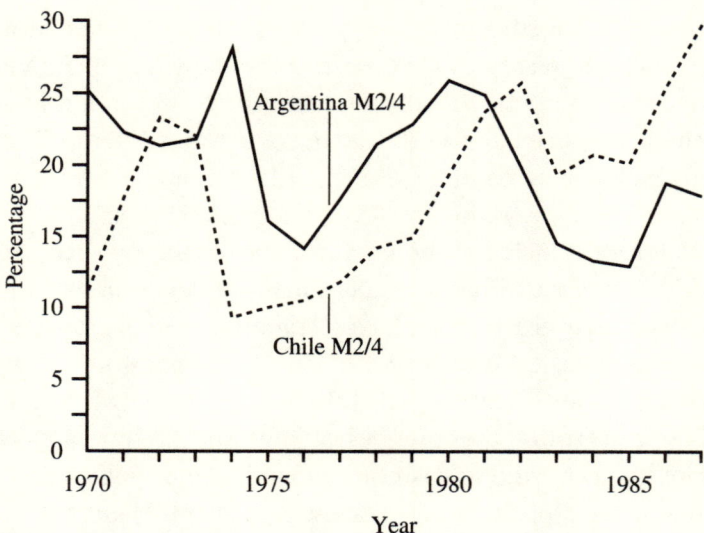

Figure 5.1. Partial Indication of Financial Deepening, 1970–1987 (M2/GDP percentages).
Source: Central banks of Chile and Argentina.

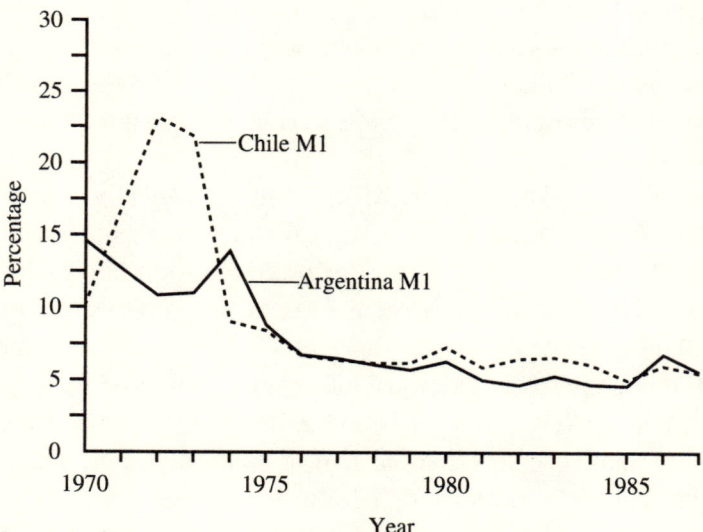

Figure 5.2. Partial Indication of Financial Deepening, 1970–1987 (M1/GDP percentages).
Source: Central banks of Chile and Argentina.

goods by coupons at fixed prices. An equivalent experience as the 1990s commence is that of the "ruble overhang" in the Soviet Union.

More specifically, increases of a country's M2/GDP can be reasonably understood as financial deepening to the extent that the M1 component is increasing at a lesser rate than is the M2. When, as in the post-Allende period (since 1974), there is little change in M1/GDP (as in Figure 5.2), but there are significant increases in M2/GDP (as reflected in Figure 5.1), financial deepening is the interpreted result. A comparison of the two graphs also reveals that significant financial deepening occurred in Argentina almost exclusively within its 1976–1981 period of financial liberalization during the tenure of José Martínez de Hoz (financial sector credit rose from 13.9 percent of GDP in 1975 to 33.2 percent in 1980).

The M1/GDP percentages illustrate vividly that any single variable is a poor guide to what is going on in an economy, even when there is a singular explanation for a particular value of that variable. In this case, the almost identical measured values are explained by the high expected alternative cost of holding cash balances (presumably mainly for transaction purposes) in both Chile and Argentina. Of course, the word "alternative" in the explanation assumes that other variables are considered. When they are, it is apparent that the reason that the opportunity cost of holding cash balances is high in Chile is dramatically different from the reason for the same phenomenon in Argentina. In Argentina, where deposit interest rates were often very negative, the alternative cost is represented by the loss in purchasing power because of the high inflation rates and/or the real return on holding foreign assets. In Chile, relatively high and positive deposit interest rates reflect the alternative cost of holding cash that is manifested in its rising M2/GDP.

Aspects of the Argentine financial system, 1970–1987. In this section some specific aspects of Argentina's financial sector are analyzed, including the financing of the public sector, interest rate spreads, competitiveness of the system, government control over financial institutions, the effects of deposit guarantees, and the solvency of the financial system.

No additional mention will be made of the share market because, in Argentina, it is relatively small and declining. For example, the number of companies allowed to issue stock has dwindled from 414 in 1970 to 206 in 1987 (Artana and Szewack 1988). It has been estimated that in 1971 the total market value of outstanding publicly traded shares was only 3.1 percent of all recorded financial liabilities in the country (Tami 1978), and the monthly average value of shares traded at the stock exchange during 1987 was only U.S. $25 million. This volume is equal to that of Peru. In Chile (with a total GDP of about one-third that of Argentina) U.S. $42 million were traded, and in Brazil the equivalent was about U.S. $400 million (Artana and Szewack 1988). Moreover, subscriptions of new shares as a percentage of GDP are negligible in Argentina. The reasons for this decline are several. The most frequently mentioned include the variability of share prices (and therefore returns) because the market is small, the lack of stable and explicit dividend policies in most business enterprises, low rates of return of the companies' net worth relative to other alternatives, and the lack of institutional investors. Among the latter only insurance companies hold and trade shares, and their holdings have also been diminishing, probably for the same reasons as those of individual investors.

In Argentina, the financial liberalization begun in 1976 more or less coincides with the beginning of a steady decline in the domestic savings rate, from over 25 percent of GDP to less than 20 percent in 1980, and a somewhat slower rate of decline in the rate of domestic investment until the final year of Martínez de Hoz's tenure as economic minister in 1981 (domestic investment as a percentage of GDP in that year fell a full 5 percent from the preceding year—from 23.2 percent in 1980 to 18.2 percent in 1981) (International Monetary Fund 1989, 203). The previously referred to record capital flight of 1981 means that the *total* savings and investment of Argentines did not decrease to that extent, but it did in the domestic (formal) economy, and that decline has continued under the heavily repressed financial system existing since 1981, descending to 10 percent of GDP accounted for by either savings or investment in 1987 (International Bank for Reconstruction and Development 1989, 181).

Argentines call the boom period before the crisis the "sweet money time." To attribute this sweetness exclusively to the financial liberalization is erroneous. It was more a product of the coincidence in time of the capital account opening and the petrodollar shock. The resulting heavy inflow of foreign resources dramatically reduced the price of tradables, including consumer durables. Real increases in consumption, by both the population and government, considerably exceeded the real increase (of about 12 percent) in GDP of the liberalization period.

The impossible public sector deficit. Financial policies in Argentina are closely linked to the financing of the public sector deficit. This deficit had been of the order of 2.5 percent of GDP in the late 1960s and early 1970s (Cavallo and Peña 1983). Perón increased it to about 14 percent of GDP during 1975, and since then Argentine governments have only been able to reduce it temporarily. Fiscal deficits, usually smaller than public sector deficits, closely follow the path of the latter.

Except for 1979–1982, which approximately coincides with the last part of the economic liberalization period, the Argentine governments financed their public sector deficits internally. On average, about half of the needed financing was obtained directly from the central bank and was therefore inflationary. The remainder was obtained from the financial system, especially from the banking sector, crowding out private sector credit. For instance, between 1970 and 1975, the share of public sector credit in the total provided by the financial sector rose from about 10 percent to approximately 19 percent, while total credit fell from 25 percent to 14 percent of GDP. Between 1980 (the last full year of the financial liberalization) and 1985 (the last year before the Austral Plan) the share of public sector credit rose from about 15 percent to almost 24 percent of GDP, while total credit dropped from 33 percent of GDP to less than

19 percent. Financial repression was so great during each of these periods of heavy government intervention in the Argentine financial market (falling M2/GDP ratios contradicting financial deepening) that, although credit to the private sector fell by over 10 percent of GDP, the public sector was still unable to increase the credit it received relative to GDP.

Presumably, the size of the budget deficits was tolerated because governments gave short-term economic growth, employment, and wage rate policies priority over fiscal and monetary discipline and did not have sufficient political power to raise tax revenues to match expenditures. Under those circumstances, voluntary financing of the deficits in domestic financial markets would have implied very high real interest rates, crowding out private sector credits. But high interest rates would have been obviously counterproductive to (short-run) economic growth and employment objectives. The alternative (adopted) solution was to intervene in the financial system; the fixing of interest rates at low, perhaps even negative, levels, and the direct allocation of credit were compatible with the short-run objectives. Moreover, the long-run real effects of such financial repression was—in spite of its own historical lessons and those from the experiences of other countries—always underestimated, except by Martínez de Hoz and his team. But their consistency in liberalizing the financial sector naturally included the freeing of interest rates. Of course, that increased public sector interest costs, thereby offsetting a large part of the gain that would otherwise have been realized. Thus did the public sector deficit, net of the cost of debt servicing, fall from 11.3 percent of GDP during 1975 to 1.8 percent during 1978, but reduce the overall deficit by only 4 percent (to 10.1 percent of GDP) (Cavallo and Peña 1983).

The pressure of the deficit on interest rates did, as noted, attract foreign resources. Though this reduced the credit crunch in the private sector, soon thereafter (during the second semester of 1979) spreads between local and foreign interest rates, computed at the existing *tablita*, increased sharply. In order to decrease pressure for an even higher domestic interest rate, the government began financing much of its deficit directly abroad. Foreign capital inflow increased sharply during 1980 and 1981, but the interest rate spread (local-to-foreign) did not decline, except temporarily during the first half of 1980. With economic agents estimating that a deficit of the prevailing size could not be financed for very long, the spread took on the risk (and corollary profit and loss) of a devaluation premium. The effects of the huge capital inflows to finance the deficit, and the relative price distortions and high interest rate spreads generated by this scheme, probably contributed to the financial problems of the business sector during 1980–1982. These, in turn, decisively affected the stability of the financial system.

Interest rates and competitiveness. As previously mentioned, the lack of financial deepening in Argentina is to a large degree explained by negative real interest rates. Ordinarily (that is, in most thoroughly liberalized economies), *real* interest rates are a function of the combination of *nominal* interest rates and inflation. A borrower of money at a given and unvarying rate of interest (the nominal rate) will experience a real cost in paying off the loan that exactly equals the nominal cost, therefore, only if the rate of inflation equals the interest rate on the loan. If the rate of inflation exceeds the interest rate, the borrower's real cost will be less than the nominal cost; if the rate of inflation is less than the interest rate, the real cost of repaying the loan will be greater than the nominal cost. Thus for any given nominal (and unvarying) interest rate, lenders are more likely to benefit from lower rates of inflation and borrowers are more likely to benefit from higher rates of inflation—insofar as we confine our cost-benefit calculation to a particular loan and do not contemplate the more general havoc associated with rampant inflation. On the basis of this "ordinary" differentiation between nominal and real costs of borrowing and lending activities, the information in Figure 5.3 reveals the inordinate difficulty that lenders or borrowers would have in agreeing on terms and entering into a contract.

A comparison of Figure 5.3 with Figure 5.4 confirms expectations:

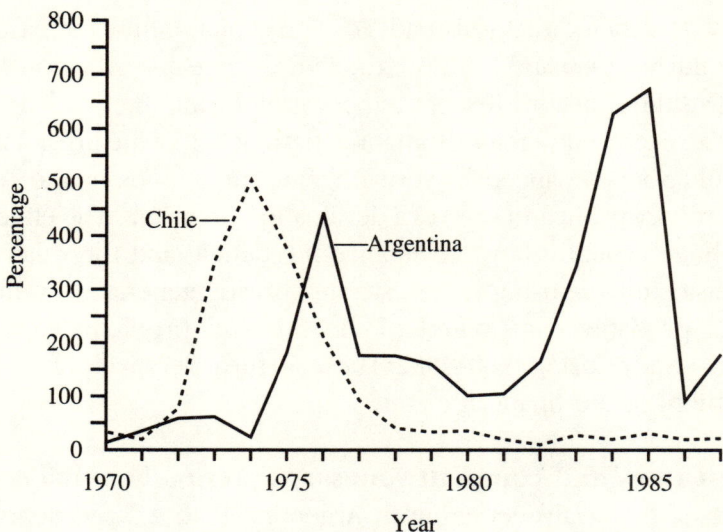

Figure 5.3. Annual Rates of Change in Consumer Price Index, 1970–1987
Source: IMF, *International Financial Statistics*, various issues.

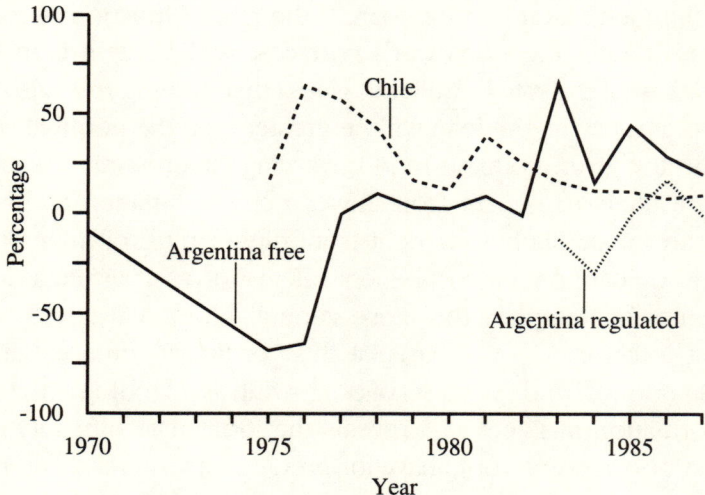

Figure 5.4. Real Short-Term Interest Rates, 1970–1987
Source: Central banks of Chile and Argentina.

The less the year-to-year change in price inflation, and the longer the period of time in which such fluctuations have been minimized, the less will be the variability over time in real short-term lending interest rates.

Several years of decreasing variability in price inflation (Figure 5.3) appear to have finally effected the same outcome in short-term lending interest rates (Figure 5.4)—in Chile. To find the same result in Argentina would probably require a study of its economy before World War II and the advent of Juan Perón. When *short*-term lending is thus affected by price instability, it is not difficult to see that *long*-term lending in Argentina might be nonexistent. This, combined with the country's moribund stock market, makes it apparent that its domestic capital market is a viable source of neither debt nor equity finance for substantial capital investments by Argentine industry. In these circumstances, the explosion of Argentina's capital flight, on the one hand, and of its foreign debt, on the other, can be understood as corresponding phenomena.

Unfortunately, it gets worse. The discerning reader will have noted that Figure 5.4 includes *two* short-term lending interest rates for Argentina, one regulated by government and the other not. The other is assumed to include lenders' calculations of the penalties that might be imposed by government officials (officially or otherwise) should their activities be detected, multiplied by the odds of that detection. With more than one *nominal* rate, then obviously there is more than one *real* rate. And, worse for Argentine lenders (and depositors), the regulated rate has been dominant since the second half of 1982, through 1987, and possibly today. Ironically, the regulated rate probably would not be dominant and possibly would not exist, but for the wealthiest Argentines being able to export their capital.

It gets worse still. There is more than one regulated rate—thus the "regulated rate" graphed in Figure 5.4 is an approximation of *average* regulated rates. In a way (that is, within the confines of a heavily regulated, as against a liberalized, economy) this makes sense. An interventionary government wanting to retain capital that would otherwise flee the country offers it special incentives to remain—hence *multiple* regulated rates.

So far is the conception of real interest rates stretched by all of this from that of the "ordinary," that we might deem the economy that fosters it to be an "economy." In lieu of those quotation marks, they are only employed (in the remainder of this paragraph) around the word *real*—in order to distinguish the foregoing, and Argentine interest rates, from the common distinction in liberalized economies between nominal and real rates. Within the universe of *regulated* rates, some groups in Argentina have had access to credit at certain rates, while others have had to pay higher rates. For instance, with compound interest on a loan of 100 in late-1970 currency, the debt obligation by the end of 1983 could have been anywhere between 895 and .82 of the same currency (Arriazu 1988). The average market rate would have yielded 122 and a foreign loan would have implied a debt of 156. If the debtor had purchased insurance against devaluation (offered by the central bank after the financial crisis), the debt would have been only 1.54. Of course, a corollary (but opposing) result would have been experienced by any depositor: a foreign-currency deposit of 100 in 1970 would have accumulated a "real" gain of 50 percent (or 150 in 1970-constant currency units), the average domestic currency deposit would yield 2.21 (a "real" loss of about 98 percent of the initial deposit!), and the best financial investment strategy would have yielded 359. Obviously, the best strategy is only known after the facts, so that the above numbers give a good idea of the average return (or cost) that might have been expected of operating in Argentina's financial market, and of the risks involved. These "real" numbers confirm that fact can indeed be stranger than fiction; they also suggest the reasons for the huge capital flight.

In addition to the spreads between foreign and local interest rates, another phenomenon important in Argentina is the high spread between interest rates on deposits and those on loans. These spreads usually reflect the competitiveness of a system, and the efficiency of the institutions operating in it. In countries with high legal reserve requirements and/or high inflation rates, they also include the foregone cost of those reserves. In Argentina, with the financial liberalization of 1977, a Monetary Regulation Account was created at the central bank to neutralize the effect of required reserves on the competitiveness of different types of financial institutions. In order to control the effect of legal reserves on interest rate spreads, however, the Monetary Regulation Account was soon used to pay interest on reserves required on time deposits. This basic mechanism is still in effect today, but spreads continue to be extremely wide. During 1978–1980, for instance, average interest rate spreads were over 20 percent per year. During late 1985 they still averaged 15 percent for the free segment of the financial market.

Several reasons exist to explain these spreads, but the most important is high operating costs. In countries with developed financial markets, commercial banks' ratio of operating costs to total assets fluctuates around 2 percent; for developing countries the average is somewhat higher and has a wider range. For instance, in Colombia and Mexico, the ratio reaches almost 5 percent. In Malaysia it is 1.2 percent. In Chile, for the larger private banks, the ratio is not different from the average ratio in the United States, and it is only slightly higher for the system as a whole (Instituto des Estudios Bancarios 1984). In Argentina, however, it reaches 8.1 percent. The puzzling thing is that Argentina has a very large number of financial institutions, so one might conclude that there must be fierce competition. There are more than three hundred financial institutions (about two hundred banks), with about five thousands offices. That is, there are only 155,000 inhabitants per bank. Japan has 780,000, Finland, 683,000, Sweden, 590,000, Italy, 395,000, and Germany 235,000. Chile has only forty banks—about 325,000 inhabitants per bank—and competition seems to have forced spreads down to nearly international levels. One possible reason for these high operating costs in Argentina is that free competition among the Argentine financial institutions and with foreign banks has never prevailed long enough to force severe cost-cutting measures.[5]

The solvency of financial institutions in Argentina. When Martínez de Hoz and his advisers changed the financial regulations in 1977, they aimed, among other objectives, at a solvent financial system. Perón had nationalized all deposits, and, until the financial reform, banks were operating for the government when collecting deposits. Although bank loans were legally made at the risk of the banks, at the highly negative interest rates prevailing at the time, the possibility of failure was almost nonexistent. The reform of 1977, although privatizing all deposits and eventually (by 1981) reducing average required reserves to only about 10 percent, institutionalized a government guarantee of 90 percent of the value of deposits above a fully guaranteed minimum. After the crisis had broken out in September 1982, required reserves of all existing types of deposits were again increased to 100 percent (in effect, similar to the nationalization under Perón). Interest rates on these deposit and reserve operations were regulated by government authority. Loans were made through rediscounting, at rates and purposes also determined by the authorities. At the same time, "free" deposits were allowed—at unregulated interest rates and without government guarantees. Initially, these deposits were allowed to comprise 3 percent of each institution's total operations. Though this percentage was to be allowed to grow rapidly, this has not been the case.

In spite of the existence of the government guarantee, of relatively high real interest rates on loans, and a rapidly growing financial system (the number of banks almost doubled between 1976 and 1981), the central bank of Argentina exercised little control over banking operations—including, most importantly, the quality of loans—during the financial liberalization period. Regulation by the government was equally relaxed in Chile, but there Minister de Castro frequently and publicly reiterated that the government would neither bail out any bank that failed nor aid its depositors. The task of the Superintendency of Banks and Financial Institutions was limited to ensuring that the financial institutions were formally fulfilling their obligations. This circumscribed focus of the Superintendency in Chile was more appropriate to its circumstance than was the same orientation in Argentina; in the absence of government guarantees, competition among banks was expected to provide market regulation of Chilean financial institutions. That Chile's government *did*, in fact, bail out financial institutions each time they appeared to be on the verge of bankruptcy (the Banco Osorno y La Union, in 1976, and Banco Español, in 1981, are two prominent examples) contributed to the assumption of an "informal" deposit guarantee during the 1974–1982 period. But this notion only emerged after the government did what it said it would not, whereas the responsibilities of the Superintendency were predicated on the government doing (and not doing) what it promised.

It appears that the transparent guarantees provided by Argentina's government presented a moral hazard for the country's financial institutions, inducing banks to take more risks on their portfolios than was socially desirable. There is also some evidence that the guarantees encouraged fraud. When numerous Argentine borrowers were unable to meet their commitments and the 1982 crisis commenced, several banks simply raised their interest rates to cover their nonperforming loans (Arnaudo and Conejero 1985). It also appears that many engaged in ever-riskier lending in hopes that the higher returns that *some* of these provided would be realized; *some* may have done so, but not enough, as none of these institutions was able to avoid insolvency and eventually intervention.

Since 1981, the governments of Argentina have implemented several schemes to increase the solvency of the financial system by improving the quality of the loan portfolios of financial institutions. As previously discussed (and reflected in Figure 5.4), one the most important of these measures occurred when the government fixed the nominal interest rate on loans and deposits while the rate of inflation was increasing rapidly, thereby effecting a drastic reduction in the real rate of interest during 1982–1983. Another important measure (also previously mentioned) was the government's introduction in 1981 of the exchange rate insurance mechanism. In contrast with Chile, the process is incomplete and ongoing—financial institutions are continuously intervened in or merged under official pressure and with its "aid." Unfortunately, there is no reliable estimate of the total cost to the government of any of these rescue operations. For any taxpaying borrower (depositor), the "real" cost (return) on the loan (deposits) is effectively increased (reduced).

Liberalization, massive intervention, and financial rebuilding in Chile. At the time the military took over the government in 1973, Chilean financial institutions were practically all state owned, interest rates were fixed, credit was allocated by the central bank, and reserve requirements were extremely high. That is, the financial system was, for all practical purposes, nationalized. Within the market orientation of the new economic policy, the system had to be radically changed. This was accomplished before 1981. Existing local financial institutions were privatized between 1975 and 1978, in such a manner that they eventually were almost all controlled by local conglomerates known as financial groups. New banks, most of them subsidiaries of foreign banks, were authorized to operate, and during 1981, 18 of the 45 existing banks were foreign. A large number of finance companies was established early during the period, although entry into the financial business continued to be regulated by the Superintendency. The operations that different types of depository institutions could perform were gradually unified, but at the same time the variety of operations allowed was enormously diversified, and the system evolved toward universal banking. The almost complete freeing of international capital flows late in this period was another way in which competition was introduced into the system. Financial institutions were allowed to allocate credit as they wished, and reserve requirements were reduced to 10 percent on demand deposits and 4 percent on time deposits. As mentioned, no formal guarantee existed for depositors. The Chilean financial market became one of the most unregulated in the developing world.

As a result, a significant financial deepening took place, some financial widening could also be observed (limited by the effect of the very high interest rates, which will be discussed later), and interest rate spreads, initially as high as those in Argentina, fell continuously, to average during 1980–1981 about 5.5 percent per year. In spite of these apparently very satisfactory results, during 1981–1982 the system broke down, the government intervened in the operation of sixteen financial institutions (about one-third of the total, but among them the largest private commercial banks), and most of the other financial institutions also had high ratios of nonperforming loans.

As in Argentina, the reasons for the financial crisis are complex. The level of interest rates in Chile was much higher than in Argentina and probably explains part of the problem. The unexpected rise in these rates to over 30 percent per year during 1981–1982 (resulting from the dollar devaluation speculation described above and compounded by distress borrowing resulting from crisis conditions themselves) provides further explanation. That explanation is made more plausible by the recognition that about 40 percent of the loan portfolio of the financial system was expressed in dollars. Thus the sharp devaluation of the peso in 1982 dramatically raised business enterprise indebtedness (the debt to equity ratio of all registered corporations increased from .61 in 1980 to .97 in 1982). On top of this, beginning in the last quarter of 1981 and continuing in 1982, economic activity levels of the country plummeted, as reflected in the GDP drop of 14.1 percent. Under such conditions, not only were many debtors temporarily unable to service their debt obligations, but also a large number of them also revised their forecasts, expecting increased foreign resource constraints (including a higher exchange rate) and a corresponding reduction of the output growth rate. Thus were lower gross of debt cash flows anticipated *in conjunction with* substantial increases in projected debt service obligations. The *combination* of these expectations made for dire forecasts. Indeed, many of the forecasters concluded that they were no longer in a position to honor their debt. This implied heavy write-offs for the financial institutions (estimated to range anywhere from U.S. $2.5 billion to U.S. $4.0 billion, out of a total asset level of the depository institutions of somewhat more than U.S. $10 billion) that their net worth could not provide (Lüders 1986a; for a presentation of the debt capitalization theory, see Harberger 1985).

Additional reasons for the financial crisis have been given by others. The most limited simply blames the Superintendency for not having exercised appropriate control over the financial system, but we have seen above that it did not have such authority. A more inclusive argument is that the loan portfolios of the financial institutions were weighted too heavily in favor of loans to firms related to the owners of enterprises that had been privatized in the post-Allende period and had thus truly become "bad" during the later 1970s. The implicit deposit guarantee (since 1974–1975 the government had, in spite of its declared policy, always bailed out the lenders and depositors of financial institutions in trouble), it is said, allowed financial institutions to roll over these bad loans by raising the interest rate level. This would explain the extremely high interest rate levels in Chile and, at the same time, the vulnerability of the financial system to the macroeconomic shock of 1981–1982. This thesis, appealing to those who are fond of conspiracy theories or who give great weight to the moral hazard issue, might explain part of the problem, but is difficult to reconcile with the low consolidated indebtedness levels, and the high profit rates, of most financial groups during 1978–1980.

Much has been written about the government intervention of the financial institutions during 1981–1982. Some have criticized the interventions as being perhaps the only important measures taken by the government, which were contrary to the spirit of a free market economy that otherwise had been implemented in Chile almost as a textbook case. This criticism would be easier to accept if the problem had affected but a single major, or perhaps a few minor, financial institutions. But, with estimated losses of the financial institutions adding up to anywhere between 25 and 40 percent of the loan portfolio, the magnitude of the problem was such that the task of sustaining *any* economy took precedence over conformance to textbook expectations. In any event, the interventions were to be definitely temporary, because the government, although willing to correct what it considered implementation errors, had no intention of changing its basic development strategy. It intervened, instead of letting the financial institutions go broke, because it judged the problem of insolvency to be of such a magnitude and so widespread that the whole financial system would have otherwise broken down, with all the implicit real costs, and possibly required many years of rebuilding. The problem, it was believed, was no longer a private problem, but a social problem, and it was therefore the government's task to solve it as efficiently and equitably as possible. The government was aware that intervention not only avoided (or, in 1982, significantly reduced) losses to Chilean depositors, but also benefited foreign lenders. This might have been fortunate for all concerned; at the time of the intervention, balance-of-payments projections suggested that Chile was going to have to renegotiate its debt and obtain new money, and any small number of private Chilean debtors in a position to purchase the foreign exchange required for debt service would have certainly exceeded the contemplated possibility of zero.

After the interventions, the government took a series of measures to restore the financial system. The solvency of the financial institutions was reestablished through a combination of actions that included: the repurchase by financial institutions of the bad loans that were purchased to their benefit by the central bank (initiated in 1981, the benefited institutions have to repurchase these loans by applying a portion of their future profits—it is expected that it will take some banks several decades to repurchase all their bad loans); the refinancing, at real interest rates of about 6 percent, of most client loans, which had originally been negotiated at much higher rates, with the funds for the renegotiations provided by the central bank; the temporary existence of a subsidized exchange rate to service the debts expressed in foreign currencies; the establishment of capitalization conditions for the purchasers of the banks that were reprivatized, or for the owners of financial institutions that were not rescued; and the application of foreign debt obligations (which debtors could buy abroad at 60 to 70 percent of their face value and to which a rationing "tax" was added) to prepay debt (Lanús de la Serna 1987). In addition, the government required financial institutions to make bad-loan provisions on the basis of a loan-by-loan evaluation procedure, which was actually begun during 1981. Financial institutions also had to reduce their loans to owner-related companies to a fraction of their net worth. The banking law was modified, and a 100 percent reserve requirement was imposed on all demand deposits that exceed 200 percent of net worth. In exchange, demand deposits are 100 percent guaranteed by the public sector. For time deposits, no such special reserve requirement exists, nor does any automatic guarantee, but financial institutions can, if they wish, buy from the government insurance for their depositors. Moreover, the time deposits of all financial institutions are classified by a commission on a monthly basis in accordance with their risk, and the classification is made public. Finally, on this front, the Superintendency is now exercising strict control over all operations (a computerized network providing it with constant, direct information), and no operation of any new financial institution has been authorized since the crisis.

On another front, the intervened institutions were either liquidated, merged, or sold. In accordance with the conception of "popular capitalism" that guided this reprivatization process, great care was taken to spread the ownership of the two large banks (Banco de Chile and Banco de Santiago) as broadly as possible. This has been complemented by the considerable attention devoted to assuring the solvency, both moral and economic, of new owners of the other banks. In view of the fact that the government neither fixed interest rates nor allocated credit even during the height of the financial crisis, once the now-solvent financial institutions had been reprivatized during 1986–1987, the financial system returned basically to its pre-crisis status, but under the surveillance of a considerably more active Superintendency and with a more explicit deposit guarantee scheme. The economic team has managed the macroconomic variables so as to avoid dramatic increases in the real interest rate relative to the LIBOR (the London Interbank Offer Rate paid by Euromarket borrowers). Striving for a risk spread for Chilean operations that more closely approximates those in the United States, the government has made progress toward that objective by means of its exchange rate policy, constant concern with the control of the level of government expenditures (and deficit), and its (indirect) management of the investment portfolio of the pension funds. The Chilean experience with interest rates (and spreads thereof) poses the definite question, and more tentative answer, of the following.

Financial liberalizations and high interest rates. From the moment interest rates were freed until the climax of the financial crisis, in 1982, one of the most puzzling phenomena of Chile's recent financial development was its persistently (and extremely) high real interest rates. Several econometric studies as well as other explanations for this phenomenon are available (see Arellano 1983, Rosende and Toso 1984, Edwards 1984, Corbo 1985, and Harberger 1985), each one applying a different model, and all obtaining reasonable results. The econometric studies are usually based on expectations models. This is as it should be, but it is also well known that the measurements required by these models are elusive. The general conclusion is that a set of factors influenced interest rate levels during those years, among which the following stand out: a sharp increase in the perceived permanent income of the country; increases in real liquidity; distress borrowing, at times, by financial groups, produced by the capitalization of the interest on loans to finance the purchase of privatized (and other) corporations; the occasional very strong expectations of an exchange rate devaluation; the level of the international interest rate; and the existing (legal and natural) market segmentation between local and foreign financial assets. Of course, the weight of these different factors varied from period to period. The mix was such that the average, highly positive, real interest rate ranged from 64.3 percent in 1976 to about 12 percent in 1980, and then rose to over 35 percent per year during 1981–1982. Such rates are, of course, unsustainable, as the extent of the financial crisis bears testimony. Since the financial crisis, the Chilean economic team has been concerned about interest rate levels as one key element of the financial recovery of the financial and business sectors. Since 1983, rates have been highly positive in comparison with those in the United States, but lower than those that prevailed during 1976–1982; real lending interest rates declined from 11.4 percent during 1984 to 7.48 percent during 1986 and 9.22 percent in 1987.

Because the lower limit of the rates was determined by the rates of return on foreign assets (to avoid disintermediation), real interest rates, if free, depend essentially on *international* as well as domestic macroeconomic conditions. Therefore, a financial liberalization does not necessarily coincide with, let alone produce, high real interest rates and spreads; at the same time, it may be more likely to incur those consequences than would otherwise be the case. The Chilean experience suggests that real interest rates be closely watched—at the very least, that attention might preclude the mis-anticipations that invariably precede "crises." The Argentine experience suggests that much more (by government) than this "very least" can compound problems while purporting to be their solution.

Another puzzle introduced by Chile's highly positive interest rates during 1976–1982 was their apparent lack of effect on the country's traditionally low savings and investment rates. From the many explanations tendered, the most plausible assumes that the development process associated with the liberalization significantly raised permanent income and, thereby, consumption demand. Since 1982, the savings rate increased to a modern-day record height in 1987. This increase has been associated with the already discussed pension funds and income tax reforms, instituted in tandem with an interest rate policy that discourages capital flights. Yet, officially recorded investment levels, even if one discounts the effects of the 1975 and 1982–1983 recessions, were relatively low. However, if one incorporates consumer durables and some other items that are typically recorded as consumption (in spite of their multiple, including nonconsumption, uses) the rate of investment since the Allende period increased significantly up to 1981. Investment rates since the financial crisis have been low, as in most Latin American countries, to a large extent because of the proportion of countries' savings that is required to service foreign debts. In spite of this, between 1965 and 1987 Chile's investment has increased from 15 percent to 17 percent of GDP, and savings have increased from 16 percent to 21 percent. In contrast, Argentina had greater percentages of GDP in both investment and savings in 1965 (19 percent and 22 percent, respectively) but, by 1987, the percentages had declined and only 10 percent of GDP could be attributed to either investment or savings (International Bank for Reconstruction and Development 1989, 180–81).

Chile's capital market. Both the size and growth prospects of Chile's share market are (relative to its past) very good, and relative to Argentina's, outstanding. During 1986, the total value of the shares of the companies traded in the stock exchange reached about 30 percent of total financial liabilities in the country and exceeded, by about 20 percent, the aggregate value of time deposits of commercial banks and finance companies. Moreover, although the trading of shares is still a minor part of the stock exchange business, it has, as a result of the institutional changes to be described below, been growing rapidly during recent years. Indeed, the real price of shares rose approximately 20 percent during 1987 alone, and the total value of shares traded in that year exceeded that of the 1980 boom year by 50 percent (Bolsa de Comercio 1988).

Part of this increase in the trading of shares is of course related to the recovery of the economy, and another part perhaps to the decrease in the real interest rates. Very high interest rates depress share values and induce borrowers to operate in the short-term market, a situation reflected in the much faster growth of Chile's depository market than of its share market during the early days of its liberalization, 1975–1980. With highly positive real interest rates, suppliers of funds also find the short-term market attractive because of its low perceived risk; the whole financial market tends to go short, and capital markets become relatively stagnant.

In 1984–1985, Chile began a series of institutional reforms that might have considerable impact on its capital market in the future. It institutionalized the professional roles of the Capital Market Agent and of eighty-three stock exchange brokers who deal in shares and bonds and act as proxies on behalf of investment bankers; by 1988, twenty-three agents were in business, six of them with foreign capital. Legal changes freeing the insurance market have also resulted in the rapid growth of its volume of business since the crisis of 1980–1982. Mutual funds, which scarcely existed before the financial liberalization, grew rapidly up to 1982, almost disappeared during the 1982–1983 crisis, but have made an impressive comeback. Although still small, each of these latter types of financial institutions has financial assets equal to about 1 percent of those of the commercial banks.

These institutional changes have been complemented by the links that exist between Chile's economy and the rest of the world. That a number of the country's most important companies are foreign-owned not only brings investment expertise into the domestic capital market, but also has probably contributed to the success of foreign debt-to-equity conversions. These swaps, in turn, have augmented the development of the capital market while allowing the level of foreign debt to be reduced. The conversions of debt to equity have contributed to the development of the Chilean capital market in at least two distinctive ways. First, several foreign commercial banks have engaged in debt conversion with the explicit objective of selling those shares later on in the local capital market in hopes of regaining the original principal and some interest return. Second, the government approved some changes in the tax code that would facilitate the operation in the country of international mutual funds, some of which plan to finance their purchases of capital market instruments through debt conversions.

The final structural change that is likely to aid the development of the capital market in Chile is the reform of the income tax law. Corporate reinvestments are only taxed at a 10 percent rate. This provides an inducement to owners of high-income shares to take their profits by way of capital gains and, in the process, spread share ownership.

Even more significant than the country's growing mutual funds are the AFPs (Pension Fund Administrations), which began operating in the early 1980s. These are private institutions that mainly manage funds from mandatory labor pension schemes on a competitive basis. The investment portfolios of the AFPs are heavily controlled by the *superintendencia* (government regulators), but the institutions have been allowed to invest in some selected SOE shares in addition to government bonds and commercial bank deposits. Though the total funds of the AFPs were estimated to have reached 15 percent of GDP by 1988, share investments of AFP-managed funds are still a relatively minor percentage of their total funds. This is expected to change in the future, however, if the experience with present investments is favorable. In the meantime, the only shares in private companies that AFPs have been allowed to purchase are those of privatized firms—SOE shares sold to the funds managed by the AFPs and then privatized. This latter process, another of the institutional changes to aid the development of the capital market, has been considerably deepened since 1986, in such a way as to spread share ownership considerably. Different names have been employed in order to distinguish and highlight distinct dimensions of this effort to broaden capital ownership: *popular capitalism* refers to the sale of the shares of the largest pre-crisis private commercial banks and of the two largest AFPs; *labor capitalism* denotes the sale, by way of special incentives, of shares to the workers of SOEs that are being privatized; and *institutional capitalism*, the already described sale of shares to the funds managed by the AFPs.

Tens of thousands of new share owners have been created, and in the process Chileans have been increasingly educated to the complementarity between assets in the economy and votes in the polity and (with broadened capital ownership), to the complementarity between economic and political freedom, and economic markets and political democracy. This educational outcome, and thus the increased *human* capital in Chile, bodes well for the sustained liberalization of Chile's financial markets, economy, and polity—beyond the Pinochet presidency, through the Aylwin presidency, into the twenty-first century. I wish the prospects were the same for my friends and neighbors in Argentina. For the new governments of Eastern Europe and elsewhere, the world certainly provides lessons; if learned they point to a successful conclusion of even the most difficult transitions. Among the lessons most worth heeding may very well be that of this Latin American contrast.

Murray Sherwin

Comment

It is a pleasure to be asked to talk about what is my favorite subject these days. Most of us who have worked through the New Zealand experience during the past few years are bearing all sorts of bruises and scars, but we still have a smile on our faces, I think.

We have tried to address issues in a rather fundamental way and have been greatly favored by a group of politicians who tell us to worry about the issues, and the politics will look after themselves. They give us all these blank sheets of paper and say, "Go away and tell us how it should be done. We want first-best solutions. Do not tell us how we have done it in the past, or how other people have done it. Just tell us how it should be done and let us worry about all the other issues."

That the focus of today's sessions is the role of capital markets and development is entirely appropriate. This is a major development issue, no question about that. I was fortunate, in late 1987, to attend a colloquium organized by the World Bank, at which the Bank staff took a group of executive directors off to some quiet spot and tried to drum ideas into our thick skulls. We went to Baltimore, and they worked us so hard we never did get to see the scenery. But the issue then was precisely that of financial markets: what is going on in financial markets in developing countries, and what should the Bank's strategies be in those areas? I was somewhat astonished and more than a little bothered to learn about the extent of the problems in the financial sectors of developing countries.

It would seem that a fairly sizable number of the Bank's borrowing clients—developing countries—has quite profound problems, although in many cases these are disguised. This situation has implications not just for resource allocation and the ineffective mobilization of savings, but also for the accumulated arrears that are very large and will be very expensive and difficult problems to address. I think the World Bank and other aid agencies are going to be spending a lot of time and effort exploring these problems over the next few years.

For are a number of reasons I think we need to be concerned about the structure and fidelity of capital markets in developing countries. Clearly, development is about mobilizing resources and investing in future output. Efficient, accessible financial markets are a key to that. But, financial markets also provide a key macro policy instrument that we need to be worried about.

A feature of governments, as distinguished from other economic agencies in an economy, is their capacity to create their own money. For developing countries, the pressure to abuse that capacity is often overwhelming.

It is also true that the capacity to create money and the evolution of monetary systems can fashion a variety of veils that enable governments to mask the true significance of many of their actions. Here, I refer to the possibility, for instance, of substituting implicit taxes in the form of inflation for explicit taxes that electorates may be more inclined to resist or react to.

So much for the little backgrounder on why we ought to talk about financial markets. I was asked to initiate the discussion on Rolf's comparative study of the experience of Argentina and Chile and to do it from the perspective of the New Zealand experience.

Anyone who has been working on the New Zealand experience has been so busy liberalizing and reforming that he has not had a lot of time to sit down and actually document what has been going on.

I have attempted to fill that gap to some modest degree. Chapter 6, on New Zealand, provides some background. I read Rolf's study with an eye to both the similarities with and contrasts to the New Zealand experience. The similarities are quite marked. Argentina, Chile, and New Zealand are all essentially agricultural nations and have relatively high incomes, particularly if you go back a little while into history. New Zealand's income was, of course, higher, and still is.

At least until the depression of the 1930s, these countries were near the forefront of international economies in terms of their capacity to provide attractive incomes for their inhabitants. But they have been in deteriorating positions relative to much of the rest of the world since then. Terms-of-trade declines, endemic in the agricultural sector (and these are all agricultural nations), account for at least part of the decline. Economic management, I would suggest, has been even more important. There has been, in response to those declines, resort in all three countries to attempts to force-feed industrialization processes through protection, through subsidies, through incentives, and through the use of parastatals of one form or another.

There have also been attempts to counter declining incomes through the use of various fiscal measures that have led to growing fiscal imbalances and ultimately to inflation. There has been increasing resort to direct government intervention to counter that inflation, the high interest rates, and all of the other inevitable consequences of lax fiscal and monetary policies.

The differences between the Argentine and Chilean experience and that of New Zealand are also marked and highly pertinent here. We in New Zealand look back with dismay at our economic performance over the past couple of decades, but we never slipped to the degree that Argentina and Chile did. The problems may be similar, but on a very different scale, obviously.

We talk about inflation problems in New Zealand and, relative to those of our OECD partners they have been substantial and difficult. But they never breached the 20 percent level. We had inflation bouncing between 10 and 20 percent for about fifteen years. But never above 20 percent. Government external debt never got above between 40 percent and 45 percent of GDP. Numbers over 100 percent, I think, were reached in many Latin American cases. Also, the New Zealand political structure is clearly more workable, more stable, and that has been important.

I do not intend to do a critique of Rolf's thesis so much as to try to raise a few issues that may be of relevance and interest to our discussion. Let me go through those.

I begin by reflecting that when I sat down to write my chapter on New Zealand, the first obstacle that I found was that it was very difficult to confine the draft to capital markets or financial markets. Rolf had the same problem, I see. You very quickly get into talking about the interrelationships between the real sector and the monetary sector. So that brings me to the first point. I suggest that, according to the New Zealand experience, to be successful, the market-based reforms must be comprehensive.

Liberalizing financial markets lifts some of the veils that I referred to earlier. It makes government actions a little more transparent. But it also forces liberalization in the real sector. Looking at the descriptions that Rolf provides of Chile and Argentina, I am tempted sometimes to focus on the glitches that they ran into and conclude that perhaps they had not gone far enough. Having started down the liberalization route, what tripped them up was an incapacity to take that through to its logical conclusion when trouble struck.

Perhaps a government loses its nerve. There may have been very good reasons for that. But if you go down the route of a particular policy framework, the crucial gaps are the ones that trip you up in the end. So perhaps you could comment on that, Rolf?

The second point, which is somewhat related, focused on the role of taxation regimes in all of this. If the major purpose of liberalizing capital markets is to mobilize savings and channel resources into areas of comparative advantage, we need to be pretty sure that the direction of the flows is not being unduly distorted by inappropriate taxation regimes.

The same argument applies to other forms of relative pricing, but I focus on the taxation regime because we are talking about highly inflationary environments here. It seems to me that, in an inflationary environment, tax systems are particularly susceptible to being eroded in important ways and producing significant distortions.

So if you embark on the liberalization route with respect to financial markets, you have also to make sure your taxation system is giving you clear, undistorted signals. That is, it must reinforce the message coming out of financial markets and channel investments in ways that might be compatible with the comparative advantages of the economy.

Third, there is the exchange rate issue. New Zealand opted for a clean float. It hoped to isolate completely the domestic monetary base from external influences. Chile and Argentina resorted to direct central bank presence in setting exchange rates, while trying to be more or less responsive to market pressures. But they maintained that presence and, for that reason, retained the direct linkage from foreign exchange flows into the domestic monetary base. Basically, they were utilizing, in the Chilean case anyway, the monetary approach to the balance of payments and seeking equilibrium through adjustments in interest rates, domestic activity, and the rest.

In Chile, as Rolf explains it, when the outflows came, pressures on interest rates and on key sectors of the domestic economy became impossible to ignore. And that is when the issues of having to sustain key industries or banks became intense. As these industries and the government came under increasing pressure, other problems were exacerbated. Paramount among these was the problem of how to finance these industries while minimizing the corresponding risk of generating quite rapid and potentially inflationary monetary growth.

From this, a twofold question emerges: How do we measure the relative merits of the two approaches to setting the exchange rate, and what lessons do we take out of the experience in Latin America?

A fourth and related point touches on the possibility of operating effective exchange controls to limit capital inflows. It is my contention, at least in New Zealand, that capital controls are no longer a feasible option. The costs of administering and compliance are too high. It is hard to establish reasonable risk management mechanisms in the foreign exchange markets to allow exporters or importers to control foreign exchange risk in the face of effective exchange controls.

The technological advances of funds transfer have really run way beyond any form of exchange control mechanism that I am familiar with at this stage. It is very easy to evade controls. So, what are the implications of the new communications technology that we see in funds transfer and foreign exchange markets? And what are the implications of that for controlling capital flows?

The fifth point is about the sequencing of reforms, a point that has been kicked around in the literature a good deal. Rolf, in his chapter, at some point refers in quite approving terms, as I read it, to the Chicago Boys in Chile who freed interest rates and international capital movements "at the right time," that is, after trade and internal financial systems had been freed. My conclusion with respect to New Zealand is that the sequence of reforms was pretty much irrelevant. Speed and comprehensiveness were more important than the exact sequencing. The government took opportunities as they presented themselves and moved very quickly on the financial sector liberalization, because it was easier to do, because we were better prepared for it, and because if they tried to wait until they had, for instance, the labor market reforms under control, they might have waited three or four years and the whole momentum, the whole mandate for change, would have been lost by then.

The other factor that I think is quite important is that liberalization in the financial sector provided pressure on goods markets to reform. I do not think we would have the attitudinal shifts now appearing in labor markets and in goods markets had we not subjected the macroeconomy to the pressures that an effective monetary policy and other external or broader protection reforms have generated.

Sixth is the issue of deposit insurance and prudential supervision. Both Argentina and Chile found themselves with enormously expensive problems when called upon to restore solvency to the financial system. Chile at least has vowed not to intervene on a number of occasions, but has been forced to do so. New Zealand has vowed not to intervene by bailing out failing financial institutions. Indeed, it has an established history of allowing financial institutions to fail, although we have never had the whole system under threat at any one point.

Supporting a banking system can be expensive. I come back to the point that Professor White raised before: if you are going to get into the process of supporting a failing set of institutions or a failing system, one needs to be very careful about how that support is funded. You must get those costs up on the table and make sure that they are funded in a noninflationary, appropriate fashion. It is a very practical problem of how to fund these issues and rehabilitate the banking systems without getting into another inflationary bind.

Let me address one final point that I think is quite important but that does not seem to have been prominent elsewhere. When we think about financial sector liberalization and the implementation of broader adjustment programs, do we need to pay any attention to the issue of central bank independence? So many of these countries have substantial inflation problems, which we seem to agree is essentially a monetary phenomenon. We may have disagreements on the extent to which it is essentially monetary, but we seem to be coming out at about that point. If the government has control over the central bank, the central bank will be unable to put a brake on its own financing of fiscal deficits and other government expenses. Then it is hard to control inflation. Is there an issue here that we ought to be thinking about in relation to developing countries? How do you structure their central banks in such a way that they have the capacity to provide a degree of restraint on government's expenditure proclivities?

Discussion

Mr. Walters: I have just one minor point that is important in this case because it is repeated elsewhere. I think the real problem in Chile was the indexing of wages on the prices of goods that people consumed rather than on the price of goods that they produced. When the price of copper dropped, the wage rate in terms of the product price went up steeply. There was an increase in real product wages. That was the real crunch.

We have done the same thing time and time again in Britain. The index should be based on what is produced, not on what is consumed. Otherwise, you will be entrapped by changes in the terms of trade. Wouldn't you agree?

Mr. Lüders: Oh, yes. I agree 100 percent.

Mr. Hanke: I am curious about this sequencing issue. *The Economist* magazine has been on New Zealand's case, as you know, Murray, indicating that the country should not have liberalized the financial markets first, saying that is bound to create a disaster eventually.

Would you both like to comment on the sequencing issue? To

what extent is it an issue in the context of financial and capital market liberalization?

MR. SHERWIN: I usually agree with *The Economist*. That is one example where I do not. It and a number of others have argued that New Zealand's appreciating real exchange rate is a direct result of our getting the sequencing wrong and that this is going to cause us major problems further down the track. As I have said, I think that the sequencing in New Zealand resulted from the circumstances we were in. We would have lost the opportunity to make the most of the changes that have been made had we tried to do it the other way.

Trying to reform labor markets, for instance, is a hellishly difficult process, particularly when, as a good British colony, you have inherited British trade union rules and British trade unionists and their habits. We have had a very difficult labor market situation. But for the first time in modern history, we are now getting some flexibility introduced into work practices, in the demarcation disputes, and in all those traditional areas that have caused problems.

We are getting reductions in manning. We are getting work practices that reflect the availability of new technology. I would not estimate how quickly that is moving, but we are getting attitudinal shifts. What is a little bothersome about all of this is that it has come at the same time as sharply rising unemployment. It would be nice to think that we could have generated some of those changes without having to go through the pain. But I suspect it is pretty hard to avoid that.

So the conclusion I think we are coming to is that you take the chances as they present themselves, and you do it quickly to limit the difficulties that may arise from liberalizing the financial sector before the goods markets. Having those financial sector liberalizations in place, being able to run an effective monetary policy and make all the changes that enable you to get the fiscal situation under control is extremely helpful in generating desirable attitudinal shifts elsewhere in goods markets.

MR. WALTERS: Can I interject something here that is not strictly relevant to this? When Mrs. Thatcher became prime minister, Fritz

Hayek went to see her. He is one of the really great men in the social sciences.

She asked Fritz Hayek what advice he had for her. This was in 1980, I think. He said, you must abolish the trade unions. [Laughter] She said she could not do that. And he declared that in that case she was finished. And, of course, she did not eliminate unions. And she was not finished. But it is interesting that the trade union reform in England has been, by any measure, an enormous success.

Mr. McKinnon: I would like to address the sequencing or order of liberalization issue again because I think it is very important for New Zealand and Chile. Should you, as Lawrence White and Mr. Sherwin suggest, do it as best you can, when you can, in any market? Or should you plan to liberalize some markets first, and then save other markets for last on the grounds that there will be problems unless you get the order right?

I think everyone agrees that you can improve the government's budget position anytime. The sooner the better. Getting rid of fiscal deficits is best done first in the liberalization process. Then very quickly move on to domestic finance, which it is possible to liberalize once the budget is under control. And in the real trade sector, the flow of imports and exports can be liberalized in parallel with domestic finance.

But what is really a wide-open question is that of exchange controls and foreign capital inflows. As New Zealand did, should you liberalize the capital account immediately because it is easy enough to do? Or should you be cautious about exchange controls on the capital account and leave it to the last as far as liberalization is concerned?

Let me give you some reasons why I think liberalizing international capital flows should be left to last. When an economy is very unsuccessful for a long period of time, as, say, Korea was between 1954 and 1964 and Chile was under Allende and then New Zealand as you have just described, that country becomes very unpopular in international capital markets. Nobody wants to lend it a nickel; and so to generate capital the country may be forced to run a net trade surplus, except for official aid or grants.

Then in comes a new broom. Suddenly, the economy that was quite moribund improves its prospects for growth. To support that new sentiment, there are liberalizations in fiscal policy, and in domestic finance, and in foreign trade. Future growth looks attractive. An economy that had been a pariah to the international bankers all of a sudden looks very attractive to them.

Bankers are much like lemmings. They are always looking at what the others do. For example, none of them would lend to Chile under Allende. If one of them decides it is a bad bet, they will all decide it. Then, after Allende, once the Chilean reforms look as if they are taking hold and will be successful, international bankers all change their minds together. They decide that Chile is a great place in which to invest, they do not want to be left out, everyone wants a piece of the action.

So the portfolio preferences of international bankers toward individual countries change rapidly. There could be an avalanche of financial capital into a newly liberalizing economy as happened in Korea in 1966–1967 and in Chile in the late 1970s. This then makes it very difficult for the real economy to adjust.

As Rolf mentioned, the capital inflow will lead to sharp appreciation of the real exchange rate. There is just no way you can avoid it. If you stay on a fixed nominal exchange rate, there will be internal inflation because of the forced increase in the domestic money supply. And if you are on a floating rate, the rate will just float up. Thus efforts to rehabilitate your export industries are likely to fail; indeed, the real appreciation is like hitting them over the head with a hammer. Having to absorb the financial capital in real terms means you have to run a big trade deficit. So governments naturally are very reluctant to allow a sharp appreciation of their currencies to occur.

Then, when the debts have to be paid back, all this has to be turned around. With real depreciation, you have to switch resources back into the tradable goods sector rather than nontradable. It is really a wrenching adjustment. And it seems to me it has happened in one economy after another.

Discussion

I think there is a case for being quite restrictive on the use of foreign capital during the liberalization process. I have actually given this talk at the World Bank a couple of times, suggesting that they should not try to buy liberalization in poor countries by saying if you liberalize and get rid of tariffs and quotas, we will give you so much money.

If such an agreement occurs, and the country does remove its trade restrictions and a big injection of foreign capital follows, there will be an appreciation of its real exchange rate and a big trade deficit. Indeed, that is the only way the foreign capital can be absorbed in real terms. And the competitiveness of the industries that were just liberalized will be undermined. Just this transfer problem itself becomes overwhelming.

There is nothing wrong with long-term inflows of foreign capital that are absorbed smoothly over a long period of time and are properly financed with long-term bond issues. But an avalanche of short-term capital at the time you are trying to liberalize, just because your economy has become very popular in the international capital markets, is something you really have to guard against. And that is why I think controls on capital flows should probably be removed last in the proper sequencing of liberalizations.

Mr. Lüders: The proper order of liberalization is an issue that comes out most clearly if one analyzes the Chilean and Argentine experiences. The negative effects of "excessive" capital flows, of course, depend on how much the economy was distorted to start with. If you have an economy that is not too distorted, you can probably liberalize international capital flows and it is not going to make such a big difference.

The case of Argentina, especially, clearly suggests that if you have a highly distorted economy, it is a big mistake to open up the capital account before you altered to the trade account. That's an important lesson. What about political opportunities? This is a typical cost-benefit problem. If the price system is not too distorted, and you have the political opportunity to do it, maybe it is advisable to liberalize capital flows before engaging in trade liberalization. This might have been the case in New Zealand. However, if you have very distorted prices, even if you have the political opportunity to liberalize international capital flows, on the basis of Argentina's experience you might be well advised not to do so. You might risk the whole liberalization experiment.

MR. SHERWIN: Just a very quick point. You better make damn sure that you know how to manage exchange controls and that you can do it effectively and in a nondiscriminatory fashion.

MR. BROCK: I want to add a point concerning the use of capital controls during the course of a liberalization. Both Professor McKinnon and Professor Lüders have argued that such controls may be desirable, at least at the early stages of the liberalization. Because this advice runs counter to the notion that liberalizing countries have a comparative advantage in growth and therefore should borrow internationally, I would like to explain why "market forces" alone should not determine how much is borrowed.

Once again, the concept of pecuniary externalities when there are incomplete markets for risk proves useful in understanding the nature of the possible problems. Professor Harberger of the University of Chicago has argued that one such pecuniary externality results from the fact that borrowing countries face upward-sloping supply curves of foreign funds because lenders to the country cannot entirely diversify away country risk (that is, there are incomplete markets for risk). Market forces will cause the country to borrow more than is socially optimal, because no borrower will take into account the consequences of his actions on the rate of interest charged to all other borrowers. In the presence of this externality, Professor Harberger argues that developing countries should tax capital inflows to limit them to the socially optimal level.

A second example is related to the government's provision of insurance to the banking system (because of the fundamental pecuniary externality of bank runs). As I noted in my earlier remarks, provision of insurance introduces the problem of moral hazard into the action of banks. Banks are encouraged to hold too little bank capital and to engage in overly risky loans as a result of government insurance of the banking system. Governments that provide explicit or implicit insurance to the banking system must be concerned about the borrowing behavior of banks, especially during the course of an economic liberalization, when the structure of the economy is in flux. Failure by the government to regulate the international borrowing of domestic banks can result in overly risky investment during the liberalization, with the possibility that the state may be forced to bail out a number of large banks whose gambles do not pay off.

One solution to this problem of pecuniary externalities is to allow the domestic banking system to be taken over by foreign banks, so that the domestic branches of these foreign banks can operate without the need for government insurance. Such a relinquishing of control over the financial sector may be politically difficult in many countries, however. But, in the absence of such a diversification of risk by a country, restrictions on capital inflows during a liberalization must be taken seriously. Professor McKinnon argues that only after a long period of time should the domestic financial market be fully integrated with world capital markets. Such a line of reasoning appears, superficially, to be illiberal. However, unregulated "market forces" working in the presence of pecuniary externalities of the sort I have described can produce much mischief. Professor McKinnon's argument to retain capital controls during a liberalization seems to me to be well founded, as does his advice to relax capital controls only as financial deepening (and increased capacity for risk bearing) takes place in the economy.

Ms. SAGARI: I am puzzled with the case of Chile in the following sense. Normally when we find problems in the financial sectors of different countries, we usually have easy explanations for these problems: lack of sound macroeconomic policy, inadequate regulatory framework, inadequate tax regime. But when you look at Chile, a successful economy with many top-notch policymakers from Chicago, you discover that firms are not resorting to the securities markets. They are not issuing bonds or equity. Managers have some concerns over loss of control, but they are not issuing preferred shares or convertible bonds or any of the other instruments. And there are only fifteen firms that are considered safe by the government for the investment of pension funds.

Banks are not interested in lending for the long term. There is no lending for more than five years in Chile. The banks say they do not have long-term sources of funds, and we ask them why they do not issue long-term instruments. They answer that nobody would buy them or that they are not interested. So the issue of long-term financing remains. Maybe we are asking for too much too soon.

But then what do we do? Do we continue to finance investment with rollovers of short-term instruments? I would like to know how Rolf Lüders sees it. What are your views?

MR. LÜDERS: Your question is extremely complex, but I think that the basic reasons that the equity market did not develop before is related to the high interest rates prevailing in the 1975 to 1982 period.

During that period, interest rates were of the order of 60, 50, and 30 percent per year. I think these levels are generally unheard of anywhere in the world. A book exists that describes the existing interest rates a long time before Jesus Christ. I don't know if you've seen it. It's a very interesting book, and provides a history of interest rates. In this book, it is difficult to find periods in which interest rates exceed 10 percent in real terms (that is, after correcting for inflation). There are a few periods, of course, where you have rates that exceed 10 percent, but not rates of 30, 50, or 60 percent per year, year after year. It's something incredible. With those rates, there's no way in which you can expect, I think, any other market but the short-term financial market to develop because it is so profitable to invest in a bank that offers you 20 or 30 percent real interest per year.

No business can give you that kind of real rate of return. So no business is going to try to finance its assets through equity that, under the circumstance, would have demanded a return of over 20, perhaps even 30, percent. There's no way in which you can develop a long-term capital market with interest rates as high as those prevailing in Chile during the late 1970s. That's why I stress the idea that, in the process of liberalization, one has to be very careful with what happens to the real rate of interest. If real rates of interest go up to those kinds of levels, you are likely to run into problems of adverse selection and moral hazard, and so on and so forth.

Ms. SAGARI: That was in 1982?

MR. LÜDERS: Yes. One also has to explain why the long-term capital market didn't develop after 1982, when the government did care about the level of real interest rates. Interest rates are still free in Chile, but today macroeconomic conditions have been managed in such a way that real interest rates are only slightly above international levels plus risk premia. The order of the real lending rate is now about 9 percent per year.

That is, for a country like ours, a reasonable interest rate. Nevertheless, the securities markets have not developed very fast. But if you have an economy that is not using its full capacity, there is less need for big investments. Only in the last two or three years has the need for new investments risen in Chile, and the available indexes show a very rapid development of the securities market since 1986. (I point this out in the chapter.) It's fantastic! Trading in the securities market now exceeds the levels of the 1980–1981 boom. This is quite incredible.

The presently reasonable interest rate levels of the financial market in Chile are allowing the very fast development of the securities market. I am quite hopeful that within the next five years or so we will see a big improvement in that market.

MR. CALLISON: I want to return to the concern you expressed earlier about opening the floodgates to external sources of capital during a period of liberalization because of the effects capital flows will have on the domestic money supply and/or the exchange rate.

I think I understand this concern in the context of Chile, but am not so sure that the case can be generalized to many other countries in Latin America. I am more aware of cases in Africa, where the economy is very depressed, where investment has not occurred because it does not make sense, where the exchange rate is highly overvalued and has been for a long time, where you have high tariff protection policies, and where you have pent-up demand for imports. In a situation like this, if you have liberalization, there is a lot of political fear that the exchange rate is going to jump very fast very far. If at the same time you have tariff reductions, that in itself would argue for further devaluation of the exchange rate.

In that situation, the typical World Bank and Agency for International Development (A.I.D.) response is to pump money into the economy in support of the liberalization program. So the same effect is achieved by the influx of foreign assistance as you mention with capital flows. It would tend to appreciate the exchange rate more than would otherwise be the case. In other words, it slows down the depreciation, which is seen as a good.

Foreign assistance also helps to provide the foreign exchange for pent-up demand for imports, many of which are essential inputs for domestic industrial processes that have been operating at maybe 20 or 30 percent of capacity. There is a premium on getting these inputs, on providing access to foreign exchange for existing industries so that the economy can start to work again, and on stimulating investment and increasing production needed to get the economy through a usually difficult transition period.

People are going to be thrown out of work. There are a lot of industries that are no longer going to be viable. You are trying to stimulate investment in industries that are going to be viable and that takes time. In a case of comprehensive liberalization, there is a very serious need for a substantial influx of capital, and not just short-term but for several years. So in other words, all of our arguments on the African side are for private capital, as well as development assistance, to slow down the process, help them get through the transition period more rapidly, and provide funds for the investments that are needed to make that transition successful.

MR. MCKINNON: I would like to address the big A.I.D. dilemma. In certain kinds of liberalization programs, there is a case for a big injection of capital at the time liberalization occurs. I have to admit that. But that is typically a second-best situation in which the government does not have control over the public finances. Then, to have a stabilization program that eliminates domestic inflation and

Discussion

the inflation tax, the government has to be given another source of finance because it is not raising sufficient internal tax revenue.

In effect, A.I.D. or some other agency has to come in with budgetary support for the government in order to bring the domestic price level under control. Although the economy overall is helped by stabilizing the price level, the large trade deficit resulting does put pressure on the newly liberalized tradable goods industries. They must operate with a higher real exchange rate than would otherwise be the case. But, if the alternative is explosive inflation because of an uncovered government budget deficit, that kind of program can be justified.

Ideally, though, we want the government's fiscal stance to be corrected, its budget to be balanced, thus making unnecessary a large temporary injection of foreign capital. Then you can have a bootstrap-type of liberalization by doing it yourself. A.I.D. and the World Bank could still give very good technical advice, but they could now avoid injecting a big dollop of capital. Perhaps a line of credit for foreign exchange could be established to be drawn on only if a calamity occurred. The line of credit would be there just to maintain the credibility of the liberalization, to support the current exchange rate and the current price level. But the authorities would seek to avoid the actual injection of capital itself.

After World War II, the Marshall Plan was very successful in unblocking inconvertibility in intra-European payments. There was a line of credit that the Americans gave to European governments that enabled them to stabilize their financial systems and engage in foreign trade. But that line of credit was not drawn on to any great extent. To establish the credibility of a stabilization program in third world countries, similar devices could be used.

MR. SPOSATO: I think there is an additional point to be made here. Reference only to the exchange rate—especially in Africa, with which I am most familiar—is somewhat misleading because, if the exchange rate falls too far, you are also raising the cost of intermediate goods and, if the capital inflows are limited, you are raising the cost of obtaining capital.

So you also raise the price of your final good. I come down on the side of Stu Callison in the case of Africa. I think there are very clear reasons—even to lower the price of final goods—that capital flow is necessary. Evidently it is an empirical question, but I think it has to be looked at in many different aspects.

Mr. McKinnon: As long as it is an official agency, and does not intend to get paid back.

Mr. Walters: When Mrs. Gandhi of India went to see Margaret Thatcher, she complained that she had not known that when people borrowed money from international agencies they did not plan to pay it back. She said if she had realized that she would have borrowed much more.

[Laughter]

Ms. Craig: I think it is important to understand the role of the exchange rate. What kind of signal is the exchange rate over time to what's going on? If the capital flow is not A.I.D. money, is not World Bank money, but is a net inflow of private monies into Chile, that's some sign that Chile has future goods to supply to the rest of the world. The world is expecting future goods, not current goods from Chile. Well, what does the exchange rate do? It should reinforce that pattern of consumption and production within Chile. The counterpart to that capital inflow should be a trade deficit.

Europe was expected after World War II to have a trade deficit, not a trade surplus. Future goods were expected, not current goods. So I'm not so sure that the appreciation of exchange rates implies that the rates are moving in the wrong direction. There may be some difficulties for companies that were exporting, but isn't domestic consumption going to pick up some of these goods?

Mr. McKinnon: Remember that, if there is a huge transfer, you need real appreciation to begin with to absorb the capital. Then when you pay it back, you have got to have a real depreciation. This heightens the financial risk and uncertainty that Phil Brock was talking about. Can the economy, can everyone in it see through that pattern? Most people half my age will be experiencing the liberalization for the first time. Can they really see through the real exchange-rate pattern into the future and make all the correct investment decisions on the basis of these large fluctuations? You have to ask yourself that question.

MR. LÜDERS: I would like to emphasize something I said before in that connection. At least the experience in Chile and Argentina has been that if you suddenly and significantly increase the foreign capital flows, the effect on the exchange rate and on purchasing-power possibilities makes people feel so much richer that they are initially willing to consume a high proportion of it. Then they start to care about investing. The signals are wrongly read, and that's very important. That's why I emphasize so much the amounts, because I do not think that net foreign capital flows of between 1 percent and 3 percent of GNP do much damage. But flows of the order of between 10 percent and 15 percent of GNP make a big difference.

MR. MCKINNON: I am going to do something unfair. At the end of Chapter 11, in a book written in 1971 [p. 169], before the inflow of capital into LDCs, I found the following quotation. It is from my own book.

[Laughter]

> During liberalization, however, the case for restricting the use of foreign short-term capital—particularly supplier credits for imports—may be quite strong as a supplement to exchange-rate policy. At the very least, the LDCs can dismantle official regulatory devices set up for the express purpose of encouraging the use of foreign short-term finance. . . .
>
> Reform-minded governments may want to go further however. A really widespread liberalization in foreign trade (including consumer goods) and finance, associated with a large discrete devaluation, and a sharp rise in rates of interest, can make temporary administrative restraint over short-term capital flows a virtual necessity. Besides rejecting stabilization loans and other extraordinary government-to-government aid, the authorities may restrict the purchase of domestic financial assets by foreigners and sharply limit the trade credit that importers are permitted to accept.

MR. WHITE: Maybe I should register my doubts about the case for capital controls. In the discussion we have heard good reasons to expect an appreciation in the exchange rate and to expect high interest rates. Yet I am puzzled by any economist—and this applies generally—who claims to have a model of exchange rates that can identify situations in which the market exchange rate is currently too high (that is, above its equilibrium level) or in which the market interest rate is too high.

Ron McKinnon asked whether private agents in the economy can see through what is happening and not be misled, but it seems to me that we have to ask the same question about those who would try administratively to set the right volume of capital flows and right interest rates and right exchange rates. I do not see what reason we have to believe that government officials are going to move us closer to the equilibrium values than are private agents whose results emerge from transactions in the marketplace.

The other thing that puzzles me is that if you really could identify cases in which the exchange rate is temporarily high and is going to come down in the future, you could make an awful lot of money. You would be out trading in the market, not advising governments.

Mr. Sherwin: I would not have a lot to add to that. The main point of going, for instance, to a floating exchange rate, at least in New Zealand's case, was that the government decided it would rather have market participants betting against one another than betting against the government.

We have had questions about the inadequacy of long-term financial flows into Latin America, even though interest rates are 30 percent real or whatever. Well, there are consumers of credit at that price and there are others who are suppliers. These are consenting adults entering into contracts. If people are worried about the inadequacy of capital flows and the burden of high interest rates, it seems to me that we should look behind those problems and find out what is generating them. It is better to look at what is causing the problems rather than trying to shoot the messenger.

Mr. Lüders: I agree that it is very difficult to say when an interest rate is too high, or the exchange rate is too low, or whatever it is. Nonetheless, it appears that, in certain circumstances, governments are able and willing to intervene in financial markets. If that is taken into account, then moral hazard, adverse selection, and other related problems are introduced. It is true that people make a lot of money if they can identify government-caused distortion; in the case of Chile, some made a lot of money by speculating against the peso!

During 1981–1982, hundreds of millions of dollars "flew" from the country before a stable exchange-rate policy was adopted, and some of those people who speculated are probably now very, very rich. The same thing is true when you mention consenting adults depositing money at high interest rates and/or getting loans at even higher rates. Those receiving loans at those rates were in general unable to service the loans as agreed. Finally the taxpayers had to come up with the difference. I think this is a political fact. Somebody already mentioned that it is very difficult to find any country in the world today that does not intervene in the financial markets once a problem becomes widespread. If this is true, then policies have to adapt to that fact. This is the whole point.

If it were possible to have a financial system in which the government never intervenes, and in which everyone knows the government never will intervene, then I would be more inclined to accept the conclusions just expressed by Larry White and Murray Sherwin. With such different premises, conclusions *should* change. With *those* premises, everything would be subject to free, competitive markets. I am inclined to agree that people would learn to adjust to the problems that would come up in such environments.

But this is not the way the world works. As soon as you have a widespread financial problem, the government intervenes. People sense that and bet on it. For example, in Argentina they purchased U.S. $30 billion in foreign assets. They bought most of those dollars probably when they were very cheap. Somebody must have lost.

Mr. Kalotra: I always have a problem when I am dealing with such qualified people who look at global issues. Much of my experience is in the trenches. From that vantage point, I see two major reasons among others that have been given for liberalization. One is that we all believe that liberalization in itself is a very good idea. The second is that, as in Chile, the view is that if you liberalize, increased confidence in the economy is likely to attract more foreign capital.

Let us look at the United States itself, the most liberal country in the world. Its deficit indicates that whether you have liberalization or not, what you do with capital is very important. And to my mind, with all the liberalization in the United States, in the next ten to twenty years we will find that a large part of the U.S. capital will be owned by foreigners. I think that has its own implications, irrespective of the fact that the country has more money at this stage than it otherwise would. But much more important is what is done with the money.

In these discussions we seem to consider the financial sector as if it is separate from the total national economic process. Regarding privatization in Africa, we talked about selling off companies to the private sector even though the total equity capital of the privatized companies is going to be much more than the total funding in the capital markets of those countries. The point I am leading to is that liberalization and sequencing must relate to the availability and use of financial capital.

How liberalized is the country in terms of the dissemination of technology? Acquiring the equipment and technology is not the crucial matter. It is using it for competitive advantages that is important. My submission to you is that liberalization of one sector in isolation from other sectors can be harmful. New technology can have a significant impact on the labor market. And efficient use of the technology will depend on the availability of essential support services. To promote a healthy economy, this interdependence of sectors must be recognized. While the United States may be able to finance consumption with deficits for a time, the developing countries, especially in Africa, will not be able to do so.

So, the view from the trenches is that we have to look at a lot of things in suggesting liberalization policies to these countries. I have said this before—and have not made myself very popular—but if the economic history of the post–World War II period is written, perhaps among the agencies that will receive major criticism will be the World Banks and the A.I.D.s of this world. If you look around the world, the white elephants of the public sector and of several technologies that have not been used have come out of money for development. Liberalization and aid is not very helpful unless and until you have the capability to use aid effectively and competitively, to have trade surpluses, and to feed your people. You cannot approach individual sectors in isolation.

MR. REILLY: I am supposed to talk about the trenches this afternoon so I would like to respond. Over and over today I find myself wondering whether I understand what other people are saying. My experience is vastly different from that of other people here in the sense that I am invited as an adviser to a government that may already have decided to do something about its capital market; at least it tells me it has.

Today, I hear repeated discussion as if developing nations can create capital markets. But when you go out to identify where capital might be used, you will find business people telling you that they cannot even get a permit to open a shop, that they cannot change prices even though the cost of goods is going up and their profit is going down.

I think the purpose of the trenches discussion, which may be frustrating to all of us, is to see whether we can put together this economic theory with what actually happens at the nuts-and-bolts stage. We are not going to do the proper thing if we do not blend theory with the nuts and bolts.

You will see many countries in which the capital market plumbing is all there. All the nuts and bolts are there. If you go to Pakistan, for example, you will discover that Ayub Khan went to Wall Street in the late 1960s and said, "I want it all!" So they gave him a stock exchange. They gave him a monopolies law. But none of it works.

Though I have no empirical evidence nor theoretical argument for it, my proposition is that if a government wishes to develop its capital market it cannot think of that as a panacea. It must understand that it has to encourage the private sector to make investments. Therefore, when you find a country that has done everything right—the Chilean example—and you ask why the economy is not growing more rapidly, you must remember there are a number of other steps to take at the micro level. Can a businessman really make an investment in expanding his product? Can he get the permit? Is the law adequate?

In Chile for example, they wrote a new law in 1981 to replace a company law that is more than one hundred years old. These are the kinds of specific, very micro steps that do not appear in the macro concepts that we are talking about here.

Rolf J. Lüders

Response

Murray Sherwin was saying that among the important issues of economic liberalizations are the sequencing of their various components and the speed with which they are implemented. There's a famous story about two Germans that really reflects the Chilean attitude toward these problems.

These two Germans are called Otto and Fritz. Well, Otto is a German who lives in Chile and, being a German, he wants to go back every year to Germany. One year he bought a cat and, not knowing what to do with the cat during the trip, he went to his friend Fritz and asked him to take care of the cat.

Otto was in Germany, in Munich, drinking beer, when he got a telex saying, "Your cat died. Come back immediately to the funeral." Otto went back and buried the cat. Then he went to his friend and said, "Fritz, you don't deliver bad news in that way. What you have to do is say first, cat is on the roof of the house. Then you say, cat fell off the roof. Next you say, cat is sick. And finally you say, cat has died. So you do it slowly."

Well, the next year Otto again went to Germany and while there, he received a telex saying, "Otto, your grandmother is on the roof of the house. . . ."

Murray stressed the similarities and differences between the the liberalization experiences of Chile and New Zealand. However, I have the impression that conditions in New Zealand in the early 1980s were very different from the conditions in Chile (and Argentina) in the middle 1970s when their liberalization programs were begun.

Both Argentina and Chile in the mid-1970s had just come out from two populist governments, Allende in Chile and Perón in Argentina. Both Perón and Allende left these countries with 500 to 600 percent rates of inflation, huge government deficits, and economies almost completely closed to international trade and finance. In Chile, practically all kinds of business, including small farms and medium-sized industries, were nationalized. I think these were very different conditions from the ones prevailing in New Zealand in the early 1980s. It might be very appropriate to go fast in a liberalization program if conditions are relatively undistorted, as they might have been in New Zealand, but it's very difficult to do so if conditions are the way they were in Chile and Argentina.

Another word before going to the issues. I think it is true that Argentina and Chile have a similar history and in many respects similar economic conditions. Both of them liberalized their economies during the second half of the 1970s, after decades of interventionist policies. However, when they both went into deep financial and economic crisis during the early 1980s, they reacted very differently.

In Chile, GNP dropped by 14 percent during a single year of its crisis, and unemployment eventually rose to extremely high rates, almost 30 percent of the labor force. In Argentina, the recession was also very deep. However, Chile maintained its efforts to liberalize trade and its financial system, while Argentina went back to an interventionist and protectionist system. Therefore, I think it is quite interesting to compare Argentina with Chile because their economic policies over the entire 1970–1987 period allow us to study two subperiods of similar policies (1970 to the mid-1970s and the mid-1970s to early 1980s) and one period of quite different policies (early 1980s to 1987 and possibly to today).

In both Argentina (from 1975–1976 to 1981) and Chile (between 1973 and 1987) financial liberalization was accompanied by a very substantial financial deepening. In that sense, the hypothesis of the McKinnon book was confirmed. For Chile, the ratio of M2 to GNP rose from somewhere around 10 percent in the early 1970s to somewhere around 30 percent in 1987. That is a very big change. In Argentina, financial deepening was also very noticeable during the liberalization period. However, if you take the total period of analysis—beginning with financial repression in 1970 and ending with the same in 1987—then the ratio of M4 to GNP (Argentina's M4 is the nearest equivalent of Chile's M2) decreased from 25 percent to 15 percent. It's impressive how true it is that financial repression, by way of fixing internal interest rates below those of the international market, which are corrected for risk, depresses deposit and credit levels.

Though not emphasized in my chapter, it also is striking how Chile's financial liberalization produced financial widening. That the same effect is not evident in Argentina may be attributed to its return to financial repression during the early 1980s.

Chile now has a whole array of financial institutions offering numerous alternatives by which people can invest their savings and a wide variety of short- and long-term credits with different types of guarantees. That financial widening should accompany financial liberalization is an expectation of Ron McKinnon's book; that it does is illustrated by Chile's recent history.

In this connection, I want to go back to the interest rate problem. Although a diverse array of credit and deposit types is now offered in the Chilean financial market, this did not happen during the late 1970s when the system was already liberalized. Today the interest rate level is reasonable; real interest rates were excessively high in the late 1970s. These excessively high interest rates concentrated the whole financial sector on short-term operations.

Another striking phenomenon brought out by the study of the Chilean and Argentine cases is the effect of financial liberalization on concentration in the financial sector. If one measures concentration by the Gini Index, Lindahl Index, or any similar measure, by 1987 concentration in Chile's financial business had diminished to but a fraction of what it had been in 1970. Argentina's banking system became less concentrated only during its liberalization phase, but reverted with renewed intervention. Today, the banking system in Argentina is as concentrated as it was in 1970. Many who oppose financial liberalization say that it produces concentration. The evidence here supports the opposite, with the largest banks' share of the financial business becoming smaller, rather than larger, with financial liberalization.

McKinnon also stressed in his book the importance of the share of total savings that goes through the financial system. Ron also suggested that we can assume that, if savings go through the financial system, they are going to be more efficiently allocated. Someone from A.I.D. pointed out, correctly, that this will be true as long as the rest of the markets are rightly in place. This is why McKinnon also emphasizes a set of policies that have to accompany financial liberalization, to make sure it will positively contribute to economic growth.

In this sense, financial deepening is a necessary, but not sufficient, condition for economic efficiency. Its necessity is illustrated by what we have observed in Chile and Argentina. The more liberalized system, which is more competitive, allows greater reductions in the costs of intermediation, reflected in the spreads between rates of interest on deposits and loans. In Chile these spreads are now down almost to the level of those in the United Sates, which is very surprising. The U.S. spreads are about 2 percent per year; those of Argentina are about 8 percent. The magnitude of the difference reflects how inefficient the intermediation system can get if it's not open to competitors.

Those are some of the lessons obtained from the study of the Argentine and Chilean financial liberalizations. Now I want to go back to some of the questions Murray posed that are really macroeconomic rather than financial system issues. First, should a financial liberalization be accompanied by liberalization in other markets? For me, the answer is obviously positive, if for no other reason than to assure an undistorted allocation of resources. I think that the experiences of Argentina and Chile bear this out. Chile liberalized practically all markets beginning in late 1973. In contrast, Argentina liberalized only between 1975 and 1981, and that brief period of liberalization was additionally confined to internal financial markets and external capital flows. Argentina liberalized little in either the international trade sector or labor market. This produced distortions, described in the chapter, that eventually contributed to the economic crisis of 1981–1982 and to the reversal of the liberalization process.

In Chile, the exchange rate was fixed (in 1979), but as Murray pointed out, this is not incompatible with economic liberalization in that this sort of monetary approach to the balance of payments means that the quantity of money moves freely according to the demand for it rather than being subject to attempts to control it by government authority. However, the combination of this fixed exchange rate with government intervention in the labor market (specifically by its indexing of wages to the Consumer Price Index [CPI]) provided a textbook illustration of how the liberalization of one market, but not others, is a recipe for disaster—in this case the economic crisis of 1982–1983. What happened was the following.

When the petrodollar recycling took place and Chile was, in the eyes of foreign investors, a very attractive place to invest, the country received huge capital inflows. These depressed the real exchange rate well below the fixed nominal exchange rate, and the "excessive" money balances brought about by the capital inflows generated an increase in the prices of nontradable goods and services. Then, when the financial crisis of the late 1970s and early 1980s occurred, foreign capital flows began to dry up, and there was some speculation against the peso. According to the monetary approach to the balance of payments, these problems should have been corrected (in the absence of government intervention) by a reduction of wage rates and costs, making Chilean exports more competitive. But the government *had* intervened in the labor market, having indexed wages to the CPI.

It was therefore very difficult, if not impossible, for the system to adjust. So I think that the policies based on the monetary approach to the balance of payments did not succeed in Chile mainly because of a labor market that was insufficiently free and certainly less free than it should have been, given the country's financial and trade policies. In Chile the interventionist labor market policies aggravated the recession, in all likelihood contributing to the deepness of the financial crisis rather than ameliorating it.

6
Murray Sherwin

Capital Market Liberalization: The New Zealand Experience

In July 1984, a Labor government was elected to office in New Zealand in the midst of an undignified flight of foreign exchange. From its first day in office, the incoming government signalled an intention to pursue a path of macro- and microeconomic policy reforms as rigorous as any seen, certainly within the Organization for Economic Cooperation and Development (OECD) group, in the postwar era. The reforms cover a wide field including the implementation of stringent fiscal and monetary policies, sweeping rationalization and reductions in import protection, the removal or substantial reduction of incentives for production or export, a fundamental overhaul of the system of taxation, new approaches to labor relations, a revamping of the machinery of government encompassing more flexible approaches to the management of government departments, "corporatization" of many government enterprises, some privatization, changes designed to introduce competition and remove competitive biases in markets generally, and a critical review of a broad range of government interventions in the economy.

This chapter describes the liberalization of the New Zealand financial markets that took place through this period, the philosophy underlying these changes, and the impact of changes to the extent that can be assessed so far. It also discusses issues such as the speed and sequencing of reforms that have had considerable currency in the literature in recent years.

Background

Although there were short-term economic problems facing the new government in 1984 that required immediate action, the more serious difficulty to be overcome was a general malaise that had long afflicted the New Zealand economy. Since 1960, per capita gross domestic product (GDP) had been growing at only 1.4 percent, by far the lowest of any OECD country. As a result, New Zealand's per capita GDP had fallen from seventh in the OECD in 1960 to eighteenth by 1984. Over the same period, New Zealand's inflation rate had averaged 8.5 percent, compared with an OECD average of 6.3 percent.

In the decade to 1984, New Zealand had experienced virtually no economic growth, current account deficits had averaged 5.3 percent of GDP, and inflation had averaged 13.5 percent. External public debt had grown from 10.7 percent of GDP in March 1975 to 36.7 percent of GDP in March 1984. Unemployment had grown from near zero to around 5 percent of the labor force.

Certainly, a sharp drop in the country's terms of trade since the mid-1970s had contributed to the lethargic economic performance. But it was also clear that the terms of trade were unlikely to recover quickly to historical norms and that the economy was not accommodating to that reality in any acceptable way.

Increasing political frustration with persistent low growth, intractable inflation, and an escalating debt burden manifested itself in two main ways. First, from 1979, the Conservative national government of Sir Robert Muldoon embarked on a series of "think big" investment projects: expansion of the Marsden Point oil refinery; expansion of the New Zealand Steel mill; construction of a factory to convert natural gas into synthetic petrol, ammonia urea fertilizer, and methanol; extensive reticulation of natural gas; and others. In total, investment in these projects amounted to N.Z. $6.4 billion (in 1983–1984 dollars), or approximately 18.4 percent of 1983–1984 GDP. Although they were large and created substantial employment, especially during the construction phase, most of these projects were of dubious economic value.

Second, from 1982, there was increasing resort to direct government interventions in pursuing the objectives of lower inflation, improved export competitiveness, and improved balance in the external accounts. The result was, by 1984, a comprehensive freeze on prices, wages, dividends, rents, interest rates (both deposit and lending rates), credit growth of most financial institutions, and the exchange rate. This freeze was instituted in the face of a fiscal deficit that reached almost 9 percent of GDP in 1983–1984. By that year, government expenditure had reached 41.5 percent of GDP, up from around 27 percent twenty years earlier.

The price freeze was effective in reducing the measured consumer price index (CPI) to around 3.5 percent over the year to March 1984, but the policy mix was clearly unstable. In order to deflect opposition to the freeze and to suppress the emergence of direct price pressures, substantial income tax cuts were announced in the budget of August 1982. There was also increasing resort to direct subsidies to support the competitiveness of agricultural and manufacturing exports. Notwithstanding enhanced direct export support, excess demand pressures were emerging in the form of a rapidly worsening current account deficit.

Financial Market Liberalization: 1984–1988

This section describes the principal decisions in the program of financial market liberalization. They are addressed in chronological order.

Interest rate decontrol. Clearly, the events surrounding the election of the Labor government in July 1984, including the foreign exchange crisis, were a major influence on the joint decisions of July 18 to devalue the exchange rate by 20 percent and to remove virtually all interest rate controls. But the behavior of financial markets during the years before 1984 provided persuasive evidence that such liberalization was desirable in any event. Increasingly pervasive interest rate controls in the years leading up to 1984 had produced all of the textbook effects: financial sector disintermediation, distorted credit allocation, higher costs of intermediation, deteriorating quality of service to consumers, and deteriorating quality of financial sector balance sheets. Moreover, the focus on reducing interest rate levels had complicated immeasurably the task of funding the government's fiscal deficit and implementing an effective monetary policy. Various devices such as inflation-adjusted savings bonds and increased compulsory holdings of government bonds by financial institutions provided some scope to counteract excessive money supply growth. But the major weight of monetary control fell by default to the current account deficit and resulting official external borrowing.

Institutionally, stringent interest rate controls spurred the growth of relatively inefficient finance companies and other fringe financial institutions at the expense of the core banking entities. There seems little doubt that this hurt the price and quality of financial intermediation and the robustness (in a prudential sense) of the core of the financial system.

More broadly, it was evident that credit allocation was also being rendered suboptimal. On the one hand the interests of the nation's net savers were being significantly impaired by the often negative real interest rate structure; on the other, pressure to provide larger volumes of relatively cheap credit to sectors such as agriculture and housing was readily capitalized into higher prices of farm land and housing, thus diminishing the benefits intended.

The early decision to remove most interest rate controls drew its immediate rationale from the foreign currency crisis the incoming government faced in 1984. Denied any scope to vary interest rates in the period leading up to the election, the capacity of the Reserve Bank of New Zealand (RBNZ) to moderate currency flight over that period was severely constrained. But the broader consequences were also clearly evident by that time. Given the new government's determination to implement a rapid and comprehensive adjustment program, including a rigorous monetary policy regime, there was little interest in retaining direct government involvement in the setting of interest rates.

The removal of exchange controls. For some fifty years, New Zealand had maintained exchange controls of various forms. Over that period, a number of attempts had been made to relax or remove them, but invariably, chronic balance of payments weakness had spurred successive governments to fall back on the controls. By the late 1970s, however, the controls were becoming increasingly ineffective, largely reflecting the changing technology of funds transfer and the increasing globalization of the New Zealand business community and its funds management techniques.

The structure of New Zealand's exchange controls had focused on outward capital movements initiated by New Zealand residents. Direct inward foreign investment had long been welcomed as an important means of relieving pressure on official external borrowing. Furthermore, in order to encourage inward investment, it was accepted that foreign investors must have guarantees of ready remittance of their funds. The controls reflected that assessment. Current transactions were also relatively unconstrained but subject to surveillance for the purposes of authentication.

This structure necessarily involved the screening of all transactions in order to distinguish capital from current transactions, to verify that export proceeds were being fully repatriated, and to verify that current remittances were indeed justified by the relevant imports of goods and services. Necessarily, such a regime was expensive in terms of direct administrative costs borne by the public sector and in terms of compliance costs met by the private sector.

Considerable efforts had been made to minimize those costs by delegating authority to the commercial banks handling the transactions, but there were severe limitations to that form of delegation, even in the comparatively compliant environment that New Zealand provides.

While the New Zealand system hinged on distinguishing between capital and current transactions, it was impossible to operate exchange controls in any partial fashion. The authentication requirement demanded universal scrutiny of transactions, thus limiting the scope for economies of administration. Moreover, the distinction between capital and current had become increasingly irrelevant. As corporate funds management techniques become more sophisticated, current transactions assume essentially the same behavioral characteristics as capital transactions—responding to interest rate differentials and exchange rate expectations in the same way as capital. This is even more the case when trading firms operate in a variety of different markets and are both exporters and importers. Earlier New Zealand businesses were characteristically either exporters or importers but not both. In those circumstances it was relatively easy to relate flows of goods and flows of funds for control purposes. That is no longer the case.

The clearest evidence of those changes was the pre-election foreign currency flight of 1984. It occurred in spite of the vigorous application of the existing exchange control regime. Subsequent evaluations could find no evidence of illegal capital flight and the entire problem seems to have been one of relatively straightforward leads and lags on current transactions.

Given that experience, the conclusion facing the new government was quite clearly that the exchange control regime was expensive but ineffective. The government's options were either to try to make it work by tightening considerably the degree of scrutiny of transactions and removing much of the flexibility that had been granted to companies in the interests of efficiency and effective management of their foreign currency flows and risks, or simply to remove the controls altogether and rely on a broader macropolicy mix to maintain external equilibrium.

Three key considerations directed the government to the latter option:

- a general philosophical bent toward market solutions
- the evidence that the existing regime was ineffective when under pressure
- a wish to move to a more market-determined exchange rate regime and the consequent desire to encourage greater exchange rate risk-management capacity within the private sector; a wish that was incompatible with the maintenance of exchange controls

The decision to remove exchange controls was announced immediately before the long Christmas–New Year break in 1984. It passed with no detectable impact on foreign exchange flows.

The exchange rate float. New Zealand's exchange rate regime had gone through many changes over the years—from a fix against sterling, to a fix against the U.S. dollar, to a fix against a trade-weighted basket, and then to a crawling peg against the basket that resulted in the New Zealand dollar's being adjusted at frequent intervals by small amounts calculated to offset inflation rate differentials.

Over the period since the 1973–1974 escalation of oil prices, in particular, the New Zealand currency had been subjected to a series of minor crises often provoked by changes in the exchange rates of important trading partners and generally resulting in discrete devaluations of the New Zealand dollar. As the inflation differential between New Zealand and its trading partners widened in the 1980s, these crises became more frequent and disruptive. They also became more costly to the New Zealand taxpayers, with the mechanism generating much of that cost being forward exchange risk cover provided by the government through the RBNZ.

Getting rid of the forward exchange risk was a high priority of the RBNZ through the early 1980s and efforts to do so highlighted many of the difficulties facing New Zealand policymakers at the time. Attempts by the RBNZ to price itself out of the forward market inevitably put pressure on the exchange rate, exchange controls, and interest rate controls.

The administered exchange rate regime had also posed numerous difficulties when attempts were made to determine what an "appropriate" exchange rate might be at any time and to maintain the rate at the appropriate level through changing circumstances so as to minimize risk to the government.

With these concerns in mind, there was a clear early preference on the part of the government (shared by its policy advisers) toward the view that a freely floating exchange rate represented the best solution. This was strengthened by the nature of the structural reforms taking place in New Zealand, together with the extreme volatility evident in the exchange rates of New Zealand's various trading partners. New Zealand's trade is spread relatively evenly among the United States, Australia, Japan, and the United Kingdom (about 20 percent each). The currencies of that group have moved in quite divergent fashion in recent years, adding to the difficulties of fixing any rate for the New Zealand dollar administratively.

The major concern confronting the government related to issues of potential volatility. Was the New Zealand dollar market sufficiently well developed, deep, and robust? Could it produce an exchange rate stable enough to meet its resource allocation role efficiently without official intervention? The counterfactual, of course, was whether the RBNZ could expect to produce a better outcome through direct interventions in the foreign exchange market. In addressing that question, it was assumed that the various sources of disturbance that might produce exchange rate volatility would exist regardless of the exchange rate regime New Zealand chose to adopt. There was no option that permitted those pressures to be avoided. Rather, the issue was one of which market could most efficiently bear those pressures.

In the event, the government opted for a completely clean float, preferring to obtain independence of monetary policy ahead of any particular target (with respect to level or rate of change) for the exchange rate. Also important were the government's desire to avoid further official external borrowing and concern to avoid the risk inherent in foreign exchange market interventions. Given that decision, its major effort before announcing the float in March 1985 was to strengthen the local foreign exchange market in readiness. Accordingly, decisions were taken to remove exchange controls, encourage greater capitalization of foreign exchange dealers, and to allow 100 percent foreign ownership of foreign exchange dealers.

The abolition of ratio requirements. Financial intermediaries in New Zealand faced a variety of balance sheet restrictions including, and most important, requirements to purchase government securities. These ratio requirements varied substantially among different institutional groups and had been imposed over the years for a variety of reasons: to provide cheap funding for central government, to moderate the interest rate consequences of monetary control, to encourage credit allocation to particular sectors, and, ostensibly at least, to improve the prudential integrity of financial institutions.

There is little dispute that ratios failed to meet most of those objectives—the major exception being the provision of cheap credit to the government (even that came at the cost of financial sector disintermediation). Moreover, the ratio requirements probably did more to undermine the prudential integrity of financial institutions than any other single government intervention did. The effect was to impose holdings of relatively illiquid assets on the balance sheets of the financial sector, to encourage excessive exposure in certain sectors (especially agriculture), and to impinge on the profitability of the financial sector. Given the new government's willingness to pay full market rates on its debt and its concerns for transparency, efficiency, and competitive neutrality, ratios were seen to be redundant or even harmful in the new climate and were abolished completely in February 1985.

The new monetary management framework. The scrapping of ratio controls and lending-growth guidelines was part of a move toward a more efficient framework for monetary management. The new approach to monetary policy relies on influencing excess demand for liquidity in the financial system and hence, in the first instance, short-term interest rates. All the funding costs of financial intermediaries are liable to be affected by sustained pressure on short-term interest rates. Funding costs are, in turn, likely to affect the interest rates at which loans can be made and hence the ability of institutions to expand credit. This approach to monetary control is likely to be effective because it cannot be undermined by disintermediation and efficient because incentive effects are neutral: there is nothing within the monetary policy framework that gives an unfair advantage to a particular group of financial intermediaries.

The RBNZ's ability to influence the excess demand for liquidity stems from the bank's position as monopoly supplier of settlement assets in New Zealand. The RBNZ, as the government's banker, specifies that all payments to government be settled in *settlement cash* and this underpins the banks' demand for cash deposits of the central bank. By influencing the supply relative to the demand for these assets, the RBNZ is able to affect short-term interest rates and, ultimately, money and credit growth. In addition to the banks' settlement cash deposits at the RBNZ, the operational reserves base definition, known as primary liquidity (PL), includes government securities on issue that can be discounted for settlement cash on demand at the RBNZ. At present, discountable securities are government securities with thirty days or less to maturity.[1]

The operation of monetary policy in the new institutional environment has involved targeting zero trend growth from year to year in the supply of PL and making discretionary adjustments to various monetary policy instruments to try to ensure a consistent degree of downward pressure on nominal demand and inflation. Zero trend growth in PL has been targeted through a policy of fully funding net public sector injections to primary liquidity through sales of medium- and long-term public debt. Following the exchange rate float in March 1985, public sector injections became the only possible source of growth in PL, and consequently, the full-funding policy was able to guarantee a stable trend level of PL from one year to the next. Open-market operations and short-term Treasury bill sales are also conducted with the aim of smoothing short-term variations in liquidity conditions. The uneven flow of government expenditure and taxation revenues through the year generates wide seasonal variations in the demand for PL. Consequently, to avoid unnecessary short-term interest rate pressures, the within-year liquidity management operations deliberately allow significant seasonal movements in the supply of PL.

From 1985 through 1988 it has become clear that a stable quantitative relationship between PL and nominal GDP or inflation is unlikely to emerge during such a period of rapid structural change and disinflationary pressure. For this reason, the policy of zero trend growth in PL has been supplemented by discretionary adjustments to the base level of PL and other monetary policy instruments. A passive medium-term approach to monetary policy with unchanged instrument settings would no doubt ultimately achieve the objective of a stable general level of prices; however, the transition path could potentially turn out to be either so lax or so restrictive as to undermine the policy's overall credibility.

The main supplementary policy instruments available for discretionary adjustment are the discount margin (the margin above market interest rates at which government securities falling within the PL definition are discounted for cash at the reserve bank), the daily target for bankers' cash at the reserve bank, and the average level of PL targeted over the month ahead. If it is desired to tighten monetary conditions using these instruments, the discount margin can be raised, and/or the daily cash target can be reduced, and/or the average level of PL for the month ahead can be lowered. Any combination of these has the effect of reducing the excess supply of liquidity in the banking system, thus putting upward pressure on short-term interest rates. Open-market operations are used to give effect to any changes in the daily cash and monthly average PL targets.

The need for a discretionary monetary policy implies that a number of monetary indicators must be monitored so as to enable judgments to be made about whether or not monetary conditions are consistently firm. The main indicators monitored are movements in the level and shape of the interest rate yield curve (an inverted rate structure is indicative of tight liquidity combined with reduced inflation expectations), movements in nominal and real exchange rates, and growth in the money and credit aggregates. Movements in these indicators are assessed against a background of other relevant economic information in order to determine the extent to which movements in the monetary indicators reflect factors other than changes in underlying liquidity conditions.

New banks. The core of the New Zealand commercial banking system consisted of four trading banks: one wholly state-owned (the Bank of New Zealand), the other three wholly or partly foreign-owned (Westpac, a branch of Westpac Australia; ANZ, a subsidiary of ANZ Australia with minority local shareholding; and National Bank of New Zealand, a wholly owned subsidiary of Lloyd's Bank PLC). Each was established by its own act of Parliament. Legislation in New Zealand protected the use of the term *bank*, reserving it for the four trading banks, the Post Office Savings Bank, and the community-owned—but state-guaranteed—Trustee Savings Banks.

In addition to these banks, there existed a wide range of other financial institutions: savings banks, merchant banks, finance companies, building societies, and credit unions, along with such finance sector parastatals as the Development Finance Corporation, Rural Bank, and Housing Corporation. Insurance companies and the finance arms of retailers were active in the various forms of financial intermediation, and professional groups such as lawyers had also acquired quite substantial roles in certain forms of financial intermediation. Interest rate regulations and government security ratio requirements provided highly uneven competitive environments for these different institutional groups, and legislation in some cases limited the range of services that could be provided or client groups that could be served.

With an eye to leveling the playing field, removing the rents that existed in some forms of legal status, and, above all, improving the range of services available to consumers while reducing their cost, the decision was taken to open access to the banking sector. This involved the introduction of a relatively straightforward set of qualitative licensing criteria under which institutions of substance, good reputation, and appropriate experience may seek to be accorded the status of *registered bank*. There is a minimum capital requirement (N.Z. $30 million; paid up to $15 million), but no restriction on the total number of institutions that may gain this status. Nor is there any particular constraint on the nature of the banking business in which they may participate, that is, there is no obligation to provide retail services, branch networks, or foreign exchange services. Access to the central clearing system is a matter for negotiation and agreement between potential newcomers and existing members of the clearing system. Wholly foreign-owned entities may establish registered banks either as locally capitalized subsidiaries or as full branches of the foreign parent.

The proximate objectives of these changes include:

- the establishment of a more competitive and competitively neutral financial sector
- the removal of regulatory incentives to establish particular forms of financial intermediaries
- the reduction of rents associated with attainment of any particular form of status conferred by regulation
- ease of entry to and exit from the financial arena in the interest of enhanced competitiveness

The regulatory changes that permitted the easier acquisition of bank status were seen to carry a requirement for enhanced official attention to prudential supervision. The framework within which this was introduced is discussed below.

Prudential supervision. Prudential supervision has never assumed a particularly high profile in New Zealand, in large part because of the predominant state or foreign ownership of the major financial sector assets. The decision to broaden entry into the banking sector coincided with increased international efforts to coordinate and integrate banking supervision networks. Accordingly, the amendments to the RBNZ Act that permitted the establishment of new banks also gave the RBNZ, for the first time, explicit responsibilities and powers of prudential supervision.

The debate preceding this development centered on the extent to which there is a useful role for central agencies in prudential supervision, the moral hazard issues entailed in undertaking supervision of any group of financial institutions, the financial hazards that could ensue, and above all, the objectives of supervision.

From that debate emerged the government's clear wish to be explicit in rejecting any notion of deposit insurance and any presumption that the failure of particular financial institutions should necessarily be prevented. Also rejected was the notion that supervised financial intermediaries should conform to a prespecified, uniform set of balance sheet ratios.

Instead, emphasis was placed on the disclosure of relevant balance sheet information and the seeking of explanations and justifications where exposures or other risk measures depart significantly from industry norms. Where information provided suggests that an institution is at risk of failing, the RBNZ has powers to assist in facilitating its orderly exit from the market. The objective of supervision is to protect the financial system, not individual participants within that system. The costs of mismanagement should fall on shareholders, managers, and depositors, but not on the state or other financial institutions.

The Consequences of Change

Major reforms of the New Zealand economy were initiated in 1984, but the process is far from complete today. Moreover, even in the New Zealand environment, where the usual lags between recognition of a problem and the analysis, decision, and implementation of new policies have been unusually compressed, four years is rather too brief a period to allow reliable evaluation of the success or

Capital Market Liberalization: The New Zealand Experience

otherwise of the new policy mix. Even casual assessments of progress are confounded by both the magnitude of individual policy shifts and of the number of fronts on which substantive change is occurring simultaneously. A volatile international environment has further complicated the analysis.

With that in mind the following sections offer descriptions of the immediate effects of the principal reforms and the consequences so far as it is possible to evaluate them.

Exchange controls, capital flows, and the exchange rate. As indicated earlier, the decision to remove exchange controls of itself had little direct impact on the nature of New Zealand's foreign currency flows, beyond lowering transaction costs. For the first time in fifty years it became possible for New Zealanders to remit funds from New Zealand to finance foreign investment, but tightened domestic monetary conditions and the associated increase in domestic interest rates left little incentive for large scale capital remittance. Instead, the tendency has been for sharply increased inward private capital flows, either in the form of foreign currency borrowing by New Zealanders or inward portfolio investment by foreigners. These inflows had always been possible under the previous exchange controls. It was the new domestic policy setting that now made them attractive.

With the exchange rate floating from March 1985, the task of funding any current account deficit fell entirely on the private sector. Far from proving difficult, as many had feared before the float, persistent upward pressure on the exchange rate has indicated no lack of willingness on the part of foreigners to assume N.Z. dollar–denominated assets in a variety of forms. Nor has there been any undue willingness on the part of local residents to bear the currency risk implicit in foreign currency borrowing.

The behavior of the exchange rate under the float has been somewhat erratic, but probably not unreasonably so given both the extreme volatility of major currencies through this period and enormous structural changes taking place domestically. Indeed, it is difficult to imagine how New Zealand could have managed its exchange rate effectively through a cycle that has seen the currencies of its major trading partners (Australia, the United States, Japan, and the United Kingdom) fluctuate through enormous ranges against one another. The number of authorized foreign exchange dealers grew from the four trading banks in 1983 to seventeen by 1987 and, during that time, turnover in the local foreign exchange market grew from around N.Z. $10 billion per month to a peak of around N.Z. $370 billion. Of that at least 30 percent is purely third-currency trading (that is, no N.Z. dollar component is involved). At that level of activity, the market is generally capable of absorbing quite considerable shocks without exhibiting undue volatility. It is, however, still subject to occasional sharp shocks, especially those involving downward adjustments of the currency. Table 6.1 indicates the degree of volatility experienced by the N.Z. dollar since April 1985 against the currencies of major trading partners. Clearly, it is rather more volatile than are its larger counterparts. What is less clear is the impact this may have had on trade volumes and welfare levels more generally. Research conducted by the RBNZ has pointed to some impact, albeit small, on trade with Australia. This trade involves mostly manufactured goods rather than the agricultural products that still dominate New Zealand's exports. There is some reason to believe that trade in manufactured goods might be more sensitive to short-term exchange rate uncertainties than is agricultural trade, for which adjustment lags are typically larger and alternatives to exporting quite limited.

If the exchange rate has been uncomfortably volatile, but ultimately tolerable, the trend in the absolute level of the exchange rate has generally provided more discomfort, at times bordering on intolerable. The trade-weighted index (TWI) of the N.Z. dollar has moved between 53.6 and 73.4, with an average of about 62.8 (1979 = 100 in the RBNZ nominal exchange rate index). That, however, masks the much greater movements in bilateral exchange rates shown in Table 6.2.

The sharp appreciation against the Australian and U.S. dollars

Table 6.1
Exchange Rate Volatility

Currency	Daily movement	Monthly movement
New Zealand dollar	1.04	3.96
Yen	0.76	3.21
Australian dollar	0.86	2.94
Sterling	0.89	2.51
Deutsche mark	0.88	2.58

Notes: The exchange rate is measured against the U.S. dollar. Volatility is measured by standard deviations of first difference in logs of daily (monthly average) exchange rates, multiplied by 100.
Source: Author's calculations.

coupled with the unfavorable inflation rate performance in New Zealand over the period have clearly affected severely the competitiveness in those two markets. This is made more significant (at least in terms of direct employment consequences) because these are New Zealand's major markets for manufactured goods. Overall, New Zealand exporters are now back to a less competitive position than they were in before the July 1984 devaluation.

Analysis of the sort provided above quickly leads to two ques-

Table 6.2
Exchange Rate Movements of the N.Z. Dollar (percentages)

	Changes through March 31, 1988, from:	
Currency	March 1985 (prefloat)	July 1984 (predevaluation)
U.S. dollar	48.1	6.8
Sterling	−15.0	−25.6
Yen	−28.7	−45.0
Australian dollar	42.4	19.6
Deutsche mark	−26.4	−37.8
Trade-weighted index (TWI)	4.6	−16.4
Real TWI[a]	29.1	10.6

[a]Changes to December 1987.
Source: Author's calculations.

tions: is the current level of the real exchange rate sustainable and, if not, what should be done about it?

Factors relevant to judgments on the question of sustainability include:

- Was the starting point appropriate? There were some who felt the 20 percent devaluation of July 1984 was greater than could be justified on competitive grounds.
- Is the current account position sustainable? The deficit has shrunk from 8.4 percent of GDP in 1984–1985 to 3.8 percent in 1986–1987.
- Is the capital account position sustainable? Official external debt ratios are now beginning to diminish, partly from the proceeds of asset sales and partly from a modest program of repayments funded directly from the foreign exchange market. Private indebtedness continues to grow. Very substantial holdings of New Zealand debt are now traded in international markets and there has been no sign of unwillingness on the part of foreign investors to acquire more risk. Judgments on how far that can proceed are notoriously difficult, and investor sentiment can be subject to abrupt, unpredictable changes.
- Have there been productivity gains to offset exchange rate pressures? Undoubtedly, there have been important productivity gains in both the public and private sectors in New Zealand. However, it is stretching credibility to suggest that these alone would compensate for a loss of exchange rate competitiveness of the scale that has occurred.

Beyond these factors, one can point to improvements in the terms of trade, portfolio adjustments in the wake of the financial sector deregulations, and the fact that, on a bilateral basis, competitiveness has improved sharply in some major markets.

None of these factors, singly or together, provides a strong basis for arguing that the exchange rate has been moving toward some sustainable longer-term equilibrium level. Perhaps it is unreasonable to expect that it could given the circumstances of the past four years. But it is difficult to put aside completely the conventional argument that different speeds of adjustment in asset and goods markets may be giving rise to exchange rate overshooting.

In the face of this, the New Zealand authorities have refrained from any direct intervention in the foreign exchange market and have maintained their firm approach to monetary policy. Given the persistence of inflationary pressures, at least until quite recently, and the surprising strength of domestic demand through much of this adjustment phase, the government's target has been to reduce inflation to low single digit levels. It is not clear that an alternative approach, which must inevitably have involved a more relaxed approach to monetary policy, could have substantially modified pressure on the tradable goods sector. Direct controls on capital flows have been judged unworkable, and progress in liberalizing goods markets has probably been proceeding about as rapidly as is physically possible. Undoubtedly that progress has been aided considerably by the competitive pressures imposed via the monetary policy and exchange rate policy mix.

Monetary policy and inflation. With the float of the exchange rate in March 1985, the RBNZ gained, for the first time, direct control of the reserve base of the financial system. The monetary policy regime exerts pressure on credit expansion via traditional quantity and price rationing, and domestic demand is influenced by the general level of interest rates flowing from the RBNZ's control of financial system reserves. Given this scope for effective monetary control, the possibility of achieving the desired degree of price stability has undoubtedly been greatly enhanced. Despite the clearer objectives and availability of strengthened instruments, the day-to-day management of monetary policy has been far from mechanical. The task of interpreting developments and developing appropriate responses has been no less complex than before.

The intention of monetary policy has been to apply consistently firm pressure to monetary conditions with the aim of reducing the underlying rate of monetary expansion and hence, eventually, the rate of price inflation. The results to date have been slow to emerge and difficult to evaluate. With respect to the main monetary indicators—in particular money and credit growth, interest rates, and the exchange rate—the relationships between the instruments of policy, the indicators themselves, and the ultimate inflation objective have undergone significant structural changes that have made it very difficult to determine the degree of monetary policy pressures being applied at any time.

The observed rates of growth in money and credit have been substantially affected by a number of factors that have tended to exaggerate the rates of growth in M3 and private-sector credit (PSC), for example. A major influence has been the process of financial sector reintermediation following the removal of quantitative and interest rate restrictions. Also contributing have been increased scope for households and corporations to increase their gearing in the wake of financial deregulation and the wealth effects of a boom in property and equity values. As a result of these factors, M3 and PSC growth reached annual rates of 29 percent and 34 percent respectively during 1985–1986 before commencing a downward trend from mid-1986.

With respect to inflation, the period through June 1985 was heavily influenced by the aftermath of the previous government's wage and price freeze. Attempts to restore appropriate relationships among wages and prices, including in particular various government charges (such as electricity and postal services), and the effects of the 20 percent devaluation of July 1, 1984, combined to push the annual rate of inflation to 16.6 percent by June 1985. Also, firm control over monetary policy was not achieved until after the exchange rate float in March 1985. Before that, capital inflows associated with higher domestic interest rates had tended to undermine attempts to restrict money and credit expansion.

The second confounding influence on the downward path of consumer price inflation, the 10 percent value-added tax introduced in October 1986, was a major obstacle to the disinflation effort through 1986–1987. The tax provided a direct inflationary impulse of around 7 percent and also stimulated pretax expenditure that sustained consumer demand in the face of declining real incomes.

Although progress in reducing New Zealand's inflation has been slower than expected, a comparison with international experience gives some reason for comfort. Even in the major industrial countries, adjustment periods between three to five years were typically required to reduce inflation to below 5 percent. Also, inflationary expectations were more deeply embedded in New Zealand—the result of a decade and a half of persistent double digit inflation.

Results are now forthcoming. For the year to March 1988, the CPI was 9.0 percent, and a figure close to 5 percent is forecast for the year to March 1989. [Actual results: 4 percent—Editor]

Financial sector structure and efficiency. The structure of New Zealand's financial markets began to change under the previous government with the decision in 1983 to widen access to the foreign exchange market. That attracted a number of additional participants, most notably a number of foreign banks that were able to establish small subsidiaries in New Zealand to operate as merchant bankers or finance companies.

With the passage of major amendments to the RBNZ Act in 1987, a number of those who established a presence earlier have taken the opportunity to attain full banking status under the Act. Also, institutions previously operating as building societies and various forms of savings and loan institutions have also become full banks, in some cases in partnership with foreign banks. New Zealand now has fourteen registered banks, rather than the previous four trading banks, but no newcomers have been attracted purely on the basis of the 1987 legislation. Some of the earlier arrivals may, however, have been anticipating the 1987 changes.

What has changed is the array of services provided by the financial sector. The rapid rate of innovation and growth in global financial markets, combined with the major changes occurring in the domestic economy, has caused an overall increase in the demand for financial intermediation and risk management services. The evidence of efficiency gains is largely circumstantial but persuasive. There has been a major reorganization of ownership and management structures and a far more aggressive approach to the marketing of financial services. Also, evidence of reintermediation indicates that the higher margins (between 8 and 10 percent) that have traditionally applied in fringe financial institutions are being competed away.

As with most of the liberalizations discussed in this chapter, it is rather too soon to make firm judgments on the full extent of gains (or losses) deriving from these changes. The first registrations under the new banking legislation occurred mid-1987. A good deal of change has still to occur in this area yet, but the first indications appear positive.

The Sequencing and Speed of Liberalization

Most commentators on the issue of the optimal sequencing of economic reforms begin their analysis with an acknowledgment of the ambiguous nature of the theoretical arguments in this field. Nevertheless, there appears to be a pronounced balance of opinion that the liberalization of international capital flows should await substantial progress in goods markets. Underlying that opinion is a concern about exchange rate overshooting arising from the ability of financial asset markets to adjust more rapidly than can goods markets. In addition, the inevitable emergence of high real interest rates in the early phases of an adjustment program, coupled with the removal of restrictions on foreign borrowing, will put upward pressure on the exchange rate at a time when an important aim of the adjustment program is to redirect resources into an efficient, competitive tradables sector. Recent experience in New Zealand appears to confirm that line of argument. The exchange rates have appreciated sharply and there has been considerable pressure on the profitability of the tradables sector. Investment in tradables has not been strong.

Capital Market Liberalization: The New Zealand Experience   231

Despite that, the experience does not provide clear evidence of an alternative and preferable sequence of reforms. The circumstances preceding the 1984 election gave good reason for prompt measures to regain stability in foreign exchange flows. Also, from the outset the suppression of inflation was seen as a crucial element in the overall economic strategy and could not be achieved without the capacity to implement an effective monetary policy. That in turn pointed to the need to float the exchange rate, which itself required the removal of exchange controls.

There seems to be little merit in arguments that the financial sector reforms should have awaited progress in goods markets. Indeed, progress in goods-market reforms appears to have been promoted in important respects by the government's early decisiveness in financial-market reforms. Substantial attitudinal shifts generated in that process have spilled over into other sectors. There can be little doubt that opportunities for real progress could have been lost had the government attempted to tackle, for example, the labor market first.

An important component of the overall reform program in New Zealand has been its comprehensiveness and the rapidity with which changes have been introduced. An agenda of financial sector reform had been under consideration within the RBNZ and Treasury Department well before the 1984 election. The implementing of those reforms was possible with little delay. By contrast, taxation reforms, labor-market reforms and protection reforms, by their nature are more difficult to bring together quickly. The credibility of the overall program required early evidence of the government's commitment to change in order to be sustained.

Even four years after the initiation of this process, major sectors of the economy have still to be addressed by the Labor government. Social policy (education, health, welfare), which in aggregate dominates government's expenditure patterns, is only now being subjected to the sorts of reviews that trade policy, labor markets, and the public sector have now seen. Even the taxation system, which has already undergone substantial reform, remains unfinished in important respects.

This unfinished business does not reflect any unwillingness on the part of the government to move on with its reforms. As much as any other factor, it reflects the physical constraints that inevitably intercede. Bureaucratic capacity to plan and implement change, parliamentary capacity to consider reforms fully, and the time required to consult with the electorate and sector interest groups all limit the speed with which changes can be implemented. Given the tyranny of a three-year election cycle, the Labor government was predisposed to move quickly with its reform program. The finance minister, Roger Douglas, also believes strongly that rapid implementation of change both makes change more likely and moderates the cost of adjustment. His belief has been supported by the behavior of key sector groups so far. For example, the acquiescence of farming groups in the removal of agricultural subsidies was conditional on more rapid progress on border protection reforms, while the move to a broad-based consumption tax gained public acceptance by way of the accompanying income tax reforms and tightly targeted welfare measures designed to protect those small groups that would otherwise have been disproportionately harmed.

Conclusions

The New Zealand capital market liberalizations have been comprehensive, rapid, and rigorous in adhering to a consistent market-oriented philosophical framework, but are just one component in a much broader macropolicy reform agenda. The program drew its initial impetus from the foreign currency flight immediately preceding the 1984 election. Those circumstances strengthened both the government's willingness to contemplate rapid and comprehensive reform and the public's willingness to accept such change. Subsequently, the maintenance of the momentum of change and attention to consistency and mutually reinforcing policy changes have been important in maintaining public support for the program.

The adjustment period has produced high nominal and real interest rates, rising but somewhat erratic real and nominal ex-

Capital Market Liberalization: The New Zealand Experience 233

change rates, increasing unemployment, flat or declining real household incomes in aggregate (but widening income distribution), rapid institutional change in the public and private sectors, and stubbornly high (but declining) inflation rates. Despite that, public support has, by and large, been maintained. The Labor government was re-elected in September 1987 for a second three-year term.

It is rather too soon to be drawing firm conclusions or lessons from the New Zealand experience. But a few points can be made.

(1) The comprehensive nature of the program has been important to its sustainability. For example, liberalization of the financial sector would have made little sense without the very stringent approach to fiscal policy. That, in turn, would not have been possible without major reductions in direct support to agriculture and manufactured exports. That, in turn, demanded reforms of border protection and, perhaps more important, taxation.

(2) The liberalization process, like the regulatory process that preceded it, feeds on itself. Just as regulations beget further regulations to close the inevitable loopholes and escape routes, the removal of regulations puts pressures on those remaining.

(3) The speed of adjustment and reform has been important in maintaining the constituency for change. Longer delays between the implementation or announcement of changes risks encouraging opposition and resistance to change.

(4) Consistency and resolve on the part of the government to pursue a reformist path have been vital to building credibility and support. The extent of change in New Zealand has been profound, and the analytical framework within which decisions are being taken has been well articulated. Interest groups find it harder to resist changes harmful to their direct interests if they know and accept the broader structure of the government's decision matrix. Indeed, the occasions when support for the government's reforms has been weakest are those on which the government itself has appeared to be divided or irresolute.

(5) The negative consequences of change have often been exaggerated before implementation.

(6) The sequencing of reforms, in terms of the theoretical model, may be less important than the physical and bureaucratic constraints or essentially practical concerns that invariably intrude. Making changes as opportunities present themselves may be more important then the precise order of decisions.

(7) A political-constitutional structure (unicameral parliament with only two major parties) that permits rapid decision making and limits the need for negotiating compromise positions on key policies has also been important to the government's capacity to pull together a reform package with tight internal consistency.

Compared with developing countries, New Zealand possesses many very important advantages that should increase its chances of bringing to fruition a successful reform program. Nevertheless, the adjustment process is proving painful. Politicians and the electorate are inevitably impatient for results, and there are strong temptations to change direction in the face of poor or negative initial responses to reforms. After four years, the positive responses in New Zealand are evident, but not yet overwhelming. The inflation rate is decreasing, the current account is improving, official external debt is being reduced, and substantial efficiency gains do seem to be forthcoming. Therefore, though the hardships of adjustment are also obvious, there is reason for optimism.

Appendix

Murray Sherwin's contribution, delivered in mid-1988 as a background perspective for his comment on Chapter 5, by Rolf Lüders, describes what became known as "Rogernomics," in recognition of Roger Douglas, who was appointed finance minister by New Zealand's newly elected Labor government in 1984. Within seven months of Mr. Sherwin's seminar presentation, Mr. Douglas was no longer finance minister. The principal reasons for his exit from that office are recounted in the first of the two *Wall Street Journal* articles that immediately follow. The second, by Mr. Douglas himself, presents "laws" of policymaking for enabling politically successful structural reform. (If these laws were read, understood, and *believed* by Mikhail Gorbachev, then it appears that other, perhaps more personal, objectives took precedence for him over politically successful structural reform.)

On October 27, 1990, New Zealand's other major political party won 68 of the single-chamber parliament's 97 seats. The new finance minister of the National party government appeared to be intent on completing the economic experiment launched by Mr. Douglas.

Previously, in 1990, a freely elected government had begun its term of office in Chile. If the new governments in New Zealand and Chile sustain and expand their extraordinary programs of economic liberalization, then continuing attention to the economic performance of the two countries should prove instructive to the rest of the world, not least to the countries of Eastern Europe.

Alternatively, if either New Zealand or Chile should abandon the path on which both embarked, while the other stays the course, then the citizens of each country might see in the other a future that might have been their own. In that event, the contrasting futures might be less vivid than that of the two Germanies, and more closely parallel to the Latin American contrast of Chile and Argentina.

New Zealand's Unfinished Economic Experiment

By TIM W. FERGUSON

CHRISTCHURCH, New Zealand—Roger Douglas may have fallen short of the brass ring in his bid to revolutionize this nation's economy, but this week he got a gold watch of sorts from the Mont Pelerin Society, an international group of free-market intellectuals meeting here.

The political-academic conference opened in the wake of Mr. Douglas's announced intention not to stand for re-election to Parliament next year. The introduction by the head of New Zealand's Business Roundtable compared the former finance minister to West Germany's Ludwig Erhard. Sure enough, Mr. Douglas in three years took New Zealand from its nadir of state interventionism in 1984 under an ostensibly conservative government and made it a laboratory of economic liberalization under the Labor Party.

In truth, Mr. Douglas's adieu is rather an anti-climax, coming two years after he suffered his Waterloo. It was the Southern Hemisphere summer of 1988 when the Douglas scheme for a 23% flat-rate income tax was shot down by then-Prime Minister David Lange. Mr. Lange couldn't in the end countenance the death of the progressive income tax, which Mr. Douglas had halved from a 66% peak, or the stripping of perverse welfare incentives, which the controversial minister had in mind as well. The PM eventually sacked him.

In the view of Colin James, a regional economic journalist, "Rogernomics as a style of setting big objectives and pursuing them in big jumps died" the day Mr. Douglas tried those last, bold steps. Mr. Douglas would stage a comeback to the cabinet this year in a lesser post and Mr.

Reprinted by permission of *The Wall Street Journal*, © 1989 Dow Jones & Co., Inc. All Rights Reserved Worldwide.

Lange would resign, but an incrementalist era of the "technical tidiers-up" had commenced. Rogernomics still provides plenty to chew on, however. "As a case study in reform," noted Bryce Wilkinson, an investment-house economist, "New Zealand offers excitement, tragedy and opportunity in Shakespearean proportions."

With the curtain beginning to fall on his two decades in politics, Mr. Douglas came in for praise at the Mont Pelerin meeting not only from the assembled outsiders, but from Ruth Richardson, a possible finance minister if her National Party is returned to power next year, as it is now favored to be. Mrs. Richardson's blessing of her rival ("who taught New Zealanders about markets and what they mean") is not really surprising given that both are "drys" within parties that are still dripping with corporatist or statist inclinations.

And, for all the bravado the Kiwi reformers still display, the country isn't exactly in their corner these days. Here, as in Thatcher's Britain, the microeconomic truths of a system of efficient, rational choice are hitting macroeconomic shoals.

The Douglas measures, which included an end to capital, wage and price controls, currency props, export subsidies, tariff protectionism and agricultural supports (in a country as farm-oriented as any in the world) nonetheless left unemployment at 7.5% and rising in a nation used to Japanlike levels; mounting social expenditures that have kept government growing as a fraction of the economy through the 1980s; and interest rates (nearly 13.9% on three-month Treasurys, vs. close to 7.6% in the U.S.) that are breeding bankruptcies (they nearly doubled from 1986 to 1988) and feeding anxiety among mortgage holders.

Mr. Douglas and a nonpartisan admirer, Reserve Bank Governor Donald Brash, protest that an anemic 1.5% economic growth rate masks sustained accomplishments, such as reducing the public deficit to nearly zero, beginning to pay down foreign debt that had reached Mexicolike dimensions (as a percentage of gross domestic product) under the previous National Party government, and cutting the inflation rate by more than half. Prices now are rising at better than a 7% clip, but earlier this year the rate was down to nearly 4%, and legislation in the works effectively would commit the authorities to 2% by 1992.

Tight money has been a source of both pride and anguish here. New Zealand didn't respond to the 1987 world-wide equity crash with a liquidity infusion, and share prices have hardly rebounded. The wealth loss has shaken big financial institutions, and investors are nervous. The downtown office construction one sees in the capital of Wellington and in the biggest city, Auckland, is a last gasp, and retail sales give hints of cascading.

A 10% consumption tax that Messrs. Douglas and Brash devised while cutting income-tax rates was bumped up to 12.5% this July as the government went looking for revenue to cover the spending growth. This added to a tax burden on Kiwi workers that already was the fourth-highest among the 23 nations of the OECD.

With compulsory unionism pervasive and arbitration requirements adding to workplace rigidity, the labor market is still sand in New Zealand's gears, just as it is in the U.K. Yet some change is evident.

"Redundancies" is part of the vocabulary here now. The government has let strikes run their course in order for a more competitive environment to emerge. And the dropoff in farming that accompanied the end of various supports also was felt at the middleman stage. Meat-processing employment, for example, fell nearly 20% between 1986 and 1988; workers in that line were paid 54% above the average wage in 1985, and only 19% above it in 1988.

Mr. Douglas says he set about free-market reforms not out of the Mont Pelerin Society's libertarian ideals—he has no philosophical objection to government doing anything that it does "efficiently"—but because he recognized, as too few social democrats have, that the state is in the business of bestowing privilege. He wanted to dismantle those artifacts of unfairness. It is thus ironic that Colin James, while a fan, believes that Mr. Douglas has left his countrymen so "shellshocked" that a populist candidate could ride the hard times to a renewal of South American-style policies next year.

But, in the meantime, Mr. Douglas holds one trump. His present cabinet post includes oversight of the nation's immigration policies. He is speaking softly about the issue—language and cultural worries are strong—but he may yet wield the stick that could draw an entrepreneurial burst out of the mulish New Zealand economy. This isolated land is one of the few places that, at least in the abstract, wants more people.

Best of all, Ruth Richardson is all for opening the country's doors. Why not a million more New Zealanders? she asks. If the nation's largest newspaper, which this week headlined a lead editorial "From Roger to Ruth," has it right, things again may be looking up down under.

The Wall Street Journal, December 1, 1989

The Politics of Successful Structural Reform

By Roger Douglas

Politicians almost universally believe that timely, appropriate and voluntary action to remedy structural economic imbalance should be avoided at all costs because it amounts to political suicide. Consequently, as studies by the Organization for Economic Cooperation and Development show, in eight out of 10 cases over the past decade, reform was left until the developing imbalance had collapsed the currency or caused some other costly economic or social disaster. This is the point at which the goverment that failed to take timely action is normally thrown out of office, and a new party is elected to carry out reforms that could (and should) have been undertaken years sooner.

The idea that governments can retain power by refusing to make necessary and valuable structural reforms is, in fact, nonsense. It inevitably leads to the downfall of those foolish enough to believe it. Rather, it is quality decisions, which strengthen the economy and improve the medium-term prospects of the voting public, that are the key to any party's hopes of re-election.

These conclusions are all supported by our experience in New Zealand, where wide-ranging structural economic reforms have been undertaken in the 5½ years since the present government won power in July 1984. Wherever quality medium-term policies have been implemented without compromise, opinion polls show that the government continues to enjoy the approval of the voting public. On the other hand, wherever our approach, for political reasons, stopped short of an uncompromising emphasis on quality, we are in trouble with the public now.

Implementing quality decisions also provides an important insight into the nature of political consensus. Most governments believe they must have consensus support for reforms before they are enacted, otherwise the actions they take will not be politically sustainable at election time. The inevitable result is compro-

---

Reprinted by permission of the author.

mised policies. Our experience in New Zealand shows consensus develops progressively, after the decisions are made and deliver satisfactory results to the public.

What then, beyond quality decisions, are the principles that form the basis of politically successful structural reform? The New Zealand experience has highlighted 10 fundamental laws of policy making that create the environment needed to support such reform:

1) *You need quality people for quality policies.* In New Zealand, this was evident politically in the caliber of new Labor Party candidates attracted in the 1978, 1981 and 1984 elections. Without politicians prepared to get their minds around complex issues and the guts to adopt policies that would achieve the results needed, the government's program of reform would have stalled. The quality of political candidates is a world-wide problem. Politics is a mess because too many people with education, vision and courage are content to criticize from the sidelines. As long as this continues, we will wait in vain for good government in democratic countries.

The importance of good people was evident also in our public-sector reform. Getting the structures and incentives right can transform the performance of many dynamic workers who were held back by the old system. But it was even more essential to replace the people who could not or would not adapt to the new environment. This applied in the private sector as well. Deregulation has forced a dramatic improvement in the quality of business and company management.

2) *Once you have defined your objectives clearly, implement reform in quantum leaps.* If you advance a step at a time, the interest groups will have time to mobilize and drag you down.

Packaging reforms into large bundles is not a gimmick but political efficiency. The economy operates as an organic whole, not an unrelated collection of bits and pieces. When reform is packaged in this way, the linkages in the system can be used to see that each action effectively enhances every other action. Large packages provide the flexibility to ensure that losses suffered by any one group are offset by gains for the same group in some other area. The public will accept short-term pain if the gains are spelled out and the costs and benefits are shared by the whole community.

3) *Speed is essential.* It is impossible to go too fast. The total program will take some years to implement even at maximum speed. The costs appear immediately while the tangible benefits take time to become visible. Move too slowly and the consensus that supports reform can collapse before the results are evident and while the government is only partway through its program. Apparent requests from interest groups to a slower pace often turns out, on closer analysis, to be resentment that government is not moving fast enough to abolish privileges still enjoyed by rival groups. Privileges impose costs on everyone else. It is uncertainty, not speed, that endangers structural reform programs.

4) *Once you build up momentum don't lose it until you have completed the total program.* Opponents find a rapidly moving target much harder to hit, and you will have plenty of opponents if you are removing privileges and protection. Staying in front allows the government to lead the public debate. Removing privileges even-handedly across the board reduces the grounds for interest groups' opposition and offers them a more constructive role in a better society.

5) *Consistency plus credibility equals economic confidence.* Maintaining credibility is essential to keep public confidence in structural reform and minimize the costs. The key to credibility is consistency of policy and communications. If the government lacks credibility, people refuse to change their behavior to fit new

policies and thus place avoidable costs on the economy. Speed, momentum, avoiding ad hoc decisions, and an unwavering adherence to medium-term objectives are crucial in establishing a government's credibility.

6) *Let the dog see the rabbit.* People cannot cooperate with the reform process unless they know where you are going. Where feasible, spell out your objectives and intentions in advance. If programs are to be implemented in stages, start by publishing the timetable. Businesses and professional analysts understand the importance of quality in decision making and the benefits of medium-term policies. In time, their increasing good will toward the programs becomes a major factor in creating a favorable climate of public opinion.

7) *Never fall into the trap of selling the public short.* Successful structural reform is not possible unless you trust, respect and inform the electors. Tell the public, and never stop telling them:

• What the problem is and how it arose.
• What damage it is doing to their own interests.
• What your objectives are.
• How you will achieve those objectives.
• What the costs and benefits of your action will be.
• Why your approach will work better than the other options.

People may not understand all the technical detail, but they have a lifetime of experiences to help them sift wheat from chaff. They know when key questions are being evaded. They respect honest responses to their questions.

8) *Don't blink; public confidence rests on your composure.* Over the past five years, ministers of the New Zealand government have announced some of the most radical decisions on structural reform in the past 50 years. Structural reform demands a major change in the ideas and attitudes most people grew up with. Such demands inevitably cause discomfort and uncertainty. People become hypersensitive to any signs of similar anxiety in the politicians responsible for these reforms. When they cannot understand the argument, they base their judgment on their assessment of the speaker's mental and emotional condition. That is another reason why it pays to make decisions of the finest quality. When you know you've got it right, that comes out through their television sets.

9) *Incentives, choice, monopoly—get the fundamentals right.* A sick economy cannot be regulated back to health. Since 1917 the concept of command economies has been tested to extinction. Government became the most oppressive vested interest of all. The role of governments today is to create a framework that widens people's opportunities for choice, improves the incentives to productive activity and sees their gains benfit society as a whole.

The abolition of privilege is the essence of structural reform. Wherever possible, use your program of reform to give power back to the people.

10) *When the pressure becomes extreme from colleagues or vested interests to abandon medium-term policies and accept an easy ad hoc compromise, ask yourself: "Why am I in politics?"*

No party holds power forever. Sooner or later we all find ourselves out of office. That is the reality of life in a democracy. We may as well use the time we have to do something worthwhile. Genuine structural reform, carried through without compromise, delivers greater gains in opportunity and living standards in the medium term than any other approach to political decision making.

What the voting public wants most from politicians is the guts and vision to make decisions of real benefit to them and to their children. Their future depends on it.

The Wall Street Journal, January 17, 1990

7   *Flora M. Painter and Robert J. Rourke*

Policy and Institutional Considerations in Equity Market Development

The 1980s saw a significant increase in interest among developing countries in the role of the private sector in economic development. They were joined in this interest, as the 1990s began, by most of the countries of Eastern Europe, and for many of the same reasons. In all of these countries, interest in the most developed economies in the world, and most especially in how they got that way, has been greatly intensified. As a result, both the accomplishments and promise of private enterprise are being extolled in parts of the world where the individual property rights essential to such enterprise have not yet been fully and legally recognized. In consequence, too, it is being increasingly understood that private enterprises can grow as rapidly and substantially as they do in developed economies because of the capital markets that have developed in tandem with their economies.

Capital markets play a critical role in economic development by encouraging domestic savings and mobilizing these savings for investment in productive activities. Many private enterprises come into being only because of capital markets that allow others, not directly involved in their operations, to invest (venture capital) in their futures. Few private enterprises can grow significantly in the absence of adequate capital markets. Conversely, capital markets can only grow and contribute to the overall development process where private enterprise is reasonably unfettered.

This chapter begins by detailing the structure of a financial market as it exists in a developed industrialized economy. Within this overall structure, a capital market (especially one with traded securities) is the component that is least likely to be developed (if it exists at all) in a developing country. This delineation at the very outset of the chapter shows the vivid contrast between the benefits that fully functioning capital markets provide economies and people in a few countries of the world and the absence of such benefits in most.

Then, after a summary of the conditions of economies that are essential to the growth of both private enterprise and capital markets and of those that have the opposite effect, the remainder of the chapter describes specific *types* of issues and market conditions that limit the development and growth of equity markets in greater or lesser degree in different countries and concludes with a consideration of potential remedies for these impediments to the development of capital markets, private enterprise, and countries.

The Structure of Financial Markets

The components of the financial markets of developed countries can be roughly grouped into money markets and capital markets.

Money markets. Money markets are a source of short-term financing. They have developed in response to the needs of governments, financial institutions, and businesses for ready access to a supply of cash to meet immediate needs and a place to put cash temporarily.

One of the best examples of the use of money markets is provided by the cash management services that banks in most developed countries offer their clients. Banks invest the cash balances of corporate clients in short-term securities such as Treasury bills for tenures that match the clients' cash flow requirements and extend short-term loans and reverse repurchase agreements to meet periodic peak cash needs such as payroll expense. Where capital markets are functioning, the yield on money market investments also serves an important function in providing a reference point, or index, for evaluating the return on investments in capital markets.

The financial instruments used in money markets include government securities, commercial paper, certificates of deposit, repurchase agreements, and banker's acceptances. Traditionally, banks were the only formal institutions participating in money markets, but there has been a significant increase within the past ten years in the number of mutual funds and dealers that invest and trade in the money market.

For the most part, money markets are nonexistent or inconsequential in less-developed countries (LDCs). Few governments rely on short-term securities to meet financing needs or, when they do, trading in the securities is not permitted. Banks in developing countries do not usually engage in "balance sheet" lending to meet the cash flow requirements of businesses, but frequently a thriving informal or "curb" market operates to provide a ready, albeit expensive, source of short-term financing.

Capital markets. Capital markets exist to provide long-term financing for start-up and expanding enterprises. Financing is obtained in the capital markets either by issuing debt instruments, typically bonds, or by selling equity in the enterprise through the sale of shares. Long-term financing raised by the sale of bonds or shares through either a private placement or a public offering is frequently referred to as "risk capital," in that the providers of funds are at risk that the enterprise will earn sufficient profit to pay dividends to its shareholders, or to pay the interest and principal on its debt.

The sources of financing in the capital market fall into two categories—nonsecurities and securities—depending upon whether or not the financial instrument used to document the financing arrangement is transferable, that is, negotiable. One way to make the distinction is by viewing the nonsecurities component of a capital market as a "closed shop."

Nonsecurities. The sources of funds in the nonsecurities component of the market are usually financial institutions or related organizations such as banks, leasing companies, pension funds, and insurance companies. Businesses seeking funds negotiate directly with these providers of funds. An institution that provides these funds may sell off a portion of its investment to other financial institutions, but the investment is not represented by a negotiable instrument that is readily available for purchase by individual investors or investor groups.

Typical forms of nonsecurities financing include term loans, leases, sale and leasebacks, and mortgages. To the extent that long-term financing is available in a developing country, it almost always is provided through term loans and mortgages, although sale-and-leaseback arrangements are also becoming important in meeting the capital equipment needs of businesses in developing countries. As one example, eighty-four leasing companies were established in Indonesia within months of a revision to the regulations permitting leasing operations.

Although sale-and-leaseback arrangements can be a useful alternative to raising funds for capital equipment purchases through bond issues or sale of equity, this financing technique is generally only available to well-established firms that offer low risk of default to the lessor. In developed countries many types of nonsecurities financing are being packaged and converted to securities (securitization).

Securities. The securities component of capital markets provides long-term equity and loan funds through the use of negotiable instruments that can be freely traded by individuals as well as institutions. This component of the market can be highly effective in mobilizing domestic capital because the securities representing the investment can be readily sold to meet cash needs or other investment objectives.

The liquidity of a provider of funds in the securities component, then, is much greater than that of institutions providing nonsecurity financing because its assets can more readily be turned into cash (which is wholly liquid). In contrast, institutions providing nonsecurity financing generally hold their investment until the final payment has been made and generally have less choice in the matter than do their counterparts in the securities component of capital markets. The liquidity of an investment in securities is not limited to shares or stocks, but holds for all investments represented by a negotiable instrument including bonds and debentures (although, of course, a recently purchased thirty-year bond is less liquid than a publicly traded stock or, for that matter, a recently purchased one-year bond or a twenty-nine-year-old thirty-year bond). The securities segment of capital markets consists of primary and secondary markets, both of which are essential in attracting savings to investment in productive activities.

Companies obtain financing for the acquisition of the plant and equipment needed for production by issuing securities (shares and stock, bonds, or equity equivalents) in the *primary market*. In developed countries, these securities are generally not sold directly to the public by the issuers, but instead are distributed by brokers or purchased by underwriters for subsequent resale to institutional and individual investors.

Financial intermediaries in the primary market—merchant, investment, and commercial bankers, as well as brokers and licensed dealers—fulfill an important role in establishing an effective market price for the securities being issued by a company. They often purchase the entire issue and, in thereby "underwriting" the sale, assure the issuing company of obtaining the entire proceeds estimated for the issue.

Once an issuing company has sold its securities, it has no further involvement in the disposition of its issues, except as the profitability of its performance and the information it provides affect the demand for shares in the company. That demand is accommodated by the trading (buying and selling) of securities in the *secondary market*, by brokers and dealers acting on behalf of individual and institutional investors.

It is somewhat ironic to call this market secondary as, without it, the primary market would be miniscule or nonexistent. It is the secondary market that assures liquidity to investors in *both* markets. Because investments made in shares or other equity instruments traded in secondary markets (stock markets, for example) can be converted into cash at almost any moment, the investment by individuals and others is more likely to be made. These are the purchasers who may also be resellers in the secondary market. Without them, without assurance of a market for *re*sale of the bonds or shares from issuing companies, underwriters and other financial intermediaries would not be willing to make the initial purchases of new issues by companies in the primary market. So, the *initial* purchase of equity shares issued by a company requires both *other* (secondary) purchasers who think they have a better idea of what those shares are worth than do those who sell them *and* a market (the secondary) in which these differing evaluations can be joined.

Once equity instruments are traded in a secondary market, the investment decisions of purchasers in that market are qualitatively different from those of purchasers in the primary market. A purchaser in a fully functioning secondary market can sell what was purchased a moment later—for cash. That is liquidity. A purchaser in the secondary market who holds onto whatever is purchased is therefore making a *series* of investments; though the purchase price was the investor's only cash outlay, any decision *not* to resell is effectively *another* investment, no less than the original outlay was, but only because of the liquidity of the investment. Being able to sell at a moment's notice is a luxury of secondary markets that is not afforded purchasers in primary markets. "Primary," therefore, is better understood in terms of risk (more) rather than time of purchase (first).

Where they occur at all, securities market activities in developing countries tend to consist principally of the trading of the limited number of issues available in the market by a small number of investors. Growth of capital markets requires continual introduction by issuers of the new debt and equity of companies seeking long-term financing. It is this important function that attracts domestic savings, provides for a wider distribution of ownership among a population, and leads to an increase in the number of enterprises and the growth of the private sector and economies.

The equity (securities) segment of capital markets provides for permanent finance without contractual payments. In contrast, reliance on debt capital carries contractual obligations to make fixed payments without regard to the profitability of the enterprise or the potential benefits of other applications of the funds. The dangers to both governments and private enterprises of heavy dependence on debt are ameliorated by securities markets and greater reliance on the equity finance that they provide.

The problems associated with reliance on debt finance have become painfully evident to governments and businesses. For governments, excessive reliance on debt finance to fund capital-intensive projects with low returns has led to debt servicing problems. For private companies, high debt-to-equity ratios have led to unbalanced capital structures and financial vulnerability during periods of economic downturn. During the 1970s, for example, the sharp increase in international interest rates almost doubled the cost of repaying foreign currency loans by debtor companies at the very same time that their capacity for doing so was greatly reduced by the dramatic increase in oil prices. In such countries as Brazil, where the government as well as companies had such extensive debt that their external accounts were exhausted, new loans were not forthcoming to finance the old. The situation was further complicated by the fact that the Brazilian government, faced with accelerating inflation and mounting public debt, abolished credit subsidies and competed with the private sector for capital, usually offering higher interest rates in order to obtain financing for itself.

These problems have contributed to a growing recognition

among the governments of LDCs that the expansion of the role of the private sector in economic development is a prerequisite for sustained economic growth, and that equity markets play a crucial role in financing the growth in private investment. As a result, more LDC governments are putting an increasing emphasis on the development of their domestic capital markets.

Requisites for Capital and Equity Markets

The development of a country's capital and equity markets will only occur as part of a comprehensive endeavor that addresses all the factors that affect the profitability and attractiveness of private enterprise for individuals. Laws, regulations, and economic policies that encourage the formation or expansion of private enterprises also contribute to the development of capital and equity markets because they increase the demand for long-term finance. The legal framework, economic policy, private sector growth, and capital mobilization, therefore, are interrelated conditions contributing to the development of capital and equity markets.

Vigorous equity markets can exist and develop only in supportive political, legal, and economic environments. Government involvement in the economy may doom the prospects for equity market growth if it inhibits the formation and growth of private sector firms. In addition, government policies—fiscal, monetary, and regulatory—can impede the development of equity markets if they distort interest rates and prices, or if they encourage inflation and price instability, or if, in pursuing short-range fiscal objectives, they create disincentives to investment in private enterprise.

Obviously, then, the development of capital and equity markets will occur only in market economies. At the same time, a free market is not sufficient for the successful development of a capital and equity market. Other factors, including conditions of political instability and social turmoil, or inadequate and restrictive laws and regulations, also increase the risk of (and expectations of return on) investments. Under these circumstances, publicly traded private companies will find it necessary to distribute most profits, and even incur losses, in order to meet the shareholders' expectation of dividends. Privately held companies have no incentive to go public under these conditions and generally divert their profits to investments in overseas markets, or in unproductive activities such as real estate development.

The willingness and ability of private entrepreneurs to invest in new operations and the expansion of existing enterprises is a key determinant of the success or failure of efforts to develop an equity market. A favorable climate for business formation and expansion will promote the development of a securities market as businesses seek ways to obtain long-term financing of capital requirements that exceed the funds available from family resources, internal profit financing, and borrowing. Conversely, a securities market will not develop and grow in an environment in which political turmoil, tax policies, regulations, or laws governing company operations discourage the formation of new companies or the expansion of existing enterprises.

Capital and Equity Markets in LDCs: Variability and Norm

Although the level of sophistication of equity markets among developing nations varies considerably, the growth of these markets in most LDCs is retarded by the lack of the requisite conditions for the development of private enterprise summarized in the preceding section. As a result, the number, volume, and variety of stocks traded in LDC equity markets is characteristically small, and sometimes even these sparse markets are dominated by government debt securities. Of course the corollary of such limited supply is the scarcity of investors in those markets and the limited volume of transactions (turnover activity). The equity raised through new public issues, therefore, is generally insignificant relative to gross national product (GNP) or to the value of funds channeled to the private sector through the nonsecurities market and other sources.

At the same time, investors more often than not exhibit a seeming preference for quick, guaranteed returns rather than long-term capital gains. That investors appear to appraise the value of equities principally on the basis of their dividend returns is indicative that the future earnings of those equities are more closely associated than are current dividends with fulfillment of the more extensive conditions for private enterprise development discussed in the previous section. One implication of this is that no amount of effort toward the development of an equities market will succeed where private property rights and economic freedom are otherwise generally distorted or repressed. Another, more positive, implication, however, is that expected future earnings will be more positively assessed by investors as the effort to fulfill the requisite conditions for private enterprise growth moves from the realm of "new initiative" to that of "long-standing commitment." Previous proclamations by governments of "today's new policies" are remembered by potential investors in almost any LDC as yesterday's experiments. Therefore, one more condition should be added to the requisites enumerated above: time. For any government wanting to realize the benefits of equity market development, the corollary of time is patience. Investors have to see a *sustained*, as well as comprehensive, commitment. Patience on the part of LDC governments might be encouraged if they acknowledge that their citizens have no difficulty in recognizing sustained commitment when they see it; otherwise, capital flight would not be a problem.

The remainder of this chapter addresses factors that are more particular to the development of capital and equity markets, as such, than are the conditions discussed to this point. Each of the two sections that follow addresses the same four critical issues in equity market development: (1) developmental and regulatory considerations, (2) institutional considerations, (3) the supply of securities, and (4) the demand for securities. The section that immediately follows addresses those factors associated with each of these issues that inhibit equity market development; its successor section provides responses to the four sets of constraints. The discussion in both sections is based largely on practical experience in the development of equity markets in a number of developing and developed countries. The two sections provide an overview of the *types* of problems and responses encountered in each of the four issue areas, in recognition of their varying significance among a diverse group of countries.

Factors Inhibiting Capital and Equity Market Development

Developmental and regulatory considerations. In most developing countries, regulatory and developmental policies and procedures affecting the securities market require substantial improvement. Reilly (1986a, 184–85) mentions some of the more common problems.

Lack of a unified government office to supervise and develop the market. In many developing countries, no single government agency is charged with coordinating capital market development activities. Generally, responsibility for the supervision and development of the capital market is segmented among different government agencies—the Ministry of Finance, the securities commission, the central bank, and so forth—whose roles may overlap or conflict and result in extensive, duplicative, and sometimes inconsistent regulations.

Such a lack was a major problem at the time of the 1979 crisis in Thailand, for example, when regulatory and developmental responsibilities were fragmented among various government agencies. According to Manas Leeviraphan, director-general of the Fiscal Policy Office of the Ministry of Finance of Thailand, this fragmentation impeded efficient policy formulation so that no single agency was able to take immediate action to resolve the crisis in the Securities Exchange of Thailand. The crisis had a detrimental impact on investor confidence for years thereafter (Leeviraphan 1986, 151).

A crisis in Singapore in 1986 was quickly resolved by the Monetary Authority's capital market section and the stock exchange. The exchange was reopened within two days of its closing.

Scarcity of adequate skills. Often, regulatory staff do not have the requisite skills to conduct regulatory work or to promote the development of the securities market. In addition, the unnecessary duplication that results from having a number of government agencies involved in securities market regulation and development often contributes to the shortage of skilled personnel.

Insufficient understanding of the markets. In many countries, existing regulatory bodies are run by officials and civil servants who have knowledge of regulation, but lack knowledge of how a market works and what will make it grow. Generally, there are few, if any, practitioners with a real understanding of how securities markets operate.

Lack of authority to enforce regulations. Even if they have qualified personnel, existing bodies often do not have enough authority to enforce rules or to promote regulations to develop the market.

Inconsistent and outdated regulations. Frequently, regulations are introduced in response to specific problems and on an ad hoc basis. As a result, regulations are often inconsistent and may even be unenforceable. In fact, some regulations are based on outdated legislation and may be at cross-purposes with goals to develop a securities market.

Overemphasis on regulation and underemphasis on development. A common problem in securities market development is that too much emphasis is placed on regulation and little, if any, on market development. An appropriate balance between regulation and development of the market is important. As Sir Kenneth Berrill, chairman of the Securities and Investments Board of the United Kingdom has pointed out, "It is essential not to divorce the objective of developing capital markets from the objective of regulating them: Markets which develop without a suitable regulatory framework will not, in the long run, operate as successfully as those which are effectively regulated. Securities commissions, and similar organizations, thus have a dual responsibility, neither of which should predominate at the expense of the other" (Berrill 1986, 160).

Experience shows that countries, such as Brazil and Korea, that have taken a developmental approach to capital market growth while attending to regulation have been more successful in their efforts to develop the market. In Brazil, associations of merchant bankers, brokers, and institutional investors have been particularly effective in making practical recommendations on how to develop the securities market (Reilly 1986b, 11).

The primary purpose of regulation is to support fair and orderly markets and to protect investors in order to maintain and increase investor confidence. The issue of self-regulation has to do with the extent to which a privately operated trading facility should establish its own rules and regulations and the extent to which government agencies should regulate the market participants. In some developing countries, trading facilities are operated by government agencies and regulations are set by them. Other countries have adopted the British approach that allows the stock exchange to function primarily on the basis of private self-regulation. Still others have followed the U. S. approach in which trading facilities are allowed to operate as self-regulatory agencies subject to oversight regulation by a government ministry or securities commission (Reilly 1986a, 182–83).

The challenge is to attain a delicate balance between a system that assures the adequate protection of investors and one that does not deter market growth. Extremely loose rules and regulatory practices (be they those of market participants or of government) can lead to speculation, heavy damage to investors, and loss of investor confidence. Rules and regulatory practices can be so stringent and demanding as to stifle private initiative and discourage companies from going public.

Equity market depth and the structure of financial institutions. Central to the development of securities markets is the question about the type of financial structure—universal banking (also known as multibanking) or specialized securities market institutions—that has a greater positive impact on the development of securities markets. The International Finance Corporation (IFC) has been at the center of this discussion. To answer this question, the IFC has conducted, in developed and developing countries, numerous case studies that have sought to relate the depth of the securities market (measured as the ratio of securities outstanding to GNP) to the structure of the financial institutions. The discussion presented below is based on the findings (Gill 1979).

Arguments in favor of universal banking systems focus on the economies of scale that should result when banking and the securities market are merged into a single institution. Even if economies of scale were insignificant, supporters of universal banking argue that if specialized institutions are as efficient as those of universal banking, universal institutions will evolve naturally into specialized systems in the absence of laws and regulations to enforce such specialization.

Proponents of specialized systems argue that laws, such as the Glass-Steagall Act in the United States, are necessary to curb abuses that might arise from conflicts of interest and undue concentration of power if banks are allowed to engage in securities market operations. Abuses could lead to a loss of confidence on the part of savers to the detriment of securities market development. Another argument in favor of specialized systems focuses on financial innovation and entrepreneurship. The argument is that specialization facilitates the entry of entrepreneurs into securities markets because less capital is required to start such operations and encourages the development of new financial instruments and techniques. Universal banking requires considerable start-up capital and banks may resist the development of securities markets in favor of traditional bank finance if monopolistic structures emerge.

In a survey of developed countries, including Germany, the United States, Canada, Japan, and the Netherlands, the IFC found that there is little evidence to support the argument that universal banking systems result in significant economies of scale leading to greater efficiency and securities market depth. In developing countries, difficulties in segregating universal banks and specialized institutions in particular countries, and in controlling for the variability of other factors such as stage of economic development and levels of political and economic turmoil, overshadowed the conclusions of the IFC. Nevertheless, the IFC found no evidence to support arguments in favor of universal banking structures in the developing countries. In fact, in developing countries with prominent securities markets, such as Korea, the Philippines, Jordan, and India, the development of the market has taken place amid distinct specialization of financial institutions.

Some exception was found in the case of Mexico and Brazil, both countries with successful securities markets and multi-function banking conglomerates. Nevertheless, closer scrutiny of the Brazilian and Mexican cases reveals that in Brazil the various activities of the banking conglomerates are managed by separate legal entities that function much like specialized institutions, and, in Mexico, independent brokers and dealers and the government have provided most of the stimulus to securities finance whereas the banking conglomerates have played only a minor role.

The single most important conclusion of the IFC, however, is that the differences among financial institutional structures are less important determinants of the level of securities market depth than are other factors, such as fiscal policies, laws and regulations, and the level of economic development.

Institutional considerations. Underlying the problems of limited demand and supply of securities are some fundamental considerations of an institutional nature. The following provides an overview of the key areas that require attention in any effort to develop an equity market.

Financial intermediaries. The principal financial and securities intermediaries in equity markets are brokers, dealers, market makers, and investment and merchant bankers. In the primary market, the role of merchant and investment banking firms is to encourage companies to raise finance through public offerings of securities. In the secondary market, brokers act as intermediaries between buyers and sellers in exchange for a fee. Market makers are dealers who buy and sell securities for their own account, to make a market for customers. Their role is very important to the liquidity of the secondary market. In addition, financial intermediaries can play an important role in the growth of the capital market by educating potential investors and offering programs to promote the ownership of securities.

In many developing countries, securities intermediaries are inadequate. Often, LDCs have few, if any, investment or merchant banking firms. The financial sector is generally dominated by commercial banks that play a relatively small role in the capital market, because their lending activities are primarily short-term oriented. In addition, in countries with a Glass-Steagall type of banking system, commercial banks are not allowed to engage in underwriting activities. Other common problems include (Reilly 1986a, 178–79):

- Inadequate capitalization. In many LDCs, brokers are underfinanced individuals, not properly capitalized firms with branch offices to serve customers and generate business throughout a country.

- Inadequate training. Often, brokers have little, if any, training in financial analysis. As a result, they cannot provide investors with sound financial advice and generally act solely as "introducers" between clients and take no responsibility for securities transactions.

- Absence of market makers. In some countries, there are no market makers who will buy and sell securities for their own account and in doing so provide liquidity for the secondary market.

- Excessive or inappropriate regulations. In some countries, stock exchange regulations or laws may restrict brokers from engaging in related activities (such as underwriting). In Indonesia, for example, brokers are not allowed to act as dealers or market makers, only as agents for clients (Reilly 1986b, 31–32). Because of the low level of market activity that prevails in most

LDCs, such a policy effectively limits profitability and, therefore, the number of brokers, while further stretching the already thin population sufficiently trained to perform any of these activities adequately. In addition, there may be limitations on selling prices and underwriting commissions and fees, all of which may encourage abuses such as free riding and insider trading. In Brazil, for example, free riding was a common practice in the 1970s. In fact, it was the largest source of profit from underwriting activities. The deliberate underpricing of issues and market manipulation that occurs with free riding leads both to a substantial reduction in the proceeds from an offering to the issuing company and in public confidence in the equities market.

- Ignorance of practice elsewhere. Often there is little awareness about the role of financial and securities intermediaries in other countries. As a result, the importance of these intermediaries is underestimated, and even downplayed by regulations that impede the healthy development of such institutions (Ferris 1971, 4).

Trading facilities. The purpose of the secondary market (this discussion is based on Reilly 1986a, 180–85) is to facilitate trading in already issued securities. Its role is critical to a properly functioning securities market for two major reasons: liquidity and pricing. The secondary market provides liquidity, so that holders of securities can sell their securities when they desire; it provides a price-determining mechanism whereby market participants interact to bring together buying and selling interests both for fair secondary market prices and to set prices on new issues of securities in the primary market.

These functions are essential to equity market development because they facilitate the mobilization of and access to equity capital for the growth and expansion of private firms. In the absence of properly functioning secondary trading facilities, there is insufficient liquidity to attract investors, securities can be priced incorrectly, prices can be manipulated, and securities intermediaries can take advantage of inside information and opportunities denied to ordinary investors.

In many developing countries, facilities for trading securities must be established for the first time. In some cases an organized market exists, but the facilities are obsolete or so antiquated as to thwart the timely trading that characterizes dynamic markets and makes them attractive to participants. In still other countries, existing market facilities are not subject to adequate standards or safeguards and operate like private clubs.

Efforts either to establish secondary market trading facilities or to correct deficiencies in their operations must address the following issues, among others:

- Governments and companies must decide on the *type* of market in which securities will be traded. They might choose an auction stock exchange as the trading mechanism for particular securities. In such an exchange all current buy and sell orders represented by brokers are centralized in one physical place or computer system and exposed to one another and the interest of market makers to produce the best possible price for each order transacted. Or, where there is insufficient infrastructure or trading volume, purely brokered transactions between customers or an over-the-counter trading market may be the only alternatives.

    In Kenya, for example, stockbrokers neither conduct an auction nor buy and sell for their own account. They are simply intermediaries for negotiations between buying and selling customers who are occasionally represented by other brokers.

    Over-the-counter markets are those in which individual security dealers make their own markets by buying securities for or selling securities from their own inventories. At primitive stages of development, over-the-counter markets can result in the setting of different prices for the same security at the same time by different brokers. With regulation and fast communication between many dealers by telephone or computer, however, over-the-counter markets can compete with auction markets in pricing efficiency and liquidity.

Both types of markets exist simultaneously in highly developed securities markets, incorporating some physical trading floors, some computer networks, and some telephone networks. The United States has both the largest auction and over-the-counter markets: the auction market on the computer-assisted trading floor of the New York Stock Exchange, and the over-the-counter market conducted through the automated quotation and trading systems of the National Association of Securities Dealers (NASDAQ).

Typically, an over-the-counter market may be developed to supplement trading on the traditional stock exchange and to attract companies that cannot meet the stringent requirements of the stock exchange. In the United States, for example, the over-the-counter market developed because many smaller companies could not meet the stringent listing requirements and costs of the major exchanges. In other environments, smaller companies not suitable for stock exchange listing and auction trading may be traded as unlisted securities on the exchange as a second tier. This has been recommended for Kenya, for example.

In some countries, an over-the-counter market is effective in establishing an investor base and a secondary market for a company. According to Mr. Kanju Sugimoto, general manager of the Nomura Securities Company Limited in Japan, "new issues opportunities and secondary market trading are in a chicken-and-egg relationship." If it is difficult to obtain financing in the equity market because the secondary market is very weak, few companies will want to list their shares. But, with few listed companies, activity in the secondary market cannot pick up. Mr. Sugimoto suggests that an over-the-counter market can be used to solve this dilemma. Listing requirements in the over-the-counter market would be less stringent and companies might not be able to obtain the same tax privileges accorded listed firms. However, when the trading volume of such shares became large enough, companies might then move to the stock exchange and comply with its listing requirements (Sugimoto 1986, 55).

Recently, the government of Indonesia decided to establish an over-the-counter market in order to supplement trading on the Jakarta Stock Exchange, which has failed to attract new listings since 1984 and has suffered from a very low level of trading activity. The new market will be open to foreign participants and will have less stringent listing requirements than those of the Jakarta exchange (Intrados Group 1988, 11).

- It must be decided whether securities trading will be subject to a *site requirement*, that is, allowed only on the site of officially recognized trading facilities. Trading might also be allowed outside the facility, on the "curb." If trading will only be allowed on the official facility, the problem then becomes one of enforcing the rule.

- In order to increase the *efficiency* of trading facilities, and thereby make them more productive and useful for securities professionals and investors, a number of issues need to be considered: (1) the timely compilation and distribution of information about transactions in the market such as volume, and opening, closing, high and low prices (market information), (2) the compilation, distribution, and analysis of information from issuers of securities traded in the market that is relevant to buyers and sellers in determining market prices (corporate information and analysis), (3) the recognition and deterrence of fraud and manipulation, (4) the development of improved procedures for trading, (5) refinements in the clearance and settlement of securities transactions, and (6) marketing and promotion to extend securities ownership among the general population.

- Another issue is to determine whether the trading facility should be private, with no government involvement, or whether the government should play the primary role in establishing, financing, monitoring, or even operating the facility.

Historically, stock exchanges in most countries were established as private bodies by members wishing to exercise monopoly control over securities trading. As markets grew, the stock exchanges imposed listing requirements, and concerned governments relied on these to protect investors from malfeasance. In addition, many countries, particularly European ones, imposed restrictions on institutional investors, prohibiting them from investing in unlisted securities. Since the birth of the concept of securities regulation, however, securities laws, disclosure requirements, standard accounting and auditing procedures, and other means of protecting investors have ensued.

Currently, the stock exchange in most countries still operates as a private body with formal requirements for listing and membership. A securities commission is generally charged with oversight responsibilities. This is not always the case, however. In Indonesia, for example, a government agency, BAPEPAM, manages the stock exchange. One important disadvantage to this arrangement is that it is difficult for a government agency to take a profit-making, private sector point of view in operating the exchange. Therefore, it has been recommended that the BAPEPAM should adopt a more traditional oversight role and allow the private sector to manage the stock exchange in Indonesia (Reilly 1986b, 10–11).

An intermediate condition existed in Jamaica from 1980 to 1988. The government subsidized the private stock exchange by furnishing a trading room and offices in the Bank of Jamaica and a bank officer and six staff members to administer the exchange.

- Finally, the *cost* of initial trading facilities can be modest. It is not necessary to establish elaborate securities exchanges;

simple trading facilities can be established that allow flexibility for growth. In Kenya, for example, it was recommended that the brokerage system be converted to an auction market: A blackboard would be purchased and one member's conference room rented for an hour each day. Exactly such a prototype already exists in Alexandria, Egypt.

Limits to the supply of securities. One explanation for the undeveloped nature of capital markets in developing countries is that the supply of securities is very limited. The lack of a market is also related to the demand for securities, but there are some specific reasons for the reluctance of companies to "go public" that are not accounted for by limited demand. Four of these reasons are discussed in the following.

Pricing interference. Government intervention in the pricing of equity issues is one of the major impediments. The price at which a company can sell its shares is a very important consideration as it determines whether the cost of capital raised through the equity market is economically attractive or not. In some LDCs, the government fixes the price at which companies and controlling shareholders can sell their shares based on the notion of "par value." In other LDCs, the government establishes an issue price on the basis of book value, without adequately taking into account current or future earnings potential. In developed markets the price of a share is established in negotiations between the underwriter and the issuing company and is affected by the underwriter's assessment of what the market would be willing to pay given the earnings record and other characteristics of the company.

Government involvement in the pricing of public issues occurs in most developing countries. One typical example is Kenya, where the government, through the Capital Issues Committee, plays a major role in the pricing of issues in an effort to "protect" the unsophisticated buying public (Ferris 1987, 9). Unfortunately, this places the government in an undesirable position of appearing to be recommending an issue at a particular price.

Equity Market Development

An issue that is underpriced may encourage free riding by financial intermediaries, a practice whereby the middleman or underwriter of an issue, knowing that the issue is underpriced, buys most of the shares for his own account and issues only a few shares to the public, selling the rest later when the price has been pushed up by increased (and easily predicted) demand. The only free ride provided by this practice, of course, is that taken by the underwriter, who essentially receives more than he paid for. The public purchasers at the higher price are penalized relative to the underwriter, but they still receive what they pay for—at a demand-determined price—and each purchaser can probably sell the day after for the same price or more. The only party definitely receiving less than paid for is the issuing company. Its ride, in comparison with that of the purchasing public and (even more) that of the free-riding middleman, is truly painful, so much so that pricing interference and its free-riding corollary is a factor limiting the supply but not necessarily the demand for securities.

Another example of the negative effects of price interference for the development of equities markets is provided by Malaysia, where companies are only allowed to issue shares at prices ranging from four to eight times their pretax earnings. According to Dato Malek Merican, managing director of the Arab-Malaysian Merchant Bank Berhad, this results in the systematic underpricing of shares, increasing the cost of going public and encouraging considerable oversubscription of shares. In consequence, an elaborate balloting system is required to select the successful applicants, "many of whom will sell their shares at considerable capital gains within a few weeks of the public listing" (Merican 1986, 136).

Indonesia presents still another example of government interference with market pricing. There, the national investment and unit trust fund, Danareksa, is said to "encourage" companies issuing public shares on the Jakarta Stock Exchange to set low prices (Reilly 1986b, 136). As a result of these and other practices, only twenty-four companies have listed shares on the Jakarta Stock Exchange since 1977 and there has been no new stock issue on the exchange since 1984.

Tax Biases and Disincentives. The supply of securities is also diminished if tax policies make the cost of raising equity funds more expensive than debt finance. Interest on debt is generally tax-deductible to a corporation, but dividends on shares must be paid out of after-tax profits. In addition, stamp duties and other transaction costs are frequently high and discourage the transfer and trading of securities. Excessively high taxes on the capital gains arising from the sale of shares also impede secondary market activity as controlling shareholders prefer to retain their shares and take out profits in dividends or illegal payments.

Tax biases against investment in securities and in favor of deposits in banks also force companies to rely on borrowing from domestic banks or other sources rather than issue bonds or sell equity interests. When interest received from bank term deposits is tax free, and dividend income is taxable, which is frequently the case in developing countries, banks can obtain funds from depositors at lower rates than companies can obtain funds through the issuance of securities. The situation is further complicated when one considers that in many developing countries, particularly in those with new or relatively inactive markets, investors are apt to prefer dividends currently received to potential capital gains from share appreciation. As a result, in order to be competitive with the banks, publicly listed companies must offer dividend rates that are equivalent to the after-tax interest rates paid by the banks. In these instances, it is less costly for firms to borrow from banks than it is to issue equity or debt securities in the market. According to the Asian Development Bank (ADB), the 1983 dividend payout ratio (total annual cash dividends plus any payments on preferred stock divided by annual company earnings) for nineteen listed companies in Indonesia reached 120 percent. Thus some publicly listed companies diminished their capital base by paying more in dividends than they gained in profits (Asian Development Bank 1985, 45).

In many countries, tax laws are poorly administered and tax requirements are not enforced rigorously or uniformly. As a result, companies may be reluctant to go public because they are afraid that the financial disclosure required for public offerings will lead to

Equity Market Development

increased tax assessments by the fiscal authorities. Dispassionate observers (including, possibly, tax authorities) might deem these companies to be no more than "cheaters" deserving of no less than full assessments of the tax codes. In a sense this is true, but it must be asked: if bankruptcy—being unable to stay in business—were the result of such rigor, might the cheating be viewed as being perhaps necessary, or at least as being less blameworthy? The interaction of moral and practical considerations posed by this issue and question is illustrated by the more extreme circumstance of most third world firms; for them, the issue is not whether their equity should be publicly traded, but whether they wish to be legally recognized at all. Many (some think most) businesses in LDCs have opted for the informality of the underground economy, subjecting themselves to few, if any, of the requirements that are expressed in the law of the land. More than tax law is involved and the effects are illustrated by the (unfortunately) not exceptional case of the Philippines:

> That country has a minimum-wage law, which most small firms evade, and sales and profits taxes, which they commonly do not pay. A small firm that pays profits tax, evades sales tax, and offers wages that are 20 percent below the minimum wage, faces a marginal tax rate of 85 percent if growth, and the official attention success attracts, forces it to start paying sales tax and comply with the minimum-wage regulations. If it cannot raise its profits by more than 85 percent, it will lose money by expanding. This example assumes that the firm already pays profits tax on its net income. If it was initially evading profits tax but had to pay a larger share of the tax as it grew, the effective marginal tax rate would be higher still. Besides the tax and minimum-wage regulations, there are other regulations which small firms can often ignore or "negotiate," but which become more effectively binding as the firm grows larger. Taking all these factors into account, the marginal tax on firm expansion can easily exceed 100 percent, providing an overwhelming incentive to remain "underground" and small (Biggs, Grindle, and Snodgrass 1988, 158).

To be publicly traded or not is thus a natural extension of another decision—to be recognized at all.

Inadequate or restrictive laws and regulations. Company law is central to the establishment and operation of companies, including their issuance of securities. For this reason, it is generally regarded as the most important law affecting securities market development. In many developing countries company laws are usually very rigid and would benefit from substantial reform (Asian Development Bank 1985, 68–69; Reilly 1986a, 186–87).

Restrictions or limitations entailed by the company laws of various developing countries apply to a wide variety of activities, including the specific approvals required for incorporation, the issuance of securities once a firm is incorporated, and the requirement of "par value" price offerings once a firm has become both incorporated and allowed to issue securities (Reilly 1986a, 186–87; Asian Development Bank 1985, 69). That is just the beginning. Additional restrictions or limitations that inhibit the development of equities markets are those on the allowance of partially paid shares and founders' shares, on the issuance of corporate bonds and debentures, transfers of shares, and on the issuance of more innovative instruments such as convertible bonds, warrants, and options. More general limitations that commonly underlie all these particulars include the lack of clear definition of the legal position of certain types of activities such as investment and merchant banking, leasing, and venture capital, as well as inadequate provisions for either the disclosure of material information about companies or the protection of minority holders in a company. Finally, though it may seem unwarranted in view of the preceding, there is a lack of appropriate enforcement powers and sanctions. We suggest that the latter will only occur where the rules and the rule-making process are themselves reasonable.

Laws and regulations that stifle the formation and expansion of private sector companies also affect the number of potential issuers of public shares and, therefore, the supply of securities. In many developing countries, extensive approvals for the set-up or expansion of private firms are required and the registration process for a public offering of shares is often cumbersome and time consuming.

A common problem also arises because laws and regulations are inadequately enforced and there is wide discretion in the actual application of such laws. Tax rates, for example, might differ from those set by law. In addition, unauthorized and ad hoc concessions, and noncompliance with government laws and regulations, can be widespread. For the private sector, inadequate or inconsistent enforcement of laws and regulations creates considerable uncertainty, and uncertainty increases the risks of doing business. In these instances the rules of the game become obscured as decisions tend to be made case by case. Opportunities for corruption increase, and the enforcement of rules might be subject to pressure from special interest groups. Moreover, the conscientious and uniform application of tax laws is important when private companies consider the advantages of going public.

Another problem arises because prevailing laws and regulations are based on legal systems, such as the Napoleonic Code, developed in other countries in earlier periods. As a result, laws may restrict unduly the activities of the private business sector and thereby impede the development of a securities market (Reilly 1986a, 186–87). In Indonesia, for example, the Commercial Code is written in Dutch and has remained virtually unchanged in nearly fifty years. To make matters worse, the number of Indonesians who read and write Dutch decreases every year.

In contrast, financial authorities in Amman, Jordan, have used company law to stimulate the supply of securities. The law requires that all companies wishing to have limited liability status must go public. According to some experts, this was a major factor in the development of the securities market in Jordan in the 1970s (Gill 1979, 36).

Inadequate protection of property rights and contracts. In many developing countries, the heads of family-owned enterprises are reluctant to share control with the public or with entrepreneurs outside the family because the legal system fails to provide adequate protection and enforcement of property rights and contractual obligations. The work of Hernando de Soto and the Institute for

Liberty and Democracy in Peru has been particularly enlightening about the costs of such legal impediments. The failure of the legal and institutional infrastructure to promote, protect, and enforce property rights and contractual agreements is found by de Soto to result in inefficiently organized production that limits economic growth (de Soto 1988, 15–47, 209–19, and his discussions throughout; de Soto 1989).

Similarly, inadequate laws affect the willingness of owners of private firms to go public. In Bangladesh, for example, it has been found that reluctance to dilute family ownership and control is one of the major impediments to going public. Frequently, even when the company is listed on the stock exchange, few shares are available for trading because most continue to be held by the original owners. Moreover, according to Khurshid Alam, former chairman of the Dhaka Stock Exchange, "even when shares are floated in the primary market on a 50:50 basis," the initial sponsors frequently buy additional shares on the market to raise their holdings to between 70 and 80 percent. This attitude is largely blamed for the limited availability of shares and the low level of trading in the secondary market (Alam 1986, 127–31).

A recent study by the Asian Development Bank found that even when a company is publicly listed, most of its securities are closely held by the original owners, relatives, or friends. The controlling shareholders, usually the founders, often prefer to finance the company from internally generated funds or bank loans (possibly through banks that they control). In several Asian countries, the percentage of closely held shares frequently amounted to between 60 and 85 percent. This constitutes a major impediment to the trading of securities in the secondary market (Asian Development Bank 1985, 44).

Limits on the demand for securities. Some of the same factors that constrain the supply of securities, such as tax biases and inadequate laws and regulations, also diminish the demand for securities. In addition, ownership of securities is often concentrated in a small, wealthy segment of the population. Most people probably do not use banks, much less a broker, to invest what little savings they have. In the Yemen Arab Republic, for example, more than 60 percent of the money supply is in the form of cash held outside the banking system.

In addition, savers often lack confidence in the financial and political stability of the country and thus require almost instant liquidity. In the most extreme cases, even a country's currency is not considered to have the liquidity of cash. The economies of some, such as Poland and Argentina, have been effectively dollarized, with a foreign currency providing domestic liquidity. In others, jewelry and cattle are common surrogates for cash. To the extent that these cash alternatives are a consequence of poor macroeconomic policies (rather than of religious or cultural traditions), they should not discourage those who wish to develop equities markets within a comprehensive program of institutional and policy reform; they do, however, highlight the need for such comprehensiveness.

Five of the most typical impediments to the growth of demand for securities are discussed in the following. The first of these, lack of investor confidence, is the most fundamental and occasions the other four. Indeed, so basic to the development of any equities market is investor confidence that it has already been introduced in the comments above. Of the other impediments, the second—inadequate accounting and auditing standards—is most central to the first. The remaining three limit the *size* of a securities market, but do not undermine its very existence. More easily remedied than the other two, they nonetheless require a government possessing the wisdom and willingness to do so.

Lack of investor confidence. As it affects willingness to invest in securities, lack of confidence in the financial and political stability of a country includes savers' fears of extraordinary regulations of business activities and of government expropriation of private property. An equities market without the confidence of investors is virtually a contradiction in terms. Confidence in equity investments is not only undermined by the factors just discussed, but also by a curious combination of both too much and too little being required of participants in what are (or might be) a developing country's securities market.

Too little information may be required of both the companies issuing securities and of the trading process for an equities market to attract the savings of many individuals and institutions. In the absence of clear (transparent), reliable, and timely information about both the firms whose securities are subject to trade and the trading activities themselves, potential investors are apt to be distrustful of corporate managers and fearful of market manipulation.

In Bangladesh, for example, the Company Law of 1913 stipulates very little disclosure of financial information. As a result, there is a lack of investor confidence that has contributed to a low demand for securities and has restricted the growth of the capital market (Alam 1986, 127). Where too little information is required of market participants, an almost ever-present corollary is the inadequacy of accounting practices.

Inadequate accounting and auditing standards. Deficiencies in accounting and auditing procedures can affect both the demand for and the supply of securities. On the demand side, inappropriate accounting and auditing standards discourage savers from investing in securities because they cannot obtain accurate information about the financial position of companies. On the supply side, companies may be reluctant to go public for fear that financial disclosure will result in higher taxes to the company. Sometimes companies whose securities are traded are audited appropriately while closely held companies are able to evade taxes.

Uniform and professional accounting and auditing procedures are central to the efficiency and effectiveness of resource mobilization and allocation through the securities market. If accounting, auditing, and financial reporting practices are inadequate, it is not possible to ascertain the true financial position and profitability of companies. As a result, resources can be misallocated and investors misinformed. Moreover, in the absence of uniform reporting requirements and generally accepted accounting principles, investors cannot draw reliable comparisons among different firms. Yet, in many developing countries, financial statements are not governed by legally binding generally accepted accounting principles (GAAP) and audits are not conducted in accordance with legally binding generally accepted auditing standards (GAAS). Problems ensuing from or associated with the absence of such standards are numerous: auditors who are not independent of the companies they audit; businesses that maintain two sets of books; one for the owners and the other for tax authorities; absence of a professional body of accountants and auditors to develop uniform principles and standards and to license and regulate the membership; lack of private or government authority with the power to enforce duties and standards; and a lack of criminal penalties for false certification by auditors (Reilly 1986a, 181–82; Asian Development Bank 1985, 52–53).

Tax biases and disincentives. Tax policies represent a powerful tool with which the allocation of savings among different types of financial instruments may be influenced. In most countries, tax policies encourage the deposit of savings in banks or investment in government savings programs. In contrast with interest earnings from those sources, dividends paid the owner of a security frequently are taxed twice, once as corporate income and again as shareholder income. Investors are effectively encouraged to be more yield conscious and to think less in terms of total return (income plus appreciation) where, as in Egypt, Kenya, Indonesia, and Sri Lanka, among other countries, tax policies place dividends at a comparative disadvantage to other forms of interest income, such as interest earned on bank deposits, postal savings, and housing bonds.

Portfolio restrictions of financial institutions. In many developing countries, portfolio composition requirements are imposed on collective and contractual savings institutions, stipulating that a certain minimum percentage of total assets must be invested in designated financial instruments. Often, governments require institutional investors, such as pension funds and insurance companies, to invest a certain percentage of their funds in low-yielding government securities. Moreover, pension funds (both private and public) are frequently barred from investing in corporate securities either through regulation or tax treatment, and insurance companies are usually subject to similar restrictions or are limited to investing only a small percentage of their funds in corporate securities. Such requirements restrict the demand for corporate securities and, therefore, the amount of financial resources available to private sector business even when these securities offer higher yields. In addition, because mutual funds and other types of investment trusts are nonexistent in many LDCs, the demand for securities remains low.

Restrictions on foreign portfolio investment. Foreign portfolio investment has become an increasingly important issue in capital market development, particularly in light of the debt crisis and the subsequent decline in commercial banking loans to developing countries. The International Finance Corporation has played an important role in recent years in the establishment of international mutual funds, unit trusts, and other collective investment mechanisms that have contributed to the internationalization of securities markets. Unfortunately, a number of developing countries still place significant restrictions on foreign portfolio investment thus limiting the demand for domestic securities.

Though the Malaysian, Chilean, Thai, and Philippine markets are relatively open to foreign investment, and Brazil, India, Taiwan, Korea, and Mexico are accessible through a variety of investment funds, these markets are exceptions to the rule. By and large, LDCs are reluctant to open their securities markets to foreign investors. The most common impediments imposed are tax and regulatory barriers, including strict limits on the repatriation of income, the prohibition against majority ownership by foreigners, the maintenance of high capital gains taxes, and restrictions on foreign exchange (Intrados Group 1988, 7–8).

The three most frequently expressed arguments against foreign portfolio investment are essentially the same as those used in opposition to direct foreign investment, that (1) it may allow foreigners to make profits at the expense of nationals, (2) it may bring in "hot money," implying that foreign investors might withdraw their capital suddenly, causing instability in national securities markets, and (3) it may allow foreigners to gain "control" of a country's economy. The second and third arguments are largely incompatible with each other. The degree to which a government concerns itself with limiting foreign portfolio investment may reflect the extent to which it is failing to redress the disincentives to securities investments by its own citizens. Nonetheless, where the issue of foreign ownership is extremely controversial, there may be a practical need for addressing it by means of laws and regulations. The risk of "hot money," for instance, has been addressed in Mexico, Korea, and Brazil, among other countries, by limiting foreign portfolio investment to closed-end or partially closed-end investment trusts. Other responses to the (incompatible) risks of both "hot money" and control have included specifying the instruments that foreign portfolio investors can buy and placing a fixed upper percentage limit on the total equity available to foreign investors. In Argentina, for example, aggregate foreign portfolio investments may not exceed 20 percent of a company's share capital, and total foreign investment may not exceed 49 percent of share capital. The issue of control has also been addressed by such measures as limiting the maximum voting rights of individual foreign shareholders (Gill 1984, 46–49).

Responses to Constraints on Equity Market Development

Many potential solutions to problems in the development of equities markets have been suggested throughout this chapter. This concluding section provides an overview of the types of solutions and recommendations insofar as they have not been explicitly expressed in the the preceding pages.

Strengthening the institutional framework.

Encouraging financial intermediaries. The combination of support and incentives employed for encouraging the establishment of securities intermediaries generally include the following components:

- Training in financial analysis in order to create a professional core of securities intermediaries is essential to creating, in turn, confidence among the investing public. It is critical, for example, that brokers are familiar with and understand the financial position of issuing companies such as is provided through disclosure reports, and can make recommendations to their customers on the basis of such information.

    In addition to training in accounting, auditing and financial analysis, government officials and private sector representatives should receive training in securities market development and operations, market making, brokerage, and regulation. Securities commissions and other supervisory agencies can greatly contribute by stimulating training programs for employees of the stock exchanges and brokerage firms. They can encourage professional examinations to set minimum standards for market operators and thus help to increase investor confidence.

    It is often recommended that training include courses at institutes that have been established for that purpose in the major market centers (such as the New York Institute of Finance, founded by the New York Stock Exchange, which offers two sessions a year for foreign professionals). It is also frequently recommended that selected candidates be sent to stock exchanges, over-the-counter regulatory organizations, and securities firms in developed countries in order to gain first-hand experience in the operations of equity markets. The need is so widespread that preparation of educational videos might be desirable. It is also recommended that delegates from both the public and private sectors of a developing country visit securities markets that have been established more recently than those of the United States, Japan, or the United Kingdom in other countries that are most comparable to their own, such as Brazil, Singapore, and Malaysia.

- Support for improvements in accounting and auditing standards and procedures is a corollary of support for the increased training of securities market professionals. Recommendations generally call for a thorough review of laws and regulations governing accounting and auditing, followed by revisions to improve financial reporting; training and the establishment of licensing requirements for accountants and auditors; the development and enforcement of generally accepted accounting principles and generally accepted auditing standards and of uniform financial reporting requirements; and the uniform enforcement of accounting requirements among publicly traded companies as well as private companies of a certain size to remove disincentives to going public (Reilly 1986a, 181–82).

- Ensuring legitimate profit making by securities intermediaries. It is commonly believed that attracting the highest quality professionals to the investment banking and brokerage community is one of the best ways to protect the investing public. Profitability attracts such individuals, but profits should not come from such illegitimate practices as free riding and insider trading. Thus, it is generally recommended that regulations that limit legitimate profit making in the securities business through the imposition of ceilings on underwriting commissions, brokerage fees, and the like should be eliminated, or the limits raised to reasonable levels. An appropriate approach is to establish underwriting rates at a respectable minimum in the early stages of development of the securities market in order to avoid destructive price cutting, while allowing negotiation between issuer and underwriter. In Kenya, for example, it has been recommended that minimum fees be mandated to preclude predatory competition in the embryonic securities industry, with final fee setting left to negotiation between issuers and underwriters. In Kenya, and in Indonesia too, it has also been recommended that brokers act as dealers or market makers, not just as agents for their clients, and that they band together to serve as underwriters. Because the level of market activity is often low, this would allow them to increase their profit potentials, thus encouraging a greater number of brokers to participate in the market and engage in broader selling efforts (Ferris 1987, 17; Reilly 1986b, 31–32).

- Government-owned banks should not compete as underwriters. Otherwise, as in Indonesia, where Danareksa is the major underwriter in the country, their dominant position in the market effectively stifles the development of private underwriters and discourages companies from going public.

- Another important issue is that adequate financing be available for equity market activities. It has been recommended in some countries that facilities be established to finance the activities of merchant bankers and securities brokers, dealers, market makers, and investors. In Indonesia, for example, it was recommended that a securities rediscount facility and a securities market finance fund or corporation be established for that purpose (Reilly 1986b, 32).

- Establishment of intermediary institutions or branches of brokerage firms in important cities outside the main urban center is also frequently recommended. India exemplifies this approach with the objective of propagating interest in share-ownership "to the four corners of India." Financial intermediaries should be encouraged to engage in a broader distribution of securities by offering their securities to suppliers and customers in different parts of the country (ibid., 31–32).

Increasing the supply of securities. Actions to increase the supply of securities generally take one of two forms: the removal of impediments, or the adoption of positive incentives. Some LDC governments, however, have also resorted to direct intervention in an attempt to encourage an increase in public issues. In some countries, foreign or joint-venture companies are required to go public after a specified number of years as a way of increasing domestic ownership. South Korea, for example, imposes fiscal penalties on companies that do not go public after government authorities have determined that they should (Hakim 1985, 21–23). Indonesia until recently limited foreign ownership to 49 percent and required sale of the foreign equity after ten years.

Revising laws and regulations. It is recommended that equity market development efforts begin with a comprehensive legal review to identify duplicative and conflicting laws and regulations that might impede the development and efficient operation of a securities market (Asian Development Bank 1985, 68–69). Such a review goes beyond those laws most directly related to the supply of securities, such as those governing the listing of securities; it includes laws and regulations governing taxes, investment, accounting, and auditing, the operations of financial intermediaries, and the formation and expansion of private enterprise. In short, the review should include all laws affecting the development of capital markets. Completion of such a review should result in the next recommendation.

Eliminating tax biases favoring debt over equity. Because companies will not go public as long as the cost of equity funds is greater than that of debt financing, this is one of the few explicit recommendations expressed in previous pages that is reiterated in this conclusion.

Liberalizating pricing. One of the most important steps to encourage companies to go public is to eliminate government involvement in establishing the price of shares. Share price should be negotiated by the underwriter or sponsoring brokers and the offeror and should follow the industry practice of giving emphasis to earnings. This assures that profitable businesses will be able to sell their shares at a fair price with the result that the cost of raising equity capital will be competitive with the cost of long-term borrowing. In addition, higher issuing prices will enable the owners to raise larger amounts of funds for future growth without concern about the extensive dilution of their ownership that would have taken place at the lower prices. In South Korea, for example, growth of the capital market accelerated rapidly in 1973–1974 when the Ministry of Finance liberalized the pricing process (Ferris 1973, 4–6).

Privatizing profitable parastatals. The supply of securities is increased if a government privatizes selected state-owned enterprises by offering shares in these companies to the public. Companies selected for divestiture should be those that are (or might reasonably be) successful, in order to attract private investors. In addition, because one of the best incentives for individual investors is hearing about others' successful investment experience, the privatization of well-known, stable, and successful state-owned enterprises could have an important demonstration effect.

The government of Sri Lanka has developed plans to promote the development of the securities market through the privatization of certain public enterprises. Bangladesh, in an effort to augment the supply of securities in its fledgling market, has also devised a policy to divest 49 percent of the shares of public companies, including those of nationalized commercial banks (Rahman 1986, 10, 59). Privatization activities entailing the sale of shares can also be complemented by debt to equity swaps, one of the new financial instruments discussed next.

Developing new financial instruments. Because investors differ on the levels of risk and return that they prefer and are willing to accept, expanding the variety of financial instruments available to them is a rather obvious means to expanding the population of investors in the securities market.

Debt-to-equity swaps and the securitization of illiquid assets are among the prominent possibilities for creating new financial instruments, promoting new investments, and assisting in the reduction of a country's foreign debt. As such, they present important opportunities to increase the supply of negotiable securities and enhance capital market activity.

In a debt-for-equity swap, a lender redeems sovereign or private debt in local currency at the central bank of the debtor's government and invests the proceeds locally. The exchange might be made at par or at an otherwise discounted value, subject to negotiations with the central bank. Debt-to-equity conversion programs have been implemented in several countries, including the Philippines, Brazil, Argentina, Mexico, and Chile (see, for example, Hanke 1987, 161–68). An advantage to the debtor country offered by these swap programs is that they accomplish two things simultaneously: retiring hard currency debts while promoting productive investment in the country. By providing an important stimulus to local capital markets, debt-to-equity conversion programs can lead to the repatriation of flight capital (Clarke 1987, 3).

An additional advantage of debt-to-equity conversions is that they can be used to support privatization through the divestiture of state-owned enterprises. In the Philippines, for example, debt-to-equity swaps were used to support the privatization of two of six government commercial banks. Forty percent of one of these, the International Corporate Bank, was sold to American Express through a debt-to-equity swap in July 1986. In the other case, the First National Bank of Boston, in 1987, accepted the conversion of $19 million of its Philippine debt (payment of which had been blocked since 1983 by a debt moratorium imposed by the country's central bank) in exchange for shares in the Commercial Bank of Manila (Arthur Young and Stanford Research Institute 1988, 7–8). The securitization of illiquid assets involves the conversion of essentially nonmarketable debt instruments into securities. In recent years, this securitization or shift of credit flows from bank lending to marketable debt instruments has become a major trend in international financial markets. Banks in the United States have used securitization very successfully for several decades to increase the liquidity of their holdings of home mortgages and automobile receivables.

There are several reasons for the growth of interest in the securitization of international credit flows, but the international debt situation has been a principal one. The presence of strong securities markets in developing countries would have enabled greater reliance on equity finance and thereby lessened the impact on the financial stability of the LDCs of the rapid escalation in world real interest rates. Instead, the debt crisis highlighted the desirability of strengthening and maintaining the liquidity and marketability of bank assets and encouraged banks to strengthen their capital base by issuing more long-term debt. The securitization or packaging for resale of otherwise illiquid assets including housing and automobile loans as well as foreign debt would create a larger pool of securities for trading and thereby contribute to the development of securities markets.

Providing fiscal incentives. Though it is preferable, generally, to promote equity market development by eliminating existing impediments and distortions so as to put all markets on an equal footing, tax incentives are often used as inducements to companies to go public. Reliance on fiscal incentives to encourage equity market development, however, can cause distortions, and most financial market experts agree that such discriminatory policies should be viewed as temporary measures.

Where tax incentives are employed, publicly listed companies typically are taxed at a lower rate than are closely held, nontraded companies. In Thailand, for example, the corporate tax rate for listed companies is 30 percent compared with 40 percent for unlisted ones. In Sri Lanka, newly listed companies are eligible for a 10 percent lower tax rate and a five- to ten-year tax holiday if they invest in priority sectors such as tourism, exporting, and fishing. Egypt gives a tax incentive to companies that list their shares on the country's exchanges. Other incentives might include accelerated rates of depreciation for listed companies for a certain number of years, tax credits or investment allowances for investments in plant and equipment, and concessions on taxes payable in the year after a new public issue of shares is made (Asian Development Bank 1985, 49).

The spectrum of tax incentives that can be applied in equity market development is broad, but none should be expected to be effective if tax laws are poorly administered and tax returns understate income. Under such circumstances, companies are unlikely to go public for fear that financial disclosure will reveal deficiencies in their tax statements. This appears to have been the case in Indonesia, when the government approved tax incentives to encourage companies to go public after the Jakarta Stock Exchange reopened in 1977. By late 1979, only two companies had gone public, even though hundreds of foreign companies were required to transfer majority ownership to Indonesian nationals and were offered tax incentives to go public. One of the main reasons so few companies responded to the incentives is believed to be the desire to avoid disclosure requirements in light of the poorly administered tax system (Dickie 1981, 91).

Increasing the demand for securities. Efforts to increase the demand for securities should be responsive to the several conditions discussed in the following.

Comparative yield. To increase the demand for securities, it is important to place dividend and interest income on an equal footing (Ferris 1987, 12). This can be accomplished in a number of ways: by removing or reducing the double taxation of dividends, removing or reducing the capital gains tax, making interest from bank deposits taxable at a rate comparable to that of dividends, and eliminating other tax disincentives to investment in securities. Thus, any effort to induce increased demand for securities should begin with a review of the tax structure to ensure that it does not discriminate against the securities market. The goal should be to ensure an after-tax return on interest income from savings deposits, corporate funds, and dividends that adequately reflects the investment risk involved.

Japan, for example, does not have a tax on capital gains from securities transactions. According to Kanju Sugimoto, associate director and general manager of the Nomura Securities Company Limited in Japan, the dramatic increase in the number of individual investors in the country is almost entirely the result of the absence of a capital gains tax (Sugimoto 1986, 75). Taiwan, Korea, and Malaysia also do not have capital gains taxes and have experienced rapid growth in the size of their securities markets. Studies by the Securities Industry Association in the United States have shown that reduced capital gains taxation can produce offsetting increases in income tax revenue to the government through the accelerated realization of gains (Securities Industry Association 1986).

Increasing investor confidence. A number of steps can be taken to increase investor confidence (Shipp 1986, 53; Reilly 1986a, 183).

- The availability and reliability of information on the financial condition of listed companies may be increased by enhancing the disclosure of material information by those firms. In consequence, it is also important that adequate accounting and auditing standards be established and implemented. Investor confidence requires the ready availability of complete and trustworthy information on the financial condition of securities-issuing companies. A brokerage infrastructure with the capacity to analyze corporate information and interpret the results in easily understood language will expand the size of the investing public.

- The effectiveness of the regulatory and supervisory environment may be improved so as to allay fears of market manipulation and other abuses. This demands the development not only of a comprehensive system of stock exchange regulations and company laws, but also an effective system for enforcing these regulations.

- Professional requirements for securities brokers would enable them to provide advice to their customers on the financial position of particular companies and take responsible actions on behalf of their customers.

- Provisions to protect the rights of minority shareholders should be required in a country's company laws. An alternative is to incorporate such provisions in the agreement listed companies make with stock exchanges.

- The public could be educated on the benefits of investing in securities and on the way in which securities markets operate through advertising campaigns in the news media, seminars, courses, and other activities. A country's securities commission can initiate this educational process, but as the securities infrastructure develops, these functions should be taken over by stock exchanges, stock brokers, companies, financial institutions, and trade associations. In the United States, for example, investment and brokerage firms have been actively involved in investor education and promotion programs through seminars and other means.

Improving investment experiences. A favorable investment experience is an important stimulus to growth in the demand for securities; few things attract new investors more effectively than reports, from friends or relatives, of successful investments. Conversely, word of an unfavorable investment can be detrimental. In the early stages of equity market development, therefore, it is generally recommended that only the shares of well-established companies with favorable earnings potential and proven management be made available to new investors. This recommendation parallels the suggestion for implementing privatization by the divestiture of *successful* government enterprises and the public distribution of their shares. Public confidence in such companies is generally higher than it is in newly formed entities. Thus, the distribution of shares in privatized companies could greatly contribute to investor interest and demand (Ferris 1973, 7; 1987, 14).

Foreign investment. Foreign portfolio investment can increase the demand for securities and provide a stimulus to the development of securities markets. The International Finance Corporation has been particularly adamant in its support for the liberalization of flows of portfolio investment across borders and has focused considerable attention on the important role of such investment in solving the third world debt crisis (Gill 1986, 9–19). As described earlier, however, many countries still place restrictions on foreign portfolio investment in local securities. Yet, the benefits of foreign investment funds are numerous. These funds help to speed up the process of equity market development (Pearson 1986, 213–16) by: (1) supplying an immediate source of previously unavailable equity capital, (2) bringing a variety of ancillary benefits to recipient countries in the form of investment technology transfers, including better research and investment marketing techniques and more advanced computer hardware and software, and (3) being, potentially, a country's first step in opening its stock market to foreign equity investors (as in Korea, and now in Thailand and India).

The Korean government adopted a series of policies in the early 1980s designed to open the stock market to foreign investors over a ten-year period. Initial steps involved the issuance of two private placement mutual funds, Korea Trust and Korea International Trust, for a total of $50 million. This was followed by the launching in 1984 of a closed-end investment trust, the Korea Fund, a second issue of which followed in 1986. To attract foreign portfolio investment, Korea adopted procedures to protect investors and establish acceptable accounting and auditing standards. In addition, Korean officials eliminated most of the fiscal barriers by reducing withholding taxes on dividends and abolishing them on capital gains (Pyun 1986, 207–10; Gill 1984, 48).

According to Peter Pearson, the managing director of Fidelity International Investment Management (Hong Kong) Limited, the Korean approach of establishing foreign investment trusts can be a catalyst for much broader and rapid development of a securities market that might follow a pattern in approximately this order: (1) investment in domestic equities, (2) the establishment of foreign investment funds for investing in bonds and equities, (3) the establishment of a domestic unit trust (mutual fund) industry employing techniques imported by the foreign fund, (4) the establishment of a limited program to allow foreign institutions to purchase selected individual shares, (5) the establishment of specialized foreign funds to invest in particular sectors of the market, (6) the establishment of domestic unit trusts to invest overseas,

(7) the complete liberalization of stock markets to permit investments by foreign institutions and individuals (Pearson 1986, 216).

Tax incentives. Just as a government's fiscal (especially tax) policies can influence a firm's choice to provide itself with additional funds by means of either debt finance (in the form of bank loans) or equity finance (by issuing securities)—as previously discussed regarding approaches to increasing the *supply* of securities—so can tax policies increase the *demand* for securities by making equities more or less attractive relative to other forms of savings.

Developing, as well as industrialized, countries have provided a wide variety of tax incentives to stimulate demand for securities. Some incentives have been more successful than others. Among developing countries, the Brazilian approach is frequently cited as one of the most successful tax incentive plans (see Teixeira da Costa 1985, 40–43; and Drake 1977, 85–86). Beginning in 1965, the Brazilian government established a series of tax incentives to foster the growth of the securities market by encouraging individuals, as well as institutions, to invest in shares or debentures of publicly traded companies. One of the most important steps the government took was the creation through Decree-Law Number 157, of special mutual funds known as "157 Funds." Tax provisions allowed individuals and corporations (but currently only individuals) to deduct a portion of their income tax liabilities as long as the amount deducted was invested in the mutual funds. To encourage long-term investment, withdrawals from these funds could not begin for at least two years. The mutual funds were in turn required to invest in company securities, particularly in new issues, but the government designated the proportion of funds that had to be invested in new issues, on the one hand, and in already traded shares, on the other.

Tax-relief provisions also allowed individual Brazilians to offset against income tax a portion of the cost of buying listed stocks or convertible bonds. Other incentives provided for the partial exemption of dividends from personal income taxation and for concessional rates of withholding taxes for shareholders in public companies that undertook to widen their equity base. These incentives led to a tremendous growth in individual and institutional demand for securities and produced impressive increases in the volume of shares issued and traded. According to IFC statistics, the number of open capital companies—those that have opened their share capital to public subscription—rose from 209 in 1968 to 551 in 1978. In addition, the value of shares traded yearly on the Rio de Janeiro and Saõ Paulo stock exchanges jumped from U.S. $131 million in 1968 to U.S. $4.818 billion in 1971 (Hakim 1985, 22).

The role of institutional investors. Institutional investors such as pension funds, insurance companies, and mutual funds can play a vital role in mobilizing savings and investing those savings. Investment trusts and mutual funds provide advantages, in particular to small investors, through diversification, professional portfolio management, and continuous supervision by professional managers. And as exemplified by the "157 Funds" in Brazil, the provision of tax incentives for investment in specialized investment trusts can provide an important stimulus to capital market development.

Development banks can also contribute to the success of mutual funds and the development of equity markets by spinning off some of their established developing company shares into closed-end mutual funds distributed to the public and managed by the development bank. This frees up development funds that would otherwise have provided additional debt financing to supply, instead, new venture capital.

Some countries, including Brazil and Korea, however, have gone beyond the provision of fiscal incentives to encourage investment in securities. In 1985, for example, Korea adopted a regulation requiring life insurance companies to invest a minimum of 5 percent of their available funds in local equities. Similarly, Brazilian pension funds are required to invest a minimum of 20 percent of their available investment funds in domestic equities (Gill 1986, 3–4).

Regardless of the success of portfolio composition requirements such as these, they are not recommended components of a strategy for stimulating the development of a securities market. These requirements, like those of institutions to invest some percentage of

Equity Market Development

their funds in government securities, in fact constitute impediments to the free interplay of demand and supply and can result in significant distortions of the market. The practice of government's effectively directing the way in which private individuals and entities spend their earnings is but a step removed from government's spending it for them. The failure of such command-and-control systems has never been more evident than it is today.

It is hoped that the considerations of this chapter will contribute to a better understanding of the policy and institutional requirements for the development of capital markets and of the links between the growth of equity markets and economic development.

Terrence C. Reilly

Comment

My topic is a subset of capital markets. We have discussed the capital market in its broad sense and placed a lot of emphasis on the deposit-taking institutions, monetary policy, and so forth. You will find me at the other end of the spectrum. I am not so theoretical. My knowledge is more of the nuts-and-bolts components of capital markets. My perspective on the chapter under discussion is also different in that I was one of the members of the Arthur Young team who contributed to it.

I am going to summarize some of the fundamental points that are mentioned in the chapter and that are part of my experience, so first of all let me tell you who I am and what I do. I am a practicing financial and securities lawyer who has been working with international organizations for the past twelve years. I respond to invitations from host countries to help develop their securities market, the stock and bond market. These countries range from Latin America to Africa, throughout the Middle East, and in the Far East. For example, my first experience was in Chile, where I met Rolf Lüders.

If you will allow me, I want to apply an adage that some

Americans use: smart people are entitled to ask dumb questions. I am going to assume that you are asking me what is the purpose of developing a securities market, because from what I have heard this morning, it seems to me there is not a great deal of common experience in what you and I do.

You are worried about macro policies. This morning somebody said that an objective of liberalization is to move away from the banking system and allow a freer financial system to raise capital through the sale of stocks and bonds. A second point indicated that you want to capture funds that are available in savings but that are not being put into productive enterprise.

What the securities market is designed to do is allow enterprises to raise long-term finance. In order for it to do that, there must be a primary market having underwriters and issuers and there must be a secondary market to provide liquidity once the securities are being issued and traded. You cannot do any of this unless you have adequate macro policies. For example, in a country where the interest rate is very high, you are not going to get long-term securities. The entrepreneur asks why he should put his money into expanding his plant when he can make more by putting it in the bank, or when he can buy government securities and get paid 22 percent.

The major thrust of the securities market is private sector growth. That is why countries wish to create them. Sometimes capital market projects are accused of focusing on the plumbing—putting in the capital market institutions, the stock exchanges, the underwriters, the brokers and dealers—but not worrying about whether there is any water to flow through the plumbing. If you find a country that is at a very basic stage of economic development, the kind of capital markets that I am involved in would not be relevant, whereas the policies discussed earlier probably would be.

The purpose of this seminar, I believe, is to devise certain considerations that international agencies might take into account in providing assistance to various countries. The first thing I would say, if you are with an international organization or loan agency, is that you should not expect the securities market to be a panacea. You should first look to see whether the underlying economy in the country is likely to prosper. If it does not have the basic macro policies that you think are relevant, those must be put in place. You should also keep in mind that there may be many economies that are basically agricultural; in these, the costs of immediate and intense securities market activities are likely to exceed their benefits. On that basis, capital and securities market development is more sensible, at the moment, in Chile than it is in Ghana.

If the country passes the test for need, then the next question addresses the government's view about the private sector. Here you find great vacillation. Governments seem to want to encourage the private sector, but at the same time maintain direct control. I do not mean by this the debate about whether you have a directed economy, which I would say India has, or whether you have a free economy. Even in a directed economy, the government allows the private sector to do certain things. But government allocates resources to control who can do what, because it supports certain priority industries. What I am talking about is the basic environment for business. Can business establish itself? Can you get a permit to start a new business, or are you competing with some government official? This underlying environment for business is crucial to the development of securities markets. In some countries people will wonder why you are interested in the development of a securities market. If you do not have the opportunity to make a profit, if you cannot get permits to expand the plant, if you must employ extra workers all the time, if you cannot fire anybody, and if there is corruption, securities markets may not seem very important. Those people are right. So, before you start worrying about a stock market and underwriters, you have to look at the basic business environment.

Assume that we have passed those hurdles. Now what are the specific problems in securities market development? The basic problem appears to be in the supply of securities. That is, companies are not used to raising long-term finance. For example, someone asked this morning why, in Chile, there are only fifteen companies raising long-term finance. The answer is that the companies are not used to doing that. The entrepreneur wants to control his business. In this country we have a separation of business ownership and management. This was first carefully examined during the 1930s in a famous book by A. A. Berle and Gardiner Means (1932). But in most parts of the world, particularly in the developing world, if you start a business, you want to own it. You do not want somebody else to have access to its profits. If you retain control, you can take care of yourself very well. You can have three cars and three houses and you can pass this wealth along in your family. So companies do not want to raise long-term finance through equity because they would then have to give away some of the ownership.

A second problem in securities market development is that banking institutions have been there all along and they have established relationships with entrepreneurs and are willing to lend funds for the short term.

Third, the tax laws encourage debt over equity. If you borrow a million dollars and you pay 10 percent interest, the interest is a deduction from pretax income. If you sold a million dollars worth of shares and paid out a 10 percent dividend, the dividend comes from after-tax income. So there is a bias built in against equity financing.

The normal situation in a developing country is that banking institutions are in place and are way out ahead. There is an imbalance against equity. My view is that what you have to do is reduce that imbalance. The government should take steps to encourage the growth of a market to provide long-term capital.

When I was first working in Chile, we asked whether the government was going to provide incentives. They gave us the Chicago School answer: no incentives; leave it alone; all we want to do is to allow people to have a greater sense of confidence in the market—which means providing some form of regulation, not incentives.

But in other countries, such as Venezuela, they give tax incentives for companies to go public. If you go public, your tax rate is reduced from X to Y. Some countries have found this does not work. But some method of encouragement to go public is probably necessary in many countries in order for the supply of securities to be substantial enough to have a market.

At the far extreme of this is Korea, which is touted as the model country in terms of securities market development. They have a policy that earlier led them to tell companies that you cannot have access to the bank market and commercial lending unless you raise long-term finance in the securities market. In 1987, I believe, Korea told fifty-six companies to go public. So we have the Chilean situation in which they make a level field through broad policies, the Venezuelan approach, in which they provide some incentives, and, at the far end of the spectrum, the Korean approach, in which they actually force companies to go public.

To have a policy for increasing the supply of securities, it is normally required that government officials be convinced that a securities market is necessary and important. Government officials are usually familiar with the banking market but do not have any familiarity with the securities market. They do not think it is terribly important because the local entrepreneurs are not after it. Therefore, a great deal of education is required in order for government officials to arrive at a position of adopting policies for encouraging the supply of securities.

The next step is to take the three traditional areas in securities market development—supply, demand, and underwriting—and see what has to be done. As I say, supply is often a tax problem. But also, owners are afraid of losing control. These problems have to be dealt with. They are very micro policies.

In the supply field, for example, you might find that it is impossible to issue preferred shares. You might urge a company to issue preferred shares because you know the entrepreneur does not wish to lose control. If he could issue a nonvoting preferred share, he would not lose control. He could redeem the share after five years. This is something that France did. You might find that no one has ever thought about issuing preferred shares. But if they did think about it, they would find out that they cannot do it because the most recent company law, based on a nineteenth century statute, says that preferred shares can pay an interest rate of only 4 percent per year (not per month), so the security will never be used.

In other countries, you will find that you cannot issue convertible debentures. Why are convertible debentures interesting? Well, they provide access to longer-term finance, but the fact that the debenture is a bond that is convertible into shares provides a sweetener for the investor. He knows he will get his interest, but he also benefits if the company does well and his bonds are converted into shares. It turns out that the government has a company law, again adapted from some earlier legislation, that says that, every time a share is issued, all of the shareholders must vote on it. That means if you want to convert your debenture, you have got to have the shareholders approve it, which is impossible. In that situation, you have got to convince the government to change that law.

Capital market development at the supply level entails many specific concerns that only emerge when you consider how to get people to issue long-term securities. Frequently, no one in the government has been doing that. When you ask why securities are not being issued even after the country has done everything right on the macro level, my answer is that no one has gone through the system and ripped out all of these impediments.

On the demand side—that is, on the matter of who is going to buy the securities—often the savers receive tax incentives to deposit their funds in the government postal service or the banks. In one country where I worked, it turned out that a company wishing to provide the after-tax yield equivalent to a bank deposit would have to offer up to 48 percent return. If I put $100 in the bank, rather than put it into shares, my bank interest would be tax-free. In order to get the same yield from a stock, I would have to receive substantially more than the company earns. The company cannot afford to pay that much, so the demand inadequacy feeds the supply inadequacy.

I can go through a litany of these problems, but they are all raised in the chapter. What I am trying to point out is that there are many small, specific factors that affect the development of capital markets. You will seldom find literature describing these factors. They tend to be a reflection of accumulated past policies that are naturally biased against the securities market.

On Wall Street there is a saying that securities are not bought, they are sold. That does not mean they are bad items, but that somebody has to make the effort. In the United States, the somebody is an underwriter who is looking for a transaction commission. An underwriter will go to General Motors and suggest that the company issue bonds or shares. If the underwriter finds the law is not adequate in the state in which the company is incorporated, he will bring pressure to have the company reincorporate in a different state, or to change the law, or both. From the 1920s to the 1930s, most of the state laws in the United States were changed because underwriters were trying to develop business and they found that state laws were impeding them. So the laws were changed.

In many countries, if you are trying to be an underwriter, you encounter tremendous difficulties. Say I am trying to be an underwriter and I recommend that you raise $10 million in the bond market, rather than borrow it for the short term. You say that you might be interested. But, before you issue those bonds, the government has to approve the price, the terms, and all the specifics of the bonds. You can see the problem this presents.

In summary, the greatest impediments to the development of a securities market may not be the macro issues discussed here. Frequently, the major obstacles are created by seemingly innocuous or minor provisions in statutes and regulations. Experience teaches us that it can be difficult to identify and eliminate these provisions. But the task must be accomplished in order to permit the operation of an efficient securities market, which is one step toward allowing individuals and countries to develop to their maximum potential.

Discussion

Mr. Lüders: I do think that tax discrimination against securities is very important in Chile, and in most of Latin America. As Terrence Reilly says, this discrimination occurs wherever individuals are not required to pay taxes on interest, but must pay taxes on dividend income.

In Chile, the tax law was changed to avoid this problem. Reinvested profits are now tax-exempt. Moreover, for all practical purposes, dividend income is eliminated from taxation for most medium and small investors. So it does not make much of a difference anymore whether you deposit at a bank or have dividend income.

Mr. Reilly: But that is from the point of view of the saver. From the point of view of the entrepreneur, he would rather maintain control and also get his tax deduction for the interest he pays.

Mr. Walters: Would it be possible to deduct the dividend payments just as they deduct interest, before they assess the tax? That would put the two on exactly the same basis.

Mr. Reilly: There is that approach. Or you could allow the recipient of dividends to deduct from his income taxes the taxes paid on his pro rata share of the company's gross income. There are arguments for doing it one way or the other. The question is, why do governments usually ignore both methods?

Mr. Walters: The only answer must be that they tolerate nonentities that hate entrepreneurs. That must be it.

Mr. Reilly: I think governments have gotten used to the tax deduction for interest. It is something that came to them—more a consequence of tradition than of design.

Mr. Lüders: But I think all that has been done in Chile.

Mr. Walters: On the firm side. You are right.

Mr. Lüders: No. Some people might have such a strong preference for being sole owners that they will not issue securities. But others, for whom profit, rather than control, is more important, now have a neutral choice available—to finance their assets with either equity or credit, as there is no longer tax discrimination against securities income.

What is very important in our case is the development of institutional investors. The AFPs, which are similar to private pension funds, are accumulating significant amounts of money that they can now invest in shares of companies controlled by the public sector. But these companies are being privatized, so the shares will very soon be shares that belong to privately controlled companies. I think that this development is very significant. I know Silvia Sagari would like to see even more progress on this point, but it is occurring at a very rapid pace without exceeding the limits of prudence.

Mr. Reilly: But the AFPs are allowed only to buy shares in listed companies. Is that correct?

Mr. Lüders: The companies have to be listed, and in addition to that, they have to be approved by a commission.

Mr. Reilly: Right. Well, regarding the businessperson who does not want to issue shares, it may be that he just does not want to expose his company to the disclosure that a public issue would bring. In this country, if you did not want to do that, which is not normally a problem, you would have a private placement with an insurance company or pension fund. Private placements do not require that you be listed. That may be an area for you to look into.

Ms. SAGARI: Yes, we have looked at that, and the regulation of AFPs prevents them from investing in firms that are not listed.

But I want to ask you about your experience with secondary or over-the-counter (OTC) markets, where firms could be traded with less disclosure of information, which I think may well be the way to go in some places.

MR. REILLY: OTC. Does everybody understand what an OTC is? Let me explain it from my point of view. OTC simply means trading that does not meet the listing standards on a stock exchange. It is simply a way to market shares for some companies that could not sell them in the past because they had to meet the listing standards of an exchange.

I think it is a good idea to allow that. I do not think there is any great cachet that comes from the listing approval of the Bangladesh Stock Exchange. I do not think any comes from the Hong Kong Stock Exchange, either. So, fine, let there be other companies, so long as people understand these are more risky companies.

A question then arises about this asymmetry in disclosure: a listed company versus a nonlisted company. There is a growing trend in developing countries to decide they ought to have listed and nonlisted companies. They often grab hold of the nonlisted approach thinking that maybe it will stimulate supply. It often does not because, in fact, the entrepreneur does not care whether his stock is listed or not listed. He just does not want to sell it.

If listing standards are very restrictive, such as a requirement for three years of demonstrated earnings of a certain percentage, and if that stops the institutional investor from buying any other security, then I would say have a second tier or over-the-counter market where companies meeting a lower standard could be traded. They did this in London with the unlisted securities market. People think it is quite successful. They are thinking about doing it in Hong Kong. I think they are doing it or thinking about it in Singapore. But I do not see it as a panacea.

Mr. Kalotra: You asked why the government should have a liberalization of policies. I do not know how many people in this room know—I did not know, for instance—it is not only the governments that need to liberalize. The African Development Bank, by its mandate, is not allowed to promote the private sector, per se, because all the colonies that contributed to the bank have specifically prohibited such activity. We have asked the African Development Bank to work on this problem. They had their first roundtable on private sector development in early 1988. Bear in mind, though, that there are wheels within wheels, so more than one government plays a role in making policy for the bank.

Secondly, being an accountant, I would like to comment on the question of taxation on risk capital versus interest. In India, dividends are not allowed as a deduction in the corporate tax computation, and there is also a tax on the shareholders when they receive the dividends. In spite of that, which is the normal practice, we have learned a lot from our British forefathers.

When the English and the Scots came to India, they realized that, even though savings in the country are very substantial, most savings are in the household sector. Today, the savings in the Indian household sector are between 23 and 34 percent of personal GDP. But cultural habits cause savers to put it in ornaments and other things or into land. You do not put it in the stock exchange.

When they started businesses in India, the British realized that they had nobody to buy shares except one community, the Parsees. (Zubin Mehta is one.) That community, as part of their historical culture, did not believe that they needed ornaments. They had always put money into shares.

The British took on one company, made it successful, established a track record, and then sold the shares and bought another company. They did that for forty companies, and the concept of what is called "managing agency houses" came into being in India. It was one way of encouraging an investment-shy public to put money into business shares.

The managing agency houses were sometimes roundly misused

by the owners. If a company was doing badly, the owner could play around with bookkeeping transfers. I was employed by a managing agency house as an accountant when I started working. The Indian law said that there could be no outstanding balances between the companies at the end of the day. We used to write checks to each other before closing so that there was no balance at the end of the day. We knew how to get around the law.

What the Indian government did was remarkable, and perhaps Chile has something to learn out of this. When the managing agency house was stopped, the Indian government realized that it was understandable that Indians were still reluctant to invest in the securities market. Five or six development banks were established. They are government owned and their main task is to underwrite issues and provide long-term finance, not short-term, because there is a large banking system.

A lot of people do not understand this. In large Indian companies, government institutions sometimes hold between 4 percent and 8 percent of equity, but they generally do not interfere in the management. In the past ten or fifteen years, they have been putting people on the company boards to look after the capital that has been provided by the government development bank. Though I am generally opposed to the use of government money in this manner, there is no doubt that what these development banks have done in India is remarkable. There would be a far smaller formal private sector in the country but for their loans and the government's allowing private enterprise to manage those projects themselves.

You talked about convertible loans. I helped issue the first convertible loans in India, and it was not immediately successful. We found out that our present results were not as good as future returns. We went to the government and convinced it that the concept of a fixed convertible loan after ten years was a good one, we sold it to the Indian public, and it is now a common instrument.

Similarly, to draw short-term capital out of a public that is used to putting money either in jewelry or in cash, we have what are called public deposits. All of a sudden, private sector and public sector companies started taking unsecured deposits directly from the public. This reduced the burden on the banking system because it tapped resources that were not previously available.

The point I am trying to make is that there are innovative ways to arrange financing. Pakistan has taken much the same approach in following the development bank concept. One has to understand and accept the cultural aspects of the people and their societies. In India, we have separate communities, if we talk about business and entrepreneurs. There are the Marwaris and Gujaratis who are entretreneurial. Go anywhere in Africa and you will find that they still control the trading community. They are part of our diversity in which different sorts of people do different things, and it is in their nature to take risks.

Having made my point, I want now to be advised and helped. One of the biggest questions in my mind is why we have so much of a problem in the formal sector of the economy. I have never seen a problem in the informal sector of the economy. In India, the informal sector of the economy is 40 percent of the formal sector. In other countries, it is between 50 percent and 60 percent. I have been studying the lessons to be learned from the informal sector of the economy.

I think somebody said that 80 percent of American employment is in firms with fewer than five hundred people, and 90 percent of the work force in developing countries are working in firms that employ fewer than fifty people. Big firms in the formal sector are the exception.

What is it then that is in the informal sector? What is in the large informal sector all over the world that we need to share with the formal sectors? How can we tap that informal money and use it for development rather than exploitation?

Mr. Birdzell: I want to respond to the question of the uses of the informal sector. If you look at the history of Western countries and even some of the postwar Gang of Four, you have a question as to whether you can introduce free-market institutions unless you already have such institutions dominating an informal sector of the economy.

The English acquired a free market by lawlessness, violence, and political corruption, as we did. Unless you have an informal market that is able to battle political forces favoring political control, it may not be strategically possible to achieve free markets in the more formal and open sections of the society. There is certainly nothing in history that gives you any encouragement to think that you will get free markets by the voluntary retirement of political forces.

The other thing that I want to touch on is the question of what difference it makes to have listed, unlisted, or no securities. In the American history of listing industrial securities, there is no point in listing unless you have people who are interested in trading. What is valuable about listed securities is their regular day-to-day operating market.

Some of the New England textile companies were listed on the Boston Stock Exchange, but nobody ever traded them because majority control in the firms was held by families of the company founders. So, the first thing you have to do if you are to have trading in securities is to dilute family ownership. Of course, that is what the organizers of trusts did. They took ownership away from the families, or at least divided it among a number of families, and thereby created a group of people who were interested in trading. Also, in setting these companies up, they sold shares to the investment bankers' customers. But, at any rate, you got a wide enough distribution of ownership that a market could operate in which companies could be usefully listed.

There are various estimates of what securities trading meant in terms of the value of the company. My recollection is that the going rate for the sale of a proprietorship was a matter of two or three times earnings in the period we are talking about. The going rate for the sale of securities in a listed company was about ten times earnings. You automatically multiplied the value of the property by two or three times when you listed it. This, of course, provided the investment bankers with an enormous margin for making offers that people could not refuse.

It is funny: some people never understood the mechanism. Andrew Carnegie always maintained that he sold his company for twice what it was worth, and the language was watered stock. But, actually, when compared with a listed company, a proprietorship was almost unmarketable.

Listing a company made stock purchase a short-term investment. It made it a short-term investment only so long as you had an active market in the stock. You could evaluate performance from day to day. If you did not like the direction in which the company was going, you did not have to wait until it was bankrupt. You could get out. You could diversify. You did not have to invest in one industry. You did not have to have your whole family fortune tied up in New England textile mills. You could distribute it across the board in small pieces.

Listing a stock converted the tremendous risk of an investment in a large, specialized, multimillion dollar factory into the much more attractive risk of a number of small investments that could be converted into cash by calling a broker. The market evaluated that at something like three to one.

Regarding unlisted securities, a lot of unlisted securities have only fictitious markets. There are not enough people to buy and sell to enable you to match what you can get out of listed securities. So, it is a sort of step down.

But as I say, experience indicates that, if you are going to have a capital market for securities, you are going to have to first get rid of family ownership of the companies. Second, you are going to have to have a fairly large number of people who are interested in churning these things. Another element you need is a difference of opinion on what companies are worth. Otherwise, you get no trade.

I think it would take a while to develop those institutions. There are nations that think all you have to do is build an exchange and open it.

MR. REILLY: I think that is right. That is why I tried to make the allusion to priming the pump. You cannot just create a securities market and say here we have it.

The attitudes of the New England families that you described encouraged the distribution and diversification of ownership. Presumably, they could find enough buyers. The underwriters there could see a profit, and there were other companies to do business with. That is different from what you are going to find in most of today's developing countries.

MR. BIRDZELL: That is one of the problems of economics. It is easy to describe the institutions you need. It is very hard to describe where you get the people that operate them.

MR. REILLY: My advice to an international agency or anybody thinking about this is to emphasize that establishing a capital market is a slow process and to repeat that securities are sold and not bought. So, the institutions should be allowed to make a profit.

Does that sound consistent with what your perception is?

MR. BIRDZELL: Oh, sure. I am not a believer in the theory that if you set up the correct institutions, everything happens by spontaneous combustion. But I do think that you must have a relationship between people. Indians, for instance, are always on the list of people that have a long trading tradition. That is why they are so very unpopular in Africa. In trying to explain why the Gang of Four has been so successful, we conclude that much of their success is because the Chinese have a long history of trade and commerce.

MR. KALOTRA: Not only that. They took over from the Brits as a trading community. Trading was the whole basis of the British Empire.

MR. BIRDZELL: So, do not take trading people and give them an institutional brace that they do not fit into.

MR. WALTERS: I would like to get some of your expertise on a question that occurs to me as being quite critical in all these things.

About fifteen years ago, it was well known that the markets of Hong Kong and Kuala Lumpur were a scandal. They were manipulated, and there is no doubt about that. In fact, I knew the manipulators. Very nice chaps, but, nevertheless, their hands were as dirty as the coal man's.

But what has been happening recently is this: There has been an increasing desire in the West to spread our portfolios and to acquire assets of all sorts in places such as Malaysia, Singapore, and Hong

Kong. These markets have been coming into contact with the big players such as Scudder, Fidelity, and so on. These big boys, as I understand it, have been saying: Look, we have got big bucks to spend with you, but you simply cannot play your little games. You have got to have an open market.

This seems to be an aspect of a general beneficial trend in capital markets. Third world capital markets are going to benefit from this enormously because of the greater contact with the West. The greater the contact with the West, the better. The financial practices that you reviewed—openness, standards of accounting, and all those other things—make the London market and Wall Street much more open and much less susceptible to manipulation than are those markets in the East.

This also occurs in other respects, for example, in the development of leasing companies. Leasing companies have been financially successful and very sound in the third world. There are all sorts of other companies, too, that have developed quite recently. That development is mainly because of contacts with the West and attempts by the managers of Western portfolios to diversify into these markets, where they see better prospects for profit than they see in the Western markets.

I believe this contact with the West is a great impetus to development and wealth creation in the third world. First, from the development of direct foreign investment because techniques, management, and expertise in many cases can be imported. Second, from portfolio investment they acquire not the techniques, perhaps, but standard international practices, which are accepted in Switzerland, London, and the United States.

You did not mention it, but I wonder if that is your impression, too, and I would like to know what your expertise tells you about all this.

MR. REILLY: I take your proposition to be that the development of these securities markets is aided by exposure to more sophisticated investors with different techniques that then get transported to the local economy. All this has a salutary effect. I suppose you could cite the following example.

When the Hong Kong Stock Exchange closed last October for four days, the criticism of it was that the decision was made by the head of the stock exchange. He represents the committee of twenty-one, which is made up of local brokers. The big foreign brokers do not have access to that decision-making process. Now that is all being challenged and questioned by the Hay-Davidson Committee, which is going to make the market a little more open and representative.

Your question is, do I think that is a good idea or a bad idea? I must say I do not start with your presumption that it is good for a market to be exposed to a London merchant bank money manager. The basis of that presumption is that they are going to learn better practices in Malaysia or Hong Kong or wherever it is. But, I do not think those better practices are necessarily tailored to that country. Maybe there are other more appropriate methods for that country that will encourage private sector growth. They may not look the same as markets in London or Hong Kong, but they may accommodate healthy private sector growth through the securities market.

If you look at the history of the Singapore securities law, for example, you would find that the attorney general decided in 1969 that speculation was inherent in the market. That embodies a cultural point of view about how the Chinese like to invest. So he was not going to rip it out. He was not going to pass insider trading rules.

My impression, without having any evidence, is that although your presumption may be true, it should be tempered by a recognition that there may be things that are appropriate in a more buccaneering economy that might be removed by too much exposure to the kinds of premises that underlie a fair market in the West.

If I were in Hong Kong and someone were making this proposition to me that my market ought to operate more like London does, I would say, oh, you mean like Morgan Grenfell and all the problems they had when they were representing the Guinness Company and manipulated the stock? How fair is that? I would say, let me in my country cheat my way, and I will develop my market my way.

MR. WALTERS: I think what I would say is simply that countries can learn from contacts. I was not suggesting for a moment that these countries should copy London. The West has developed techniques and institutional mechanisms. It has developed them by making mistakes. The third world, in my view, can learn a hell of a lot from this. We can learn a little from the third world on other things, too.

MR. REILLY: I would limit my earlier rejection of the proposition to the area of securities regulation. Do not try to make these markets in developing countries poison-clean like a hospital because it will not work. But I will agree with you on techniques such as trying convertible debentures in Mexico, or some place. Someone can tell them about that.

I was recently in Bangladesh, and I found out that the equivalent of the underwriting house gets shares from the company going public and sells them off five years after the company has been nurtured. But it is required to sell those shares at par value. That did not sound right to me because they have nurtured this company. I ended up in a long conversation that turned into sort of a mutual congratulation society. Someone said, you mean I can sell them for more than par, the market value? They thought it was just a tremendous discovery. I think that kind of exposure is very constructive.

MR. WALTERS: I found that a fund that has been set up to promote Malayanization has the legal right to buy any stocks it fancies at par value. In other words, it is licensed to expropriate. Now of course, there is great reluctance on the part of Western portfolio holders to buy into this market knowing that their holdings can be expropriated. Relating this back to the other point: I think it is very important to realize that the instruments we use in the West are not necessarily the right ones for those countries. I remember when we were in Malaysia, Ed Shaw and I both agreed that one of the best instruments you could develop in Malaysia would be a five- to seven-year certificate of deposit. There is nothing like that in the West at all.

Discussion 309

MR. REILLY: You will find something similar to this in the Arab world in things called Musharakahs and Mudarabahs, which are Islamic instruments. You do not find any public companies floating securities, but you will find there is a fund somewhere in Geneva that has half a billion dollars representing Saudi investors in these little certificates because they want to invest Islamically.

MR. WALTERS: I would like to come back to the point about the gap that has appeared in providing long-term capital of various sorts. About ten or twelve years ago, there was an attempt to fill this gap in five- to seven-year capital supply. The way in which it was to be implemented was through the development financial institutions or corporations (DFIs or DFCs). The idea in setting them up was that the governments would get them going. Eventually, however, they would attract a lot of private sector capital through deposits and develop substantially as private sector operations.

We have had some experience now for the past decade. We can look back on not a happy experience at all. First, those institutions did not develop private sources of capital. On the contrary, they became more and more dependent upon flows of concessionary borrowing from the World Bank, A.I.D., and from government. They failed as institutions that raised capital.

That is the one side of it. The lending side looks even worse, I am sorry to say. The expectations were that somehow lending would provide capital for up-and-coming firms. It would be the engine of development according to relative advantage. Exactly the opposite occurred. Generally speaking, the capital has been supplied to large well-established firms at concessional interest rates with credit rationing. Those firms have been politically well placed.

These funds have been channeled into the old traditional firms. Just like any other civil servants, the lenders do the same thing that they have always done: it becomes an issue of precedent. In fact, many of the firms are in great financial difficulties. There are exceptions, some outstanding exceptions, that have done well. But on the whole, they are in very bad straits.

There is an argument that we should walk away from them and

specify that only competitive institutions able to raise money on the markets will be allowed to receive these long-term injections of cash. That is one way of dealing with it. Politically, though, it would be very difficult indeed. But clearly something must be done about these institutions. I would like to know what views you have. What you would do about them?

MR. REILLY: My experience is that they behave just the way you have described them. I have come to the conclusion that development financial institutions are irrelevant for purposes of securities market evolution not only for the reasons you have mentioned but because often the local government does not allow them to raise money in the local market. In addition to that, when they are speaking to the entrepreneur—I am told by various of these entities—and looking for some equity to make a longer term investment, the entrepreneur simply says no. So DFIs were frustrated.

Your question goes to what could be done about it. I may be insulting some by saying I tend to favor unsubsidized credit markets. Maybe instead of walking away, you should slowly creep away because the more you are there the more subsidized credit is going to be considered an indispensable crutch.

In one country I worked in, the subsidized credit was so badly used that only the most ridiculously speculative company ever went to the securities market. For example, it was clearly understood that if you wish to build a hotel you organize a $10,000 company. Then you go to various DFIs and obtain subsidized credit to import the goods needed for the hotel. Next you go abroad with a $5 million credit from the DFI. You buy $4 million worth of goods and are billed $5 million to allow for your "commission." The goods are delivered and the hotel goes bankrupt. You lose the original $10,000, but you make a million. Why? Subsidized credit.

I am very pessimistic about those arrangements. But there are other ones in India that are apparently much more successful at doing what they should do.

MR. KALOTRA: Looking at success stories to find out what made them successful, we can learn valuable lessons that may be relevant to numerous countries.

India's first DFI was the Industrial Development Bank of India (IDBI), seen by the government as an extension of its central bank or reserve bank. Staff from the central bank was assigned to IDBI. Within one year, the government realized this was not the way it could assist the private sector. So it set up yet another institution, realizing that you could not change the culture of this first institution at all except by example.

The second industrial bank employed professional people from the financial world who had never worked in government. They were told that, for all practical purposes, they were not a part of the government except that some part of their money would come from government. The rest would have to come either from the Indian public or other sources. The bank could lend openly in the international markets and work it out. The advantage of establishing the new unit was that it was run by professionals who knew what they were doing. The net result was that there was competition between this bank and the first (IDBI), to the betterment of the first.

Then, realizing the need to attract far greater resources, the government established what is called a Unit Trust of India in which the public could invest. That became successful and professional.

None of this was easy, and it seems that much could be gained by our sharing the experiences of India and other countries with one another. Perhaps those having the most trouble are encountering very nearly the same difficulties as India overcame. It would seem worth finding out.

We cannot take away the political issues. We cannot take away the kickbacks. But experience has taught me that if people in the country can find even one or two success stories within their country or a comparable country, there is a better chance of replicating them. This is all I am recommending. It is difficult, but it is doable.

Mr. Walters: I think a competitive structure and raising capital from the private sector at market rates are critical ingredients in any success we have seen in the DFCs.

Ms. Sagari: On the issue of DFCs, I fully agree with you. We are trying to figure out what is a good way to fill this gap. Obviously all the subsidies should be eliminated, and maybe one should look for some better institutional arrangements that would improve the performance of these corporations. In particular, trying to get more professional bankers and fewer civil servants to manage these institutions may help. The discouraging fact is that we have looked in detail at the private banking sector in many countries, and I am afraid we have to report that the condition of the long portfolios of these private banks is not much better than that of the DFCs.

I have a very specific question, though. In the United States you can buy insurance for municipal bonds. We have been considering the possible implementation of some bond insurance schemes. I believe in some of the developed countries such as England there is insurance for bonds issued by private corporations. But I know nothing about these issues, and I wonder whether you know of any successful experience with bond guarantees. This would be for bonds issued in the market. You would buy insurance against the return involved and the face value of the bond.

Mr. Reilly: The municipal bond is already a government instrument, right? So somebody is already standing behind it with government power. How are you going to apply that to a private sector issuer? Once you do that, you are altering the market forces because the buyer looks at the guarantor.

Ms. Sagari: Well, you could think of a scheme where a specialized agent analyzes the information about a firm and guarantees the face value of the bond. Some academicians have suggested that guaranteed bonds could be marketed in such a way that you would pay the issuer to buy insurance. The rate at which the bond is issued plus the fee paid to the insurer would be less than the rate for nonguaranteed bonds.

Mr. Reilly: The purchaser of the bond is looking at the creditworthiness of the guarantor. So, therefore, he is demanding a lower return on the bond and the issuer is paying a lower rate. But my question is, what is the benefit of all of this and who actually stands behind the bond? It is not the issuer anymore, it is the person issuing insurance.

Ms. SAGARI: I would say it is both. There is a primary person issuing the bond. And then there is a second agent who is willing to guarantee the bond.

MR. REILLY: How do you fund this guarantor? It seems to me the guarantor has got to go back to the DFI or DFC that obtains government funds and subsidized funds, or else it has got to get its money from the market. It is difficult to see how it would get its money from the market. Maybe it is an insurance company. I am not saying it would not work, but maybe I am expressing my bias again. I do not purport to have a lot of answers to these things, but I think some rocket scientist in a merchant bank might be able to find a way to put this together and sell it. I am not against that. He might find some barrier, some impediment, some little wrinkle that is not right. But I have not seen insurance offered.

MR. LÜDERS: In the last few years a possibility for developing securities markets has emerged that relates the privatization efforts of some countries with their high levels of foreign debt. Money-center banks are acquiring, through debt-to-equity swaps, substantial shares of equity stock in companies of the indebted countries. Because these banks are seldom in the business of running industrial and other nonfinancial companies, they are eventually willing to divest these shares in the local capital markets. This has been going on in Chile.

Let me be more specific. Let's say that ABC Bank in New York has Chilean debt. It can then transform Chilean debt into equity in state-owned enterprises that are being privatized. Later on, this bank can sell those shares in the local market to get its capital back.

This bank is in fact performing a function similar to that of Morgan and the trusts in the case of the United States. Eventually, the money center bank wants others to assume part of the risk it is taking and to bring its own capital back home. By so doing, it spreads the ownership of the local companies and helps to develop the local capital markets.

Mr. Walters: The essential element, Rolf, is to make use of securities, correct? Then you can spread ownership instead of having it concentrated.

Mr. Lüders: Yes.

Mr. Reilly: I think again that that is an idea that is worth pursuing. I am not specifically familiar with any banks that acquire equity with the commitment to have a public issue later because there is probably not much interest in the market for that company's shares.

Mr. Lüders: I will give you an example. Bankers Trust bought a relatively small electricity company in Chile through a debt-for-equity swap. The bank is not interested in the electricity business, per se, but in eventually selling those shares on the local capital market. Whatever it receives for those shares will be instead of the principal and interest that might have been received in repayment of the debt that was swapped.

Mr. Reilly: Would it sell them to the AFPs or somebody else?

Mr. Lüders: Right now it cannot sell them to the AFPs so it holds those shares for some time until it can, or until other investors can be found. Slowly, it is already selling shares off and getting their capital back.

Mr. Hanke: Rolf, to what extent is the privatization of social security aiding this whole process of securitization?

Mr. Lüders: I think it's aiding very much. Right now the only shares the private funds can buy are shares of state-owned enterprises. As this occurs, of course, the SOEs are being privatized, and the pension funds will end up owning shares of privatized companies. The government wants the pension funds to provide ownership by individuals in private companies, and this is being accomplished as the process continues.

Eventually, this process will be very significant because the pension funds are going to have financial assets equivalent to the GNP. In a country that has a GNP of $25 billion, if only 20 percent of the funds' assets is put into equity, it amounts to $5 billion in equity, which for Chile is a lot. There are many funds competing with one another, so they are very competently managed. That should aid the entire process.

MR. HANKE: Just one follow-up on this. You privatize social security, in effect, and the available funds then begin eating away at the state-owned enterprises.

MR. LÜDERS: What you do, first, is privatize the management of the social security funds, because social security is still mandatory. Then you allow those funds to have shares of SOEs. As those shares are sold to funds and other investors, at some point, over 50 percent of a SOE's shares will be privately owned and control of the SOE is transferred to the private sector. Through this process, a significant capital market is institutionalized.

MR. HANKE: Right. You privatize the management. You have allowed them to buy shares and that investment will be increasing over time. So what is it now? Is it 10 percent of their portfolio?

MR. LÜDERS: That's right. Of course, it's increasing. It can increase eventually to 20 percent of pension fund portfolios according to the law.

MR. HANKE: So as an outside investor, it would seem to me that this would make the Chilean market very attractive because you know this pension fund money is going into the equity market.

MS. SAGARI: The problem is that, according to the law, pension funds cannot invest in any firm that has a concentration in ownership above 50 percent. There cannot be any one single shareholder (except the government in state-owned enterprises) holding more than 50 percent of the shares. It used to be 20 percent, but in August of 1987 it was increased to 50 percent. The problem is that there are only about nine firms that fulfill this requirement and are actually issuing shares.

With bonds, the requirements are slightly different. But even for bond investments, there are only fifteen eligible firms. So investment of these tremendous amounts of funds being accumulated in pension plans poses a contradiction. Though the social security system has been privatized, because of regulations that may be reasonable to protect these mandatory savings, the only investments these "private" pension funds can have are in government securities and shares of government firms that are in the process of privatization, so it sounds a bit funny sometimes.

MR. LÜDERS: Let me defend it on market grounds. What should happen is that eventually through demand-pull pressures on equity share prices, the rate of return on share ownership gets down enough to make the issuing of shares sufficiently attractive for companies that today have relatively concentrated ownership. This is the idea. I think one should give these processes time. That is why I like the joke about Otto and Fritz, because these things don't happen overnight.

Ms. SAGARI: That is why I was wondering whether we were asking for too much, too soon. I do think that this is the case with Chile. Everybody is very anxious to succeed. But I do think that these things require time. There is a process of learning, of people getting used to issuing these types of instruments. Today the AFP people are going around to firms that have been authorized to sell securities and asking them to issue bonds. They want to buy their bonds.

MR. LÜDERS: Up to two years ago we had excess capacity, so why would these firms seek additional equity capital? Today, the average rate of return for the listed shares of the stock exchange is over 30 percent in real terms per year. So who is going to issue shares at that cost, when they can go to a bank and get a loan at 9 percent?

MR. KALOTRA: I have a point to raise with the World Bank and A.I.D. participants. I think that one of the major problems with DFCs, and I am talking about most of the A.I.D. and Bank projects, has been the obsession with large projects—construction projects, large fertilizer plants, etc.—and, in terms of the financial sector, with lending. We have done a study for the World Bank in which we looked at three hundred World Bank and A.I.D. projects. We found the projects that entailed lending were either dismal failures or, at best, suboptimal.

We investigated thoroughly the real costs. I think there are problems with the things we have been talking about because there have been no findings. One problem is that when we do lending, we also provide what is called business advisory services. But for a $35 million loan, we have three business advisory service people in different parts of the world.

We seem to believe that credit is the only factor of production. I think that A.I.D. and the World Bank may still believe that. We realize that the world has moved away from extractive industries—from a manufacturing or industrial revolution to an information revolution. Even though, for instance, 80 percent of the employees in IBM have nothing to do with manufacturing; some of the institutions have not realized the importance of the services sector.

Services improve the capability of running a microenterprise or running a DFC or a large enterprise. There is only one A.I.D. project in Jordan that specifically improves industrial services. We have suggested that the Bank and A.I.D. lending of $35 million perhaps should be reduced to $27 or $28 million, and those $7 to $8 million saved should be used to increase the capability within the country to provide needed services. Whether it is rudimentary management, marketing, or technological assistance depends on what sort of an industry we are talking about. To use the $27 million most effectively is the central objective.

We have to respond to the changing information technology to create capabilities in countries to use the funds available or to manage the products manufactured. It is my request that we identify what has enabled large enterprises to be successful, whether it be better management, better user technology, or whatever. I think more money from these institutions should go to strengthening service skills in developing countries over a long period of time. Would anybody like to react to that?

MR. SHERWIN: Let me respond to that. The issue of World Bank lending to DFCs, as a number of people have pointed out, is one that has led to all sorts of strife. You look at the DFCs we have been so busy funding in various parts of the developing world and discover that their balance sheets indicate they are in quite a state, a fact that has also been pointed out.

Reference was made to the obsession with big projects. I think part of our problem with DFCs has been an obsession to get away from the obsession with big projects to try to step down to smaller-scale operations. But the Bank, I think, is singularly ill-equipped to do so. It is Washington-based, expensive, and has all sorts of impediments that make it an inappropriate vehicle to reach small- and medium-sized enterprises or whatever other catchphrase you wish to use for the sorts of target audiences we might be trying to get at.

We pour a lot of money into development finance banks of one sort or another, and then three or four years later we come along and help clean up their balance sheets because they have had to contend with exactly the problems that we were trying to avoid. That may be something of an exaggeration, but it does not seem to me to be a wholly productive way to proceed. I am not sure what the answers are. IFC (the International Finance Corporation) has been trying to get to small- and medium-sized enterprises in various ways.

A few weeks ago, the World Bank board considered a new initiative in Africa, which first acknowledged that it will be expensive to get to this target group. Second, it regarded as small- to medium-sized businesses in Africa those requiring loans starting at about $100,000 and running up to about $1.5 million. In the African context that seemed to me to be large to very large industry and still leaves the bulk of the private sector in Africa untouched.

When I—in my brief experiences in Africa—looked at the private sector, a lot of government officials told me, "We do not have one, so why do you keep telling us to do something about it?" They do have one, but it happens to consist of small farmers, or small traders, or taxi drivers, who have small needs—a $200 loan might be just what they need to get going.

This brings us back to the issue of the informal sector that has been referred to on a few occasions. It seems to me that perhaps the smartest thing institutions such as the World Bank and other development agencies can do is to encourage governments to pull their sticky fingers out, not assist expressly, but try to remove some of the impediments and some of the negative policy structures that trip these sectors up. Just let them breathe a bit.

MR. MCKINNON: I have a kind of conundrum that maybe somebody can help me with. I think the development of equity markets is very important, but it comes fairly far along in the development process. The economy has to reach a certain level of per capita income and have a degree of financial stability before it is worthwhile to make a big effort to develop a securities market. But then if you have a fairly successful economy, such as the Korean economy, with a number of big groups, the industrial companies for one reason or another are reluctant to go public on their own. The Korean government has actually forced them to issue shares through one device or another, quite Draconian to begin with. There are also ongoing regulations that force new equity issues by Korean enterprises. The question I have is: does this make sense? Is there a case for government to step in and force fairly well-established companies to sell shares to outside holders?

MR. REILLY: I think the operative question is, are there really "good" reasons? I can only give my biases. If the purpose is to increase the availability of long-term finance to industry in general, then it seems to me that it is a reflection of the policy to get the market more developed. To motivate people or make them used to investing.

If that is a valid policy, which I think it is, then the tools should be looked at in terms of that policy and not just in isolation. Looking at it in isolation makes it sound a bit strange. Bechtel is one of the largest privately held companies in the United States. No one is going to tell Bechtel to go public. But in this country we are not trying to create a greater mobilization of savings and allocation to the capital market. In Korea, they are. Developing capital markets could be an argument for it. The analogy would be that it is like an antitrust argument. That there are certain principles you wish to implement and this is one of the tools. I am not an expert on Korea, and obviously I can only repeat what other people have told me.

There is a similar provision in Philippine company law that says the National Economic Development Authority can declare any company to be of national significance, in which case it can be told to raise funds in the capital market of the country. When I looked at the history of that, I found that the debate on the floor of the Philippine legislature was full of assertions that it was a terrible idea. Why should I as an entrepreneur, who built my company, be forced to sell it? It is expropriation. You do not ask me to sell my house, do you? So there is a strong argument against it. I think you have to look at the purpose behind such a law and ask whether you are creating a tool that really is going to foster that purpose.

That is about the best argument I can make for it. The argument against it is that it seems a bit of expropriation. But in my little nuts-and-bolts field I must say it stands out as something I am very attracted to. But I have never been able to sell it to anybody and prove it really is the right thing.

MR. MCKINNON: I accept your argument about the problem of getting started with securities trading. But if a company has no outstanding common shares, everything is run by insiders. Then there is a signalling problem: Outside shareholders will be very suspicious of any new equity issue.

Suppose Hyundai in Korea has been private for a long period, and then, out of the blue, decides to issue new equity. The signalling effect is quite adverse here, causing outsiders to be suddenly very suspicious that the insiders might have information that the fortunes of this company are about to turn down and are just trying to unload. So the outsiders will be very suspicious of actually buying these shares.

Indeed, we know that mature U.S. companies issue very little new equity. Earned surplus accumulates internally but relatively little new equity is issued as a means of ongoing finance. People have explained that, on the basis of this adverse signalling argument, if an established company tries to sell shares, people will often be suspicious of its motives.

So the time when you want to go public or issue equity is when you have an easily explainable reason for doing so. There could be a major new project that needs finance. But if there is none immediately available, maybe you could claim the government is forcing you to go public, which would then diminish the adverse signalling.

MR. REILLY: Actually, you see the latter in places such as Indonesia when you try to find out the purpose of an offering, and they say they are going public to be consistent with the policy of the government that we should be public.

MR. MCKINNON: Right. So then the outsiders believe the chances are better that nothing adverse is going on.

MR. REILLY: Is the signalling problem a reason not to pursue the policy, or is it a reason to deal with how to prevent the missignal by means of adequate disclosure? Adequate disclosure is a problem in all of these countries. But presumably it could be dealt with through disclosure that would be sufficient for an institutional investor. In that case, other people might rely on a broker who has made an analysis similar to that made by the institutional investor. I can see the problem you have, but I do not know whether it overcomes the other positive objective, which is to get the securities market going.

There may be another objective: If all these companies are held privately, you may have many zaibatsus all over the place, and maybe that power and the economic return on those assets should be spread in the economy. This is a political question. I must say the signalling problem sounds interesting, but it seems to be manageable and not necessarily sufficient to overcome the other positive arguments.

MR. WALTERS: I think one or two conundrums or paradoxes have arisen. Virtually all of us in this room have been interested in capital markets per se. One of the important requirements for such markets mentioned by Ron McKinnon and others is that we need a suitable environment. I will come back to that in a moment.

The major concern is that somehow we have got to inject a large quantity of savings, between 20 and 25 percent, into the processes of intermediation in order for it to find its way into more efficient use. It is rather like going from barter to a price system or from the informal sector to the fully intermediated system. However, there are worries. There are great worries in my view as to whether that is going to be ultimately an efficient way to go.

Let us suppose that we follow the McKinnon rule: Most of us would agree that if we get interest rates up it encourages people to put their money on deposit in the banking system or other markets. That is to say, we would not continuously rob them of their assets by maintaining low interest rates. Most of us would agree that that is a good step. But then I point out that we would be taking resources out of the informal sector and putting them into the formal sector.

The government, having done that, starts wasting those resources. Those resources might well have been better employed in the informal sector. By encouraging intermediation, we may develop a more efficient way for government to lay its hands on more resources and waste them. Before you start the process of increasing interest rates for deposit liabilities of the banking system and encouraging more intermediation you had better be sure that you do not have an African, or, indeed, Latin American syndrome, where funds were taken by the government and substantially wasted.

The other point that has not been dealt with is one that I think is extraordinarily important. This arises from the fact that much of the developing world is and has been for many years under more or less continuous financial crisis. To put it in a nutshell, their banks are broke. Many of the firms are broke. It is not just a problem of illiquidity. It is a problem of solvency. In many cases insolvency has been associated with very big foreign borrowings under conditions in which the borrowers thought that negative real interest rates would persist. The negative interest rates turned out to be very positive real interest rates from 1979 onwards.

Chile and many other countries have been caught by changes in relative prices: a fall in the price of exports relative to the price of imports. Large fractions of their commercial sector, the banking system, and indeed industrial systems were broke.

While they are broke, and while these issues are not resolved, the incentive system is massively distorted, just as it is in the Texas savings and loans industry. But similar and much more important distortions appear also in these developing countries. I think that Texas in this respect is a member of the third world. (I hope there are no Texans here.)

[Laughter]

Ms. CRAIG: Actually, I'm not a Texan, but I have a deposit in a Texas S&L, so I'm not likely to share your objectivity.

[Laughter]

MR. WALTERS: We have seen this in many financially distressed countries. No one knows how the bankruptcy laws are going to be imposed. No one knows who is going to be saved. People sit around and capital is left idle because no one knows whether they will be rewarded for using it. They might be robbed.

These uncertainties hung like a cloud over Chile. Eventually Chile resolved them, and I think rather well. They still hang like a cloud over many other countries. I should guess in Latin America probably a majority of the banks are in fact insolvent. I suspect in Africa, also, most banks are bankrupt and a pall of uncertainty hangs over them. No one is clear about how this problem is going to be resolved, and consequently there is an enormous amount of capital and associated labor left idle.

It is a paralysis. Let me give you the case of Chile. No one knew how the mortgage issue was going to be resolved with respect to housing. So there were something like twenty thousand houses left idle. The owners did not know what to do. The homes were just left vacant. The rendering of most of your capital idle by these uncertainties is in my view absolutely critical. The main thing to do is draw the line and specify which are to be saved and which are to go under so certainty is reintroduced. There are lots of problems about how that line is to be drawn, how much it will cost, and which industries or firms will be dissolved. In most cases, the government, for political reasons and maybe for good economic reasons, has to step in and resolve the issue.

That, I think, is quite a critical issue in the development of capital markets and the financial markets generally. Otherwise, you have all this capital hanging around idle. We had not looked at that very vexing problem: what happens if you do not do it?

If you do not settle those issues, your financial institutions—development finance corporations and banks—will continue to channel funds in exactly the same way they have before. There is no change in the distribution of capital. There is no redistribution of assets from what you should not be producing to what you should be producing as a consequence of changes in relative advantage, changes in relative prices and, of course, the discrediting of management. Your financial institutions will be taking funds and channeling them straight into the old avenues. All the resources will be devoted to simply bailing out old friends.

We have not talked about that issue. It seems to me, however, to be a central problem in the majority of developing countries, certainly in Latin American, most African, and many South Asian ones. So the issue of financial repression lies heavily on my agenda.

I would like to go back to what we might call the framework within which capital markets can develop. I entirely agree with much of what Ronald McKinnon says except that I think differences arise regarding what sort of framework should be developed, what sort of monetary exchange rate institutions should be developed in LDCs.

I think there is a historical model: the currency board system. It is a model to which I think New Zealand is tending. It has worked very well in the past. Currency boards were extraordinarily important in colonial Africa and Asia. They exist now only in Hong Kong, Brunei, and Singapore. Hong Kong, Brunei, and Singapore have developed quite well.

Mr. McKinnon: And Panama until a few months ago.

Mr. Walters: Panama does not have a currency board. It uses the greenback. That is a greenback system, I believe.

Mr. McKinnon: But the balboa is issued as pocket change.

Mr. Walters: If you count that you would count also Liberia. But let me develop the currency board idea for a moment. The currency board is a very simple system. It was inaugurated by the Bank of England and the Bank Act of 1844.

The Bank Act set up the issue department of the Bank of England to behave like a currency board. The idea of a currency board can be illustrated by the case of Hong Kong's currency board based on the U.S. dollar. If you want to get Hong Kong dollars, then you bring U.S. greenbacks to the currency board, plop them on the table, and for every greenback you turn in, you get 7.8 Hong Kong dollars, and vice versa.

This monetary mechanism worked very well in all British Africa and much of Asia. The French colonies had a variant of the currency board system. It does not prevent countries behaving badly in all sorts of ways such as overborrowing. But at least it does save you from dramatic inflation. Hong Kong, for example, stays with the dollar. It does prevent governments from simply debasing the currency; the bane of the Latin American or, more recently, of the African countries.

If a fixed exchange rate system is adopted, then all the consequences of the administrative institutions needed to validate that exchange rate system must be created and accepted. The currency board is an institutional mechanism that will give you complete validation of that fixed exchange rate system. The best alternative to a fixed-rate currency board system is a free-floating system.

The IMF has drawn attention to this in recent reports. It draws attention to the fact that currency boards are fairly successful. The IMF does not exactly recommend adoption of them, but it says that they are very successful and that there is much to be said for them. Between those two extremes, and, alas, many of the Latin American countries fall between those two extremes, any sort of creeping rate or crawling peg is an invitation to all sorts of capital flow speculation and, of course, creates problems with interest rates. On balance, I think the extreme solutions are best.

That is the issue on the exchange rate monetary side. On the other side, I agree entirely with Mr. Reilly: The environment—the economic, regulatory, legal and, indeed, moral environment—is enormously important in development. The main point I would make here is that a necessary condition for development is a very simple one. It is that the rate of return on capital in a country be allowed to be reasonably profitable.

It does not matter whether it is foreign capital or domestic. You will then avoid capital flight. Capital will not fly if it can make money at home and foreigners will come in to make money. I think it is terribly important to the game. This issue has not been raised. It is not related directly to capital markets, but it is a very important condition for the import of foreign investment.

Direct foreign investment has a bad name in developing countries. It has a bad name also in the West largely because people have invested and then been caught by expropriation. But direct foreign investment has enormous advantages. It brings management and technical expertise. I cannot see why developing countries are so against it. The investing country puts all its assets in the LDC's lap. Foreigners own the industries, but the host country controls it.

I think that direct foreign investment has enormous effects on capital markets, too, because, once direct foreign investment is involved in a country, you get much more participation by foreign capital markets and all sorts of other foreign contacts.

Nobody mentioned MIGA, the Multinational Investment Guarantees Association. It is probably appropriate you did not mention it. Anyway, we will leave that to those who believe in moral hazard and adverse selection. I think those are the sort of major issues on which I detected some gaps in our discussion and things I thought would come up naturally, but for some reason did not.

Ms. CRAIG: I have a question that has not been considered. Is there a size requirement for an economy? That is, when is an economy large enough to underwrite, in any sense, an equity market? This is related to the question of foreign investment. Is the right approach to try to develop a completely domestic equity market? Should the developers of any equity market be concerned about the role of foreign investors in that equity market? Should they consider the development of something like regional equity markets? Is there some subset of countries that can underwrite a regional equity market or would that make sense from historical perspective? What happened in the West? Did each country develop its own market or was there some sort of regional development?

Mr. Reilly: Theoretically you could have a regional gulf cooperation council or securities market among the United Arab Emirates (UAE), Yemen, Saudi Arabia, Kuwait, and so forth. This would assume that any member of that group is willing to have its company's shares traded and subject to the vulnerability of a market outside of its control. It has not happened, but it has been discussed.

ASEAN (the Association of Southeast Asian Nations) last year agreed at the Council of Foreign Ministers' meeting in 1987 that there should be cross-listing among ASEAN member countries. So the idea is there. But are you suggesting that if there is some minimal base that a country needs in order to have a capital market—that is, enough companies and enough investors—that the problem of insufficient stocks and shareholders might be overcome by having a regional market? Is that how you are coming at it?

Ms. Craig: Yes. Because it occurs to me that a country such as Brazil may be large enough to support a diversified capital market. But, if you look at Texas, it is not highly diversified, and its capital market is dominated by one or two industries. There are some great advantages to having a portfolio that is spread over many industries.

Mr. Reilly: You mean, if you are living in Texas and can only buy one or two companies, you would prefer to go to a regional market to invest?

Ms. Craig: Or someone from Texas who has money to put into a savings and loan might want to know that the S&L could invest not only in Texas, but also in other states.

Mr. Reilly: But this really happens anyway informally. I mean you just pick up the telephone.

Ms. Craig: But does it happen this way internationally? When we have countries that do restrict who participates in equity markets, I think that is a hurdle you have to consider. You also have to consider the rules against or in favor of foreign investors in an equity market. You wrote a little bit about this.

Mr. Reilly: Sure. For purposes of discussion I am assuming that if you had cross-listing, it is the same as having it all listed in one place. If you are trying to set up an ASEAN regional market, you are going to have a problem in the Philippines where only a certain percentage of the shares can be owned by foreigners. Consequently, only certain kinds of certificates can be traded outside of the region. I do not see that as a plus or a minus in terms of whether you could have the regional market.

Ms. CRAIG: That is not the question I was asking. Is a regional equity market something that should be part of a broader capital market development strategy? Should planners consider that, when the local base of savers or buyers of equities is quite small, there may be someone in Singapore who might be interested in Philippine stock? Would that give an incentive for more issuance of stock?

MR. REILLY: I will give you my impressions. The impression I have is that for such people, who are interested in cross-border investment and who do not find an opportunity in their own country, they do it anyway; they just simply call up Singapore, or they call up the local branch of the Singapore broker. So they make the investment. As a result there has not, so far as I have seen, been a clear, felt need for someone to set up a regional market other than in a country such as Bahrain that says, we would like to be like an offshore financial center. But they have not proceeded too far.

I think that it is not necessarily an economic analysis of market development you are going through. It is a political analysis. Does someone want this to happen? Now the ASEAN countries apparently want closer interlinking of trade and so forth, so they say, why not have capital be available from one to the other?

The Gulf Cooperation Council countries have the same instinct. And there will probably be a broader Arab impulse to do this. But it has not arisen in my experience as a tool to solve one country's need to make greater long-term finance available to its industry.

There is nothing to stop a Bahrain company or a Singapore company from selling in another market. Last year, one of the major Singapore companies sold shipbuilding facilities in the Philippines. In order to finance those, it went to the Philippine market with a public issue of the local shares. Perhaps I have not thought it through the way you would like, but the need has not really arisen. I suppose it could be something a country might want to try.

One question I would like to get people's impression on is whether a securities market should be the last thing that comes or should it come earlier. Does anybody have a view based upon their experience or bias? Should an international agency be pushing securities market development?

MR. MCKINNON: I think if it is an individual economy starting from low per capita income, with financial development on its own, then the securities market comes last. But there are examples from the colonial era in which a beginning economy had access to, say, the London capital market. If you wanted to set up a rubber plantation in Malaysia, you could issue equity shares in London to finance it. But that sort of thing is pretty hard to organize within a single national economy that does not have that external connection. You then have to rely more on domestic financial intermediaries at the initial stages. At a certain level of maturity, however, you can develop equity finance domestically.

MR. REILLY: Perhaps you will allow me to argue that a little bit. You said this is the way it has happened. I wonder if it has happened that way because there have been biases against securities markets and biases in favor of bank mobilization of finance and lending. If so, one should take a vigorous approach to overcome those biases. Is it right that it has happened that way? Or, is it perhaps something we should not allow, that we should discourage from happening?

I accept the contention that in some countries the economy is not developed enough to have a securities market. But I am baffled by the proposition that because events have transpired one way previously, that is what you should expect to happen in the future. My experience tells me it has happened that way in many places because there have been biases in the system.

MR. MCKINNON: That is true, but there are economies of scale, considerable economies of scale in equities markets. If you are small it is hard to develop that domestically.

Mr. White: I do not think this is the sort of question we can answer a priori. It is the sort of development for which we have to let the market show us the appropriate institutional structures. International agencies should not be trying to push any particular institutional structure but rather encouraging a change in the rules of the game—namely, toward stricter legal respect for the rights to own and to exchange freely all manner of financial instruments and property titles—so as to remove impediments to the emergence of whatever is the best nuts-and-bolts solution.

Mr. Reilly: Then let me just take you one step further. I am sorry to dwell on this but, if an international agency is interested in the privatization of parastatals, then that seems as a corollary to call for the development of the local equity market. When you cannot sell these enterprises to the public—if you sell them back into a small group—you are going to concentrate power. If you are not going to sell them to a small group you have got to create enough demand and enough liquidity for a securities market. It seems to me that, if you are saying parastatals should go and the economy should be open for opportunity, the necessary corollary is the development of a capital market. Can you take me out of that conundrum?

Mr. White: Other people, particularly Steve Hanke, know more about this than I do, but my impression is that parastatals have been auctioned off in places, such as Bangladesh, which certainly do not have developed securities markets.

Mr. Reilly: Yes. But was there not a problem with a lot of companies being auctioned off through Corfu and the procedure led, in Chile, to concentrations of power that were very disadvantageous. If that is true, then one would argue that capital market growth would be a good thing because it would distribute the securities broadly. When I was working in Chile in the early 1980s, people said, "Look at this paint company for sale; we should buy it. We do not know about paint but it is a distress sale. We should buy it. We will create a paint company, and a this, and a that, and the other thing." It led to the concentration of power.

Mr. Hanke: I hate to open up anything new at this juncture, but I will just mention one mechanism available even when you do not have an organized capital market: You can get into arrangements such as employee stock ownership. That is one mechanism. Ultimately it is nice to have a capital market so there is liquidity after the employees get the shares.

MR. SHERWIN: Professor White has given the answer I would have given. I have been a little bothered by some of the discussion. We seemed to be pushing development of various types of markets because someone decided that they are beneficial. I do not think that case has necessarily been made.

It seems to me that markets develop when a need is evident. I would be much more inclined to see agencies concentrating on the broader policy setting. They should spend a lot more time trying to level the playing field and to create environments where people can see whether development of a particular market structure is likely to be beneficial. Then the various parties to the market can come together as they wish. In other words, agencies should worry about the need for particular forms of market structure when the need becomes a little more evident.

MR. BROCK: I want to discuss the comments made by Barbara Craig on the need to link a developing country's capital markets with the rest of the world. I think that not enough has been said today about the importance of these linkages. Given the small size of many developing countries, our discussion of the importance of internal financial market development in these countries would be equivalent to a discussion of the importance of capital market development in the hypothetically independent countries of Ohio, Kentucky, Texas, Rhode Island, and so on.

In my earlier comments, I tried to emphasize that undiversified risk poses a fundamental problem for the functioning of capital markets in countries the size of individual states of the United States. I do not intend to argue that the existence of pecuniary externalities associated with this undiversified risk justifies the web of government interventions in financial markets that we see in developing countries. But the existence of such externalities does provide a starting point for our understanding the origin of financial controls in these countries.

It would obviously be better to integrate a country's financial markets with those of the rest of the world than to suffer the problems of financial instability in a Texas-sized sovereign country. Chile has been mentioned a number of times as a country that is now following good financial policies. However, Chilean social security companies can only invest in Chile and are prohibited, for example, from buying stocks on the New York Stock Exchange, even though a portfolio of foreign stocks would yield a more stable flow of retirement income than would a portfolio made up entirely of Chilean investments.

In contrast to Chile, production in Texas is carried out by a large number of foreign (out-of-state) companies and by increasing numbers of out-of-state banks. In addition, Texans are not restricted to holding their retirement funds in Texas companies or in government bonds issued by the Texas government. As long as developing countries will not permit diversification of production risk via the foreign ownership of banks and companies, and as long as these countries do not permit their citizens to diversify their portfolios to insure a smooth consumption stream, the pecuniary externalities that I have discussed will create large problems for the successful development of capital markets in developing countries. However, in the presence of externalities created by undiversified risk, policymakers who wish to reform capital markets in developing countries must be careful not to embrace the view that all governmental interventions in financial markets are purely the consequence of rent-seeking behavior by pressure groups seeking cheap credit.

MR. WALTERS: I think the development of technology, the globalization of technology and the globalization in capital markets confer an enormous benefit. Somehow the third world must be linked to those benefits of technology and cheap capital.

The essence of it is simply freedom. Freedom of people to participate. Freedoms for them to buy foreign equity or foreign funds. That is one of the essential elements that we look for. How it will develop, who knows? Markets develop in all sorts of ways.

Economists are the last to predict ways in which markets develop. We are awful at it. If we were any good we would be making money in the markets rather than rotting away in our ivory cellars or wherever we are.

I would like to go through the major points we have discussed. We all agree, I think, that the environment must be right for development of capital markets. I have a list of things that help. First, do not get your real exchange rate too wrong, at least not by intervention. Do not try to control your real exchange rate to rob the farmers or reward your political allies. Try to keep a reasonably efficient real exchange rate.

Second, get your fiscal balance broadly right. In other words, do not get into a state in which 10 percent of GNP is devoted to covering the fiscal deficit. A fiscal deficit of perhaps 3 percent is not too bad, but clearly 6 to 7 percent is such that governments will dominate the capital markets with all sorts of bad effects.

The third point is to not get your real interest rates too different from those in international markets. Do not try to rob your depositors or to unduly subsidize your borrowers. All these things will give rise to trouble in your financial and capital markets. They will lead to financial repression and probably an absolute contraction of your financial sector as you have seen in Mexico, Brazil, and so on.

The fourth point is to remove restrictions. There are many restrictions that inhibit development of capital markets. Removing restrictions does not sound very interesting but in many cases it is absolutely essential.

Fifth, improve laws and the administration of the laws. The law about bankruptcy for instance is most important. The law about repossession in the case of mortgages and various other types of chattel loans is quite crucial.

The next lesson one learns—which is most relevant for A.I.D., the World Bank, etc.—is not to try to impose what you think is right.

Because what you think is right is unlikely to be what is suitable for a developing country. Try little things and see whether they work, whether they fit in with the mores and beliefs of the people. Simply try to create the conditions within which people in these developing countries can come to mutually agreeable arrangements.

The seventh one is more problematical. This is the problem of sequencing. The basic lesson is to beware of freeing up the market before you have got the signals right. If the signals are pointing in the wrong direction, freeing up your market will send your resources down the wrong avenues. That seems to be another lesson that has come out of this discussion.

A final or eighth lesson is that financial markets should not be dealt with separately from the general issues of property rights and legal reforms. Neither should they be ignored, as indeed the World Bank and other development institutions ignored them for so long. Capital markets should be allowed to adapt to market signals elsewhere in the world, as should technology, communication, taxation, and other elements of the environment in developing countries. I think the great lesson we learn is that no country should be an island unto itself. Albania is not a role model for anybody.

8

Khurshid Alam

The Dhaka Stock Exchange: Expanding Equity in the Development of Bangladesh

Dependence on easy debt financing provided by government agencies, government-controlled development financing institutions (DFIs), or domestic commercial banks has proven painfully counterproductive throughout the developing world. With financial sectors in a deepening crisis as a result of debt recovery problems and the increasing stringency of terms on both domestic and international loans, the urgency for mobilizing domestic resources by means other than debt finance has greatly intensified.

The principal alternative to debt finance, of course, is equity finance. But, whereas it is easy to participate in debt finance (though interest rates and terms of repayment may be severe), and virtually everyone has some experience with it, most individuals in developing countries have little experience with equity finance. Indeed, experience is not only slight, but also difficult to gain in the absence of well-developed equity markets.

The Capital Market in Bangladesh

Because capital comes from savings, and the savings rate in Bangladesh is low, its capital market is necessarily underdeveloped. This low level of savings is attributable, in part, to very low per capita income. At the same time, savings might be higher at *any* level of income if the capital market afforded greater opportunities for individuals to increase their future income by saving in the present.

The domestic savings rate in Bangladesh, according to World Bank estimates, was about 2.6 percent of gross domestic product (GDP) in 1987–1988. When remittances from the earnings of Bangladeshi workers abroad are taken into account, national savings rise to about 6 percent of GDP. Foreign savings, mostly in the form of external aid, stood at 6 percent of GDP in 1987–1988 compared with 11.5 percent in 1981– 1982, and the share of fixed domestic investment financed by foreign capital fell from 76.7 percent of GDP in 1981–1982 to 51.3 percent in 1987–1988.

Given that the existing stock of capital depreciates at an annual rate of 10 percent, and that the population is increasing by between 2 and 3 percent yearly, the savings rate must be raised to at least 12 percent in order for sustained economic growth to be possible. Yet, the combination of a low level of savings and declining foreign capital inflows yielded a decline in gross investments (both public and private) from 15 percent of GDP in 1981–1982 to 11.8 percent in 1987–1988.

The capital market in Bangladesh, as of today, consists of the DFIs, such as Bangladesh Shilpa Bank (BSB), Bangladesh Shilpa Rin Sangstha (BSRS), the investment/merchant banks including Investment Corporation of Bangladesh (ICB), National Credit Limited (NCL), and Bank of Commerce and Investment (BCI), the commercial banks, and the Dhaka Stock Exchange (DSE).

Constituting the country's secondary security market, the DSE is one of the critical parts of the capital market in its entirety. At the same time, its operations are greatly influenced by how other operators in the capital market function. For example, BSB and BSRS offer mostly debt financing with limited equity support for industrial investment activities. ICB provides underwriting and bridge and debenture financing facilities to the industrial sponsors. It also operates mutual funds, unit certificates, investors' accounts, and the like—all schemes intended to tap savings, including those from the household sector, for investment in securities in the capital market. The number of certificate holders of ICB's mutual funds (closed-end securities as their portfolio) and unit fund stood at about one hundred thousand on June 30, 1989. Besides, the ICB has about forty thousand investment account holders who invest in securities through the corporation. Two other private investment banks—NCL and BCI—are also supporting investment activities in the capital market.

Though commercial banks and insurance companies also have roles in the promotion of the capital market in many other less-developed countries (LDCs), their operations have not become a direct component of the capital market in Bangladesh. Nonetheless, the phenomenal growth of deposits with commercial banks in recent years (standing at 170 billion taka on December 31, 1988), are deployed to meet the credit needs of various operators in the economy, and the banks thereby contribute, albeit indirectly, to the growth of the country's capital market.

Indicative of the *potential* for increasing both the savings rate and the productivity of investment in Bangladesh is what amounts to hidden savings (and lower productivity investments) in the country's very active informal (curb) markets. These reflect a demand for (and supply of) funds that is not being provided by the financial instruments and institutions of the formal market. The very existence of curb markets, therefore, poses an explicit challenge to those desiring the development of the capital market and economy of Bangladesh: Make the formal market more attractive to savers and borrowers than the curb is. The magnitude of curb markets contradicts the standard excuse for the underdevelopment of LDC capital markets, that is, that low income accounts for low savings that, in turn, account for too little demand (capital) for the development of corresponding markets. This is putting the chicken before the egg, as the Bangladeshi curb markets attest.

The Operation of the DSE: An Overview

After the emergence of Bangladesh, the Dhaka Stock Exchange (DSE) practically ceased to operate because most major industrial and financial units, such as the jute, textile, banking, and insurance industries, were nationalized. But about five years after independence, the government began assigning the private sector greater operational leeway and the DSE was reactivated in 1976. The share market commenced operations with nine listed companies having a paid-up capital of 137.52 million taka.

With activities expanding very slowly, DSE had to maintain its operations in order to expand them at all. Patience was rewarded, in December 1982, by the government's shift in economic policy toward the private sector, including its return of the jute and textile mills nationalized in 1972 to their erstwhile Bangladesh shareholders. In phases, the government also sold many other enterprises to the private sector. This policy change had a very favorable impact on the share market, resulting in the addition of fifty-six new companies in the mid-eighties, and raising the total number of companies listed with the exchange to eighty-two (with a total paid-up capital of 2.65 billion taka and market capitalization of 5.73 billion taka at the close of the 1986 calendar year). Total turnover in the exchange's Ready section was 849,144 shares amounting to 47.85 million taka, and forward trading had commenced on the trading floor in September, 1986.

In the three years between 1984 and 1986, forty companies offered shares to the public, amounting to 599.130 million taka. The public response of 866.357 million taka represented an oversubscription of more than 44 percent. This reflection of the absorption capacity of the country's capital market is not surprising. The response to the creation and institutionalization of investor opportunities in the formal capital market merely echoes the observations made above on the success of curb markets.

By the close of the 1988 calendar year, the operational base of the DSE had expanded to 111 listed securities, including 101 companies, 6 mutual funds, and 4 debenture issues. The issued capital of the 101 listed companies was 3.664 billion taka and their market capitalization was 13.556 billion taka. In 1988, the 21 new public issues for a total amount of 302.96 million taka met with subscriptions of 721.54 million taka, more than twice the value of the available issue and an oversubscription of 138.16 percent.

Along with an expanding operational base, the turnover of shares on the floor of the DSE has also increased. Total turnover reached its peak in the 1987 calendar year at 1,876,326 shares and debentures, amounting to 177.66 million taka. In 1988, there was a slight decline to 1,823,936 shares and debentures and a value of 130.03 million taka. This partly represented the recessionary situation of the flood-impacted economy in the year.

The share market has also achieved some depth as a result of the satisfactory level of dividends declared by many listed companies. In 1984, thirty-five of the fifty-eight listed companies paid dividends ranging from 10 percent to 110 percent. As many as eight listed companies in 1984 issued bonus shares, ranging from 20 percent to 100 percent. In 1985, forty-one of the seventy-two listed companies declared cash dividends ranging from 5 percent to 60 percent, and, in 1987, cash dividends ranging from 5 percent to 80 percent were declared by forty-eight of the ninety-two listed companies.

Though the DSE has shown some buoyancy, it is still in its rudimentary stage. Several factors inhibit the development of the stock exchange: (1) notwithstanding the government's divestment operation, the public sector enterprises that it owns still dominate the organized industrial sector, (2) the interlocking family directorates that are generally popular among new entrepreneurs in the early stage of industrialization have not yet given way to public companies that allow the stock exchange to fulfill its role as a mobilizer of savings and thereby allow the middle class to participate in the industrial development of the country, (3) low liquidity of shares, and (4) incomplete and otherwise inadequate income and balance sheets as well as other gaps in information about corporate operations. The combination of these factors makes the small size of the corporate sector and of the stock exchange in Bangladesh unsurprising.

It should be stressed that the broadening of the shareholder base can alone encourage "mass capital." If holdings are broadened, the fruits of industrialization pass to the common investor. Broadening the base will not only provide better accountability but also will ensure a more equitable distribution of wealth, strengthening both social stability and the meaningfulness of political democracy. Indeed, as I survey the countries of the world, both present and past, I am struck by the strong correspondence between the extent to which their equity markets are developed and the degree to which they are characterized by equity in the more inclusive sense (as in equity of opportunity). The experience of the communist countries today only dramatizes the correspondence, albeit suggesting a stronger proposition: The absence of equity (capital) markets precludes the expansion of equity (opportunity) in society. Bangladesh's experience upon attaining its independence appears to be but one of many instances that support this stronger proposition.

Government Policies, Privatization, and the Capital Market

After independence, the nationalization of large industries relegated the private sector to a very minor role in the Bangladesh economy. Industrial policy has undergone several changes during the past eighteen years. The first notable change in the policy was made in 1975–1976 and the most significant (the New Industrial Policy, or NIP) occurred in 1982. NIP gave a distinctive emphasis to private enterprises, and the economy was further liberalized by Industrial Policy 1986, which provides the basis for the process of industrialization in Bangladesh at the present time.

Measures for developing the capital market by mobilizing private savings for individual investment include the establishment in October 1976, of the Investment Corporation of Bangladesh (ICB) to provide equity finance and underwriting facilities. The decision to promote the gradual divestment of smaller private enterprises from government to private ownership also provided immediate investment opportunities to the private sector. In 1980–1981 another important decision was taken to allow private commercial banks to operate side by side with the nationalized commercial banks.

Various institutional developments have taken place in the 1980s to support the private sector. The private sector was allowed to set up entirely locally owned commercial banks and insurance companies. Seven new private sector banks are already in operation in the country. In addition, two previously nationalized commercial banks (NCBs) have been reprivatized and partial divestment has taken place in one other NCB in which the government now retains only 51 percent of the equity ownership. Several life and general insurance companies have also come into operation.

Another new business is the Industrial Development Leasing Company (with 45 percent foreign ownership), which finances the procurement of capital equipment by leasing (with option to buy) to potential investors. Another investment leasing company is also scheduled to begin full-scale operations with the support of the Asian Development Bank. Furthermore, investment banks have been permitted in the private sector, and two investment and merchant banks are already engaged in business.

Though the government's policies do aid the growth of equity, relative to debt and finance, Bangladeshi companies remain more likely to raise capital by profits from their operations and by borrowing from DFIs and commercial banks than by public sales of their equity (which is noninflationary investment financing). As of June 30, 1988, most companies listed with the office of the Registrar of Joint Stock Companies were the 16,057 private limited companies, representing primarily family-owned enterprises. Of the 1,981 public limited liability companies registered with the office, only one hundred or so were listed with the stock exchange. Furthermore, even when a company is listed on the stock exchange, few shares are available for trading as most continue to be held by the original sponsors. The original sponsors often buy additional shares in the market to raise their holdings to as high as 70 percent or 80 percent though shares are floated in the primary market on a fifty-fifty basis.

The government recognizes that the highly skewed ownership structure of Bangladeshi companies is a fundamental constraint to the growth of the capital market and has adopted several policies intended to broaden both the supply of shares available to the public and the shareholder base. These measures include: (1) a 5 percent rebate of corporate tax on publicly traded companies—those whose shares are held by a large number of shareholders at a rate of five shareholders for every 100,000 takas of shares, (2) a lowering of the corporate tax over the past five years, (3) a waiver of the taxation of dividends at the shareholder level, (4) the requirement that any new industrial enterprise be publicly traded in order to receive credit from Bangladesh financial institutions, and (5) the requirement that newly issued shares be sold at par value.

In practice, these measures have neither increased the supply of shares nor broadened their ownership to an extent that will rapidly increase either private relative to government investment or equity relative to debt financing. In fulfilling the fourth requirement, for example, the norm for newly traded companies is to rely on debt for about 80 percent of their finance and on the sale of publicly floated shares for about 10 percent, with the remaining 10 percent being accounted for by the investment of the initial sponsors' purchase of share ownership.

It should be noted that those who contend that poor countries must become richer before they can reasonably expect significant growth of their equity market have dismissed the growth of the Dhaka Stock Exchange as being no more than a consequence of the fourth and fifth requirements noted above. From the perspective of these critics, governmental requirements have simply guaranteed the expansion of the DSE. At least four responses are appropriate:

first, although those requirements do contribute to the number and paid-up capital of companies listed with the DSE, they cannot account for the increased volume of trading of those shares *subsequent* to their initial par value issuance; second, previous government mandates (the nationalization of industries and abolition of stock exchange activities upon independence) may well have prevented the magnitude of DSE operations from being greater than either they are (with today's favorable policies) or would have been (in the absence of both yesterday's negative and today's positive policies); third, were it not for the inconsistency between the government's trying to maximize the sale price of newly privatized firms while requiring other newly traded firms to issue shares at par value, both DSE operations and share ownership would be much greater than they are; and fourth, the public offerings of the related companies under the holding company divestment program have *also* been oversubscribed even though these shares (as discussed below) have been clearly overvalued (overpriced). In short, the critics should not expect to have it both ways; the positive contributions of some government policies to the expansion of the Bangladeshi equity market should be recognized in tandem with, not in lieu of, other policies having the opposite effect.

As just suggested, it must be recognized that the several means by which privatization can be accomplished have diverse economic effects. The one thing they all have in common is that government must act; privatization, then, is a political process with economic consequences, and the choice of means by which privatization is to occur is extremely important.[1]

Many people have expressed concern about the concentration of wealth in a relatively few hands as a result of privatization. Divestment through the public offering of securities and shares can help avoid concentration. In the United Kingdom, a portion of the sale of such securities has been allocated to or reserved for the workers. A similar provision can be made for the clients and customers of the units to be divested. One can also add a restriction that no individual or institution can hold more than, for example, 5 percent of the shares or securities under divestment operation. There are indeed various ways in which to address the issue in an initial offering. Another way to decentralize ownership and concentration can be to discount shares sold to employees or to give shares to employees outright. It is important for the government to set regulations to ensure competition for the newly privatized entity so that it will not become a monopoly and allow inefficiency to continue. Another variant on privatization is simply to allow private business into areas where it has been forbidden.

Divestment operations, under which the shares or securities of public sector enterprises are offered for public subscription, can help strengthen the process of promoting an industrial democracy. Such a move in a developing country such as Bangladesh is also necessary to develop confidence and investment habits among small investors and relieve the pressure on public resources. However, as in most of the less-developed world, privatization through the sale of shares to the public has not been much practiced because the (equity) capacity of the capital markets is either nonexistent or rudimentary.

The reprivatization of government-owned enterprises has been more common in LDCs, especially in the earliest stages of privatization programs. Bangladesh is no exception. The initial major move in privatization was made under the New Industrial Policy (NIP) of 1982 when the government returned jute and textile mills to their former Bangladeshi owners. The government's return of two nationalized commercial banks—Uttara and Pubali—to their previous shareholders also exemplifies reprivatization. Even before the NIP, privatization had commenced in the late 1970s in Bangladesh with the outright sale through open competitive bids of abandoned and taken-over or vested public enterprises to buyers in the private sector.

Privatization in the developing countries of Asia (as in many other countries, including those of Eastern Europe) has become a principal (perhaps the preeminent) orientation of government policies. Fortunately, the accessibility and distribution of share ownership among citizens has become the preeminent emphasis of these policies.[2]

In the second half of the 1980s, the divestment operation under the Holding Company Scheme began. The scheme has a direct bearing on the equity component of Bangladesh's capital market because it entails the incorporation of public sector enterprises as public limited companies and the floating of shares in these companies for public subscription. This scheme provides for the retention of the government's equity ownership at 51 percent, with the remaining 49 percent of its shares made available for public subscription. Of the 49 percent of shares available for public offering, 15 percent is kept reserved for the employees and the remaining 34 percent is available to the public.

The official account (as of July 31, 1989) showed that 489 public sector industrial enterprises had been divested at a combined sale price of 1.73 billion taka, of which 1.21 billion taka had already been realized. During 1989–1990, eight more public sector enterprises were to have their shares publicly floated under the Holding Company Scheme, bringing the total number of holding companies to fourteen.

Notwithstanding the encouraging response from investors to the public issues of holding companies already in operation, it is necessary to signal some cautions here. Capital structuring of public-sector enterprises under the Holding Company Scheme at high and unremunerative levels has led to extremely high sale prices of the related units to the detriment of their profitability and capacity to pay dividends. The consequent decrease in the price of traded shares and increase in the discouragement of the initial investors have not been abated by the retention, under the Holding Company Scheme, of the corporate management structures of the enterprises.

If the Holding Company Scheme is to live up to its promise, it is essential that the capital restructuring of its components occur, and that they be converted into real corporate units with complete accountability to their boards of directors without any exogenous influence. Emphasis must now be placed on the realistic valuation of the assets of units scheduled for divestment under the scheme. It is also imperative that the sequence of disinvestment under the scheme proceed from the most to the least profitable units, rather than vice versa (or somewhere in between). Units that are clearly profitable and are most likely to provide attractive dividend yields should be offered for public subscription in the first phase of operation. A supply of high quality shares can go a long way to strengthen the operations of the capital market. An increase in the supply of attractive issues will improve both liquidity and sectoral coverage in the market and ensure wider participation by investors. Demand that is now evident in both curb (debt) markets and in the oversubscription of overpriced shares of holding companies simply requires the supply of better alternatives. And so too does the development of Bangladesh.

9   *Steve H. Hanke and Alan A. Walters*

Confidence and the Liberal Economic Imperative

In developing countries, there is considerable debate about the desirability of moving away from a controlled economic order and toward a more liberal one. This debate represents a major change in thinking. Several developments have motivated this change. An accumulation of unambiguous scholarly evidence has shown that central control and interventionism retard economic progress (Scully 1988). Today's observations provide a booming echo of yesterday's scholarship. Interventionist developing countries have registered substandard performances, and their leaders have witnessed the collapse of the socialist economies of Eastern Europe. In addition, the deregulation and globalization of markets, as well as the accompanying innovations that have exploded during the past decade, have altered the international economic setting. In this new economic environment, even the most ardent dirigistes have been forced, as a matter of survival, to embrace some aspects of the liberal economic order.

There is considerable agreement, therefore, about the desirability of the liberal economic order and the elements of reform that would produce such an order. But there is much dissension about the proper sequencing of such reforms (Krueger 1984). The debate about sequencing is serious and warrants attention because there are unresolved issues. However, contrary to the conventional view, we conclude that the sequencing issues should hold a position of secondary, not primary, importance.

The primary issue concerning liberal reforms is that of confidence or credibility; confidence that the reforms will be implemented and produce a liberal economic order. If confidence is established and maintained, most of the problems that are alleged to be caused by the "improper" sequencing of reforms simply disappear.

To appreciate the validity of this conclusion, we might consider that most of the problems that allegedly arise from improper sequencing result, in fact, from a loss of confidence. For example, many argue that capital markets should not be liberalized before domestic labor and goods markets are deregulated. Those who hold this position contend that a premature liberalization of capital markets will result in capital flight, which will inhibit further reforms. This line of reasoning is usually incorrect. Indeed, when the liberalization of capital markets appears to trigger capital flight, the flight has usually been caused because individuals do not have confidence in the government's liberalization package or in the willingness or ability of the government to deliver the liberal reforms, regardless of their sequence.

The flight of capital occurs because asset holders expect that they cannot earn a rate of return that will match that available in Miami or Zurich. But if the liberalization of domestic markets is really expected, so that appropriately high rates of return are assured, it is unlikely that any capital will flee. Indeed, on the contrary, capital will flow *in*. This was the experience in the United Kingdom after the abolition of capital controls in 1979: Instead of a depreciation in sterling, which most economists predicted, there was a massive real appreciation. New Zealand had a somewhat similar experience in 1984–1985.

Confidence and credibility are, therefore, of primary importance. As Keynes argued in the *General Theory*:

> The *state of confidence*, as they term it, is a matter to which practical men always pay the closest and most anxious attention. But economists have not analyzed it carefully and have been content, as a rule, to discuss it in general terms. In particular it has not been made clear that its relevance to economic problems comes in through its important influence on the schedule of the marginal efficiency of capital. There are now two separate factors affecting the rate of investment, namely, the schedule of the marginal efficiency of capital and the state of confidence. The state of confidence is relevant because it is one of the major factors determining the former, which is the same thing as the investment demand schedule.
>
> There is, however, not much to be said about the state of confidence a priori. Our conclusions must mainly depend upon the actual observation of markets and business psychology (1936, 148–49).

Economic theorists and econometricians have completely ignored this passage in the *General Theory*, because, of course, confidence is difficult to define and insert in any formal abstract model. Econometricians find it impossible to quantify and to measure. Keynes admitted as much. Perhaps this explains the failure of economists to consider confidence and the misdirection of their attention toward sequencing issues. Yet, it is clearly unsatisfactory to confine analysis only to definable and quantifiable magnitudes and to ignore an important determinant of behavior simply because it cannot be encapsulated in any neat definition or be measured by government statisticians.

Unlike Keynes, we suspect that there is much to be said a priori about the state of confidence. For example, it seems likely that confidence is determined by the general credibility of government policy. Therefore, to reach the goal of a liberal economic order, we offer the following menu (drawn heavily from Harberger 1984). If it is chosen and pursued with vigor, the government's general credibility and the public's confidence will be established, enhancing the prospects for liberal policy implementation and economic growth.

(1) Private property and contract rights must be universally accepted and established. This is the first and most important fundamental step in any economic liberalization program, particularly in countries that were previously socialized (Eastern Europe). Without universal and secure property rights, all liberalization policies will be jeopardized.

(2) Budget deficits and government spending must be kept under adequate control. Although budgets need not be balanced at all times, there are severe limits to the budget deficits that can be incurred year in and year out with impunity. Governments and politicians must say no to spending requests, so that public spending, as a share of the economy, is kept at modest levels and so that large budget deficits are not realized on a regular basis or taxes increased to stifle growth.

(3) Inflationary pressures must be kept under reasonable control. To encourage economic development, inflation rates must not be highly variable and should be kept predictable and low. For many developing nations, this inflation objective can best be achieved by abolishing their central banks and replacing them with currency boards.

(4) The advantages of open international trade must be exploited. Liberal trade policies facilitate the efficient allocation of resources and stimulate economic growth. This is particularly true in small economies, where real competition can only be obtained through liberal trade policies that allow foreign producers to compete freely in domestic markets. For the sake of its own industries, a country should ensure that they are *not* protected. In the financial sector, entry and operational restrictions imposed on foreign banks and securities dealers should be removed.

(5) Excessive tax rates must be avoided. Excessive tax levels and rates distort behavior and create large disincentives to economic activity, while yielding little revenue. In the financial sector, discriminatory implicit and explicit taxes on financial intermediation and private bond and equity markets must be abolished.

(6) Excessive subsidies and tax incentives for private industry

must be avoided. Subsidies and tax incentives, which are designed to achieve particular objectives, may or may not actually assist in obtaining those goals. However, one thing is certain: they distort economic choices, resource allocation, and retard economic growth.

(7) Union privileges and immunities must be avoided. State-created monopoly privileges and immunities for unions—such as exclusive representation, compulsory union membership, and immunity under antitrust laws—should be avoided. These monopoly privileges and immunities distort labor markets and create an artificial and unfair advantage over nonunion members, mainly the poor. In consequence, monopoly privileges for labor unions act as a drag on economic growth and a source of poverty creation.

(8) Price controls must be avoided. Price controls, including interest rate ceilings, cannot be justified on economic grounds. They tend to vitiate the signalling role that prices should play. Hence, price controls impede the movement of resources from lower-valued to higher-valued uses and result in resource misallocation and slower economic growth.

(9) Market interventions and restrictions on competition must be avoided. Market intervention and restrictions on competition—such as the use of marketing boards—result in the politicization of economic life, in inefficient enterprises, resource misallocation, and slow economic growth.

(10) State-owned enterprises must be privatized. State-owned enterprises are inefficient. For example, sales, adjusted profits, and productivity per employee are lower for nationalized enterprises than they are for private firms. Taxes paid per employee are lower, sales per dollar of investment are lower, profits per dollar of assets are lower, wages and operating costs per dollar of sales are higher, sales grow at a slower rate, and, with few exceptions, state-owned enterprises for which accounts are presented properly generate accounting losses that are passed on to taxpayers.

(11) Unclear boundaries between public and private activity must be avoided. When boundaries between the public and private sector are unclear, it is symptomatic of poorly defined property

rights. Ill-defined property rights distort resource allocation and retard economic growth. Government bailouts of insolvent private firms are but one example of unclear boundaries between public and private activity.

(12) The manipulation and repression of private capital markets must be avoided. The manipulation and repression of private capital markets distort and promote capital flight and the savings and investment process. They repress intermediation, inhibit saving, and prevent funds from flowing to their most valuable use. In the first chapter of this volume, we analyzed the primary means used to manipulate and repress capital markets. We itemize the major features that must be eliminated:

- selective credit policies, such as interest rate ceilings on deposits and loans, selective rediscounting by central banks, direct subsidization of financial intermediaries, and credit floors and ceilings
- discriminatory taxes on financial intermediation, such as special explicit taxes, portfolio requirements on intermediaries, and high reserve requirements
- restrictions on competition, such as entry and operational restrictions on foreign banks and security dealers, as well as on indigenous operators
- specialized credit institutions and state-owned banks
- restrictions on private bond and equity markets

Once a government embraces the menu of liberal reforms, its general credibility will be enhanced. In consequence, public confidence will become established. Once confidence is established, the liberal reform package can be implemented and a liberal economic order built. This will occur regardless of the precise sequence in which the individual elements are introduced and emphasized.

If confidence is not established, it is unlikely that liberal reforms, regardless of their sequencing, will be successfully introduced and a liberal economic order established. It is important to recognize that à la carte liberalism is destined to fail. By such picking and choosing of liberal reforms, politicians cannot gain the public confidence that is essential to the successful introduction of *any* of their choices. Not unlike a bridge partially built, liberal economic reforms require their whole in order to reach the other side.

The Soviet Union's leaders are discovering the hazards of employing an à la carte approach to liberal economic reforms, including the failure to capture public confidence. (Note that most of the piecemeal reforms that are being debated in the Soviet Union are not very liberal in any case; see, for illustration, Aslund 1989.) More precisely, public confidence is not captured because the approach does not *allow* for confidence by any public other than one (unknown to us) that is too stupid to care, anyway. Hence, à la carte liberalism is fatally flawed because an *absence* of public confidence is its inevitable consequence. As a result, Mr. Gorbachev is learning that his attempts to change the Soviet Union's command economy to one that is a bit more liberal is analogous to going down the Niagara River in a canoe: Above and below Niagara Falls, the waters are rather calm, but the transition is a bitch.[1]

Notes and References

1. Jerry Jenkins, "Capital Markets and Development: Essential and Irrelevant"
Notes

I appreciate comments on a previous draft of this chapter by Philip L. Brock, Steve H. Hanke, Jill Jenkins, Stanley Laughridge, Steven Nittler, Tom Shinal, Bryan E. Snyder, John D. Sullivan, Lawrence H. White, and Neal S. Zank. I alone, however, am responsible for the published product.

1. Conversely, the irrelevance of capital markets and, especially, of securities markets to economic growth in all but perhaps the past hundred years in today's developed countries is suggested by the argument that "most nineteenth-century manufacturing enterprises were too small to sustain an active market in their shares. The emergence of larger enterprises had to precede the shift to incorporation and marketable securities" (Rosenberg and Birdzell 1986, 223).

The extended discussion of the development of capital markets, in their extremely valuable book, *How the West Grew Rich*, resulted in Birdzell's luncheon presentation to those attending the seminar on which the present volume is based. The expectation that he would expand the historical perspective of the proceedings was richly fulfilled. In addition to analyzing the size of enterprises, he imparted information about a second factor contributing to the late emergence of stock markets in today's developed countries: the appreciation of currencies in the nineteenth century.

That second factor is emphasized in this, the introductory chapter, and accounts for the *irrelevant* in its subtitle. The twentieth-century depreciation (and debasement) of currencies accounts for the word *essential*. The reader should know that Mr. Birdzell did not make the latter extension and might not concur with it. To me, the combination of the two factors is important. More specifically, the greater the rate of depreciation of a currency, the greater the likelihood that a shift to incorporation and marketable securities of an enterprise of any size will *become* beneficial both to the enterprise and to the society where, under circumstances of appreciating or more stable currency, it might not.

2. On declining prices and their economic implications during the nineteenth century, see Rosenberg and Birdzell (1986, 164–65).

3. Shares in stock had been traded for centuries before 1900, but their availability did not afford the opportunity for responding to (let alone satisfying) "the desire of individual investors to apply insurance principles to investments. . . ." (Rosenberg and Birdzell 1986, 229). A reminder that stocks were traded long before 1900 *and* of the absence of opportunity for individuals to diversify risk are *both* served by recalling the South Sea Bubble of 1720. Interestingly, equity *and* debt finance are so thoroughly intertwined in this case as to both buttress the thesis of the text and reinforce its differentiation between the "riskiness" of markets and individuals. For a summary accounting of the overlap between debt and equity finance in the South Sea case, see William B. Willcox (1971, 48–50).

4. Well above the $3.38 average price of industrial common stocks in 1900 (see U. S. Bureau of the Census 1960, 657).

5. Although most individuals would probably object that *their* particular choices have had, and can have, no real influence on currency matters, the objection ignores their *non*choices, or, more precisely, their choosing neither to choose nor to act.

6. This discussion of retarded capital markets parallels Ronald I. McKinnon's excellent delineation (1973) of "fragmented" economies. His definition of fragmented economies assumes the continuing devaluation of currencies, and I sought a more inclusive term. Indeed, it is unknown whether economies that most closely conform to the description of fragmentation would conform at all had their currencies not been nationalized.

7. On this, see Thirsk (1991) and the ensuing discussion of his paper.

8. On the correspondence between the provision of credit within informal economies and underground success, see Landa (1988).

9. Manuel F. Ayau (1989, A17) reports that, "in Guatemala, of an adult population over age twenty-five of 3.2 million, only thirty-two thousand are registered income-tax payers."

10. Before the "trust busting" crusades by the U. S. government had begun, markets were providing their own regulation during the 1890s:

> The merged companies were seldom able to maintain their initial market shares. Sometimes they were unable to keep up with the rate of growth of their industries, sometimes they learned the hard way that maintaining their share of

the market was incompatible with attempting to control prices. In Stigler's words, 'almost invariably the share of the merger in the market declined substantially as time went on [1968, 102].' The trusts had other problems than a decline in their shares of the market. Even so prototypical a trust as Standard Oil made its profits principally by reducing its own costs and then charging the same price as its competitors—and the trusts that lacked a way of reducing costs fared badly (Rosenberg and Birdzell 1986, 227–28).

11. See also White's path-breaking study (1984), *Free Banking in Britain: Theory, Experience, and Debate, 1800–1845*, and a more recent collection (1989) of his works, *Competition and Currency: Essays on Free Banking and Money*.

12. As indicated by the judgment of William A. Niskanen, a recent convert to the aim of the reforms ("George Selgin has convinced me that my conservative acquiescence to the contemporary role of central banks has been misplaced. . . ."):

> May I suggest . . . that it is counterproductive to argue about end-states in the public arena. The optimal *strategy*, I suggest, is to make the case for an initial sequence of steps that would be valuable and low risk, whether or not the subsequent steps lead to the end-state that you believe may be desirable. Free banking, privatizing the Federal Reserve, and repeal of deposit insurance may be the best end-state, but that debate, at this time, is best left to the academic journals. The more important task is to determine the most important next steps (1989, 469).

These remarks were offered in comment on a paper in the same volume by George A. Selgin (1989). It is unclear, however, whether Niskanen's conversion is attributable to that particular paper; it might have already occurred from reading Selgin's book, *The Theory of Free Banking: Money Supply under Competitive Note Issue* (1988).

As an increasing number of economists (especially monetarists, and most notably, Milton Friedman) have been persuaded of the preferability of the free banking end-state over that of government money, the debate over how has intensified. It is entirely possible (as observed in the text of this essay) that the time consumed by this debate will preclude the end-state from ever occurring; this possibility is suggested by the fact that another convert, while acknowledging "his mistaken view at that time" (in a public debate with Friedrich A. Hayek in September 1976), proposes another government intervention—albeit international this time (see Coats 1990, 11, fn. 2).

13. That the possible evolution of international private money might be precluded by international government, thus echoing the earlier preemptions by national governments is suggested by the recent proposal prepared for the International Monetary Fund (IMF) by Warren L. Coats, Jr., an adviser in its Treasurer's Department (1990).

14. The possibility that something like this might occur is suggested by Richard W. Rahn (1989, 353–62). What the currency provider in the example "decides is most prudent" must be responsive to the preferences of those using the currency;

otherwise, its units could fall into disuse as those of more responsive providers increase in circulation.

15. "A second Act the next year froze the authorised note issues of the Scottish banks as well, and obliged them to maintain 100 percent marginal reserve ratios against further issues.... Free banking in Scotland had been sacrificed to satisfy Peel's desire to unify the U.K. monetary system" (Dowd 1989, 129).

16. This is not to say that central banks do not perform useful functions. With the centralization of the reserves of member banks, they are able to serve as a clearinghouse that enormously reduces the transactions and associated costs that would otherwise be required, conceivably, between each bank in the system with every other. The provision of such a valuable service does not require the existence of a central bank. The clearinghouse function was occurring anyway and was preempted, not created, by central banks. On this, see particularly Selgin and White (1987, 439–57).

17. If, that is, the new order provides sufficient inducements, as did the Bank Acts of 1844 and 1845. Dowd explains:

> Much of the agitation for free banking had come from bankers, and the Acts effectively made note issuing a cartel by banning new entrants and freezing market shares. The suppression of competition was thus a windfall gain to existing note issuers, and this went a long way to silencing any other criticisms they might have made of the Act (1989, 129–30).

References

Ayau, Manuel F. 1989. "U. S. Forces Wrong Medicine Down Latin American Throats." *Wall Street Journal* (February 24): A17.

Bird, Richard M., editor. 1991. *More Taxing Than Taxes? The Taxlike Effects of Nontax Policies in LDCs*. San Francisco: ICS Press.

Coats, Warren L., Jr. 1990. "In Search of a Monetary Anchor: A 'New' Monetary Standard." Washington, D.C.: International Monetary Fund, Treasurer's Department, April 13.

Cumby, Robert, and Richard Levich. 1987. "Definitions and Magnitudes: On the Definition and Magnitude of Recent Capital Flight." In *Capital Flight and Third World Debt*, edited by Donald R. Lessard and John Williamson. Washington, D.C.: Institute for International Economics.

Dowd, Kevin. 1989. *The State and the Monetary System*. New York: St. Martin's Press.

Hanke, Steve H., and Alan A. Walters. 1990a. "Reform Begins with a Currency Board." *Financial Times* (February 21): 17.

———. 1990b. "East German Currency Board." *Financial Times* (March 7): 19.

Hetzel, Robert L. 1990. "Free Enterprise and Central Banking in Formerly Communist Countries." Federal Reserve Bank of Richmond, *Economic Review* (May/June): 13–19.

International Finance Corporation. 1990. *Emerging Stock Markets Factbook 1990*. Washington, D.C.

Landa, Janet T. 1988. "Underground Economies: Generic or *Sui Generis*?" In *Beyond the Informal Sector: Including the Excluded in Developing Countries*, edited by Jerry Jenkins. San Francisco: ICS Press.

McKinnon, Ronald I. 1973. *Money and Capital in Economic Development*. Washington, D.C.: Brookings Institution.

Niskanen, William A. 1989. "Rethinking the Case for Central Banking." *Cato Journal* 9, no. 2: 467–79.

Rahn, Richard W. 1989. "Private Money: An Idea Whose Time Has Come." *Cato Journal* 9, no. 2: 353–62.

Rosenberg, Nathan, and L. E. Birdzell, Jr. 1986. *How the West Grew Rich: The Economic Transformation of the Industrial World*. New York: Basic Books.

Selgin, George A. 1988. *The Theory of Free Banking: Money Supply under Competitive Note Issue*. Totowa, N.J.: Rowman and Littlefield.

———. 1989. "Legal Restrictions, Financial Weakening, and the Lender of Last Resort." *Cato Journal* 9, no. 2: 429–59.

Selgin, George A., and Lawrence H. White. 1987. "The Evolution of a Free Banking System." *Economic Enquiry* 25 (July): 439–47.

Sullivan, John D., ed. 1987. *Building Constituencies for Economic Change: Report on the International Conference on the Informal Sector*. Washington, D.C.: Center for International Private Enterprise.

Thirsk, Wayne. 1991. "Financial Institutions and Their Quasi-Taxes: A Little Bit of Craziness." In *More Taxing Than Taxes? The Taxlike Effects of Nontax Policies in LDCs*, edited by Richard M. Bird. San Francisco: ICS Press.

U. S. Bureau of the Census. 1960. *Historical Statistics of the United States, Colonial Times to 1957*. Washington, D.C.: U. S. Department of Commerce.

White, Lawrence H. 1984. *Free Banking in Britain: Theory, Experience, and Debate, 1800–1845*. Cambridge: Cambridge University Press.

———. 1989. *Competition and Currency: Essays on Free Banking and Money*. New York: New York University Press.

Willcox, William B. 1971. *The Age of Aristocracy, 1688 to 1830*. 2d ed. New York: Heath.

Wonnacott, Paul, and Ronald Wonnacott. 1986. *Economics*, 3d ed. New York: McGraw-Hill.

2. Steve H. Hanke and Alan A. Walters, "Financial and Capital Markets in Developing Countries"
Notes

1. For an extended discussion of the currency board system, see Walters (1987).

2. For completeness, it is necessary to note that those countries that were not colonies, or were largely untouched by a colonizing power, did not share in this remarkable development. Examples in Africa are Liberia and Ethiopia. These countries did have stable financial regimes (for example, Liberia used the U. S.

dollar), but it appears that the absence of a colonial administration was no great spur to their development. The classic studies about the development process in colonial Africa and Southeast Asia were written by P. T. Bauer (1948; 1954).

References

Bauer, P. T. 1948. *The Rubber Industry.* Cambridge, Mass.: Harvard University Press.
———. 1954. *West African Trade.* Cambridge, Mass.: Harvard University Press.
Fry, Maxwell, J. 1988. *Money, Interest, and Banking in Economic Development.* Baltimore, Md.: Johns Hopkins University Press.
Holst, Jurgen U. 1985. "The Role of Informal Financing Institutions in the Mobilization of Savings." In *Savings and Development*, edited by Denis Kessler and Pierre-Antoine Ulmo. Paris: Economica.
Myrdal, Gunnar. 1957. *Economic Theory and Under-Developed Regions.* London: Duckworth.
Rabushka, Alvin, and Steve H. Hanke. 1988. *Toward Growth: A Blueprint for Economic Rebirth in Israel.* Jerusalem: Institute for Advanced Strategic and Political Studies.
Scully, Gerald W. 1988. "The Institutional Framework and Economic Development." *Journal of Political Economy* 96, no. 3: 652–62.
Walters, A. A. 1987. "Currency Boards." In *The New Palgrave: A Dictionary of Economics*, edited by John Eatwell, Murray Milgate, and Peter Newman. New York: Macmillan.
World Bank. 1989. *World Development Report 1989.* Washington, D. C.: World Bank.

3. Steve H. Hanke and Kurt Schuler, "Keynes's Russian Currency Board"

References

Carley, Michael Jabara. 1983. *Revolution and Intervention: The French Government and the Russian Civil War, 1917–1919.* Kingston, Ontario: McGill-Queens University Press.
Demsetz, Harold. 1968. "Why Regulate Utilities?" *Journal of Law and Economics* 11 (April): 55–65.
Foreign Office. United Kingdom. 1918. *General Correspondence, Russia.* F.O. 371, 3344, 3295. Wilmington, Del.: Scholarly Resources. Microfilm.
———. 1919. *General Correspondence, Russia.* F.O. 3969, 3970. Wilmington, Del.: Scholarly Resources. Microfilm.
Hanke, Steve H., and Alan Walters. 1990a. "Reform Begins with a Currency Board." *Financial Times* (February 21): 17.
———. 1990b. "East German Currency Board." *Financial Times* (March 7): 19.
Hanke, Steve H., and Alan A. Walters. 1991. "Financial and Capital Markets in Developing Countries." This volume.

Hetzel, Robert L. 1990. "Free Enterprise and Central Banking in Formerly Communist Countries." *Federal Reserve Bank of Richmond Economic Review* (May/June): 13–19.

Ironside, William Edmund. 1953. *Archangel: 1918–1919*. London: Constable.

Kennan, George F. 1967. *U.S.–Soviet Relations, 1917–1920, Volume 2. The Decision to Intervene*. New York: Atheneum.

Keynes, John Maynard. 1913a. "[Review of] *Departmental Committee on Matters Affecting Currency of the British West African Colonies and Protectorates Report. Minutes of Evidence*." *Economic Journal* 23, no. 89: 146–47.

———. (1913b) 1971. *Indian Currency and Finance*. Reprinted as vol. 1 in *The Collected Writings of John Maynard Keynes*, 30 vols. London: Macmillan.

Rhodes, Benjamin D. 1988. *The Anglo-American Winter War with Russia 1918–1919: A Diplomatic and Military Tragicomedy*. New York: Greenwood Press.

Spring-Rice, Dominick. 1919. "The North Russian Currency." *Economic Journal* 29, no. 115: 280–89.

U.S. Department of State. 1932. *Foreign Relations of the United States. 1918. Russia*. 3 vols. Washington, D.C.: Government Printing Office.

Walters, Alan. 1988. "Currency Boards." In *The New Palgrave: A Dictionary of Economics*, edited by John Eatwell, Murray Milgate, and Peter Newman. Cambridge: Cambridge University Press.

4. Lawrence H. White, "Money and Capital in Economic Development: A Retrospective Assessment"

Notes

Thanks are due to Jerry Jenkins, Alan Stockman, Michael Todaro, and Bernard Wasow for discussion. They are blameless for the views expressed in this paper.

1. This distinction is one that I have elsewhere (White 1987) expressed by contrasting "outside" with "inside" money. In light of Gurley and Shaw's different usage (1960), those terms are probably better avoided here.

2. As with any tax, the revenue-maximizing rate of seignorage is finite. At too high a rate of monetary expansion, the tax base of real money holdings melts away. For a clear exposition see McCulloch 1982, 5.

References

Andreski, Stanislav. 1966. *Parasitism and Subversion: The Case of Latin America*. New York: Pantheon Books.

Bauer, P. T. 1971. *Dissent on Development*. Cambridge, Mass.: Harvard University Press.

Böhm-Bawerk, Eugen von. 1959. *Capital and Interest*, 3 vols. South Holland, Ill: Libertarian Press.

Cameron, Rondo, et al. 1967. *Banking in the Early Stages of Industrialization*. New York: Oxford University Press.

Cameron, Rondo, ed. 1972. *Banking and Economic Development: Some Lessons of History.* New York: Oxford University Press.

Caves, Richard E. 1974. "Review of *Money and Capital in Economic Development.*" *Journal of International Economics* 4 (May): 223–24.

Danthine, Jean-Pierre, John B. Donaldson, and Lance Smith. 1987. "On the Superneutrality of Money in a Stochastic Dynamic Macroeconomic Model." *Journal of Monetary Economics* 20 (December): 475–99.

Darby, Michael R. 1976. *Macroeconomics.* New York: McGraw-Hill.

Diaz-Alejandro, Carlos. 1985. "Good-bye Financial Repression, Hello Financial Crash." *Journal of Development Economics* 19 (September-October): 1–24.

Edwards, Sebastian. 1985. "Stabilization with Liberalization: An Evaluation of Ten Years of Chile's Experiment with Free-Market Policies, 1973–1983." *Economic Development and Cultural Change* 33 (January): 223–54.

Fisher, Irving. 1930. *Capital and Interest.* New York: Macmillan.

Fry, Maxwell J. 1978. "Money and Capital or Financial Deepening in Economic Development?" *Journal of Money, Credit, and Banking* 10 (November): 464–75.

———. 1988. *Money, Interest, and Banking in Economic Development.* Baltimore, Md.: Johns Hopkins University Press.

Fuglesang, Andreas. 1984. "The Myth of People's Ignorance." *Development Dialogue*: 42–62.

Goldsmith, Raymond W. 1969. *Financial Structure and Development.* New Haven, Conn.: Yale University Press.

Grubel, Herbert G. 1974. "Review of *Money and Capital in Economic Development.*" *Canadian Journal of Economics* 5 (May): 333–35.

Gurley, John G., and Edward S. Shaw. 1960. *Money in a Theory of Finance.* Washington, D.C.: Brookings Institution.

Harris, John R., and Michael P. Todaro. 1970. "Migration, Unemployment, and Development: A Two-Sector Model." *American Economic Review* 60 (March): 126–42.

Hayek, F. A. 1948. "The Use of Knowledge in Society." In *Individualism and Economic Order.* Chicago: University of Chicago Press.

———. 1978. "Competition as a Discovery Procedure." In *New Studies in Philosophy, Politics, Economics, and the History of Ideas.* Chicago: University of Chicago Press.

Kirzner, Israel M. 1973. *Competition and Entrepreneurship.* Chicago: University of Chicago Press.

Lavoie, Donald C. 1985. *Rivalry and Central Planning: The Socialist Calculation Debate Reconsidered.* Cambridge: Cambridge University Press.

Leijonhufvud, Axel. 1981. *Information and Coordination: Essays in Macroeconomic Theory.* New York: Oxford University Press.

Loong, Lee Hsien, and Richard Zeckhauser. 1982. "Pecuniary Externalities Do Matter When Contingent Claims Markets Are Incomplete." *Quarterly Journal of Economics* (May): 171–79.

Lüders, Rolf. 1974. "Review of *Money and Capital in Economic Development.*" *Journal of Finance* 29 (March): 298–300.
———. 1991. "Latin American Contrast: Capital Markets and Development in Chile and Argentina." This volume.
McCulloch, J. Huston. 1982. *Money and Inflation: A Monetarist Approach*. 2d ed. New York: Academic Press.
McKinnon, Ronald I. 1973. *Money and Capital in Economic Development.* Washington, D.C.: Brookings Institution.
———, ed. 1976. *Money and Finance in Economic Growth and Development: Essays in Honor of Edward S. Shaw.* New York: Marcel Dekker.
———. 1980. "Financial Policies." In *Policies for Industrial Progress in Developing Countries*, edited by John Cody et al. New York: Oxford University Press.
———. 1982. "The Order of Economic Liberalization: Lessons from Chile and Argentina." *Carnegie-Rochester Conference Series on Public Policy* 17 (Autumn): 159–86.
———. 1986. "Financial Liberalization in Retrospect: Interest Rate Policies in LDCs." Center for Economic Policy Research Discussion Paper No. 74 (July).
McKinnon, Ronald I., and Edward S. Shaw. "Policies in Restraint of Development." N. d.
Meier, Gerald M. 1984. *Leading Issues in Economic Development*, 4th ed. New York: Oxford University Press.
Moore, Basil J. 1975. "Review of Edward S. Shaw, *Financial Deepening in Economic Development.*" *Journal of Money, Credit, and Banking* 7 (February): 124–30.
Nichols, Donald A. 1974. "Some Principles of Inflationary Finance." *Journal of Political Economy* 82 (March–April): 423–30.
North, Douglass C. 1979. "A Framework for Analyzing the State in Economic History." *Explorations in Economic History* 16: 249–59.
Price, Ralph B. 1974. "Joint Review of *Money and Capital in Economic Development* and *Financial Deepening in Economic Development.*" *Kyklos*: 188–89.
Reubens, Edwin P. 1974. "Review of *Money and Capital in Economic Development.*" *Journal of Economic Literature* 12 (June): 500–501.
Rimmer, Douglas. 1973. *Macromancy: The Ideology of "Development Economics."* London: Institute of Economic Affairs.
Sargent, Thomas J. 1986. *Rational Expectations and Inflation*. New York: Harper and Row.
Schumpeter, Joseph A. [1934] 1974. *The Theory of Economic Development*, translated by Redvers Opie. Reprinted London: Oxford University Press.
Selgin, George A. 1987. "The Stability and Efficiency of Money Supply Under Free Banking." *Journal of Institutional and Theoretical Economics* 143 (September): 435–56.
Shaw, Edward S. 1973. *Financial Deepening in Economic Development.* New York: Oxford University Press.
Simons, Henry. 1936. "Rules versus Authorities in Monetary Policy." *Journal of Political Economy* 44 (February): 1–30.

Smith, Adam. [1776] 1976. *An Inquiry into the Nature and Causes of the Wealth of Nations*, edited by R. H. Campbell, A. S. Skinner, and W. B. Todd. Oxford: Oxford University Press.

———. 1978. *Lectures on Jurisprudence*, R. L. Meek, D. D. Raphael, and P. G. Stein. Oxford: Clarendon Press.

Stark, W., ed. 1952. *Jeremy Bentham's Economic Writings*. 3 vols. London: Allen and Unwin.

Stigler, George J. 1982. *The Economist as Preacher and Other Essays*. Chicago: University of Chicago Press.

Stockman, Alan C. 1981. "Anticipated Inflation and the Capital Stock in a Cash-in-Advance Economy." *Journal of Monetary Economics*. 8 (November): 387–93.

———. 1982. "Comment on the McKinnon Paper." *Carnegie-Rochester Conference Series on Public Policy* 17 (Autumn): 187–92.

Tobin, James. 1965. "Money and Economic Growth." *Econometrica* 33 (October): 671–84.

Waters, Alan Rufus. 1974. "Review of *Money and Capital in Economic Development*." *Southern Economic Journal* 41 (July): 161–62.

White, Lawrence H. 1987. "Privatization of Financial Sectors." In *Privatization and Development*, edited by Steve H. Hanke. San Francisco: ICS Press.

5. Rolf J. Lüders, "Latin American Contrast: Capital Markets and Development in Chile and Argentina"

Notes

This chapter draws heavily on work by others as well as on two reports written by the author on the financial liberalizations of Argentina and Chile. These are, respectively, "Lessons from the Financial Liberalization of Argentina: 1977–81" (1986b, 1986c) and "Lessons from the Financial Liberalization of Chile: 1974–82." The information presented in these two reports is extensively employed in the present discussion, but without repeated reference to them. The reader who desires more extensive statistical information and source documentation than is provided here is referred to these two reports.

1. Another country whose experience parallels that of Argentina and Chile in many of the aspects that are studied in this paper is Uruguay. During the second half of the 1970s, in particular, Uruguay also advanced an economic liberalization policy that included its financial markets. It experienced, along with Argentina and Chile, an economic and financial crisis in the early 1980s. Many of the lessons that can be drawn from the Uruguayan experience in financial market liberalization do not differ significantly from those drawn in this work.

2. The effect of this event was different for holders of foreign and domestic assets. The "gross" external debt increased and, in so doing, generated a redistribution of income from domestic to foreign asset holders.

3. Although the unemployment rate rose somewhat during these crisis years, the increase was relatively modest in comparison with that in Chile. Different wage rate (and unemployment) policies can explain these effects. Argentina allowed the real wage rate to fall drastically at the beginning of the crisis, while in Chile the wage rate adjustment was delayed and only took place over a span of several years.

4. See various issues of ECLA, "Balance Preliminar de la Economia Latinoamericana."

5. Other reasons given for the high spreads, besides those in the text, are the low degree of financial deepening of the Argentine economy, the short terms of the deposit and credit operations, and the inflexibility of the wage readjustment arrangements of the banking sector. However, these same conditions exist in other countries where spreads (corrected for the effect of the reserve requirement cost) are much lower.

References

Arellano, J. P. 1983. "De las liberalización a la intervención: el mercado de capitales en Chile 1974–83." *Colección Estudios CIEPLAN* 11 (December): 5–49.

Arnaudo, A. A., and R. Conejero. 1985. "Anatomía de las quiebras bancarias de 1980." *Desarrollo Económico* 24, no. 96: 605–16.

Arriazu, H. R. 1988. "Mercados informales de crédito." X Jornades de Economía Monetaria y Sector Externo, Banco Central de la Republica Argentina. Buenos Aires. (April). Memo.

Artana, D., and E. Szewack. 1988. "Regulaciónes del gobierno en la económica Argentina." Chapter 3 in Regulaciónes en el mercado de capitales. FIEL (Fundacion de Investigaciones Economicos Latinoamericanas) Buenos Aires. (April). Unpublished memo.

Baliño, J. T. "The Argentine Banking Crisis of 1980." X Jornadas de Economía Monetaria y Sector Externo, Banco Central de la Republica Argentina. Buenos Aires. (April). Memo.

Bolsa de Comercio de Santiago. 1988. *Reseña de Valores.* Santiago, Chile: Bolsa de Commercio de Santiago.

Cavallo, D., and A. Peña. 1983. "Déficit fiscal, endeudamiento del gobierno y tasa de inflación: Argentina 1940–1982." *Estudios* 6, no. 26: 39–78.

Corbo, V. "Reforms and Macroeconomic Adjustments in Chile during 1974–1984." *World Development* 13, no. 8: 5–15.

De Long, J. Bradford. 1987. "Have Productivity Levels Converged?: Productivity Growth, Convergence, and Welfare in the Very Long Run." Working paper no. 2419. Cambridge, Mass.: National Bureau of Economic Research.

Economic Commission for Latin America (ECLA). United Nations. *Balance preliminar de la economía latinoamericana.* Published annually.

Edwards, S. 1984. "Monetarism in Chile 1973–1983: Analytical Issues and Economic Puzzles." Paper presented at the annual meetings of the American Economic Association, Dallas, Texas.

———. 1985. "Money, the Rate of Devaluation and Interest Rates in a Semi-Open

Economy: Colombia 1968–1982." *Journal of Money, Credit and Banking* 27 (February): 59–68.

Edwards, S., and S. van Wijnbergen. 1983. "The Welfare Effects of Trade and Capital Market Liberalization: Consequences of Different Sequencing Scenarios." CPD discussion paper no. 1984-36 (November).

Hanke, Steve H. 1987. "The Necessity of Property Rights." In *Privatization and Development*, edited by Steve Hanke. San Francisco: ICS Press.

Harberger, A. C. 1985. "Observations on the Chilean Economy, 1973–1983." *Economic Development and Cultural Change* 34, no. 3.

Ibañez, P., and R. J. Lüders. 1983. "Hacia una moderna economía de mercado, diez años de política económica 1973–1983." *Politica* (November).

Instituto de Estudios Bancarios. Guillermo Subercaseaux. 1984. "Eficiencia del sistema financiero: una evaluación empírica." Memo, 53–58.

International Bank for Reconstruction and Development. 1989. *World Development Report 1989*. New York: Oxford University Press.

International Monetary Fund. 1989. *International Financial Statistics Yearbook*. Washington, D.C.: International Monetary Fund.

Khan, M., and R. Zahler. 1985. "Trade and Financial Liberalization Given External Shocks and Inconsistent Domestic Policies." International Monetary Fund staff papers (June).

Lanús de la Serna y Asociados. 1987. "Saneamiento de Bancos." Buenos Aires. (August). Memo.

Lüders, Rolf J. 1976. "The Economic Commission for Latin America: Its Policies and Their Impact." Paper read at the Carnegie-Rochester Conference on Fiscal Policy. (April).

———. 1986a. *Auge y desaparición de los grandes conglomerados Chilenos 1975–1982*. With annexes "La razon de ser de la intervención del 13 de enero." "Algunas notas en torno al problema del endeudamiento interno." "¿La plata qué se hizo?" Santiago, Chile: forthcoming.

———. 1986b. "Lessons from the Financial Liberalization of Argentina: 1977–81." Washington, D.C.: World Bank.

———. 1986c. "Lessons from the Financial Liberalization of Chile: 1974–82." Washington, D.C.: World Bank.

McKinnon, R. 1973. *Money and Capital in Economic Development*. Washington, D.C.: The Brookings Institution.

———. 1982. "The Order of Economic Liberalization: Lessons from Chile and Argentina." In *Economic Policy in a World of Change*, edited by K. Brunner and A. Metzler. Carnegie-Rochester Conference Series on Public Policy 17. Amsterdam.

Mussa, M. 1983. "The Adjustment Process and the Timing of Trade Liberalization." CPD discussion paper no. 1984-15 (October).

Rosende, F., and R. Toso. 1984. "Una explicación para la tasa de interes real en Chile en el periodo 1975–1983." *Cuadernos de Economía* no. 62 (April): 25–36.

Tami, F. 1978. *Estudio del sector financiero de Argentina*. Washington, D.C.: Interamerican Development Bank.

6. Murray Sherwin, "Capital Market Liberalization: The New Zealand Experience"
Notes

Substantial contributions to this chapter were made by Grant Spencer and David Carey, respectively chief manager, Economic Department, and research manager at the Reserve Bank of New Zealand. Naturally, the responsibility for errors remains with the author.

The introductory section and the sections, "The New Monetary Management Framework" and "Monetary Policy and Inflation" draw extensively on work by Spencer and Carey (unpublished as of this writing).

1. Primary liquidity (PL) is defined to include bankers' cash balances at the reserve bank plus discountable government securities (that is, government securities with one month or less to maturity). Before December 1984, all government securities were discountable at the reserve bank. During the year to December 1985, only government securities within six months of maturity were discountable at the reserve bank. This qualification was phased down to one month by April 1986 and has since remained at that level. The definition of PL was narrowed in April 1986 so as to increase the transparency of monetary policy.

7. Flora M. Painter and Robert J. Rourke, "Policy and Institutional Considerations in Equity Market Development"
Notes

This chapter is derived from a more extensive report prepared by Arthur Young under contract with the United States Agency for International Development (A.I.D.), Bureau for Program and Policy Coordination. The report identifies a range of issues and questions that confronts A.I.D. in promoting the development of equity markets and suggests approaches that the agency might consider for incorporation within its more comprehensive strategy for encouraging and assisting the development of market-led growth in LDCs.

The report and this chapter are based on an outline prepared for Arthur Young by Terrence C. Reilly, an internationally recognized specialist on securities market development. Many of the ideas and the types of issues discussed here have been adapted from early work by Mr. Reilly for Arthur Young and other clients including A.I.D. The authors also benefited greatly from the work and practical experience in equity market development of several other experts in the field, especially George M. Ferris, Jr., chairman and chief executive officer of Ferris & Company, a regional investment firm headquartered in Washington, D.C., and Robert M. Bishop, retired senior vice-president of the New York Stock Exchange. Both Mr. Ferris and Mr. Bishop reviewed the report and provided valuable comments for which the authors wish to thank them. The authors also benefited from studies on capital market development conducted by the Asian Development Bank and the International Finance Corporation. The authors alone are responsible for any errors of omission and commission.

References

Alam, Khurshid. 1986. "Securities Market Development in Bangladesh." In *Capital Market Development in the Asia-Pacific Region*. Manila: An Asian Development Bank Symposium.

Arthur Young and Stanford Research Institute. 1988. "Liberalization and Privatization of the Financial Sector: Guidelines and Case Studies." Draft report for the Agency for International Development, Bureau for Program and Policy Coordination (November).

Asian Development Bank. 1985. *Capital Market Development in Selected Developing Member Countries of the Asian Development Bank*. Unpublished report. Manila: Asian Development Bank.

Berrill, Sir Kenneth. 1986. "A Regulatory, Legal and Supervisory Framework for Capital Markets." In *Capital Market Development in the Asia-Pacific Region*. Manila: An Asian Development Bank Symposium.

Biggs, Tyler, Merilee S. Grindle, and Donald R. Snodgrass. 1988. "The Informal Sector, Policy Reform, and Structural Transformation." In *Beyond the Informal Sector: Including the Excluded in Developing Countries*, edited by Jerry Jenkins. San Francisco: ICS Press.

de Soto, Hernando. 1988. "Constraints on People: The Origins of Underground Economies and Limits to their Growth" and "The Informal Path to Transformation." In *Beyond the Informal Sector: Including the Excluded in Developing Countries*, edited by Jerry Jenkins. San Francisco: ICS Press.

———. 1989. *The Other Path: The Invisible Revolution in the Third World*. New York: Harper and Row.

Dickie, Robert B. 1981. "An Examination of Equity Sharing Policies: What Causes Them to Fail—and Succeed?" *Columbia Journal of World Business* 6, no. 2.

Drake, P. J. 1977. "Securities Markets in Less Developed Countries." *Journal of Development Studies* 13, no. 2.

Ferris, George M., Jr. 1971. "FUMCAP—Securities Aspects: Brazil."

———. 1973. "Further development of Korean Securities Markets."

———. 1987. "Kenya: An Action Plan for Capital Market Development and Capital Mobilization." Report prepared for Arthur Young under contract to the Agency for International Development (April).

Gill, David. 1979. "Some Thoughts on the Implications of Different Financial Institutional Structures on Securities Market Development." Paper presented at the conference, Las instituciónes financeras, il mercardo de capitales en Chile, Chile.

———. 1984. "The Interdependence of National Securities Markets." Paper presented at the Ninth Annual Conference of the International Association of Securities Commissions and Similar Organizations, Toronto.

———. 1986. "Considerations for Furthering Securities Markets." Paper presented at the Eleventh Annual Conference of the International Association of Securities Commissions and Similar Organizations, July, Paris, France.
Hakim, Jonathan, ed. 1985. "Securities Markets." International Finance Corporation occasional paper. Washington, D. C.: International Finance Corporation.
Hanke, Steve H. 1987. "The Anatomy of a Successful Debt Swap." In *Privatization and Development*, edited by Steve H. Hanke. San Francisco: ICS Press.
Intrados Group. 1988. *Swaps: The Newsletter of New Financial Instruments* 2, no. 2.
Leeviraphan, Manas. 1986. "Recent Developments in the Thai Capital Market." In *Capital Market Development in the Asia-Pacific Region*. Manila: Asian Development Bank.
Merican, Data Malek. 1986. "Recent Capital Market Development in Malaysia." In *Capital Market Development in the Asia-Pacific Region*. Manila: Asian Development Bank.
Pearson, Peter. 1986. "Foreign Investment Funds from an International Investor's Viewpoint." In *Capital Market Development in the Asia-Pacific Region*. Manila: Asian Development Bank.
Pyun, Gong-Soo. 1986. "Some International Aspects of Korea's Capital Market Development Efforts." In *Capital Market Development in the Asia-Pacific Region*. Manila: Asian Development Bank.
Rahman, Mistafizur. 1986. "Commentator Remarks." In *Capital Market Development in the Asia-Pacific Region*. Manila: Asian Development Bank.
Reilly, Terrence C. 1986a. "Regulatory, Legal and Supervisory Issues for Capital Market Development." In *Capital Market Development in the Asia-Pacific Region*. Manila: Asian Development Bank.
———. 1986b. "Initial Discussion Memorandum on Policy for Capital Market Development in Indonesia." Draft report prepared for Arthur Young under contract with the Agency for International Development (July 7).
Securities Industry Association. 1986. *Securities Industry Trends* 12, no. 8.
Shipp, Arnold. 1986. "Commentator Remarks." In *Capital Market Development in the Asia-Pacific Region*. Manila: Asian Development Bank.
Sugimoto, Kanju. 1986. "The Role of Fiscal and Monetary Policy to Promote the Capital Market Development." In *Capital Market Development in the Asia-Pacific Region*. Manila: Asian Development Bank.
Teixeira da Costa, Roberto. 1985. *Brazil's Experience in Creating a Capital Market*. Bovespa: São Paulo Stock Exchange.

8. Khurshid Alam, "The Dhaka Stock Exchange: Expanding Equity in the Development of Bangladesh" Notes

1. "Privatization as Politics," therefore, is a most appropriate title for Manuel Tanoira's contribution to *Privatization and Development*, edited by Steve H. Hanke

(San Francisco: ICS Press, 1988, 53–64). As former President Alfonsin's appointed minister for privatization in Argentina, Tanoira knows whereof he speaks.

2. At a seminar on privatization and investment in Islamabad, Pakistan's former prime minister, Benazir Bhutto, said that the expansive privatization program of her government would offer shares in state-owned enterprises to the general public in accordance with the "popular capitalism" model of the British rather than to those who could afford to purchase the greatest number of shares. Malaysia has also prepared a program under which a Privatization Act is planned to codify legal procedures common to all privatizations. A total of 246 projects worth 16.34 billion Malaysian ringgits were to be privatized under the plan during the 1980s and early 1990s, mostly through the sale of shares to the public.

9. Steve H. Hanke and Alan A. Walters, "Confidence and the Liberal Economic Imperative"
Notes

1. Niskanen (1989, 468) attributes this analogy to a "leading agricultural economist" who was addressing the transition costs of ending farm subsidies in the United States.

References

Aslund, Anders. 1989. *Gorbachev's Struggle for Economic Reform*. Ithaca, N.Y.: Cornell University Press.

Harberger, Arnold C. 1984. "Economic Policy and Economic Growth." In *World Economic Growth*, edited by Arnold C. Harberger. San Francisco: ICS Press.

Keynes, John Maynard. 1936. *The General Theory of Employment, Interest and Money*. London: Macmillan.

Krueger, Anne O. 1984. "Problems of Liberalization." In *World Economic Growth*, edited by Arnold C. Harberger. San Francisco: ICS Press.

Niskanen, William A. 1989. "Rethinking the Case for Central Banking." *Cato Journal* 9, no. 2: 467–79.

Scully, Gerald W. 1988. "The Institutional Framework and Economic Development." *Journal of Political Economy* 96, no. 3: 652–62.

Contributors

Khurshid Alam is past chairman of the Dhaka Stock Exchange and currently president of the Bangladesh Center for Economic Growth.

L. E. Birdzell, Jr., an attorney and legal scholar based in Newport, Rhode Island, is also the coauthor, with Nathan Rosenberg, of the book *How the West Grew Rich*.

Steve H. Hanke is professor of applied economics at Johns Hopkins University and chief economist for Friedberg Commodity Management, Inc. (Toronto). He also serves as personal economic adviser to the deputy prime minister of the Socialist Federal Republic of Yugoslavia, and as adviser to the president at Deloitte Ross Tohmatsu International/Eastern Europe (Brussels). His many writings include those in *Privatization & Development*, and *Prospects for Privatization*, which he also edited.

Jerry Jenkins is president of the Sequoia Institute. Some of his previous work is contained in another volume in this series, *Beyond the Informal Sector*.

Rolf J. Lüders, professor of economics at the Catholic University of Chile, was minister of finance and minister of economics during the 1982–1983 crisis discussed in his chapter in this volume.

Ronald I. McKinnon is a professor of economics at Stanford University who has served as a consultant to governments throughout the developing world as well as to the World Bank and other international development agencies. His numerous publications include the seminal volume, *Money and Capital in Economic Development*, which inspired the retrospective assessment in the present book.

Flora M. Painter and **Robert J. Rourke** are with Ernst & Young's International Management Consulting Group and have consulted widely throughout the world with both national and international government agencies regarding capital market development.

Terrence C. Reilly is an internationally recognized specialist on securities market development, consulting throughout the world from his London base (with a U.S. firm).

Kurt Schuler is a Durell Fellow in Money and Banking in the Department of Economics at George Mason University.

Murray Sherwin has extensive experience in a variety of positions with the Reserve Bank in New Zealand as well as serving as executive director at the World Bank and its affiliates for numerous countries, including New Zealand, Australia, and Korea.

Sir Alan Walters was the personal economic adviser to former Prime Minister Margaret Thatcher. He is a director of Putnam, Hayes, and Bartlett, Inc., and is vice-chairman and director, AIG Trading Corporation. He is also a senior fellow at American Enterprise Institute and professor of economics at Johns Hopkins University. His voluminous publications include *Money in Boom and Slump*, *An Introduction to Econometrics*, *Noise and Prices*, *Microeconomic Theory* (with R. Layard), *Britain's Economic Renaissance*, and *Sterling in Danger*.

Lawrence H. White teaches economics at the University of Georgia. The first volume of his collected works, *Competition and Currency* (1989), follows by only five years his initial, pathbreaking book, *Free Banking in Britain*.

Seminar Participants

Alan Batchelder, A.I.D.
L. E. Birdzell, Jr.
Philip L. Brock, University of Washignton
Charles Buchanan, A.I.D.
Stuart Callison, A.I.D.
Ed Clarke, A.I.D.
Barbara Craig, Virginia Polytechnic University
Christopher Culp, Competitive Enterprise Institute
Raquel Fernandez, Boston University
Sandra Frydman, A.I.D.
Steve H. Hanke, Johns Hopkins University
Jerry Jenkins, Sequoia Institute
Jayant Kalotra, International Business and Technical Consultants, Inc.
Rolf J. Lüders, Catholic University of Chile
Roger Magyar, Sequoia Institute
Donald McClelland, A.I.D.
Ronald I. McKinnon, Stanford University
Flora M. Painter, Arthur Young
Mario Pastore, Ithaca College
Terrence C. Reilly
Neal Riden, A.I.D.
Robert J. Rourke, Arthur Young
Silvia Sagari, World Bank
Murray Sherwin, World Bank
Dick Sines, A.I.D.
Steven Sposato, A.I.D.
Mike Unger, A.I.D.
Alan A. Walters, Johns Hopkins University
Warren Weinstein, A.I.D.
Lawrence H. White, University of Georgia
Robert Young, A.I.D.
Neal S. Zank, A.I.D.

This book is a product of one of the seminars in a series addressing critical issues of foreign development and its assistance. The series, entitled

INCLUDING THE EXCLUDED:
Extending the Benefits of Development

is conducted by the Sequoia Institute, with the sponsorship of the Agency of International Development. Contributions of the following academic advisers to the Sequoia Seminar Series have distinguished the series and its publications:

Robert H. Bates
   Political Economy Center
   Duke University

Brigitte Berger
   Department of Sociology
   Boston University

Peter Berger
   Director
   Institute for the Study of
     Economic Culture
   Boston University

Richard M. Bird
   Department of Economics
   University of Toronto

L. E. Birdzell, Jr.
   Coauthor,
   How the West Grew Rich

Philip L. Brock
   Department of Economics
   University of Washington

William O. Chittick
   Director,
   Center for Global
     Policy Studies
   University of Georgia

Hernando de Soto
   President
   Institute for Liberty
     and Democracy
   Lima, Peru

Robert Higgs
   Department of Business
   Seattle University

Han S. Park
   Director,
   Development Studies
   Sequoia Institute

Douglass C. North
   Director,
   The Center in
     Political Economy
   Washington University

Elinor Ostrom
   Co-director,
   Workshop in Political
     Theory and Policy Analysis
   Indiana University

John P. Powelson
   Department of Economics
   University of Colorado

Lawrence H. White
   Department of Economics
   University of Georgia

Index

Accounting standards
  effect of deficiencies in, 270–71
  recommendations for improvement of, 275
AFPs. *See* Pension Fund Administrations (AFPs): Chile
African Development Bank, 300
Aid to Industry Fund: Israel, 31
Alam, Khurshid, 268, 270
Alfonsín, Raúl, 145
Allende, Salvador, 146–47, 204
Andreski, Stanislav, 74, 78
Arellano, J. P., 171
Arnaudo, A. A., 165
Arriazu, H. R., 152, 162
Artana, D., 143, 156
Arthur Young, 279
ASEAN. *See* Association of Southeast Asian Nations (ASEAN)
Asian Development Bank, 264, 266, 268, 271, 277, 280, 341
Aslund, Anders, 353
Association of Southeast Asian Nations (ASEAN), 327–28

Auditing standards
  effect of deficiencies in, 270–71
  recommendations for improvement of, 275
Austral Plan, 145–46
Avenol, Josef, 60
Ayau, Manuel F., 356n1.9

Balance of payments: New Zealand, 210, 213
Baliño, J. T., 144, 146
Bangladesh Shilpa Bank (BSB), 336–37
Bangladesh Shilpa Rin Sangstha (BSRS), 336–37
Banking Shares Collapse: Israel, 32
Banking system
  effect of reform in Korea for, 124–25
  free entry, market-driven, 133
  government intervention in Israel in, 31–32
  moral hazard in, 107–8, 132, 190–91

Banking system (*continued*)
  See also Development banks: India; Development finance corporations(DFCs); Free banking concept
Banking system: Argentina
  government guarantee against failure in, 164–65
  present status of, 206
  relationship to central bank of, 164
  reserve levels of, 143
Banking system: Chile
  foreign banks in, 166
  foreign-owned banks in, 174
  market and government regulation of, 164–65
Banking system: developing countries
  lack of competition in, 35–36
  nationalized, 37–38
  repression of, 86–92
  role of commercial banks in, 81–82
Banking system: New Zealand
  additions with liberalization to, 220–21, 229
  foreign banks in, 229
  prudential supervision of, 221–22
Bank note issue, 67–68, 70
Bank of Commerce and Investment (BCI), 336–37
Bank of England, 48, 52, 325
Bauer, Peter T., 73, 359–60n2.2
BCI. See Bank of Commerce and Investment (BCI)
Bentham, Jeremy, 68, 114–15
Berle, A. A., 292
Berrill, Kenneth, 252
Biggs, Tyler, 265
Bird, Richard, 133
Birdzell, L. E., Jr., 7, 355n1.1, 356n1.2, 356–57n1.10
Böhm-Bawerk, Eugen von, 67
Bolsa de Comercio, 173
Bond insurance schemes, 312
Bond market
  repression in developing countries of, 28
  role in developing countries of, 38–39
Brest-Litovsk peace treaty (1918), 45

BSB. See Bangladesh Shilpa Bank (BSB)
BSRS. See Bangladesh Shilpa Rin Sangstha (BSRS)

Cameron, Rondo, 69–71, 86
Capital gains tax, 281–82
Capitalism, institutional, 175
Capitalism, labor, 175
Capital market
  auction market as form of, 258–60
  conditions for development of, 137, 248–49, 333–34
  effect of broadening shareholder base of, 340
  effect of fragmentation of, 76
  effect of retarded, 9–14
  factors inhibiting development of, 251–53
  government intervention: Israel, 30–32
  link to world for developing country, 331–32
  McKinnon theory of internal repression of, 103
  nonsecurities as source of financing in, 244, 245
  not a panacea, 201–2
  over-the-counter market as form of, 258–59
  possible effect of liberalization on, 348
  role of, 1–2, 4, 21–22, 241–42
  securities as source of financing in, 244
  underdevelopment in Bangladesh of, 336
Capital market: Argentina, 136, 161
Capital market: ASEAN regional, 327–28
Capital market: Bangladesh. See Dhaka Stock Exchange (DSE)
Capital market: Chile, 136, 175
  effect of interest rates on, 192–93
  emergence of, 151
  See also Capitalism, institutional; Capitalism, labor; Pension Fund Administrations (AFPs); Popular capitalism; Stock market

Index

Capital market, developing countries, 249
  effect of interventionist policy on, 79–80
  forms of inflow of external capital, 193–98
  informal, or curb market as, 128–29
  methods to encourage, 40–41
  regulatory and developmental problems of, 251–53
  requirement for trading facilities for, 257–62
  role of financial intermediaries, 255–57
  timing of liberalization for, 42
  See also Equity market; Securities market
Capital market: Korea, 124–27
Capital market: New Zealand, 348
Capital Market Agent, 174
Capital markets, world, 40–41
Capital movements
  in Argentina, 142, 152, 156–57, 161–62
  causes for, 348
  in Chile, 148–49, 166, 188, 199
  effect of foreign assistance versus private capital as, 193–98
  effect of removal of controls in liberalization sequencing on, 187–91, 193–94, 230
  in informal, or curb market, 12–14
  in New Zealand, 213, 227
  when capital market is retarded, 12
Carley, Michael J., 47
Cavallo, D., 141, 157, 158
Caves, Richard, 97
Central bank
  in Argentina, 164
  in Chile, 166
  effect of credit policy of, 29–30
  independence in developing countries for, 183
  in newly independent nations, 28
  proposals to eliminate, 15–18
  proposal to abolish for developing countries, 41
  replaces currency board, 26, 28, 58
  See also Free banking concept
Chalmers, Robert, 59
Chenery, Hollis, 102
Chicago Boys, 147, 182
Clarke, 279
Coats, Warren L., Jr., 357nn1.12, 13
Company Law of 1913: Bangladesh, 270
Competing-asset effect of money, 85
Conduit effect of money, 85
Conejero, R., 165
Confidence, or credibility, 109–10, 348–49
  See also Investor confidence
Corbo, V., 171
Coup d'état
  in Argentina (1976), 139
  in Chile, 147
Credit allocation
  inefficiency of government in, 133
  in less-developed countries, 129–30
Credit institutions, specialized, 37–38
Credit markets, world, 40–41
Credit policy
  effect of government intervention in, 29–34
  effect of selective, 30–34
  government control in newly independent nations of, 28
  in Israel, 30–32, 39
Credit rationing, 107–8
  for fund allocation, 69
Cumby, Robert, 13
Curb market. *See* Informal, or curb market
Currency
  alternatives to use of, 14–16
  characteristics of developing country, 43
  decline in real value of, 2
  devaluation in Argentina of (1981), 143
  devaluation in Chile of, 149, 167
  elements of efficient, 43
  See also Informal, or curb market; Monetization
Currency board
  advantages and attributes of, 26–27, 43–44

Currency board (*continued*)
  disadvantages of, 15
  franchise for private, 57–58
  in Hong Kong, Brunei, and
    Singapore, 58, 324, 325
  mechanism of, 324–25
  proposal for present-day Soviet
    Union to initiate, 57
  proposal to replace central bank
    with, 41, 43
  role in developing countries when
    colonies, 26
  use of fixed exchange rate by, 26,
    57
  See also National Emission Caisse
    (North Russia); West African
    Currency Board
Currency issue scheme: North Russia,
  55–56
  correspondence related to, 59–63
  See also National Emission Caisse
    (North Russia); North Russia
Currency reform, developing
  countries, 43

Danthine, Jean-Pierre, 84
Darby, Michael, 89
Debt, external
  in Argentina, 141–42, 144–45, 161
  in New Zealand, 180
  renegotiation of Chilean, 151
de Castro, Sergio, 147, 149, 164
Deficit, domestic
  financing in Argentina of, 157–59
  financing in Israel of, 34
  levels in Argentina of, 141–42, 147
  in New Zealand, 211
  removal in liberalization sequence
    of, 187
  in United States, 200
de Fleuriau, Aimé-Joseph, 60
De Long, J. Bradford, 138
Demsetz, Harold, 57
Deposit insurance
  effect combined with free bank
    entry, 108–9
  lacking in Chile, 107
  New Zealand's policy for, 183
  pricing of, 132–33

  proposal to eliminate guarantee of,
    133
  provision by government of, 190–91
  substitute in developing countries
    for, 120
de Soto, Hernando, 267–68
Development banks: India, 301, 311
Development finance corporations
  (DFCs), 37–38, 309, 311–13, 316–
  18
Development finance institutions
  (DFIs), 309–11, 336–7
Dhaka Stock Exchange (DSE), 336
  economic performance of, 10
  effect of Holding Company Scheme
    on, 345
  factors limiting development of,
    339–40, 342
  listings on, 341–42
  market capitalization of, 7–8
  operation of (1976 to present),
    338–39
Diamonds Fund: Israel, 31
Diaz-Alejandro, Carlos, 66
Dickie, Robert B., 281
Disinflation, 110–11
Donaldson, John B., 84
Douglas, Roger, 232, 235–40
Dowd, Kevin, 358nn1.15, 17
Drake, Paul, 285
DSE. *See* Dhaka Stock Exchange
  (DSE)

Economic development
  domestic capital markets for
    developing countries, 102
  importance of policy choices for,
    73
  import-substitution approach to,
    102–3
  record in Chile of, 146
  use of monetary system for, 102
  ways to raise surplus capital for,
    102–3
Economic performance
  in Argentina, 138
  with capital market liberalization,
    76
  in Chile, 138, 146

Index

in Chile's 1981–82 economic crisis, 167
in countries with government intervention, 347
in New Zealand, 179, 210
Economic policy
  interdependence of all sectors in liberalization, 200–201
  sequencing of liberalization in, 185–87, 189
  use of foreign capital in liberalization of, 188–89
Economic policy: Argentina
  during economic crisis, 204–5
  effect of financial liberalization, 204–6
  liberalization of, 140–41, 207
  role of government in, 135–36
Economic policy: Chile, 135–36
  during 1981–82 economic crisis, 204–5
  effect of financial liberalization, 204–6
  liberalization including all economic sectors, 147, 207–8
  link to world economy by means of, 174
  See also Social market economy: Chile
Economic policy, developing countries
  interventionist policies in, 78–81
  sequence and timing in liberalization of, 189–90
Economic policy: Korea, 125–26
Economic policy: New Zealand
  effect of reforms in, 222–30
  sequencing and timing of liberalization of, 182, 186, 230–32
Edwards, Sebastian, 66, 141, 171
Enterprises, foreign-owned: Chile, 174
Enterprises, state-owned
  in Argentina, 139, 143
  auctioning in Bangladesh of, 330
  privatization in Chile to develop capital market, 137
Equity market
  components for, 255–62
  conditions for development of, 248–49

disclosure in, 321
factors inhibiting development of, 251–53
importance of insurance principle in, 6–8
issues in development of, 250
lack of investor confidence in developing country, 269–70
with privatization of state-owned enterprises, 330
recommendation for intermediate institutions for, 276
recommendations for financing activities of, 276
repression by newly independent governments of, 28
role in developing countries of, 38–39, 248
size of economy to support, 326–27
Exchange rate system
  alternative methods for control of, 181–82
  currency board use of fixed, 26, 57
Exchange rate system: Argentina, 140–42, 165–66
Exchange rate system: Chile, 149
  See also Foreign exchange: Chile
Exchange rate system: New Zealand, 223–27
  rationale for and effect of floating, 198, 215–17, 223–25
  removal of controls on, 213–15
Export incentive: Korea, 125

Ferris, George M., Jr., 257, 262, 276, 278, 281, 283
Fidelity International Investment Management (Hong Kong) Limited, 284
Financial analysis training, 274–75
Financial institutions, nationalized or state-owned, 37–38
Financial instruments, 278
  See also Swaps, debt-to-equity
Financial intermediaries
  effect of free entry for, 108
  effect of taxes on, 34–35
  recommendations for establishment of, 274–76

Financial sector
  components of market in, 242–48
  contraction in Latin America of, 128
  discriminatory taxes on
    intermediaries in, 34–35
  effect of stabilization of, 106–7
  idea of liberal policy for, 67–69, 73
  relation to economic development
    of, 68–71
  See also Banking system; Capital
    market; Capital market,
    developing countries; Equity
    market; Securities market; Stock
    market
Financial sector: Argentina
  as capital market, 136
  crisis in (1981), 142–43
  deepening of, 138, 155, 159, 205
  government control of, 152
  liberalization in, 156–58
  repression of, 152, 157–58
Financial sector: Chile
  bailout by government of
    depositors in, 149, 150, 165
  as capital market, 136
  crisis in (1981–82), 167–71
  deepening and widening of, 137,
    153, 155, 166–67, 205
  financial institutions in, 205
  gradual freeing of, 152–53, 166–67
  liberalization of, 137
  privatization of state–owned
    institutions in, 166
  reestablished after 1981–82 financial
    crisis, 169–71
  See also Capital market: Chile;
    Pension Fund Administrations
    (AFPs)
Financial sector, developing countries
  effect of government intervention
    on, 39–42
  effect of restrictions on, 28–29
  goal to supplant regulated
    monetary system with, 109
  link to outside financial centers,
    41–42
  noncompetitiveness of, 35–37
  repression of, 86–92, 98–99, 103
  sequencing of reform for, 42

types of intervention in, 29–30
Financial sector: Israel, 30–32
Financial sector: Korea, 104
Financial sector: New Zealand
  changes in, 229–30
  sequence in liberalization of, 186,
    187, 211–22
Fiscal deficit. See Deficit, domestic
Fiscal policy
  effect of reform in Chile for, 109,
    137
  reform in Korea for, 104
  structured for equity market
    development, 280
  See also Deficit, domestic; Inflation;
    Tax system
Fisher, Irving, 77
Foreign exchange: Chile, 150–51
Foreign Office (United Kingdom), 46–
  47, 48, 49–55, 59
Free banking concept, 15–16, 67–68,
  70–72, 107, 109, 132–33
Friedman, Milton, 357n1.12
Fry, Maxwell J., 29, 66, 72, 89
Fuglesang, Andreas, 77

Gandhi, Indira, 196
Gill, David, 254, 267, 273, 283, 284,
  286
Goldsmith, Raymond, 68–69
Government intervention
  in Argentina, 143, 158
  in Bangladesh, 342–43
  in Chile, 146–47, 167–69
  condition for financial market, 199
  consequences in developing
    countries of, 35–37, 73–78, 347
  in credit market, 29–30
  effect on financial sector of, 39–42
  to increase issue of securities, 277
  in Israeli financial and capital
    markets, 30–32
  in Japan, 113–14, 116–19
  land redistribution as form of, 79
  in New Zealand, 211
  rationale of newly independent
    nations for, 27–28
  in securities pricing, 262–63

See also Banking system;
Enterprises, state-owned;
Financial sector; Import-
substitution policy
Government-owned enterprises. *See*
Enterprises, state-owned
Government role: Argentina, 135
Government role: Chile, 135
Grindle, Merilee, 265
Grotius, Hugo, 67
Grubel, Herbert G., 97, 98, 99
Gulf Cooperation Council, 328
Gurley, John, 103, 361n4.1

Hakim, Jonathan, 277, 286
Hanke, Steve H., 15, 30, 43, 44, 279, 370n8.1
Harberger, Arnold C., 168, 171, 190, 349
Harris, John, 76
Harvey, Ernest M., 48
Hayek, Friedrich A., 77, 88, 186–87, 357n1.12
Hetzel, Robert L., 15–16, 44, 57
Holding Company Scheme: Bangladesh, 345–46
Holst, Jurgen U., 40
Human capital: Chile, 176

Ibañez, P., 146, 148
ICB. *See* Investment Corporation of Bangladesh (ICB)
IFC. *See* International Finance Corporation (IFC)
Import licenses, 79
Import-substitution policy
in Argentina (1940–70), 138–39
in Chile (1940–73), 146
See also Enterprises, state-owned
Indonesia, 267, 321
Industrial Development Bank of India (IDBI), 311
Industrial Development Leasing Company: Bangladesh, 341
Industrial policy: Bangladesh, 340
See also Privatization: Bangladesh
Inflation
in Argentina, 144, 145, 147, 204
in Chile, 148, 151–52, 204

control of, 109
as implicit tax, 178
in New Zealand, 179–80, 210, 227–29, 231
See also Austral Plan
Informal, or curb market
in Bangladesh, 337–38
in Chile, 153
effect of government intervention on, 39–40
effect of selective credit policies on, 32–33
emigration of money by means of, 12–13
function as capital market of, 39–40, 128–29
interest rate levels in, 86
lessons of, 302
Information asymmetry, 122
Instituto des Estudios Bancarios, 163
Insurance market: Chile, 174
See also Deposit insurance
Inter-American Development Bank, 151
Interest rate as a price, 131
Interest rates
ceilings as form of repression, 86–87
effect of selective credit policies on, 32–33
limits and controls for, 114
Interest rates: Argentina
effect of high, 142–43, 158–59
with government intervention, 158–64
regulated and unregulated, 161–64
spread between deposit and loan, 162–63
Interest rates: Chile
effect of high, 137, 148–49, 167–68, 172–74, 192–93
factors influencing high (post-1982), 171–72
fixed (1973), 166
narrowing of spreads among, 167
Interest rates: New Zealand, 212–13
Interest rates, real: Argentina, 159
Interest rates, real: Chile, 193
International Bank for Reconstruction and Development (IBRD), 157, 173

International Finance Corporation (IFC), 8
  establishment of financial instruments by, 272
  goals of, 318
  securities markets studies by, 253–55
  support for transborder portfolio investment by, 283
International Monetary Fund (IMF), 151, 156
Interventionist economic order. See Government intervention
Intrados Group, 260, 272
Investment, developing countries
  effect of selective credit policies on, 32–34
  rates of return in, 78
Investment, direct foreign
  advantages of, 326
  in Chile, 151
  interventionist policy toward, 79–80
  in New Zealand, 213, 223
Investment, public: New Zealand, 210–11
Investment Center: Israel, 31
Investment Corporation of Bangladesh (ICB), 336–37, 341
Investment rates
  Argentina, 138, 144
  Chile, 138, 173
Investment trusts, foreign: Korea, 284
Investor confidence
  lack in developing countries of, 269–70
  proposals to increase, 282–83
Investors, institutional, 286
Ironside, William E., 49, 54
Isaacs, Rufus D., 59

Jakarta Stock Exchange, 263, 281

Kennan, George F., 46
Keynes, John M., 44, 48–49, 59, 349
Khan, M., 141
Kirzner, Israel M., 80
Korea
  economic reforms in, 103–4
  repression of financial system in, 124–26

Krueger, Anne O., 348

Labor market
  dual, 76
  government intervention in Chile in, 207
  in New Zealand, 186
  Ranis-Fei model of distortions in, 102
Landa, Janet T., 356n1.8
Land reform: Chile, 146, 148
Lanús de la Serna y Asociados, 145, 152, 170
Lavoie, Donald C., 88
Law for the Encouragement of Capital Investment: Israel, 30–31
Leeviraphan, Manas, 251
Leijonhufvud, Axel, 86
Levich, Richard, 13
Liberal economic order
  in colonies of developed countries, 25–27
  conditions for, 348–53
Liberalization. See Economic policy
Long-Term Export Fund: Israel, 31
Loong, Lee Hsien, 121
Lüders, Rolf, 67, 97, 138, 146, 148, 168, 190

McCulloch, J. Huston, 361n4.2
McKinnon, Ronald I., 65, 66, 67, 71–100, 141, 190, 197, 356n1.6
Macroeconomic policy: New Zealand, 232
Managing agency houses (India), 300–301
Manne, Alan, 102
Martinez, Isabel, 139
Martínez de Hoz, José, 140–41, 155, 156, 158, 164
Mathieson, Donald J., 67, 72
Means, Gardiner, 292
Meier, Gerald M., 66
Merican, Dato Malek, 263
Monetary policy: Argentina. See Austral Plan
Monetary policy: Chile, 149
  See also Exchange rate system: Chile; Social market economy: Chile

Index

Monetary policy: New Zealand, 217–20
Monetary Regulation Account: Argentina, 163
Monetary system, developing countries, 102
Monetization
  in Chile, 153, 155
  in developing countries, 69
Money and Capital in Economic Development, 65–99
Money creation, developing countries, 178
Money market, 242–43
  See also Informal, or curb market
Moore, Basil, 76
Moral hazard, 107–8, 132, 190–91
Mudarabahs, 309
Muldoon, Robert, 210
Multinational Investment Guarantees Association, 326
Musharakahs, 309
Mussa, Michael, 141
Mutual funds
  to attract foreign investment in Korea, 284
  in Chile, 174–75
  International Finance Corporation development of, 272
Myrdal, Gunnar, 27

National Credit Limited (NCL), 336–37
National Emission Caisse (North Russia)
  closing of, 53–55
  effectiveness of, 55–57
  function and operation of, 48–53
Nationalization: Chile, 147
Nationalized commercial banks (NCBs): Bangladesh, 341, 344
NCL. *See* National Credit Limited (NCL)
Nichols, Donald A., 95
Niskanen, William, 357n1.12, 370n9.1
North, Douglass C., 79
North Russia
  Allied invasion and provisional government of, 45–46
  British currency-issue scheme of, 47–49

North Russian currency. *See* Currency issue scheme: North Russia

Oil price shock
  effect in Argentina of, 157
  effect on New Zealand of, 215
Overseer of the Capital Market: Israel, 31
Over-the-counter market (OTC), 258–59, 299

Parastatals. *See* Enterprises, state-owned
Patrick, Hugh, 103–4
Pearson, Peter, 284–85
Peel, Sydney, 59
Peña, A., 14, 157, 158
Pension Fund Administrations (AFPs): Chile, 175, 192, 298, 314–16
Perón, Juan Domingo, 139, 157, 164, 204
Petrodollar shock. *See* Oil price shock
Pinochet, Augusto, 140, 149
PL. *See* Primary liquidity (PL)
Political structure: New Zealand, 180
Poole, Frederick, 60
Popular capitalism, 175
Poverty
  lack of high-payoff capital as cause of, 78
  so-called vicious circle of, 27–28
Price, Ralph B., 73, 97, 98–99
Primary liquidity (PL), 218–19
Private sector
  effect of encouragement of, 248
  role in developing countries of, 241
  under social market economy in Chile, 150
Private-sector credit (PSC), 228
Privatization
  in developing countries, 344–45
  economic effects of, 343–44
  as means to augment securities markets, 278
  of Philippine banks, 279
  use of debt-to-equity swaps for, 279
Privatization: Bangladesh
  effect on stock market of, 338
  industrial policy to encourage, 340–41, 344

Privatization: Chile
  policy of, 150
  of state-owned enterprises, 137, 148, 314
Profitability
  recommendations for ensuring, 275–76
  unexploited, 78
Property rights, 241, 267–68
Protectionism
  in Argentina, 139, 140, 147
  arguments in developing countries for, 105–6
  in Chile, 146–47
  effect in developing countries of, 103
PSC. *See* Private-sector credit (PSC)
Public offering of shares. *See* Stock market
Public sector deficit. *See* Deficit, domestic
Pyun, Gong-Soo, 284

Rabushka, Alvin, 30
Rahman, Mistafizur, 278
Rahn, Richard W., 357n1.14
Ratio requirements. *See* Securities, government: New Zealand
RBNZ. *See* Reserve Bank of New Zealand (RBNZ)
Registrar of Joint Stock Companies: Bangladesh, 341
Reilly, Terrence C., 251, 253, 256, 257, 261, 263, 266, 267, 271, 275, 276, 282
Rent-seeking behavior, 74, 75, 78–79, 119–20, 121, 131
Reserve Bank of New Zealand (RBNZ), 213, 215–16, 218, 227
Reubens, Edwin P., 97, 99
Rhodes, Benjamin D., 53
Rimmer, Douglas, 67, 74
Robinson, Joan, 103
Rosenberg, Nathan, 7, 355n1.1, 356n1.2, 356–57n1.10
Rosende, F., 171

Sargent, Thomas J., 92

Savings
  effect of selective credit policies on, 32, 39
  methods in poor countries of, 9–10
  method with government intervention for, 39–42
  nationalization in Israel of, 31–32
Savings rate
  in Argentina, 138, 144
  in Bangladesh, 336
  in Chile, 138, 172–73
  in Japan, 127
  in Latin American countries, 127
  in United States and Europe, 127–28
Schumpeter, Joseph A., 68
Scully, Gerald W., 29, 347
Securities
  actions to increase supply of, 276
  impediments to demand and supply for, 262–73
  ways to increase demand for, 281–87
Securities, government: New Zealand, 217
Securities Industry Association, 282
Securities market
  effect of foreign portfolio investment on, 283–85
  factors affecting development of, 291–95
  function of and conditions for, 290–91
  increasing demand and supply of securities in, 276–87
  limit to supplies in, 262–68
  primary and secondary markets in, 245–48
  Sri Lanka and Bangladesh policies to augment, 278
Securitization
  of illiquid assets, 278–80
  of international credit flows, 279–80
Seigniorage
  capture by colonial currency boards of, 44, 49
  expropriation by newly independent governments of, 28–29
  as revenue source, 94–95
Selgin, George A., 84, 357n1.12, 358n1.16
Sergent, Charles, 60

Index

Shaw, Edward S., 66, 68, 71–72, 76, 85, 103, 361n4.1
Shipp, Arnold, 282
Simons, Henry, 121
Smith, Adam, 67–68, 107–8, 114–15
Smith, Lance, 84
Snodgrass, Donald R., 265
Social market economy: Chile, 147–50, 166–76
Social security system: Chile, 314–15
Spring-Rice, Dominick, 44–45, 46–48, 59
Stanford Research Institute, 279
Stark, W., 68
Stigler, George J., 67
Stiglitz-Weiss credit rationing model, 107–8, 132
Stockman, Alan, 84, 97
Stock market
  in Argentina, 156, 161
  in Chile, 173–74, 191, 193
  in Hong Kong, 307
  in Pakistan, 201
  public offering of shares for, 343–44
  See also Dhaka Stock Exchange; Equity market; Securities market
Subsidies, 79–80
Sugimoto, Kanju, 259–60, 281
Sullivan, John D., 13
Superintendency of Banks and Financial Institutions: Chile, 164–66
Swaps, debt-to-equity, 278–79
  to develop capital market in Chile, 137, 174
  uses of, 313–14
Szewack, E., 143, 156

Tablita. See Exchange rate system; Exchange rate system: Chile
Tami, F., 156
Tanoira, Manuel, 370n8.1
Tariffs, 79
Tax system
  effect of economic policies on, 34–35

  policy must avoid distortion by, 180–81
  policy to stimulate demand for securities, 285
Tax system: Chile
  change to avoid securities discrimination, 297
  income tax reform in, 150, 175
Teixeira da Costa, Roberto, 285
Thatcher, Margaret, 186–87, 196
Thirsk, Wayne, 356n1.7
Tobin, James, 83
Tobin effect, 83, 84, 85
Todaro, Michael P., 76
Toso, R., 171
Trade policy: Argentina, 141
  See also Protectionism
Trading partners: New Zealand, 216

Underground economy. See Informal, or curb market
Underwriters, 276
United Kingdom
  effect of capital control abolition in, 348
  privatization in, 343
U. S. Bureau of the Census, 8–9, 356n1.4
U. S. Department of State, 47, 51, 59

van Wijnbergen, S., 141
Victorica, Marcos, 12–13

Walters, Alan, 15, 43, 44, 49, 359n2.1
Waters, Alan Rufus, 97
West African Currency Board, 48
White, Lawrence H., 16, 70, 88, 357n1.11, 358n1.16, 361n4.1
Willcox, William B., 356n1.3
World Bank, 39, 151

Yemen Arab Republic, 269
Young, G. R., 53–54

Zahler, R., 141
Zeckhauser, Richard, 121